Power

and

Prejudice

The Heavy Burden of Racial Slavery
(source: Collection of the Musée de l'Homme)

The past as a precise idea has meaning and value only for the man who is aware that he has a passion for the future.

—Paul Valéry

We have given much thought to the problems arising from the invention of the atom bomb which threatens the future of mankind. Yet we forget that the forces generated by the maladjustment of human racial relations are perhaps equally powerful and an equal threat to the future of the world. The mind of man is more powerful than matter.

—Vijaya Lakshmi Pandit

Power
and
Prejudice

THE POLITICS AND DIPLOMACY
OF RACIAL DISCRIMINATION

Paul Gordon Lauren

Westview Press
BOULDER & LONDON

The frontispiece is printed by permission of the Musée de l'Homme, Paris. The photograph is no. C.35.1495.467 in their collection.

Copyright © 1988 by Westview Press, Inc.

Published in 1988 in the United States of America by Westview Press, Inc., 5500 Central Avenue, Boulder, Colorado 80301

Library of Congress Cataloging-in-Publication Data
Lauren, Paul Gordon.
   Power and prejudice: the politics and diplomacy of racial discrimination/Paul Gordon Lauren.
     p. cm.
   Bibliography: p.
   Includes index.
   ISBN 0-8133-0678-7.   ISBN 0-8133-0679-5 (if published as a paperback)
   1. Race relations—History—20th century.   2. World politics—20th century.   3. Racism—History—20th century.   4. International relations.   5. Civil rights (International law).   I. Title.
HT1521.L33 1988
305.8'00973—dc19
                                                                                        88-5752
                                                                                        CIP

Printed and bound in the United States of America

(∞)   The paper used in this publication meets the requirements of the American National Standard for Permanence of Paper for Printed Library Materials Z39.48-1984.

10   9   8   7   6   5   4   3   2   1

For my daughters,
Sandy and Jeanne,
with love

Contents

Acknowledgments

One of the great pleasures for any author is the opportunity that publication provides to acknowledge publicly those who contributed so much for so long. This book is the result of the generosity of many individuals and institutions that provided essential assistance along the way. I am most grateful

- for access to rare materials and archival collections to the U.S. National Archives and Manuscript Division of the Library of Congress in Washington; Public Record Office and British Museum in London; Hoover Institution at Stanford University; Institut für Zeitgeschichte in Munich; Franklin D. Roosevelt Library in Hyde Park; Archives de la Société des Nations et Collections Historiques and the Collections des Nations Unies in Geneva; Ministère des Affaires étrangères, Bibliothèque nationale, and the Musée de l'homme in Paris; Politisches Archiv des Auswärtiges Amt in Bonn; and the Leo Baeck Institute and the United Nations in New York;

- for library resources and numerous courtesies to the staffs of the Maureen and Mike Mansfield Library and Law Library at the University of Montana, Green Library at Stanford University, Columbia University Library and Law Library, Dag Hammarskjold Library at the United Nations in New York, the Bibliothèque des Nations Unies in Geneva, Bodleian Library at Oxford University, Suzzalo Library at the University of Washington, Universitetsbiblioteket of Copenhagen, Harvard University Library, University of Tokyo Library, and London School of Economics Library;

- for financial assistance and support to the Rockefeller Foundation for a year as a Rockefeller Foundation Humanities Fellow, the Carter Rogers Montgomery Fund for the Study of International Relations, the University of Montana, and the Mansfield Foundation;

- for the opportunity to personally attend their meetings and deliberations to the delegates and staff members of the United Nations

General Assembly and Third Committee, Committee on the Elimination of Racial Discrimination, and the Sous-Comité sur le racisme, la discrimination raciale, l'apartheid et la decolonisation du Comité spécial des ONG pour les Droits de l'homme;

- for personal interviews and sometimes lengthy conversations to official delegates to the United Nations, including J. M. Makatini as Chief Representative of the African National Congress, Hania Semichi of the Algerian Mission, T. C. Ragachari of the Indian Mission, Dragan Mateljak of the Yugoslav Mission, and Jerome J. Shestack of the U.S. Mission as Representative to the United Nations Commission on Human Rights, and a number of other diplomatic officials who wish to remain anonymous;

- for time in discussions to former President Jimmy Carter and to Sandra Vogelgesang and John Salzberg of the Division of Human Rights and Warren Hewitt as Director of the Bureau of International Organization Affairs in the U.S. Department of State;

- for interviews to officials of the Centre for Human Rights of the United Nations, including Enayat Houshmand as Chief of the International Instruments Unit, Emmanuel Palmer as Chief of the Racial Discrimination Task Force, Emmanuel Mompoint as Chief of the Research and Prevention of Discrimination Section, Lucy Webster, Jakob Moller, Thomas McCarthy, Joseph Stephanides, Elise Smith, and Pilar Downing;

- for assistance to officials of the Commission and the Economic and Social Committee of the European Communities, and the U.S. Mission to the European Communities in Brussels;

- for time and energy spent reading portions of the manuscript to John Louis Gaddis, William Roger Louis, Bert Lockwood, Jr., Olatunde J.B. Ojo, William Hoisington, Howard Tolley, Jr., Richard Drake, Harry Fritz, David Emmons, Frederick Skinner, Robert Lindsay, Peter Koehn, Leo Moser, Chandra Mudaliar, and the late Thomas A. Bailey, recognizing that any errors of fact or interpretation remain mine alone;

- for permission to cite from Crown-copyright materials in the Public Record Office to the Controller of Her Majesty's Stationery Office, and for permission to use materials previously published in an earlier form in *Diplomatic History* to Scholarly Resources, Inc., and in *Human Rights Quarterly* to Johns Hopkins University Press;

- for various forms of help and encouragement to Susan Matule, Kate Saenger, John O. Mudd, James Lopach, Julie McVay, James Frederick Green, John P. Humphrey, Charles Palm, Leonard Jeffries, Bryce Wood, Agnes Peterson, Sybil Milton, Sally Marks, the late Hedley Bull, the Atlantic Council, Amnesty International in London, and the Foundation Jan Masaryk in Geneva;

- for assistance and understanding to Barbara Ellington, Miriam Gilbert, Libby Barstow, and Marian Safran of Westview Press;

- and, for loving support throughout this long project to my wife, Susan, and to our daughters, Sandy and Jeanne, to whom this book is affectionately dedicated.

Paul Gordon Lauren

Power
and
Prejudice

Introduction: "The Problem of the Twentieth Century"

> THE PROBLEM OF THE TWENTIETH CENTURY [will be] the problem of the color line—the relation of the darker to the lighter races of men in Asia and Africa, in America and the islands of the sea.
>
> —W.E.B. Du Bois

It is extraordinarily tempting to entitle this book *The Problem of the Twentieth Century*. Few issues in our own time have possessed such an overwhelming impact upon the world as race and its most easily identifiable characteristic—color. Indeed, the racial problem has profoundly influenced most of the major developments in contemporary international politics and diplomacy. These include the search for peace and security, the creation of empires and then their destruction, the white "Westernization of the world," two world wars and numerous other armed conflicts, the Cold War rivalry between the Americans and the Soviets and its accompanying tensions between West and East, the emergence of the Third World, decolonization and national liberation movements throughout non-white Asia and Africa as well as Latin America, massive shifts in global power structures, distribution of wealth and resources among the "haves" and "have-nots" and corresponding division between North and South, the challenges to state sovereignty by international organizations seeking to intervene in domestic racial affairs, the intensification of global concern for human rights, and the passionate worldwide attention now focused upon the problem of apartheid.

When, at the beginning of the century, W.E.B. Du Bois, the famous publicist and activist for the cause of racial equality, made his celebrated statement about race, he could not, of course, have foreseen all of these developments. Nor could he have anticipated the other major global

1

problems that confront us in the late 1980s or the other forms of prejudice and exclusiveness such as nationalism and religion. It is difficult to justify the singling out of one factor or one issue as being *the* most important in the world at the exclusion of all others. But with remarkable prescience, Du Bois understood nearly ninety years ago that as the world became smaller and as contacts between peoples of different races increased, the deep and emotional tensions caused by racial prejudice and discrimination would become acute. He knew of the heavy burden of the past wherein skin color frequently had served as the badge of master and subject, of the free and the enslaved, and of the conquerors and the conquered.

Du Bois also recognized that those who had suffered for so long from slavery, colonial conquests, immigration quotas, and various forms of exploitation because of the darker color of their skins would contest white domination, demanding justice and using whatever means might be available to them, including armed violence if necessary, to obtain their freedom and equality. Moreover, he understood that those responsible for such discrimination on the basis of racial prejudice would not abandon their attitudes, or their practices, or their power lightly. This book is an account of the modern historical struggle between these powerful forces, of the political and diplomatic uses and abuses of the concept of *race*, of the impact of racial and antiracist ideology, and of how so many among the planet's non-white majority, in the words of one observer, came "to put the race issue at the front and center of all current and prospective world conflict."[1]

The global importance of race through time can hardly be questioned. For example, after Will and Ariel Durant completed their monumental and multivolume study, *The Story of Civilization*, they singled out racial tensions as one of the most influential factors in all of human history.[2] Claude Lévi-Strauss, the well-known French scholar, reached a similar conclusion in his suggestive essay entitled *Race et histoire.*[3] Other thoughtful writers from a wide variety of perspectives and persuasions concurred with these judgments, describing the impact of race upon the world as nothing short of "profound."[4] Over several decades, perceptive scholars and political leaders on their own accord have echoed the opinion of Du Bois many years before and concluded that racial relations represented "the problem of the century"[5] and "the central question of the twentieth century."[6] One author went as far as to maintain that the struggle between the white and non-white peoples of the world "is the major preoccupation of mankind."[7] Another wrote in thought-provoking words: "Race operates at every level and in almost every context. . . . Today, transcending everything (including even the nuclear threat) there is the confrontation between the races. This will spiral on, inexorably, as the twentieth century moves to its end."[8]

To recognize the profound effect of race upon history and the contemporary world, however, is not the same as saying it is the most important factor in international relations or as reaching agreement upon its meaning or definition. Racial awareness by differences in color of skin or other physical characteristics lies in the eye of the beholder and, as we shall see, has always been subject to a wide variety of cultural, religious, political, economic, and scientific influences over time. Emotionally charged and imprecise terms such as *race, racism,* and *racist* comprise some of the most misunderstood words in our vocabulary, often used and deliberately abused by individuals and nations for their own purposes. Around these words swirl many of the rationalizations, self-deceptions, and mythologies by which people pattern their stores of pride or debasement, of elevation or rejection of others or of self.[9] For this reason, wrote one observer, these expressions have lent themselves to what could only be described as "witchcraft" and made the concept of race "man's most dangerous myth."[10] Moreover, in its long history, racial prejudice has had—and will continue to have—a multiplicity of manifestations. Not every form of subtle racial discrimination, it is necessary to acknowledge, is a preamble to genocide. Thus, throughout this book, attitudes and actions toward race will be seen—as they must be—within their own particular historical context; and contemporaries will be given many opportunities to express their venom, hatred, anger, frustration, concern, or compassion in their own words.

Given these many differences and difficulties, we might find it helpful for our part to recognize the setting of the subject of race and to accept a general working definition of terms. Racial prejudice cannot always be singled out as a clearly identifiable and independent variable, somehow completely isolated from the other sources of behavior such as cultural arrogance, religious fervor, nationalistic pride, materialistic greed, ideological conviction, and linguistic or ethnic distinctiveness.[11] It is an integral part of an intricate, complex, and often changing set of interrelated threads composing the tapestry of politics and diplomacy. Hence, to provide distinguishing characteristics, we might usefully follow the suggestion of scholar Hugh Tinker who has maintained that we have a *"racial* factor" in international relations when one group of people, united by their own perception of inherited and distinctive racial qualities, are set apart from another group with (supposedly) separate inherited and distinctive racial qualities. At the same time, we have a *"racist* factor" when one group claims a dominant position justified by the supposed inferiority of the other group on the basis of physical characteristics of race like skin color but reinforced by a further claim of spiritual and mental superiority.[12]

Both these racial and racist factors, as we shall see throughout the following pages, have profoundly influenced global politics, diplomacy, and discrimination. They have greatly affected the relationship among states of different races, made racial conflicts a significant threat to international peace and security, motivated domestic groups concerned with racial discrimination to exert noticeable pressure upon the foreign policy of their own governments and to seek the active support of other nations for their protection, and propelled the issue of race high on the contemporary international agenda.[13] The first global attempt to speak for equality focused upon race. The first human rights provisions in the United Nations Charter were placed there because of race. The first international challenge to a country's claim of domestic jurisdiction and exclusive treatment of its own citizens centered upon race. The first binding treaty of human rights concentrated upon race. The international convention with the greatest number of signatories is that on race. Within the United Nations, more resolutions deal with race than with any other subject. And certainly one of the most long-standing and frustrating problems in the United Nations is that of race. One recent international conference attended by representatives of more than 120 governments, for example, went as far as to conclude that racial discrimination and racism represent the most serious problem for the world today.[14] For them, and for others, there exists substantial evidence to demonstrate that the power and the prejudice surrounding "the problem of the century" not only has dramatically influenced past politics and diplomacy of racial discrimination but is likely to influence our future as well.

1

The Heavy Burden of the Past

WHEN THE EUROPEANS CHOSE THEIR SLAVES from a race differing from their own which many of them considered as inferior to the other races of mankind, and any notion of intimate union with which they all repelled with horror, they must have believed that slavery would last forever, since there is no intermediate state that can be durable between the excessive inequality produced by servitude and the complete equality that originates in independence.

—Alexis de Tocqueville

The Tradition Begins

Discrimination is ancient in its origins. From the earliest periods of human existence, groups developed prejudices toward others and then discriminated against those whom they regarded as different or inferior. In their attempts to maintain or increase power, prestige, or wealth, groups found it easy to invent or accept the idea that others were somehow inferior to them and thus not deserving of equal treatment.[1] Among the many differences that could be (and were) used as a basis for discrimination, people quickly discovered that physical appearance was the easiest to identify. It required no careful contemplation, no subtle analysis, and no agonizing assessment of individual worth, but only a superficial glance at those visual, phenotypical features that would later be used to identify "race": the shape of another's nose or skull, skin fold of another's eyes, texture of another's hair, thickness of another's lips, and especially the color of another's skin. This helps to explain the nearly universal nature of what we now would call "racial" consciousness, which has been independently discovered and rediscovered by various white and non-white peoples alike, and has emerged in widely diverse places and in many different times throughout history.

Rudimentary drawings on the walls of prehistoric caves and paintings in Egyptian tombs, for example, readily demonstrate an early awareness

5

of racial differences. The origins of the Hindu caste system similarly indicate that the broad categories of division are based upon symbolic *varna*, or color. In descending order these include white (Brahmans), red (Kshatriyas), yellow (Vaishyas), and finally black (Shudras), with great preference given to light over dark. Many other cultures in pre-Columbian Asia, Africa, and the Americas show similar and very early patterns of prejudice based upon color and reveal the existence of race thinking long before the emergence of modern racism.[2] Systematic ideologies of racial superiority emerged only after the passing of much time, but the experiences of these societies clearly demonstrate what has been called "the impulse to inequality" as they began a tradition wherein skin color served to greater or lesser degrees as the badge of master and subject, of the free and enslaved, and of the dominators and dominated.[3]

Among these many cases of racial prejudice that led to discrimination, however, none has come even close to eclipsing that of the white, Western world in historical or international importance. Here the tradition began in embryonic form at the source of Western civilization itself, the Greeks of antiquity.[4] Facing economic and social needs beyond the limits of their own immediate resources, members of the city states found themselves increasingly dependent upon slavery. The majority of these slaves, wrote classical scholar M. I. Finley, "were not Greeks at all, but men and women from the races living outside the Greek world."[5] Small wonder, then, that slaves and foreign barbarians would become identified with each other and that efforts were made to justify this practice as part of the natural arrangement of people. No less an authority than political philosopher Aristotle, for example, asserted in his *Politics* that "barbarian and slave are by nature one and the same." Inhabitants of the colder regions of Europe he described as "deficient in skill and intelligence" and those of Asia as lacking "in spirit, and this is why they continue to be peoples of subjects and slaves." "It is nature's intention," wrote Aristotle, "to erect a physical difference between the body of the freeman and that of the slave," thus making some naturally superior to others as man is to an inferior beast. He stated his conclusion directly enough: "It is clear that just as some are by nature free, so others are by nature slaves, and for these latter the condition of slavery is both beneficial and just."[6] This position, maintained authority Michael Banton in his highly regarded work on race, represents the beginning of a "racist" feeling of prejudice used for many centuries to justify the status quo and as the "proof" of the natural superiority of the powerful. "Aristotle's doctrine," he wrote incisively, "was thus of major significance as a justification for patterns of racial relations maintained by force."[7]

Doctrines of inherent biological differences gained even wider acceptance in the classical world through the works of historians, geographers, and other commentators when they described races dwelling beyond the boundaries of the Mediterranean area. In this regard, wrote scholar Frank Snowden, "color was obviously uppermost in the minds of the Greeks and the Romans." Black Africans, or Ethiopians, he observed, provided "the yardstick" by which antiquity measured colored peoples everywhere, using skin color "as the most important distinguishing criterion."[8] The association of color with behavior followed quickly. None other than the "Father of History," Herodotus, informed his readers that Ethiopians fed on serpents, lizards, and other reptiles, were incapable of speaking any human language, and hence made sounds "like the screeching of bats." Libyans he described as a people who "burn the veins at the top of their heads," and other areas of Africa as inhabited by wild men and women, creatures with dogs' heads or no heads at all with "their eyes in their breasts."[9] Greeks and Romans held similar views of those who lived in India and the Far East.[10]

Such fantastically negative images of races to the south and east, accepted uncritically by Roman encyclopedists like Pliny, appeared particularly brutal when contrasted with images of the white-skinned peoples to the north. Even the great Roman historian Tacitus praised the Germans for possessing those physical characteristics "which we so much admire" and for being "not mixed at all with other races through immigration or intercourse" and "free from all taint of intermarriages with foreign nations."[11] It was this combination admired by Tacitus, like Aristotle before him, of physical criteria, mental qualities, and notions of superiority, wrote scholar Jacques Barzun, that provided "the model" for all subsequent theories of race.[12]

Early attitudes such as these extended far beyond the confines of time and place in antiquity. Awed and highly influenced by some of the keenest minds of Greece and Rome, authors who followed in their footsteps readily incorporated conclusions of fantasy having little basis in fact. While reinforcing ideas and myths of the past, they frequently added embellishments of their own, particularly at a time when the human species was not yet clearly defined. The popular third-century geographer, Solinus, for example, wrote in his *Collectanea rerum memorabilium* that certain black peoples of Africa represented "a bastard people among nations," and described the inhabitants as creatures who "go around like four-footed beasts."[13] Still others, he asserted, resembled dogs with "long snouts," whereas some had no noses, no mouths, or no tongues. Although he urged compassion for these unfortunate souls, even Saint Augustine described these strange and grotesque creatures of different colors as "the monstrous races."[14]

Racial distinctions proved to be of even greater importance in Muslim society. According to David Brion Davis in his pioneering works on the problem of slavery in Western culture, Arabs significantly reordered the slave trade patterns of the ancient world and thereby strengthened the growing correlation between color and domination. That is, black African slaves became far more numerous in the Arab world than in the Roman Empire. Although Muslim jurists regarded slavery as an unnatural condition that could be justified only in extraordinary circumstances, they tended to relax their standards as Arab traders moved into the interior of Africa and returned with ever larger numbers of black-skinned captives. Muslims not only began to accept the legitimacy of black enslavement in this process but also to consider Africans as an inferior and contemptible race born to be slaves. Indeed, the Arabic word for slaves, *abid*, was increasingly confined to blacks alone. The more the Muslims witnessed black Africans in captivity, the more they assigned to them a variety of derogatory physical and characterological traits. Arabic literature of the eighth and ninth centuries, for example, revealed black skin color as having been associated with offensive odor, repulsiveness, mental deficiency, uncontrolled sexuality, savagery, and evil. "From these premises," wrote Davis about the Muslims, "it followed that the enslavement of blacks was as natural as the domestication of beasts of burden." This led him to conclude in his most recent and brilliant book, *Slavery and Human Progress:* "The similarity between Muslim and later Christian racial imagery tells us less about black Africans than about the common pressures felt by a 'white' ruling race intent on celebrating its own progressive civilization while keeping slaves or an underclass of freedmen in a state of permanent subordination. Racial stereotypes, in both instances, were clearly nourished by a long-term flow of slave labor from sub-Saharan Africa."[15]

These several ideas and attitudes of the Greco-Roman experience and those transmitted from the Arab world helped to establish in Western civilization a tradition of ways of thinking about race. It is too much to assert that these ideas constituted an elaborate racist ideology or unambiguous and uninterrupted racism in the modern sense of the word. They clearly did not. At least some observers have believed that despite their attitudes, the Greeks and Romans practiced little racial discrimination in policy.[16] Their opinions of other races, however dim and sporadic, nevertheless did begin a pattern of thought about racial superiority. The fact that these notions were expressed by the most respected authorities of antiquity like Aristotle, Herodotus, and Tacitus, among many others, gave them unparalleled and unchallenged credibility.

When the classics were rediscovered, revived, and read, the ideas about races passed from one generation to others over centuries. Political treatises, historical essays, literary works, and travel accounts of unknown lands during the medieval period and Renaissance carried the heritage even further. Thus, long before they ever set foot in any significant way on other continents or established permanent diplomatic contact with other peoples, Europeans possessed an extensive tradition of certain negative images, attitudes, and practices toward other races of the world. As late as the end of the fourteenth century, they still could consult the renowned Catalan Atlas and read that the inhabitants of the Indies comprised "a people different from any other . . . who are black and without rational faculties. They eat white strangers whenever they can."[17] At the same time, the noted historian and thinker of Muslim North Africa, Ibn Khaldun, reserved his most pejorative comments for blacks: "To the south of the Nile there is a Negro people called Lamlam. They are unbelievers. . . . The people of Ghana and Takrur invade their country, capture them, and sell them to merchants who transport them to the Maghrib. They constitute the ordinary mass of slaves. Beyond them to the south, there is no civilization in the proper sense. They are only humans who are closer to dumb animals than to rational beings. . . . They frequently eat each other. They cannot be considered human beings."[18]

Blackness, in fact, began to assume a particular aesthetic and moral meaning. In an age that believed so strongly in symbolism, no other color except white conveyed so much emotional impact: Black came to represent evil, depravity, filth, ugliness, baseness, wickedness, danger, death, and sin. Europeans sometimes referred to the ultimate Christian symbol of evil, the devil, as the "black horseman" or the "great Negro."[19] The black arts, black magic, and the Black Death carried this sinister and dangerous image even further. White, in contrast, consistently denoted purity, cleanliness, beauty, virtue, virginity, beneficence, and holiness. Christianity itself, as did Islam, increasingly became associated with complexion.[20] When Europeans took such emotionally charged and intensely suggestive connotations of color (however abstract, ambiguous, and fantasy based), applied them to human races, and then combined them with additional preconceptions of foreign peoples, the results often proved to be catastrophic for those who were not white. This could be seen as the Europeans set out to discover and explore the wider world.

If the frontiers of thought regarding race remained constricted and confined during this period, those of geography burst beyond imagination. Equipped with the caravel ship design, magnetic compass, astrolabe, and firearms and possessed with the prospect of commercial gain, curiosity for the unknown, missionary zeal, and the hope of finding an ally against the Turkish enemy, explorers in the fifteenth century sailed off across distant oceans. They set into motion one of the most significant movements in the history of man: the European discovery, exploration, and eventual domination of the farthest parts of the globe. Slowly and cautiously easing out of the familiar Mediterranean and known coastal waters of the past, Portuguese sailors under the leadership of Prince Henry the Navigator conducted explorations southward around Africa. In 1434 they passed the dreaded, reef-encrusted Cape Bojador, ten years later they passed Cape Verde, and then the mouth of the Senegal River. The pace quickened, and they crossed the equator in 1473, rounded the Cape of Good Hope, and within a few years Vasco da Gama crossed the Indian Ocean, establishing the first direct commercial link between Europe and the Far East. Spurred by these successes of their rival, the Spanish sponsored expeditions to the west across the Atlantic, and by 1492 Christopher Columbus brought exciting word of a New World. In less than a single century, the Portuguese reached Africa, Asia, and Spanish America, thus discovering more territory in seventy-five years than had been discovered in the previous one thousand.

In none of these new territories did Europeans encounter whites quite like themselves. Each voyage brought them instead into contact with larger and larger numbers of people scattered across the continents, people with what they considered to be black, brown, yellow, and red skin colors. This fact was to have enormous consequences for the diplomacy of the world. In sharp contrast with the nearly exclusive intra-European and racially homogeneous relationships of Renaissance diplomacy,[21] diplomatic relations now began to expand in geographical scope to become international in fact. Thus, international relations—as we shall see by their very nature—slowly, but increasingly and inextricably came to be interracial relations as well.

Yet despite increased contact with other continents during this first part of the age of discovery, Europeans' attitudes about race demonstrated little change at all. Growing familiarity did not result in greater toleration, compassion, or acceptance, and the old stereotyped images showed tenacious persistence. The chronicler of Prince Henry's discovery, Gomes Eannes de Azurara, continued to write during the fifteenth century of blacks to the south as a tainted, inferior people destined to be slaves: a race that "should be subject to all other races in the world."[22] Editions of Pierre Cardinal d'Ailly's popular *Imago Mundi*, a compilation of astronomical and geographical knowledge, still asserted the existence in the West of "savage men who eat human flesh and have depraved and frightening faces . . . [whose] bodies are of abnormal complexion and poor and repulsive of physique. Therefore, they are base in manner and savage in speech, and there are men or beasts in these places who present such a dreadful aspect, that one can tell only with difficulty whether they are men or beasts, according to what the blessed Augustine says."[23] Columbus himself reinforced this image, for his reports rapidly abandoned the initial impression of the aboriginal islanders in the Indies as simple and gentle noble savages and emphasized the vicious man-eating Caribs, violent in their behavior and brutal beyond description.[24]

Following the initial stages of exploration, Portuguese and Spanish state leaders confronted a critical choice about the nature of their future relationship with these different peoples and races. Should they establish embassies, exchange accredited ambassadors, respectfully observe the sovereign rights of others, and follow the modalities of diplomatic behavior as practiced by the courts of Europe? Or should these tribes considered as uncivilized, barbaric, militarily weak, non-Christian, and fit for slavery be treated very differently? The answer came quickly. Through a series of papal decrees and diplomatic negotiations resulting in the Treaty of Tordesillas (1494), these two powers on the tiny Iberian Peninsula drew a line of demarcation around the globe, granting to Portugal all of Africa, India, Japan, and Brazil and to Spain all the rest of the Western Hemisphere. By means of diplomacy they divided the world between themselves, as they said, for "dominium"[25]—not so much for knowledge and discovery, but rather for domination and conquest.

Conquest and Captives

A dramatic example of this approach changing from mere discovery on the one hand to exploitation on the other can be seen in the first two Portuguese voyages to India. When Vasco da Gama reached the port of Calicut on the western coast of India, he anchored in the harbor as a peaceful friend interested in the spice trade and Christian converts. When he returned to the same port on his second voyage, he came as a conqueror and bombarded the city. Pressed by a government and merchants anxious for power and profits, he and his successors desperately wanted to eliminate the Muslim monopoly over trade in the Indian Ocean. "The Portuguese immediately realized that they could break it by brute force and not by peaceful competition," wrote historian C. R. Boxer. "This they proceeded to do with complete ruthlessness and astonishing speed."[26] To achieve this objective, Portugal needed strategically located naval bases and commercial entrepôts and seized the important island of Goa in 1510, captured Malacca the next year, and then wrested control of Ormuz. These three choke points ensured Portuguese domination of the Persian Gulf, Indian Ocean, and access to the Java and South China seas. Such acquisitions, when added to the emerging footholds on the west coast of Africa and the Swahili ports in East Africa, strongholds in the Moluccas and Macao on the edge of the Pacific, and new settlements along the Brazilian littoral, provided Portugal with the beginnings of its expansive and lucrative seaborne empire. From this empire the Portuguese grew powerful and wealthy, trading in goods and black slaves, exploiting native peoples, and demonstrating a behavior throughout the entire process that the eminent scholar, J. H. Plumb, described as nothing short of being "intensely racist."[27]

Only the spectacular triumphs of the Spanish could match this Portuguese experience in the early sixteenth century. Regarding the Treaty of Tordesillas as their legal claim for exploiting lands in the New World, the Spanish immediately began to establish settlements on Hispaniola and then on Cuba, Puerto Rico, and Jamaica. More significant by far, however, was the launching of the campaigns for conquest by the conquistadores. Motivated by material greed, ambition to strike down the pagan religion and win souls for Christ, and the love of great deeds, the first of these, Hernán Cortes, set out in 1519 toward the high central plateau of Mexico. Within less than three years the ancient civilization of the Aztecs lay in ruins at his feet and its wealth of gold and precious stones at his disposal. Encouraged by these riches, Pedro de Alvarado subsequently led a well-equipped force in a brutal campaign against the Mayas of Guatemala. Then, with a rapacity and ruthlessness that shocked even his own men, Francisco Pizarro attacked the Incas of Peru. His treasures and those that followed provided the main source of bullion for Europe during the next three centuries. In this conquest, the Spanish possessed an unquenchable confidence in their own racial, religious, and cultural superiority. "To the conquistador," wrote one authority, "an Indian was a heathen and a savage, little better than an animal" to be defeated, exploited, and enslaved.[28]

The inhuman treatment of these native peoples horrified many who witnessed it directly and indelibly marked the character of what has been perceptively called the "first widespread meeting of races."[29] For the Spanish in particular it gave rise to the *leyenda negra*, "Black Legend," of extraordinary cruelty.[30] Repulsed by the massacres and sufferings inflicted upon the Indians, a number of influential Spaniards openly condemned their government's brutal policies. The noted jurist, Francisco de Vitoria, delivered a series of stinging lectures at the University of Salamanca firmly and unequivocally rejecting conquest, arguing instead for a new international law among nations involving rights and duties for all peoples. The official reprimand that he received for this unorthodox position provoked other critics to push even further, including the Dominican priest, Bartholome de Las Casas, with his shocking account of atrocities entitled *Brief Relation of the Destruction of the Indies*. Both in this work and in his great 1550 debate before the Congregation of Valladolid with the leading Spanish scholastic of his day, Juan Gines de Sepulveda, he argued for constraints based upon religious precepts and vehemently rejected the proposition that red-skinned natives were a race condemned by nature to servitude in accordance with the Aristotelian doctrine of inferior barbarians. "The Indians are our brothers," he argued, "and Christ has given his life for them. Why, then, do we persecute them with such inhuman savagery?"[31]

Such challenging words publicly confronted a major European power over its professed Christian ethics and policy of conquest. In the end, however, only slight reforms resulted, and the people with vested interests in exploitation used the vast distance between policy in Spain and implementation in the New World to full advantage. "To insist with Las Casas that Indians should be won over by persuasion only," wrote scholar J. H. Parry, "was to abandon all future conquests and admit the injustice of past ones. The full implications of either theory were more than any self-respecting government of the time could stomach."[32] Consequently, with few effective restraints, exploitation continued apace. One authority estimated that in Mexico alone, the Spanish Conquest resulted in the decimation of the Indian population, which fell from 4.5 million in 1519 to 3.3 million in 1570 to only 1.3 million by 1646.[33] As the Indians of the New World thus languished, died out, or were exterminated, Spanish and Portuguese settlers found themselves desperately in need of a labor force to clear the land and work the fields. As a solution, slavers descended upon Africa for captives.

Slavery, of course, was an ancient tradition that ranged from the Western Hemisphere to Africa, the Middle East, and Asia. It was neither invented by white Europeans nor confined exclusively to black Africans. In fact, whites themselves had known enslavement on both the Christian and Muslim shores of the Mediterranean and Black seas, in what is now Eastern Europe and Russia, in European colonies, and in Africa and Asia.[34] But what began to emerge during the sixteenth century dramatically transformed slave patterns of the past. In terms of total numbers, focus upon a particular race, and tragic brutality, it had no parallel in human history. This new black slave trade, wrote one authority, "was larger, crueller, more systematic than anything Europe had known before. In many ways it was the most inhuman aspect of European history—for the middle passage remained for centuries one of the most brutal experiences inflicted by man upon men."[35]

Black slavery took root in the Americas not from carefully concerted planning, vast historical design, or racial destiny, but rather from innumerable local and pragmatic choices made in four continents over time. But during the latter three-quarters of the sixteenth century, ample and cumulative evidence mounted that the fortunes of white conquerors in the New World increasingly depended upon black captives from Africa.[36] Traders consequently fell upon the "slave coast" of West Africa, taking victims either by force or by barter and bribe (often with the assistance of local native rivals) from the Jolofs and Mandinga tribes of Senegambia, the Ardra and Yoruba of Lower Guinea, and then from natives of the Congo and Angola, sending their human cargo bound on ships across the Atlantic. In the event that profits alone would not sufficiently justify this slave trade, slavers could always use arguments about racial inferiority or saving heathen souls when dealing with these black savages described as "almost beasts in human form."[37] "Almost everyone is convinced," wrote one Jesuit missionary on the West African coast, "that the conversion of these barbarians is not to be achieved through love, but only after they have been subdued by force of arms."[38]

Opinions of this kind, when combined with the exploitation and brutality of the early slave trade, demonstrated that power and prejudice reinforced each other and greatly deepened a consciousness of global racial differences. Not only increased contact between one continent and another but also the very nature of that contact where captives were sold into slavery simply reinforced existing stereotypes throughout the sixteenth century about the presumed superiority of the white race. As argued by one Portuguese civil servant with intimate knowledge of Africa, blackness represented an outward sign of God's contempt for Africans and slavery was a punishment for natural inferiority. "The inhabitants of this region," he wrote, "have the faces and teeth of dogs and tails like dogs; they are black and shun conversation, not liking to see other men."[39] The noted geographer André Thevet claimed in his *Cosmographie universelle* (1575) that black Africans were "stupid, bestial, and blinded by folly."[40] "All these dusky races," continued the influential Jesuit missionary Alexandre Valignamo in diplomatic reports to his superiors, "are very stupid and vicious, and of the basest spirits."[41]

Asia presented a somewhat different case. There the landmass was dominated by East Asians, who had a well-defined, ancient civilization and the power to keep foreigners at bay. For over two hundred years visitors from Europe did not enjoy victor status as they did elsewhere but stayed in East Asia on sufferance or were sometimes expelled at will. Interestingly enough, many Europeans at first regarded the Chinese and Japanese as essentially "white." But, through time, as historian Donald Lach observed in his monumental, multivolume study, Europeans developed clearly identifiable racial attitudes about Asians. After examining countless numbers of diplomatic despatches, missionary reports, pamphlets, commercial assessments, and literary works of all kinds, Lach concluded that "in the eyes of Europe, the image of Asia was constantly changing in detail while remaining surprisingly constant in general outline. . . . While visual distortions became fewer in the Renaissance and the sixteenth century, the concrete and the fantastic continued to be intermingled."[42] In their "composite picture," he wrote, the peoples of Asia

> are divided roughly into types by color: black, shades of brown, and white. The black people are the Africans, the natives of South India, and the East Indians. The indigenous people of north India and continental southeast Asia are often described as being tawny or swarthy. Japanese and Chinese are white both to the merchants and to the missionaries. That their colors are related to habits and abilities is most clearly brought out. . . . The black peoples are generally conceived of as being inferior, incapable of improvement, and hopelessly sunk in superstition.[43]

These images and the attitudes that produced them generally went hand in hand with the unrivaled victories of the Portuguese and Spanish in defeating and exploiting those of different races. Although their staggering successes generated envy among other states eager to enjoy the benefits of empire, overseas affairs possessed little importance for European diplomacy as long as these two Iberian kingdoms satisfactorily demarcated their respective interests and no other powers contested their claims. Yet, by the seventeenth century the English, Dutch, French, Danes, Swedes, and then the Prussians sought to make clear their determination to fight for a share of the spoils in territories ranging all the way from the shores of the Cape of Good Hope in southern Africa to the eastern coast of North America and from the East Indies in the Pacific to the West Indies in the Caribbean. They sent out privateers to prey on treasure ships, navies to interdict trading routes, armies to conquer territory, adventurers to secure colonies, and merchants to capture profits. "Trade," wrote one leading government official of the time in introducing a major new theme to modern diplomacy, "is the cause of perpetual combat in war and in peace between the nations of Europe."[44] Religion added even greater intensity to this fierce struggle, as the seapower of these challengers rested almost entirely in the hands of militant Protestants eager to strike blows against Catholicism through diminishing the power of Portugal and Spain. The onslaught and penetration of these other Europeans resulted in the further expansion of white-controlled empires in Africa, Asia, and the Americas.

Whatever their practical intentions or purposes, the white Europeans did not confront indigenous peoples in these many lands with neutral opinions about race. As we have seen, certain preconceptions and images about people of color had become the common property of the West, thereby constituting a distorting lens through which the Europeans assessed the potential and predicted the fate of those non-white natives they encountered. These beliefs, it must be emphasized, were not yet racist in the nineteenth-century sense of the term because they did not entail an explicit doctrine of genetic or biological inequality. In addition, circumstances did not always allow the Europeans to act strictly in accordance with these ideas, nor were the images so fixed and unambiguous that they could not be modified by practical experience. But, as scholar George Fredrickson correctly observes in his comparative study entitled *White Supremacy*, they did establish a mode of thinking about racial differences that helped to set the parameters of white response and provided a basis for considering some categories of human beings inferior to others in ways that made it seem legitimate to treat them differently.[45] It was not that white Europeans held the only attitudes about racial prejudice in the world, but that they possessed sufficient power for conquest to make others suffer accordingly. This could be seen in its starkest form in the taking of captives for the slave trade.

Of all the many prizes of power and profit to be gained in international competition, the opportunity to trade in human slaves was the most coveted, most promising, and most lucrative in the eyes of contemporaries.[46] Colonization in the sparsely populated New World created a burgeoning demand for workers to clear the land, dig in the mines, and especially to work in labor-intensive agriculture. Booming sugar, tobacco, and then rice production, in particular, fueled the market to unprecedented proportions. Attempts to enslave Caribs and Indians seldom succeeded, and indentured servants provided only temporary assistance. Plantation owners from English and French possessions in North America to Portuguese and Spanish holdings in South America thus needed massive numbers of slaves that could be worked hard and bonded for life. This led ambitious traders readily to conclude "that Negroes were very good merchandise."[47] With the gradual introduction of slavery into the new colonies and the important *asiento de negros*, or formal concession to supply the older possessions of Spain with African captives, what had been a mere trickle of slaves across the Atlantic in the past turned into a veritable flood by the seventeenth century. Added to these dictates of the marketplace were the dicta of law, as even Hugo Grotius, "The Father of International Law," provided legal justification for black African slavery.[48] The result proved to be one of the most profitable—and tragic—enterprises in human history and one that would plague international race relations for centuries.

Atlantic civilization and its achievements, wrote historian Robert Herzstein, "rested on the backs of African slaves, and the products of colonial plantations were enjoyed by complacent Europeans who gave little thought to the millions of blacks whose labor made these products possible. The capture, transportation, and sale of 'black ivory,'" he concluded, "became one of the most lucrative branches of transatlantic commerce. The Portuguese, Dutch, French, and English competed for the privilege of supplying plantation owners, from Brazil to Virginia, with blacks who had been carried away by force from their African homelands to toil in the white man's service."[49] Indeed, for the New World as a whole, from Brazil and the Caribbean to the Chesapeake Bay, the importation of black African slaves far surpassed the flow of white European immigrants during the first three and one-third centuries of settlement. As Davis concluded, "black slavery was an intrinsic part of 'the rise of the West'" and for states to refrain from participating in it "was almost as unthinkable as spurning nuclear technology is in the world of today."[50]

In order to take full advantage of the financial opportunities of this trade in humans, investors formed companies specifically to maximize the profits of slaving. Some of the largest and most successful business organizations of all time resulted, including the Company of Cacheo and the Grao-Para and Maranhao Company of Portugal; the Dutch West India Company and East India Company; the British East India Company and Royal African Company; the Guinea Company and Compagnie de Rouen of France; and the Brandenburg Company of Prussia, among others. The Board of Trade meeting in London accurately reflected the opinion of businessmen in many other capitals when the board members ruled that it was "absolutely necessary that a trade so beneficial to the kingdom should be carried on to the greatest advantage."[51] Official policy, often accompanied by investments from the royal families of Europe, guaranteed even further financial successes. Not only did ports like Bristol, Liverpool, and Nantes enjoy a new prosperity from the slave trade, but also Europe as a whole experienced an enormous accumulation of capital and the emergence of commercial capitalism. The precise nature of the relationship between slavery, racism, and capitalism eventually became a subject of great debate.[52] Slavery and racial attitudes, of course, antedated capitalism; but there can be little doubt that capitalism, in turn, strengthened them both. Later, as we shall see, this argument assumed much greater proportions than mere scholarly discussion, for the politics and diplomacy of discrimination in the twentieth century pitted Communist countries eager to exploit this past against those with capitalist systems reluctantly pressed to acknowledge their own historical role before the majority of the non-white world.

One of the most fateful features of this entire development was the fact that by the seventeenth century, Europeans and Africans met each other in the distorted context of slavery. By this stage, they met not as diplomatic equals or political peers, but rather more often than not as conqueror and captive, master and slave—as white and black. Such a warped, asymmetrical relationship naturally led the strong (in contrast to the weak) to emphasize differences and not similarities. The degradation of blacks could serve, of course, to bind together the white population, or segments of it, to create a sense of community and solidarity, especially if outnumbered.[53] But it also could be used with devastating effect by those seeking to rationalize or justify the slave trade and with it the casting aside of heretofore acceptable legal and ethical norms of behavior. Europeans increasingly set Africans *apart* from themselves, describing them as "heathens" and "pagans" in religion, "bestial" and "brutish" in behavior, and "lewd" and "lustful" in sex, and thus fit only for enslavement.[54]

Among all the distinctions, however, nothing was greater than color. As scholar Winthrop Jordon wrote in his study of racial attitudes, blackness proved "the most arresting characteristic" of all and the one that exerted a "powerful impact" upon negative perceptions when some of the fairest-skinned people of the world came face to face with some of the darkest.[55] Some white observers described the black complexion of Africans as a "natural infection" plaguing an inferior, "polluted" people.[56] Others accepted the widely held notion that black Africans were descended from Noah's son Ham whose curse from God, as interpreted from the Old Testament account, supposedly made him not only black but destined to be a "servant of servants." Many Europeans found in this "curse of Ham" not only a direct association between blackness and slavery but also an unfolding of divine purpose that took precedence over teachings of Christian compassion and provided justification for exploitation and enslavement.[57] These several components of attitude, in the haunting words of Jordon, created "that sense of *difference* which provided the mental margin absolutely requisite for placing the Europeans on the deck of the slave ship and the Negro in the hold."[58]

Racial Slavery and Separation

With the growth of the international slave trade and racial slavery in the seventeenth century, the theories of colored inferiority gained wider acceptance. Indeed, the concomitance of racial prejudice and the power to enslave blacks suggests a strong mutual relationship between the two. Both were, after all, twin aspects of the debasement of blacks from people into property; and race relations obviously developed not only from ideas but also from a particular legal and social order in which racial contact occurred. But rather than slavery strictly causing a prejudice of race, or vice versa, they seem instead to have been equally cause and effect, appearing constantly together and continually reinforcing each other over time.[59] The more that whites observed blacks in captivity, the more the whites believed they possessed empirical evidence of their own superiority. The more that slavery expanded, the more strident became the rhetoric about race and the policies of discrimination for separation. As Fredrickson wrote, the experience of enslaving non-whites, more than any other factor, established a presumption "that whites were naturally masters," and this slaveholding mentality "remained the wellspring of white supremacist thought and action long after the institution that originally sustained it had been relegated to the dustbin of history."[60]

The similarities among European slave traders and New World slave owners in regard to racial separation were far more striking than any national differences.[61] Portuguese settlers, for example, long familiar with the concept of *pureza de sangue*, "purity of blood," when applied to Jews in Iberia, now increasingly distanced themselves from the *racas infectas*, "contaminated races,"[62] and, in the words of one authority, created a caste system "based on white supremacy and the institution-alized inferiority of colored slaves."[63] The Spanish Crown likewise promulgated specific laws to "prohibit contact and communication be-tween Indians and Mulattoes, Negroes, and similar races."[64] French slave laws, known as the *code noir*, stressed discipline, punishment, and keeping the races apart.[65] As one official despatch explained the discriminatory regulations: "This law is hard, but it is both wise and necessary in a land of fifteen slaves to one white. Between the races we cannot dig too deep a gulf. Upon the Negro we cannot impress too much respect for those he serves. This distinction, rigorously upheld even after enfranchisement, is the surest way to maintain subordination; for the slave must thus see that his color is ordained to servitude, and that nothing can make him his master's equal."[66]

Colonists from England acted in a similar fashion, gradually separating whites from blacks by a screen of racial contempt and law, including the Act to Regulate the Negroes on the British Plantations, which declared blacks as "of wild, barbarous, and savage nature to be controlled only with strict severity."[67] They further constructed legal structures designed to make blacks enslaved "for life," prohibit miscegenation or interracial marriages, and grant an owner, in the words of the Fundamental Constitutions of Carolina, "absolute power and authority over his Negro slaves."[68] The Dutch in their enslavement not only of Africans but also of peoples from Indonesia, Mozambique, Madagascar, and the Bay of Bengal region, despite greater permissiveness toward sexual relations between races, also developed policies that conveyed, in the words of one authority, their "innate conviction of white superiority."[69] Moreover, in their own separation of the races, Dutch settlers introduced to the world the concept, if not the precise word, that many years later would charge the politics and diplomacy of discrimination with intense emotion: apartheid.

These policies provided fertile soil into which the roots of racial slavery could thrust themselves still deeper during the eighteenth century. As France and Britain extended their overseas empires and ascended in global power, the number of slaves grew within their possessions in the Caribbean and on the North American continent. In the process, they extended their slave codes even further to buttress racial exclusivism and protect privileged positions. French plantation owners in Martinique, Saint-Domingue (now Haiti), and Guadeloupe enforced rigid regulations and harsh treatment of slaves and imposed an obdurate policy of discrimination against men and women of color.[70] "The safety of the whites," declared the governor of one of the colonies, "requires that the Negroes be treated like animals."[71] Even in metropolitan France strong racial policies aimed against blacks prevailed, as evidenced by specific laws prohibiting miscegenation and restrictions upon admitting Negro slaves into the country for fear, in the words of the king, of "the mixing of black blood in the kingdom."[72] Such racial legislation confronted even Charles Cornier, the mayor of Saint-Louis in Senegal, who was refused entry into France in April 1789 because of his color.[73]

The British met, if not exceeded these policies of discrimination, particularly in their American holdings. The swelling size of a slave population and a growing determination to extend enslavement steadily committed the colonies to the institution of slavery and to patterns that would plague both their black and their white heirs for generations. Fearful of slave revolts and insurrections, interracial sexual union, and challenges to the existing social and economic structure and political authority, slaveowners and others sought to impose legal codes against blacks. Indeed, by the middle of the eighteenth century, not one American colony remained without laws dealing specifically with the governance of blacks and legally making them different from whites, even though in Britain no such statutes existed.[74] Placing these regulations in the text of binding law also provided the opportunity for delineating the presumed characteristics of blacks in such a way as to justify the discriminatory measures against them. As the framers of the South Carolina code stated in a preamble borrowed from an earlier Barbados statute, special laws were necessary due to the "barbarous, wild, savage natures" of blacks, which rendered them "wholly unqualified to be governed by the laws, customs, and practices of this Province" protecting other citizens.[75]

Just as these political, economic, and social factors of the era extended slavery, the intellectual tenor of the time also helped to develop and strengthen an existing image of racial superiority. Eighteenth-century naturalists and men of letters, in their efforts to understand the avalanche of disjointed information coming from the world about them, possessed a compulsion to bring order out of chaos by categorizing objects of nature. They applied new classification schemes to plants, animals, and even men, in seeking to determine the relationship of one species to another in a great chain of being. In this endeavor, purely physical differences among peoples acquired heightened significance as there emerged a concept of human inequality based upon climatic, cultural, and especially racial criteria. For the classifiers of mankind, European/ American whiteness and the African's blackness afforded two opposite polar positions from which they could calculate the colors—and, hence, the hierarchical value—of all the peoples of the globe.[76]

In his listing of the races of man in *Systema naturae* (1735), for example, the famous Swedish naturalist, Carol von Linnaeus, placed Africans last, next to a category he called monstrous, and described them as crafty, indolent, and governed by caprice.[77] The great German physiologist and comparative anatomist who is often called the founder of anthropology, Johann Friedrich Blumenbach, introduced the term *Caucasian* in his *De generis humani varietate nativa* (1775) and argued that in an international comparison of the races, "the white color holds the first place," while the the others like black, yellow, and brown are merely degenerates from the original.[78] Numerous French writers asserted that blacks represented the link between the orangutans and humans.[79] The Dutch anatomist, Peter Camper, pioneered the idea of "facial angle" and expounded the notion of a hierarchical arrangement of skulls from apes and black Africans at the bottom, through orientals in the middle, to white Europeans at the top.[80] "Ascending the line of gradation," wrote the English surgeon Charles White in a similar vein in his *Regular Gradation of Man, and in Different Animals and Vegetables* (1799), "we come at last to the white European; who being most removed from brute creation, may, on that account, be considered the most beautiful of the human race. No one will doubt his superiority. . . ."[81] Even the highly regarded first U.S. edition of the *Encyclopaedia Britannica*, under the entry on "Negroes," referred to blacks as "this unhappy race" and described their behavior as characterized by "idleness, treachery, revenge, cruelty, impudence, stealing, lying, debauchery, nastiness and intemperance, [which] are said to have extinguished the principles of natural law and to have silenced the reproofs of conscience. They are strangers to every sentiment of compassion, and are an awful example of the corruption of man when left to himself."[82]

Added to these widely respected opinions of the scientific and intellectual community were those of political philosophy. Most ironically, at a time when some of the greatest minds of the Enlightenment generated democratic principles of liberation, equality, toleration, natural rights, and respect for the dignity of man and challenged the traditional assumption that a privileged few had the God-given right to rule over the vast majority of the population, these same thinkers confined much of the application of these principles to their own white race alone. The noted philosopher David Hume, who also served as under secretary of state for Britain and dealt with colonial affairs, wrote blatantly:

> I am apt to suspect the Negroes and in general all the other species of men (for which are four or five different kinds) to be naturally inferior to the whites. There never was a civilized nation of any other complexion than white, nor even any individual eminent either in action or speculation. No ingenious manufactures amongst them, no arts, no sciences. . . . In Jamaica indeed they talk of one Negro as a man of parts and learning; but 'tis likely he is admired for very slender accomplishments like a parrot, who speaks a few words plainly.[83]

This attitude of racial superiority received further confirmation from other philosophes such as Montesquieu who described people of Africa as "savage and barbarian" bereft "of industry" and who "have no arts."[84] Diderot and Condorcet expressed similar opinions. Although these men argued against the institution of slavery in theory, in practice they were cautious, ambivalent, or even supportive. John Locke, the celebrated philosopher of human liberty, was actually a shareholder in the Royal African Company. Voltaire, too, owned stock in the Compagnie des Indes, the fortunes of which came in part from the slave trade, and wrote that blacks possessed only "a few more ideas than animals" and that as "a result of a hierarchy of nations, Negroes are thus slaves of other men."[85] In the United States, the passionate advocate and great national leader for freedom and democracy, Thomas Jefferson, not only owned slaves himself, but went as far as to hazard the thesis that "blacks, whether originally a distinct race, or made distinct by time and circumstances, are inferior to whites in the endowments of both body and mind."[86]

Such opinions seeking to justify racial discrimination and slavery, however, did not go unchallenged. During the last three decades of the eighteenth century, organized agitation grew appreciably, particularly from within reformist churches, to advance the belief that slave labor was an intolerable obstacle to human progress and an offense against Christian morality. Protestant spokesmen like Granville Sharp, Benjamin Rush, James Ramsay, and John Wesley, among others from the Quakers, Methodists, Baptists, Congregationalists, and Presbyterians, presented their attacks upon slavery as a vindication of Christianity, moral accountability, and the unity of mankind. They passionately argued that emancipation of slaves was fundamental to the message of love and compassion from the Gospels, Christ's mission "to proclaim freedom to the captives," and the vision of resurrection and redemption. For them, the struggle against slavery presented an opportunity for Christianity to redeem itself as a progressive force for mankind and posed a decisive test for religion and moral philosophy.[87] If black slavery, wrote James Beattie in *Elements of Moral Science* (1793), be "excusable, or pardonable, it is vain to talk any longer of the external distinctions of right and wrong, truth and falsehood, good and evil."[88]

With the explosions and upheavals of the American and French revolutions at the end of the eighteenth century, these religious voices found themselves joined by others. Despite the fact that many of the most influential authorities still supported racial discrimination and slavery, political critics charged that in new times these practices and the attitudes that supported them were cruel, repulsive, and grossly out of place. It appeared to the critics that many of their "revolutionary" leaders and fellow whites wanted to restrict and control the liberating political thought of the Enlightenment about natural rights in such a way as to underwrite greater freedom for themselves without weakening their dominance over imported slaves or conquered indigenes.[89] For this reason, abolitionists on both sides of the Atlantic organized themselves as the Society for Effecting the Abolition of the Slave Trade, in Britain; the Société des amis des noirs, in France; and the Society for the Relief of Free Negroes Unlawfully Held in Bondage, among others, in America; to campaign actively for the elimination of slavery and the slave trade.

Although both visible and vocal, these religious and abolitionist groups lacked sufficient power in politics and diplomacy to bring about the immediate changes they so desired. For example, even though the new U.S. Constitution of 1787 authorized Congress to outlaw the slave trade, it prohibited any action for twenty years, did not prevent Americans from engaging in the traffic between Africa and other countries, made no clear distinction between property rights and human rights, and essentially provided official sanction for the practice of slavery itself. Even though the activists of the French Revolution extended the rights of citizenship to those of color in 1791 and shortly thereafter abolished slavery in the colonies, they did so, as scholar William Cohen observed, "not due to a fundamental reappraisal of the black man, but . . . rather the result of political and strategic exigencies."[90] Napoleon quickly reversed these changes and reinstituted both restrictive racial legislation in France and slavery in the colonies.

The prominent political and intellectual leaders of the Enlightenment and the Age of Democratic Revolution thus preferred to speak of freedom and democracy for themselves—but not for their slaves nor those of other races. Fearful of what the future would bring, Jefferson painfully agonized: "Indeed I tremble for my country when I reflect that God is just; that his justice cannot sleep for ever; that considering the numbers, nature and natural means only, a revolution of the wheel of fortune, and exchange of situation, is among possible events."[91] His fears of bloodshed and changed power relations soon developed a remarkable basis in fact as the United States and the world moved into the nineteenth century.

Even though the revolutions in North America and France failed to abolish slavery or the slave trade, they did provide sufficient impetus to spark the first successful revolt by black slaves and what has been called "the first great shock between the ideals of white supremacy and race equality" in history.[92] In Saint-Domingue thousands of blacks seized firebrands and machetes to rise up against their white masters and mulattoes. The leader of the rebellion, a full-blooded black ex-slave named Toussaint L'Ouverture, described himself as the "first of the blacks" and the "black George Washington." Under his direction, the rebels fought first the French slaveowners, then British and Spanish expeditionary forces, and finally the allegedly invincible armies of Napoleon sent against them. These foreign attempts to crush the rebellion, stop its bloody slaughter, and regain control of colonial holdings ultimately failed. On New Year's Day 1804 the victorious rebels declared the Republic of Haiti as the first independent black nation in the world. Standing before a crowd of shouting followers, the new black ruler, Jean-Jacques Dessalines, seized the old tricolor in furious hatred and dramatically tore from it the band of white. Shortly thereafter he ordered the massacre of remaining whites.

This momentous revolt provoked enormous alarm. Blacks successfully rising up against whites posed the specter of similar slave insurrections elsewhere, the loss of empire and its profits, and brutal retribution for past racial discrimination. The Saint-Domingue revolution thus decisively strengthened negrophobia by reinforcing a by then centuries-old image of blacks as savage barbarians. The French quickly imposed new legislation against blacks in France and in its colonies.[93] Extremely fearful that the disease of slave revolts so uncomfortably close to home might spread, a number of U.S. states immediately moved to place restrictions on the entry of blacks and other people of color from the West Indies. For good measure, the United States adopted a policy it would use with even greater frequency in the twentieth century when facing a distasteful regime: it refused to grant diplomatic recognition to the "Black Republic" of Haiti for fifty-eight years. The brutality of this revolt paradoxically also caused a marked decline in the fervor of those in the antislavery movement who now confronted the possible explosive consequences of emancipation and feared, as they said, "the effects experienced from the ungovernable rage and violence of the Blacks on Saint-Domingue."[94] For this reason, many abolitionists during the first part of the nineteenth century turned their attention and energies away from the politically volatile issue of slavery at home and toward what at least seemed to be the diplomatically fruitful area of the slave trade abroad.

The best example of this shift in focus occurred among the active and energetic British abolitionists. Led by such charismatic and indefatigable crusaders as Thomas Clarkson and William Wilberforce, they sought to direct public attention toward a clearly definable political goal: an act of Parliament outlawing the previously favored slave trade. They argued that at least half of the international trade was in British hands and that those profiting from this traffic in human cargo would not cease unless they were deprived of the economically artificial and morally corrupting supply of black slaves. A lengthy and bitter struggle ensued, both inside and outside of Parliament. In this contest, the abolitionists found that the moral and intellectual force of their arguments gained startling support, especially among those segments of the public influenced by a sense of national guilt over the past, the crusading zeal of evangelical Christianity, the self-interests of a nation at war, and new economic interest groups either unconnected with or even hostile to the slave trade. This support—most importantly—began to translate into domestic political power. By March 1807 the strength of the abolitionists and their supporters had reached such proportions that they could apply sufficient pressure on Parliament to pass an act declaring the African slave trade illegal for British citizens. The exuberant bishop of London responded by exclaiming that this momentous law would soon bring "a total change in the condition of one quarter of the habitable globe," eliminating a greater quantity of evil and producing a greater quantity of good than any act since the beginning of the world.[95]

As it turned out, of course, such claims for the parliamentary act and its effect on the international slave trade proved to be highly exaggerated. Nevertheless, encouraged by this initial success, the abolitionists sought to bring additional pressure to bear upon the British government to use all means at its disposal to persuade other, "morally inferior" nations to follow Britain's lead.[96] For them, the perfect opportunity to do precisely this and secure the condemnation and renunciation of the slave trade appeared to arise with the military defeat of Napoleon and the restructuring of the international order with the Congress of Vienna in 1814-1815.

All major international attempts to reduce racial discrimination and promote human rights, as we shall see, have come in the wake of wars and revolutions. Upheaval and chaos, particularly if accompanied by significant shifts in power, provide the opportunity for reassessment and change. The abolitionists appeared to understand this principle and the relationship between power and prejudice well, especially after the French Revolution and Napoleonic wars, and thus mounted a vigorous campaign to arouse public opinion and to influence the diplomats in their efforts to reshape Europe and establish a lasting peace. Wilberforce, for example, launched a series of petitions to Parliament, initiated motions in both the House of Commons and the House of Lords, and even arranged for private meetings with Czar Alexander I of Russia all to stress the importance of using the Congress of Vienna as the forum for the international abolition of the slave trade. His colleague, Clarkson, prepared a special abridgment of *Evidence on the Subject of the Slave Trade* that could be read quickly and had illustrations of crowded conditions and shackles for restraining or punishing the helpless victims that drew quick attention to the horrors of the trade. This pamphlet was then translated into Italian, Spanish, French, and German and contained a preface addressed to all potentates and their representatives scheduled to meet in Vienna.[97] Lord Castlereagh, the chief British representative at the congress, found this pressure and interference to be particularly irritating and complained bitterly that it was wrong "to force it [the abolition of the slave trade] upon nations, at the expense of their honor and of the tranquility of the world."[98]

Despite his resentment and over his objections, however, British domestic opinion and the political pressures that it could mobilize forced Castlereagh to make the abolition of the slave trade a major issue at the Congress of Vienna. If, during the course of negotiations, he seemed to be less than committed to this goal, the passionate abolitionists would remind him of the moral and intellectual dimensions of their arguments. If that were not sufficient, those with new economic interests would inform him that with the British West Indian sugar planters now deprived of their own regular supply of cheap black African labor, their rivals at least should be put on an equal footing; and that if Africa were to be opened up as a market for manufactured goods and a source for raw materials, it was important to bring about the slave trade's demise. For a variety of motives, therefore, the British and their chief negotiator Castlereagh attempted to persuade others to renounce the slave trade.[99]

The politics and diplomacy of racial discrimination during 1814 and 1815 ran a tortuous route, as both prejudice and profits influenced international bargaining. British diplomats learned that only through a combination of threats and bribes could they even approximate their goal, for the negotiators bartered their consent to, or support of, abolition in order to obtain sacrifices or assistance in other areas. The Dutch agreed to end their participation in the slave trade not because they changed their attitudes toward blacks, but rather because they could be bought off with the cession of the East Indies. Sweden, when handsomely paid, followed suit. Prussia, Austria, and Russia, having acquired little or no interest in the commerce of slaves, adopted an attitude of benevolence (not unmixed with skepticism), in exchange for British support in other areas of greater importance to them. France, no longer a supplicant, resisted a series of financial and territorial offers and finally consented only to partial limitations. The two nations engaged in the slave trade for the longest period of time, Spain and Portugal, proved to be the hardest bargainers and agreed to halt their own slave trade only north of the equator and only after having been bought off with a substantial bribe.[100]

In the end, these negotiations resulted in the first multinational agreements ever signed on the issue of the slave trade. Britain, France, Spain, Sweden, Austria, Prussia, Russia, and Portugal joined in an Eight Power Declaration asserting that this trade was "repugnant to the principles of humanity and universal morality," that "the public voice in all civilized countries calls aloud for its prompt suppression," and that all colonial powers acknowledged the duty and necessity of abolishing it as soon as practicable.[101] This declaration was not only attached to the Final Act of the Congress of Vienna but also served to stimulate another treaty provision in which Britain, Russia, Austria, Prussia, and France pledged to consider further measures "for the entire and definitive abolition of a Commerce so odious and so strongly condemned by the laws of religion and nature."[102] Britain and the United States similarly declared in the Treaty of Ghent, also ratified in 1815, that the traffic in slaves "is irreconcilable with the principles of humanity and justice" and agreed to use their "best endeavors to accomplish so desirable an object" as abolishing the slave trade.[103]

Such solemn declarations in international treaties, as we also shall witness, can be highly deceiving. Especially when dealing with the sensitive subject of racial discrimination and human rights, nations might be willing to sign general statements of principle but will firmly resist any effort by others to interfere in what those who signed regard as sovereign jurisdiction and power over their own affairs. The states party to these agreements on the slave trade not only demonstrated this characteristic plainly but also sanctioned its practice as a pattern for the politics and diplomacy of racial discrimination for generations to come. In fact, this precedent, as we shall see, was clearly and explicitly remembered more than a century later during the Paris Peace Conference of 1919.

Many abolitionists naturally praised these international pledges to outlaw the slave trade as tremendous accomplishments, and others subsequently hailed them a "great" and "an all-important step in the progress of human society."[104] The pledges certainly indicated a willingness and an ability by powerful, sovereign nations to discuss openly a most difficult and emotional subject. Yet, those who believed that simply making a statement or signing a declaration against an evil would cause the evil to disappear found themselves sadly disappointed. These negotiations accomplished only the recognition of the principle that the trade was an evil that, however profitable, must be ended for humanitarian reasons. The final texts did not declare the slave trade to be illegal, fix a time limit for abolition, make a commitment for further action, or even sanction the arrest of slavers. It was particularly important that the texts provided no machinery for enforcement. They indicated, in the words of one historian, that "while all were ready to concur in benevolent declarations, no one was prepared to take any action with teeth in it."[105] A conference of ambassadors meeting to monitor compliance, according to another scholar, "affected little" and did no more "than exchange courtesies and amicable little pieces of information."[106] Further negotiations at the Congress of Verona, as described by the directors of the African Institution meeting in London, yielded only "vague generalities of verbal reprobation, which as experience teaches, bind them to no specific efficient measures."[107]

Nations simply refused to cooperate on this matter and protested against any infringements on their sovereignty or freedom of trade on the high seas. Although the British established in the Foreign Office a special section entitled the Slave Trade Department to concentrate on this problem,[108] they worked nearly alone to suppress the trade and were successful in negotiating treaties with only a few states like Portugal, Spain, the Netherlands, Sweden, and France for a limited right of search of suspected slave ships on the seas. Portugal and Spain refused, nevertheless, to allow searches to be conducted in the critical area south of the equator. The United States consistently refused to sign any meaningful international agreement, even though Congress technically had declared the slave trade to be illegal several years before.[109] Perhaps this followed from the lucrative results of such trade, for as at least two authors emphasize, by mid-century "most of the slave ships . . . not only flew the American flag but were owned by American citizens."[110] As Secretary of State John Forsyth asserted, the United States was determined not to become "a party of any Convention on the subject of the Slave Trade."[111] As a result of this and the flouting of both the letter and spirit of treaties negotiated by the diplomatic community presumably abolishing the slave trade, the numbers of humans exported from Africa to the Western Hemisphere and Arabia actually increased.[112] One respected contemporary estimated the figure to be as high as 100,000 slaves each year when the slave trade was legal, and 200,000 per year by 1839 after it had been outlawed.[113] A more recent scholar even concluded that "during the 1840s the transatlantic slave trade probably reached an all-time peak."[114]

With this successful commerce in contraband human cargo *after* the closing of the slave trade, it is hardly surprising that the total number of blacks enslaved in the world would increase in the first half of the nineteenth century. The number of slaves doubled in Brazil, tripled in the United States, and expanded by sevenfold in Cuba.[115] It is conservatively estimated that Brazilian sugar and coffee plantations alone absorbed over 875,000 blacks from 1821–1850 to be bound into slavery, while Cuba imported 286,000 slaves during the same period.[116] Official figures from the British Foreign Office run considerably higher.[117] The most dramatic increase by far, however, occurred in the United States where the emergence of the Cotton Kingdom and fear of importing potentially rebellious new Africans led to a unique phenomenon in the whole history of slavery: the rearing or reproduction of a native-born, black, slave population.[118] Notwithstanding abolition in the northern states, slavery in the United States at this time not only endured but even expanded without any substantial importations. Reliable estimates placed the numbers in 1790 at fewer than 700,000 Negro slaves, in 1830 at slightly more than 2,000,000, and only thirty years later, double that figure at 4,000,000.[119]

Staggering increases such as these in the number of slaves were accompanied by the obvious entrenchment of the institution of slavery, the extension of slave codes to further separate blacks from whites, and frequently a more determined effort by proslavery forces to justify enslavement on the basis of racial inferiority. Although differences occurred in practice between one geographical area and other,[120] the resulting attitudes indicated an unmistakable pattern varying only in degree rather than conception. Historian Carl Degler correctly warned about the dangers of generalizations between countries, for instance, and demonstrated the contrast in the case of Brazil where the comparatively harsher system of slavery did not become so closely associated with race or skin color as elsewhere.[121] Yet, he also acknowledged that racial prejudice existed there as well, and from an international perspective recognized the essential unifying fact: Modern Atlantic slavery "was imposed upon colored people only" and "white people were never slaves."[122] As we have seen, the Spanish, Portuguese, British, French,

Dutch, Danes, Swedes, and Prussians all justified slavery on the basis on the assumed superiority of whites. At the height of slavery in the United States, southern supporters of the slave system likewise increasingly defended their arguments on racial grounds.[123] Traveling across America, Alexis de Tocqueville witnessed discrimination north and south and solemnly predicted that if this land of democracy could not resolve its pervasive racial prejudice, "great calamities may be expected to ensue."[124]

By midcentury the situation appeared even worse as tentative political compromises yielded few peaceful results, violence exploded in new territories to the west, and the Supreme Court handed down its fateful *Dred Scott* decision that blacks who descended from slaves could never become citizens of the United States. Referring to blacks as "beings of an inferior race," Chief Justice Roger Taney wrote that the founding fathers knew the Declaration of Independence and Constitution "would not in any part of the civilized world be supposed to embrace the Negro race, which, by common consent, had been excluded from civilized Governments and the family of nations, and doomed to slavery."[125] As distinguished scholar John Hope Franklin concluded from this judgment, "With the highest court in the land openly preaching proslavery doctrine, there was little hope that anything short of a most drastic political or social revolution would bring an end to slavery."[126]

The emancipation of slaves indeed did require this kind of revolutionary upheaval. "The question of abolishing slavery," explained David Brion Davis, "was ultimately a question of power."[127] As with the other great emancipation movements of the century, including those of class and religion,[128] the institution of slavery changed only when the structure of political, military, or economic power changed. Even though religious and ideological factors often inspired abolition, the decisive elements proved to be domestic and international power transformed almost always by means of either revolution or war. Slavery in Spanish America ended only when the massive empire itself fell to what historian and diplomat Salvador de Madariaga called "the eagles of power."[129] El Salvador, Guatemala, Honduras, Nicaragua, and Costa Rica abolished slavery in 1824 only after Spain had suffered armed invasion from the French army on land, humiliation from the British navy at sea, uprisings from revolutionaries at home, and military defeats during wars for independence in Central America. Britain emancipated slaves in its colonies in 1833 only after a dramatic shift in domestic power frequently described as nothing short of a "revolution."[130] France ended slavery in its colonial possessions only after bloody chaos of the Revolution of 1848. Civil and foreign wars surrounded the abolition of slavery in Colombia, Argentina, Venezuela, and Peru during the 1850s. The United States freed its slaves by the Thirteenth Amendment of 1865 only after the Civil War had inflicted what remains to this day the most devastating conflict in the nation's history. Only Cuba and Brazil retained slavery in the Western world longer than the United States; they did not free their slaves until additional wars and struggles forced them to do so in the late 1880s.[131]

These upheavals, by and large, finally ended the slave trade as well. Several decades of nearly single-handed effort by the British, inspired by both moral principle and the profit motive, had achieved only limited results. Through the use of their determined diplomats and powerful naval squadrons, they had secured several unique bilateral treaties, commissions of inquiry, and various accords with other governments since the Congress of Vienna; but these only restrained certain portions of the trade in piecemeal fashion and, even then, proved particularly difficult to enforce due to maritime rights, colonial and commercial rivalry, national sovereignty and pride, and continued suspicions over British motives.[132] The necessary prerequisite for genuinely abolishing the slave trade abroad, of course, was emancipation at home. Once nations outlawed slavery within their own domains, the slave trade had no market; and once they withdrew either active support for or passive acquiescence in the trade, this commerce in human cargo no longer could exist.

By 1890 this natural and intimate relationship between emancipation and the fate of the slave trade had become so apparent and such a part of the international agenda that the major Western powers sought to confirm it by means of a convention known as the Brussels Act. They realized that politically, diplomatically, economically, intellectually, and morally they could no longer sustain the slave trade. For these several reasons, delegates from seventeen nations, including those that had been most actively engaged in slave trading, gathered together in Brussels to draft a comprehensive act with the professed intention "of putting an end to the crimes and devastations engendered by the traffic in African slaves, of efficiently protecting the aboriginal population of Africa, and of securing for that vast continent the benefits of peace and civilization."[133] The resulting landmark Brussels Act bound the signatories for the first time to take practical steps in repressing slave trading at places of origin as well as along inland caravan routes and at sea, punishing offenders, and exchanging information that would be accessible at international offices.

Seen from one point of view, this convention marked the triumphant culmination of the struggle to associate all the major powers with a comprehensive agreement to end the African slave trade. It embodied the principle that above and beyond the sordid and selfish aspirations of individual powers, "trusteeship" and "native welfare" were an international responsibility, and it took an important step by establishing moral standards for international behavior, standards by which the powers might judge each other and the rest of the world judge them; both of which, as we shall see, set significant precedents for the League of Nations and the United Nations in the twentieth century. Yet, seen from another angle, the Brussels Act was a formalization of the ironic marriage between antislavery and the phenomenon that we shall explore below known as imperialism. It provided the opportunity for Western powers to use the maritime traffic in slaves as an excuse to take military action against those engaged in internal slave trading and to extend an imperial rule to Africa more suitable for political control and economic exploitation than for the protection or humanitarian uplift of "native peoples."[134]

Regardless of the mixed motives or reasons for abolishing the slave trade, however, in the end the record of the burden of the past spoke for itself. The black slave trade lasted for more than four centuries; involved the peoples of Europe, Africa, the United States, the Caribbean, and South America; seared itself into the historical consciousness of these same peoples; and counted among its victims perhaps as many as twenty million human beings.[135]

Ideology, Immigration, and Imperialism

The abolition of slavery ended the institution but not the ideology that subjected one race to another. Emancipation and its consequences quickly revealed the perceptiveness of Tocqueville's observation that "you may set the Negro free, but you cannot make him otherwise than an alien to the European. Nor is this all," he continued, for "we scarcely acknowledge the common features of humanity in this stranger whom slavery has brought us. His physiognomy is to our eyes hideous, his understanding weak, his tastes low; and we are almost inclined to look upon him as a being intermediate between man and the brutes. The moderns, then, after they have abolished slavery, have . . . prejudices to contend against, which are less easy to attack and far less easy to conquer than the mere fact of servitude. . . . Slavery recedes," Tocqueville wrote, "but the prejudice to which it has given birth is immovable."[136] "If I were called upon to predict the future," he concluded, "I should say that the abolition of slavery . . . will, in the common course of things, increase the repugnance of the white population for the blacks."[137]

The accuracy of this statement could be seen in the fact that loss of slave status did not bring with it loss of caste status, for emancipation often exaggerated and exacerbated existing prejudices of race.[138] The emancipation of the slaves in the West Indies, for instance, prompted

British historian Thomas Carlyle to write his infamous essay "On the Nigger Question," arguing that blacks were created in order to permanently serve their white European masters.[139] Even many of those who worked so ardently to end slavery would not accept the premise that racial equality should follow freedom. Indeed, for some, emancipation held out the prospect of simultaneously eliminating two evils: slavery and blacks. Those antislavery members of the American Colonization Society, among others, for example, set about to free slaves, but instead of integrating them upon manumission or emancipation, sought to ship them back to Africa and completely out of U.S. white society.[140] Augustin Cochin, a leading Protestant abolitionist in France, praised the freeing of the slaves but continued to view blacks as an "inferior race."[141] Even more telling is the comment of Alfred Michiels, the abolitionist translator of Harriet Beecher Stowe's *Uncle Tom's Cabin*, who asserted that blacks in their natural habitat "far from all European influence" revealed themselves as "the most stupid, the most perverse, the most bloodthirsty of all human races."[142] This kind of prejudice helps to explain the context in which explicit ideologies of racial superiority could grow and flourish.

Particular attitudes toward blacks and others of color in the minds of whites, as we have seen, evolved over a period of several centuries. Racial thinking had developed in rough proportion to the amount and kind of contact established among various races around the world. Although definite images and patterns of thought about race emerged, some ideas tended to be vague and perhaps at least partially attributable to general ethnocentrism and the clash of cultures. This increasingly changed in the second half of the nineteenth century after emancipation. Precisely during this period in the United States, Canada, Britain, Australia, Germany, the Low Countries, France, Sweden, and Switzerland, among others, racism emerged, in the words of one authority, as a "well-defined ideology," distinct from ethnocentrism and attained the status of a "firmly established, respectable orthodoxy" supported by the natural and social sciences.[143]

Ideology is a treacherous term, used and abused by historians and others in a variety of ways. This results in part from the fact that although an ideology might be taken for granted by those who have internalized its tenets, it does not lend itself to rigorous precision or to the verifiable truth it claims to represent. Thus, David Brion Davis concluded astutely that ideology ought to be considered "an integrated system of beliefs, assumptions, and values, not necessarily true or false, which reflects the needs and interests of a group or class at a particular time in history."[144] This recognized that since ideologies are modes of consciousness, containing criteria for interpreting social reality, they attempt to define as well as to legitimate collective interests and justify particular policies; hence, the continuous interaction between ideology and the material forces of history, as demonstrated in the case of racial prejudice.

The nineteenth century produced or exacerbated two great paradoxes relating to race. In the first, racism actually increased as democracy expanded.[145] The extension of freedom and democratic practices in Europe by the French Revolution and in the United States by Jacksonian democracy was accompanied by a more determined effort than earlier to deny the equality of blacks. In the second paradox, racism grew as science advanced. Enormous strides in the sciences produced not only the expansion of knowledge of the world, the unlocking of secrets heretofore hidden, and the harnessing of energy for technological power, but ironically, the creation and enhancement of what is widely known as "scientific racism." In its simplest and most obvious form, racism became not merely a dogma of prejudice, but a belief that the superiority or inferiority of human beings is actually determined by organic, genetically transmitted, biological differences of race.

It obviously was not easy to reconcile these paradoxes, but in an effort to square a circle and do so, some sought to arrange a marriage of democratic egalitarianism with biological racism through the concept of what is called "*Herrenvolk* democracy," that is, appealing both to democratic sensibilities and to racial prejudices by arguing for equal citizenship for all whites and a servile status for all non-whites on the grounds that there exist innate differences in group capacities for self-government. The contradictions between the principles of the Declaration of Independence and the Declaration of the Rights of Man on the one hand and the practices of racial slavery and segregation on the other might be overcome by developing the idea that only whites were deemed to be "men" in the sense that they qualified for natural rights. By placing a heavy stress upon biological differences, whites thus could conceive of themselves as being democratic while at the same time being racially exclusive.[146]

In this endeavor, the tools, techniques, theories, and especially the reputation of the rising biological sciences, which sought to explain everything in terms of biology and race, provided enormous assistance.[147] For example, the noted British anatomist Robert Knox (described as "the real founder of British racism" and a "key figure" in Western racist thinking)[148] published *The Races of Man* (1850) in an attempt to prove beyond doubt the superiority of whites over all others of color, especially the "despised race" of Negroes.[149] Josiah Nott, a physician and widely read exponent of ethnology in the United States, wrote in *Types of Mankind* (1854) that "scientific truth" demonstrated polygenesis, or the separate creation of the races as distinct species, in which Caucasians emerged as the most superior and blacks as the most inferior of all mankind.[150] Louis Agassiz, the famous Swiss-born biologist, lent his considerable reputation to the same theory.

The newly emerging discipline of anthropology focused its attention primarily upon the physiological differences among races as the chief determinants of their fates. Through the prestigious Société d'anthropologie de Paris, for example, the French scientific community openly championed the theory that statistically verifiable measurements of skulls could prove the greatness of the white race over all others. Both the physical anthropologist Paul Broca and the influential sociologist Gustave Le Bon strongly supported phrenology's study of cranial capacity and brain weights, arguing that the evidence proved the superiority of the white race, followed by the Mongol race, and finally, the race with the smallest brains, the blacks.[151] These and similar points of view about biological determinants and a hierarchical arrangement of races were propounded with the certainty of science and exploited the human tendency to be unduly impressed with things easily measured. They thereby gained wide acceptance throughout most countries in the Western world.[152]

This period of scientific measurements from balances, compasses, and calipers in the further development of value-laden racial theories also produced more explicit opinions about Jews. Even though Europeans long had persecuted and discriminated against those of the Jewish faith, writers of previous centuries who stressed "purity of blood" almost always placed Jews within the white race. They were a phenotypically indistinguishable group, and hence religious customs and belief made them different, not the color of their skin. After their general emancipation from many restrictions in the nineteenth century, however—as in the case of black slaves—opinions decidedly racist came to the fore. Linguists, genealogists, naturalists, philologists, historians, and other men of letters increasingly began to marshal evidence in attempting to demonstrate that Jews belonged to an "inferior race." Indeed, as Leon Poliakov, perhaps the world's leading authority on anti-Semitism, wrote, it was precisely during this time that scientific and intellectual opinion transformed Jews from a religious and historic group into a "physiological race" like other races of mankind and renamed it "Semitic."[153] This launched the beginning, he observed, of "The Aryan Epoch" of racial thinking, which presumed the superiority of the blond-haired, blue-eyed, white, "Aryan" race over all others.

Among all those who participated in this evolution of racial theories, perhaps none is better known than Count Arthur de Gobineau. Frequently described as the "father of modern racist ideology," this French diplomat, politician, and prolific author published between 1853 and 1855 a two-volume book entitled *Essai sur l'inégalité des races humaines.*[154] In that work, he synthesized and systematized ideas already deeply rooted in his time in a new and popular way around one central theme: Race provides *the* motivating force behind all human historical experience. Race, he wrote, "dominates all other problems of history and holds the key to them all." Gobineau believed that racial groups were biologically unequal and endowed with different characteristics and capabilities. "History shows," he wrote, "that all civilization derives from the white race." Among these, Gobineau viewed the "Aryans" as superior, as the only one capable of producing civilization, and as possessing a "monopoly of beauty, intelligence, and strength." The "yellow race" he saw as feeble, passive, lacking energy, uninventive, and tending toward mediocrity in all things. The "black race," he wrote, "is the lowest, and stands at the foot of the ladder." He feared that civilization would collapse due to the "contamination" of white Europeans by inbreeding with these "inferior races."[155] The acclaim accorded to such views of sweeping scope brought Gobineau out of the wings and on to center stage where his work became nothing short of a classic for racial theories. Through the sale of many copies in French and translation, the praise of numerous political and academic leaders, and the formation of Gobineau societies, his ideas spread and came to have a highly influential place in Western thought.[156]

Gobineau was not the only great synthesizer of the midnineteenth century, for in this regard he shared that position with two others: Karl Marx in economics and Charles Darwin in biology. Surprisingly enough, these two giants of thought contributed in their own, and possibly unintended, ways to racial thinking as well. As the founder of communism, Marx obviously focused his attention upon the role of class struggle and dialectical materialism in history. Although he supported an end to the slave trade and emancipation of slaves in bondage, he, like so many other abolitionists of his day, nevertheless would not divorce himself from racial prejudice. In *Das Kapital* (1867) Marx spoke of "race peculiarities" and elsewhere left little doubt about his belief in the inferiority of blacks and his ironic anti-Semitism.[157] Neither he nor his collaborator, Friedrich Engels, demonstrated any aversion at all to using the derogatory expression "nigger."[158]

Darwin's monumental *Origin of the Species* (1859) contributed even more directly to racial thinking, due to the implication of the subtitle, *The Preservation of Favored Races in the Struggle for Life.*[159] The theory that biological evolution and "natural selection" toward higher forms of life stemmed primarily from the conflict of varieties and species, with the resulting "survival of the fittest" and disappearance of the unfit, possessed an obvious suggestion for those who wanted to believe that some human races had a more exalted destiny than others.[160] Darwin's subsequent *Descent of Man* (1871) seemingly removed any doubt about the application of his doctrine to human "varieties" when he wrote that shortly "the civilized races of man will almost certainly exterminate and replace the savage races throughout the world."[161] It required little imagination to take such ideas and use them to rationalize or justify racial discrimination against non-whites in the emerging policies of immigration exclusion and imperialism.

As a result of massive technological power produced by the Industrial Revolution, transportation underwent a dramatic change. Steamships and railroads revolutionized the ability to transport people, particularly immigrants, from one continent to another as never before. Thousands upon thousands of Europeans sought relief, opportunity, or adventure unavailable at home and emigrated to Canada, the United States, South Africa, Australia, and New Zealand, among other areas. But Europeans were not the only ones who wanted to move. The British Empire provided a framework within which its various subjects might travel, especially those from India. The Chinese and other Asians wanted to spread throughout the Pacific region, from Canada in the north to New Zealand in the south. In this way the demographic history of the world began to change dramatically. Those who moved wanted freedom to enter the country of their choice, but many quickly discovered that their reception might be based solely upon the color of their skin.

Prior to the era of explicit racial ideology, immigration had never emerged as a serious problem of international relations. Europeans, it is true, had been excluded from Japan in the seventeenth century, as had Jews from Russia, Muslims from old and new Spain, and Protestants sometimes from French colonies; but these instances never involved massive numbers of people. More common were the cases in the developing countries of the Western Hemisphere like Brazil and the British colonies of settlement in Australia, New Zealand, and South Africa that desperately needed manpower and eagerly welcomed those immigrants who wanted to work. In fact, various official efforts actively promoted the unrestricted flow of peoples from other lands to come and help mine the recently discovered goldfields, settle frontier regions, farm land, or construct railroads. Newcomers always faced xenophobic suspicions toward "foreigners" and prejudice against strange languages and customs—but not exclusion—that is, not until the last part of the nineteenth century. A depressed worldwide economy and the growth of union organizations fearful of competition from cheap immigrant labor, when combined with prevailing prejudices against people of color, led to a pattern of racial violence in white cities like Victoria, Sydney, Durban, Vancouver, San Francisco, and Los Angeles. This agitation and bloodshed focused, not on all immigrants, but primarily on those other than Caucasians, accompanied by cries against "Mongolian filth," "yellow barbarians," "coolies," "inferior beings of color," and reminders of the need to maintain "racial purity."[162]

Political pressure mounted from these demonstrations, and as a result of determined resolve to restrict non-white immigration, there emerged a series of racial exclusion laws. In the United States, President Rutherford Hayes wrote: "I am satisfied that the present Chinese labor invasion . . . is pernicious and should be discouraged. Our experience in dealing with the weaker races—the Negroes and Indians, for example—is not encouraging. . . . I would consider with favor any suitable measures to discourage the Chinese from coming to our shores."[163] Within three years, Congress passed the 1882 Chinese Exclusion Act, the first legislation of its kind. The same year, the Canadian prime minister, Sir John A. Macdonald, confessed, "I share very much the feelings of the peoples of the United States and the Australian Colonies against a Mongolian or Chinese population in our country as permanent settlers. I believe that it is an alien race in every sense, that would not and could not be expected to assimilate with our Aryan population."[164] By 1885 Canada had a Chinese Immigration Restriction Act. During the same period, each of the several colonies in Australia and New Zealand passed stringent acts restricting Chinese immigration. In 1885 Queensland placed restrictions on Polynesians entering its territory, sometimes referring to them as "blacks." The Registration of Servants law of 1888 in Natal similarly classified immigrants from India as members of "an uncivilized race" and set into motion a number of restrictions against them.[165] These policies toward immigration represented only one facet of the emerging international problem of race, however, for the same steamships and railroads that carried immigrants from one shore to another also could transport troops to foreign lands for imperialistic conquest.

From an international perspective, one of the most striking and significant features of the second half of the nineteenth century was the tremendous outburst of imperialistic interest and activity by Europe. During these years, Europeans made greater efforts to subjugate and control other lands and non-white peoples than they had during the entire three previous centuries. There had been, to be sure, an extension of influence by the British in India and South Africa, the French in Algeria and Southeast Asia, and the Russians in central and northeast Asia, and both China and Japan had been forced to partially open their doors to outside Westerners. Nevertheless, such expansion generally appeared sporadic, cautious, and not particularly concerned with the acquisition of extensive territory or direct control.

After Darwin and his Social Darwinist and pseudo-Darwinian followers, who sought to apply biological principles to human behavior, and after the intensely bitter wars of nationalism at midcentury, this casual attitude of the past dramatically changed. The creation of a powerful German state, a united Italy, a humiliated France, an isolated Britain, and a growing Russia generated a passionate desire to maintain or recover national prestige and strength. If nations and races progressed only through fierce competition, then they had no choice but to participate in the struggle for survival of the fittest. Paul Leroy-Beaulieu, the French economist heavily influenced by Darwinist thought about racial competition, gave expression to the feelings of many when he argued that imperial expansion was nothing short of "a matter of life and death."[166] The theories of race thus easily fit and reinforced the prevailing political and strategic requirements of Realpolitik, the economic interests of overseas investments and profits, and the missionary urge to "civilize" and Christianize the heathen throughout the globe. Not all of those who believed in racial ideologies supported imperialism, but those who did held the power of politics and diplomacy in their hands. Thus, with mixed theories, interests, and motives, Europeans feverishly launched the "new imperialism" with little regard for the expense or danger involved and began what is known as the era of "European world hegemony."[167]

Nowhere could this intensity for imperialism be seen better than in Africa. As late as the last part of the 1870s, most of the African "Dark Continent," except for various coastal settlements, remained unknown to Europeans and free from white penetration. Then, suddenly, with a rush that is still astonishing to recall, explorers, missionaries, soldiers, and businessmen arrived from Europe and within twenty years had carved up nearly all of Africa into their own imperial possessions.[168] The British seized Egypt, pushed into the interior with control of Nigeria and the Gold Coast (now Ghana), consolidated their possessions in Gambia, moved from the Indian Ocean into British East Africa (now Kenya) and Uganda, defeated the Zulu chieftain Cetewayo, and advanced northward from South Africa into Bechuanaland, Rhodesia, and Nyasaland, dreaming all the while of an uninterrupted empire that would extend from Cairo in the north all the way to Cape Town in the south. France fought its way up the Ubangi River into the region of Lake Chad, expanded its settlements in Senegal, Dahomey, and Guinea, moved up the northern side of the Congo River to forge French Equatorial Africa, and took French Somaliland on the Red Sea coast and Tunisia in North Africa. The Belgians occupied the Congo, one of Africa's richest mineral-bearing regions, and exploited the natives with a ruthlessness that horrified even their fellow imperialists.

Germany seized German East Africa (now Tanzania), the Cameroons, Togoland, and German South-West Africa (now Namibia). Portugal consolidated its holdings in Angola and moved against Mozambique. And, finally, the Spanish secured their claims in Rio de Oro on the Atlantic coast, while Italy captured Italian Somaliland and Eritrea, and the white Boer settlers, descended from the Dutch, extended their domination over blacks in South Africa and the Transvaal. This colossal extension of European power transformed subsequent African history. Moreover, the sharp contrasts between European victories and black African defeats, European strength and black weakness, helped to reinforce existing racial prejudices of the superiority of whites over blacks. As one European political leader described the prevailing attitude toward black Africans in the 1880s: "The colored people are generally looked upon by the whites as an inferior race, whose interest ought to be systematically disregarded when they come into competition with our own, and who ought to be governed mainly with a view to the advantages of the superior race."[169]

Not content with these staggering successes against Africans, the powers of Europe rushed to conquer non-white peoples in Asia and the Pacific as well. There, as in Africa, the Europeans' accumulated wealth and military power gave them an even greater relative advantage than the one they had enjoyed when the Portuguese first fired their broadsides against Calicut several centuries before. Britain tightened its grip on the Indian subcontinent by crushing local mutinies and by giving Queen Victoria the resounding title of Empress of India, an act inspired by Prime Minister Disraeli, a firm believer in the importance of racial considerations in history. "All," he wrote, "is race."[170] British troops then moved into Burma, Tibet, Afghanistan, part of Canton, Malaya, and various islands in the Pacific to secure the approaches to Australia and New Zealand including northern Borneo, the Fijis, and the territory of Papua.

Russia made swift advances into Turkestan, Manchuria, and Mongolia, reached the borders of Persia and India, and established a naval base at Vladivostok. France joined in this scramble and sent forces into Annam and Tonkin (parts of Vietnam), Cambodia, Tahiti, the Society Islands, Tuamotu Archipelago, and Marquesas. The Germans seized the Bismarck Archipelago and part of New Guinea, while the Dutch also carved out a portion of New Guinea to add to their extensive holdings in Borneo and the Celebes and Molucca islands (now Indonesia). All sought to make further advances into China and extract concessions favorable to trade. White settlers in Australia and New Zealand launched attacks against aboriginal peoples occupying land that the whites wanted. This vigorous and aggressive wave of imperialism by Europeans in Asia and the Pacific possessed characteristics similar to those of the assault against natives in Africa, accompanied by the same extensive arguments about how the "lesser breeds" and "inferior races" must make way for advanced white civilization.[171] One difference could be seen, however, for in Asia and the Pacific the Europeans found themselves joined by the United States.

Imperialism as a deliberate foreign policy presented an uneasy dilemma for a number of U.S. citizens, in part because the creation of their own country had followed a successful rebellion against an imperial power. Yet the sentiment for territorial expansion, desire for Great Power status, and a belief in the superiority of their own race proved in the end to be stronger. Moving westward across a vast continent, the United States appeared convinced of its "Manifest Destiny" to expand and conquer because of political, economic, cultural, geographical, and biologically determined racial forces that could not be held off. Moreover, after the threats of British and Mexican intervention faded due to war and diplomacy on the frontier, Americans felt less need to conciliate the Indian tribes. In this setting, earlier images of the proud, independent, "noble savage" gave way to the attitude described by Senator (later Secretary of State) William Seward, that Indians—like blacks—presented "a foreign and feeble element," "incapable of assimilation" into the white man's society, and thus fated for extermination.[172] The same theories of race used with respect to blacks were applied to those of red skin color. Whites viewed Indians as a decayed, degenerate, and inferior race, unable and unwilling to adjust to the modern world. "To Darwinians the red men were retarded offshoots of the mainstream of human evolution," wrote U.S. historian Ray Allen Billington, "a living example of a species destined to extinction in the continuing struggle of the survival of the fittest."[173]

Once again, policy followed and then reinforced this attitude. Constantly arguing that the biological inferiority of Indians made particular actions necessary, the federal government sponsored forced removal from tribal homelands, expropriation of land, massacre of women and children, disregard of previously signed treaties, and confinement to reservations as permanent wards of the state. These assaults became part of a well-documented legacy.[174] As Francis A. Walker, U.S. commissioner of Indian affairs, explained official policy: "There is no question of national dignity, be it remembered, involved in the treatment of savages by a civilized power. With wild men, as with wild beasts, the question whether in a given situation one shall fight, coax, or run, is a question merely of what is easiest and safest." If these "aborigines of the continent," he continued, "stand up against the progress of civilization and industry, they must be relentlessly crushed. The westward course of population is neither to be denied nor delayed for the sake of all the Indians that ever called this country their home. They must yield or perish and there is something that savors of providential mercy in the rapidity with which their fate advances upon them."[175] The justification for domination by whites in the midnineteenth century sounded much the same, whether it came from Europeans or Americans, and applied to all native races, whether in Africa, Asia, the Pacific, or the western United States.

This "Europeanization of the world" by the powers of Europe (including Russia) and their cousins in the United States had profound global consequences. Wherever they went with imperialism, these white conquerors encountered many millions of non-white peoples who had created unique civilizations of their own, had made great contributions to human development in earlier times, and in some cases were proud bearers of historical and cultural traditions that antedated those of Europe itself.[176] A single machine gun produced by the Industrial Revolution, however, could decimate entire armies of fighting men if they were armed only with spears, swords, or antiquated firearms. Even though the Europeans brought a number of medical, technological, and educational benefits, they destroyed many native peoples in the process. Other non-Westerners found themselves forced to adapt to the white Western world simply in order to survive. Thus, international relations increasingly became interracial relations as well, particularly when so much power was held in the hands of those with such intense and explicit racial ideologies.

For those subjected to this emerging feature of international relations, diplomacy appeared to hold out little promise for relieving or resolving their plight. In fact, diplomatic institutions and practices as employed by the West did just the opposite. Negotiations produced "unequal treaties" in the Far East and India with special provisions for "extraterritoriality," or exemptions from local laws for whites. International agreements supported statements of general principles on human rights but rarely included enforcement provisions to implement them. Diplomacy frequently provided a ruse to conceal real intentions from native populations, as U.S. behavior toward Native Americans or European behavior in Africa has shown. Foreign ministries refused to deal in any meaningful way with immigration restrictions. Furthermore, diplomatic conferences actually sanctioned the partitioning of islands in the Pacific, the carving up of spheres of influence in Asia, and the seizing of territory in Africa. During the Conference of Berlin in 1884-1885, for example, diplomats from Europe agreed among themselves on ways to legalize their occupation and conquest of the entire continent of Africa. One participant at the congress revealed the arrogance of both power and prejudice by asserting that the newly acquired possessions were "full of savages thirsting for the plunder of the white man's property."[177] Little deference was given to the inhabitants and no African representative received an invitation to attend. Such policies, described by the *Lagos Observer* as "high-handed robbery,"[178] and the attitudes that produced and accompanied them, would not be soon forgotten by either the victims or their descendants.

*   *   *

This past proved to be a very heavy burden for the world to bear. Its extent, depth, and duration made it so. From antiquity to approximately 1890, the Western world demonstrated an evolution of definite patterns in thoughts and actions toward those of other races. There were, it must not be forgotten, courageous individuals who fought for emancipation, labored to eliminate the slave trade, opposed imperialism, and believed that the Christian faith taught the brotherhood of all men and women. During this long period, however, they most often represented a minority, lacked sufficient influence, or remained silent. The majority supported, participated in, or benefited from colonization, slavery, immigration restrictions, imperialism, and the propagation of racial ideologies. These people enslaved the black, excluded the yellow, dispossessed the red and the brown, and subjugated them all. These developments occurred not on the fringe but rather at the center of Western civilization, as demonstrated by the active participation of many of its greatest philosophers and thinkers, explorers and soldiers, scientists and scholars, political leaders, statesmen and diplomats, businessmen and investors, clerics and even missionaries. It is precisely for this reason that so many of the values and institutions of the West came to be challenged and rejected by non-white peoples throughout the globe, including the economic system of capitalism and the religious faith of Christianity. The problems created by this heavy burden of power and prejudice from the past would be seen even more clearly as the world began to move into the twentieth century.

2
The Rising Tide

ONE THING IS CERTAIN: THE WHITE MAN WILL have to recognize
that the practically absolute world-dominion which he exercised
. . . can no longer be maintained. Largely because of this very
dominion, colored races have been drawn out of their traditional
isolation. . . . The rising tide of color has . . . been beating, and
will beat yet more fiercely as congesting population, quickened
self-consciousness, and heightened sense of power impel the
colored world to expansion and dominion. . . . Unless some
understanding is arrived at, the world will drift into a gigantic race-
war.

—Lothrop Stoddard

Ideology of Racial Struggle

Ideologies of race, as they had developed in the West up through the
nineteenth century, tended to focus upon one major theme: the inequality
of human races. Building upon prejudices dating back to antiquity, the
ideologies sought to provide new systematic and scientific proof that
the superiority or inferiority of people was determined by organic,
inherited, biological differences of race. In the resulting hierarchical
arrangement, whites appeared at the top, blacks at the bottom, and
those of other skin colors somewhere in between. By the end of the
century the truth of this proposition appeared self-evident and in little
need of further documentation. Hence, the indefatigable energies of those
thinking and writing about race centered around the development of
another theme emerging with great force between 1890 and World War
I: the struggle for existence among these various races.

In the history of the world, few secular ideas can challenge the
magnitude of the influence unleashed by Charles Darwin's *Origin of the
Species* and *Descent of Man*. Many scientific discoveries affected ways
of living more profoundly but perhaps none so revolutionized fundamental
patterns of thought as did evolution. The idea of "natural selection" in
a competition among species and a "survival of the fittest" provided

such a dramatic new approach to nature that others seemed impelled to exploit its insights for the understanding of society through schemes of evolutionary development and organic analogies.

Through the efforts of such Social Darwinists as the English publicist Herbert Spencer in *The Principles of Sociology* and his compatriot Thomas Huxley in *Man's Place in Nature*, the Austrian sociologist Ludwig Gumplowicz in his *Der Rassenkampf* on the struggle of the races, the Russian writer Nicolas Danielevsky, and the American sociologist William Graham Sumner, the biological theories of Darwin were applied to the human social and political realm and then popularized through most of the Western world.[1] By the last decade of the nineteenth century these ideas had created a powerful intellectual atmosphere and acquired enough prestige to command widespread attention and thus influence many others to come. *Darwinismus* provided a loose, but comprehensive, worldview encompassing everything from protozoa to politics; the stature of such a viewpoint could buttress all kinds of opinions with the dignity of scientific truth.[2] It offered a scientific explanation for those who wanted to understand nature, a rationalization for rugged individualism and competition, an excuse for immigration quotas and imperialism, and a justification for viewing racial struggles as a fundamental part of the "inevitable" unfolding of biological destiny.

Europeans eagerly seized upon this biological conception of survival of the fittest and used it to advance further the idea of a struggle for existence among the races of mankind. The contributors to this particular ideology of race, in fact, were legion. Among many others, they included Otto Ammon, Ludwig Woltmann, and Ernst Haeckel in Germany; Gustaf Retzius and C. M. Furst in Sweden; Gustav Schimmer and Augustin Weisbach in Austria; Hans Steensby in Denmark; Iakov Novikov in Russia; Rudolfo Levi, Cesare Lombroso, and Giuseppe Sergi in Italy; Federico Oloriz y Aguilera in Spain; Emile Houze in Belgium; and Lucien Chalumeau in Switzerland.[3] Several authors from Latin America contributed to this thinking about racial struggle as well.[4] From England Thomas Huxley, Alfred Wallace, Charles Pearson, and Benjamin Kidd added further literature expressing concern about the competition between the blacks, browns, and yellows of the world with the whites. An article appearing in *Saturday Review*, entitled "Biological View of Our Foreign Policy," noted, for example, that in the global "struggle for existence," strong races advanced while "feeble races are being wiped off the earth."[5] Joining his countrymen Gabriel Tarde and Gustave Le Bon in France, the famous anthropologist Georges Vacher de Lapouge published a study entitled *Les sélections sociales* (1896) in which he argued that race and racial development represented "the fundamental factor of history."[6] Encouraged by the reception to this book, he wrote another shortly thereafter and asserted even more directly: "The conflict of races is now about to start openly within nations and between nations, and one can only ask oneself if the ideas of the fraternity and equality of man were not against nature."[7] "I am convinced," he determined with a prescience that is frightening, given its subsequent accuracy under the Third Reich, "that in the next century people will slaughter each other because of a difference of a degree or two in the [racial] cephalic index. It is by this sign . . . that men will be identified . . . and the last sentimentalists will be able to witness the most massive exterminations of peoples."[8]

Among the numerous European contributors to the ideology of racial struggle in the last decade of the nineteenth century, none could approach the influence of Houston Stewart Chamberlain. Son of an English admiral, reared in France, educated in Switzerland, domiciled in Austria, and eventually revered in Germany, he gathered the ideas of his time from many sources and then refracted them through his own particular prism of racial ideology. His wide-ranging intellectual curiosity sweeping from botany to history and from philosophy to music, when combined with the time to write afforded by inherited wealth, resulted in the publication of the famed *Die Grundlagen des neunzehnten Jahrhunderts* (The foundations of the nineteenth century) in 1899. Acknowledging his intellectual debt to Charles Darwin, whom Chamberlain described as the "incomparable master," he pursued what he termed "rational anthropology" and a "new science" based upon "intuition born of ceaseless observation." Synthesizing the work of many fields of inquiry and covering centuries of the historical panorama with great style, he argued for the primary role of race in human history. "Nothing," he wrote, "is so convincing as the consciousness of the possession of race. . . . Race lifts a man above himself, it endows him with extraordinary—I might almost say supernatural—powers, so entirely does it distinguish him from the individual who springs from the chaotic jumble of peoples drawn from all parts of the world."[9]

Chamberlain's ideas of racial struggle, racial purity, the racial inferiority of Jews and Negroes, and the racial superiority of white Aryans (or, as he preferred to call them, "Teutonics" or "Germanics") struck a responsive chord throughout Europe and the United States. Numerous editions and multiple translations followed, and in the book's first English edition it was hailed as "one of the masterpieces of the century."[10] Of importance to those conducting international relations, such diplomats as Lord Redesdale of Great Britain and Count Ulrich von Brockdorff-Rantzau of Germany circulated Chamberlain's book widely throughout the diplomatic community.[11] Kaiser Wilhelm II enthusiastically described Chamberlain's theories about race as a "magic wand" that created "order where there was chaos and light where there was darkness"[12] and began a personal correspondence with him that lasted for over twenty years. Later, Adolf Hitler would declare the same kind of praise, and Chamberlain, in turn, would provide Hitler with early support.

This extensive development of an ideology of racial struggle quickly turned from theory into practice. Encouraged by Chamberlain and others, Europeans increasingly placed those of the Jewish faith outside the white race and maintained that Jews constituted a separate, degenerate, physiological racial group. Early Jews, it was averred, had spoken a Semitic language and hence all their descendants belonged to a "Semitic race" much different than "Aryans." They existed as a "race in the midst of another race," which could not be assimilated,[13] a dangerous contaminating threat like "bacilli" in the struggle for survival of the fittest and "a cancer slowly eating into the flesh of other races."[14] This ideology gave new vigor, direction, and respectability to anti-Semitic sentiment and policy. Violent pogroms and repressive legislation in Russia forced an estimated 300,000 Jews to leave that country during the single year of 1891. The parliamentary electoral success of the ultraconservative army chaplain Adolf Stoecker, on a plank of anti-Semitism, encouraged the flowering of new hatred in Germany. The 1894 conviction in France of Jewish army officer Alfred Dreyfus on false charges of espionage split the country apart, provoked riots, and fanned the flames of popular prejudice. In Austria, the election of anti-Jewish Karl Lueger as mayor of Vienna in 1895 encouraged such passions and notions of racial competition even further.[15]

Americans as well appeared enamored with this ideology of struggle among the races. The appeal of Darwinism seemed irresistible to those who believed that in the natural selection of the species they would win. The popular and influential Josiah Strong, using biological analogies with the passion of an evangelist, wrote in his 1891 edition of *Our Country: Its Possible Future and Present Crisis* that the world was poised on the brink of "the final competition of races." In this struggle, he viewed the white Anglo-Saxons as representing "the largest liberty, the purest Christianity, the highest civilization" and as "having developed peculiarly aggressive traits calculated to impress its institutions upon mankind, [to] spread itself over the earth. If I read not amiss," he stated, "this powerful race will move down upon Mexico, down upon Central and South America, out upon the islands of the sea, over upon Africa and beyond. And can there be any doubt that the result of this competition of races will be the 'survival of the fittest'?"[16]

Other writers like John Fiske in his *The Discovery of America* (1893) and Brooks Adams in *The Law of Civilization and Decay* (1896) expressed similar opinions about racial struggle in the rise and fall of civilizations.[17] The massacre of several hundred Indians at Wounded Knee, South

Dakota, in 1890 made these ideas all the more poignant. As Theodore Roosevelt wrote in reflecting upon this kind of treatment, the coming of the whites could be stayed no more than a racial war to the finish against "scattered savage tribes, whose life was but a few degrees less meaningless, squalid, and ferocious than that of the wild beasts." All must appreciate the "race importance" of this struggle, he maintained, and recognize that in the end the elimination of inferior races would work "for the benefit of civilization and in the interests of mankind."[18] These opinions were to possess even greater force once Roosevelt became president and began to conduct foreign policy.

The thinking about race in the United States, of course, looked not only outward upon the world at large but also inward toward the particular U.S. domestic situation with blacks. Here the full triumph of Darwinism in U.S. thought coincided with the 1890 census. The statistical evidence from this census seemed to demonstrate that blacks were falling behind in their birthrate when compared with whites and this, in turn, readily fit into the thesis of the "survival of the fittest" in the "struggle for existence" among the races. "As a result," wrote George Fredrickson, "the 1890s saw an unparalleled outburst of racist speculation on the impending disappearance of the American Negro."[19] The distinguished natural scientist, Joseph Le Conte, for instance, applied Darwinian theory to the census in a study entitled *The Race Problem in the South* (1892), observing that "in organic evolution" the destiny of inferior races is either "extinction . . . or else . . . relegation to a subordinate place in the economy of nature; the weaker is either destroyed or seeks safety by avoiding competition. Not only is this result inevitable," he concluded, "but it is the best result for both races, specially for the lower race."[20] The following year a physician by the name of Eugene Corson contributed to the debate a paper called "The Vital Equation of the Colored Race and Its Future in the United States." He maintained that blacks were destined to disappear as victims of "the struggle for existence against a superior race" in a world "where the Caucasian is supreme, and all else must give way before him."[21] Using the census figures with a fashionable statistical analysis, Frederick Hoffman published *Race Traits and Tendencies of the American Negro* (1896), one of the most influential contemporary discussions of the race question to appear. He too argued that blacks, like Indians, were part of an inferior race destined to be eliminated by the stronger whites in the natural competition for survival.[22]

Hoffman's books not only became a prized source of information and conclusions for writers on race for many years to come but also had the practical effect of helping to convince most white insurance companies that they should deny coverage to all blacks on the grounds that their race constituted an unacceptable actuarial risk.[23] Yet this was not all.

One of the paradoxical features of this development could be seen in the fact that although the ideology of racial struggle implied the eventual extinction of blacks by a natural process, actual policy actively and aggressively intervened to enforce discrimination against them. When fear of black competition in the marketplace and fear of black votes in the polling place combined with beliefs about Darwinian struggle, the result proved to be a full flowering of racist demagoguery and segregation. Efforts to disfranchise blacks in several states led the way, for once the vote was removed everything else necessary for white supremacy in the South could be done. Thus, precisely during these years of the 1890s, blacks witnessed legal disfranchisement, the passage of rigorous Jim Crow ("for whites only") laws, the rise of blatant race-baiting politicians, an all-time peak number of lynchings, and a series of race riots in both the North and the South against largely defenseless blacks.[24]

The highest court in the land (which only a few years before had denied Indians the right to vote) confirmed this policy of segregation in the 1896 landmark case of *Plessy* v. *Ferguson*, placing the Supreme Court's approval on "separate but equal" treatment. Writing for the majority of the court, Justice Henry Brown argued that the U.S. Constitution and its amendments passed during Reconstruction "in the nature of things could not have been intended to abolish distinctions based upon color" and that enforced segregation of the races "neither abridges the privileges or immunities of the colored man."[25] Justice John Harland, disputing this opinion, claimed that all citizens should be equal before the law, that the Constitution was "color blind," and that any notions of superior or inferior races should be soundly rejected. He could not persuade his colleagues on the bench, however, and voted alone as an isolated voice. This case paved the way for increased segregation and an even more intense consciousness of racial differences.

With this rising tide of ideology about racial struggle being implemented through policies of discrimination, an intense consciousness about race appeared. Those who discriminated on the basis of color did so with a growing awareness of their own race. Those who were discriminated against developed an even more acute racial consciousness, as constant reinforcement came each and every time they confronted these new barriers of racial prejudice. As a consequence, the victims of racial discrimination, in defense or as compensation, steadily developed their own sense of pride of race and determination to fight back.

Precisely at this time when anti-Semitism reached a fever pitch in Europe, Theodor Herzl, an Austro-Hungarian Jew, came forward with his plan for Zionism. Arguing that Jews really were a separate and distinctive group, he believed that they deserved special treatment not accorded to others.[26] His movement grew, held international congresses, and enlisted an ethusiastic following among Jews in many lands. Ironically, as we shall see, during the politics and diplomacy of racial discrimination in the later twentieth century, the international community, as represented by the United Nations General Assembly, ruled that Zionism itself was a form of racism. The rising tide of resentment against racism demonstrated by Herzl also could be seen among certain U.S. blacks.

Interestingly enough, in the same way that Zionists wanted to band tightly together and escape to a separate state of Palestine, so did a number of blacks join in Back-to-Africa movements to support the dream of a major exodus away from white America.[27] Others, led by the determined and talented W.E.B. Du Bois, who had been educated in the United States and Germany, met in 1905 to organize the Niagara Movement for aggressive action to secure full citizenship and the abolition of all distinctions based upon race. This movement, in turn, inspired the formation of the National Association for the Advancement of Colored People (NAACP) within only four years. The "work of the Negro hater has flourished in the land," stated an early resolution of the movement in condemning "the stealing of the black man's ballot. Never before in the modern age," rang out its words, "has a great and civilized folk threatened to adopt so cowardly a creed in the treatment of its fellow-citizens, born and bred on its soil. Stripped of verbiage and subterfuge and in its naked nastiness, the new American creed says: fear to let black men even try to rise lest they become the equals of the white. And this in a land that professes to follow Jesus Christ. The blasphemy of such a course is only matched by its cowardice."[28]

Such rhetoric and organized resistance created a furor and seemed to aggravate racial tensions even further. After the turn of the century a flurry of writings appeared in the West further emphasizing the importance of struggle among the races. The attention given to eugenics or, as preferred by some, "race hygiene" and "racial science," on the best selective breeding techniques for racial superiority increased dramatically.[29] In the United States a Eugenics Record Office opened to safeguard against "degenerate breeding stock," and a number of extreme manifestations of negrophobia appeared, including new aggressiveness by the Ku Klux Klan and the outbreak of additional race riots.[30] Charles Carroll's inflammatory book, *The Negro a Beast* (1900), spoke against all those of color, especially blacks, and attempted to provide "convincing Biblical and scientific evidence that the Negro is not of the human family."[31] William B. Smith followed with *The Color Line* (1905) about the necessity for blacks to "vanish" before superior competition and await the doom of extinction "prepared in like measure for all inferior races."[32] Similar opinions about race could be found in the pages of *L'Action française* written by Charles Maurras in France and in the writings of Moeller van den Bruck in Germany.[33] Klaus Wagner's *Krieg* (1906) stressed a "policy of racial power" in warfare and asked, "Have Gobineau, Darwin, and Chamberlain lived in vain?"[34]

These many ideas about racial struggle served both to express and to aggravate many international problems preceding World War I. Considering the fever of rabid nationalism in this period, it is hardly surprising that passionate patriots would confuse biology, linguistics, culture, and politics, with the loose use of words and slogans, and speak of such things as the "Germanic" or "Teutonic race," "Anglo-Saxon race," Nordic race," "Celtic race," "Latin race," "Gallic race," "Slavic race," "American race," and so on.[35] This nationalistic rhetoric of presumed "racial" differences among whites, however, was quickly challenged by those who pressed for a closing of the white ranks when confronting non-white peoples. Expressing the importance of this kind of solidarity, John Fiske wrote that Englishmen, Frenchmen, Greeks, and all other Caucasians "belong to the same race; and that is when we are contrasting them as white men with black men or yellow men."[36] With attitudes of racial struggle on their minds, wrote one observer, many in the Western world believed that they "must stand shoulder to shoulder against the colored hordes of black, red, and yellow men whom they have aroused from their ancestral torpor in the name of civilization, else European culture—or, rather, Civilization itself—is doomed."[37] The effects of this kind of opinion, and the rising tide of resentment against it, could be seen readily in immigration and imperialism.

Immigration and Racial Exclusion

These ideologies of racial struggle appeared to be particularly intense in the places where one race confronted another not simply in theory but in actual practice. This occurred both when white Europeans or Americans moved out to conquer the non-white world in imperialism and when non-whites moved in to enter the white world as immigrants. What had been a mere trickle of migrants in the past began to reach flood proportions by the end of the nineteenth and beginning of the twentieth centuries. The lure of new opportunities and the revolution in transportation technology increasingly enabled workers and their families to travel around the globe. Those who were Caucasian found themselves confronted with xenophobia and suspicion in their adopted lands, but they could recover from these and eventually assimilate. Those with non-white skin colors, however, found themselves confronted with racial prejudice at the borders and barriers preventing their entry altogether. They quickly discovered that those initial immigration restrictions of the 1880s against race now served as inspiration for new dikes against a rising tide of color, thereby transforming ideas of racial struggle into policies of racial exclusion.

In the international effort to restrict immigration on the basis of race, the unquestioned leadership fell to those of British descent. Ironically, although these people were particularly proud of their Christian faith and democratic principles, among them the determination to bar the free entry of colored immigrants reached unparalleled dimensions. "The strong feeling of antipathy to Asiatic races [and others of color] that is now so marked a feature of the British speaking people," wrote one contemporary observer, demonstrated an intensity unprecedented in the history of the world for "race hatred."[38] The attitude of racial superiority and the fear of economic competition from cheap imported labor found expression in public statements about the possible extinction of their white race by "being flooded by undesirable immigrants from India" or "submerged under an Asiatic wave of immigration."[39] Such sentiments from self-governing territories found much sympathy in the corridors of power in London but also proved to be the source of public embarrassment, especially when the statements involved peoples from within the empire itself. Any open discrimination would belie the stated imperial philosophy of the equality of all British subjects, provoke liberal opposition at home, and cause great indignation in areas like India. As one Colonial Office minute summarized the dilemma: "The whole subject is perhaps the most difficult we have had to deal with. The Colonies wish to exclude the Indians from spreading themselves all over the Empire. If we agree, we are liable to forfeit the loyalty of the Indians. If we do not agree we forfeit the loyalty of the Colonists."[40] In the end, the British government sided with those of its members' own race and stood back to allow immigration restrictions to be erected.

The new model for racial exclusion emerged with the Restriction on Immigration of 1897 in Natal. Qualifications for entry appeared to have nothing to do with race, for the law spoke only of property and knowledge of a European language. Borrowing a page from the book of U.S. literacy tests for black voters, any immigration officer simply could determine by his own discretion that a colored applicant did not know a language of Europe sufficiently well enough to gain entrance. This simple device, known as the Natal formula, effectively excluded all non-whites not wanted. Its success encouraged similar laws to appear shortly thereafter in Cape Colony, the former Dutch republics of the Transvaal and Orange Free State, and in Southern Rhodesia, where the attorney general described them as "the last link in that chain which must form the cordon around the white people of South Africa."[41] When the Union of South Africa was established in 1910, its leader Louis Botha again applied the formula from Natal to create a uniform policy of racial exclusion and then institute a series of discriminatory statutes to establish the power of a white-minority regime. The subsequent Union Immigrants Regulation Act prohibited the entry of anyone deemed to be "unsuitable," and this naturally excluded those of non-white races.[42] Such a "color bar," predicted the *Times*, would cause more problems than any other issue in the politics and diplomacy of the Imperial Council; yet the editors concluded that the best way to resolve the matter was to make the black, brown, and yellow of the world "realize that . . . inequality [is] inevitable . . . not due to inferior *status* but to facts of race."[43]

Successful results of the restriction of immigration in southern Africa encouraged residents of Australia and New Zealand to follow suit. The earlier exclusion of Chinese immigrants had done nothing to resolve the problem of the "Yellow Peril" from Japan, and resentment seemed to grow with every passing year. Moreover, the negotiations between Britain and Japan for commercial agreements appeared too conciliatory on immigration questions. The issue became so important, in fact, that a special Australasian premiers' conference in 1896 refused to accede to the Anglo-Japanese convention. In accordance with a resolution of the conference, a number of states passed Colored Races Restriction and Regulation bills excluding the native inhabitants of Asia, Africa, and the Pacific Islands.[44] Voices spoke publicly of the "leprosy" of "colored races" and the danger of hybridization from "inferior races" like Asiatics and blacks, while the *Sydney Daily Telegraph* declared: "If we want a homogeneous Australia, we must have a white Australia. . . . It is not much use . . . to shut out Chinamen, and leave the door open to millions of Hindoos, Arabs, Burmese, Angolese, and other colored races which swarm British Asia."[45]

This "White Australia" policy proved to be a powerful unifying force around which Australians could rally. Indeed, in the opinion of the British Foreign Office, the desire for uniform exclusion laws served as "one of the main factors" in uniting the various Australian states into a single commonwealth in 1901.[46] A series of sweeping immigration statutes followed to secure White Australia as a bastion by excluding the colored races of the earth. As writer C. H. Kirmess expressed the attitude behind this policy in *The Australian Crisis* (1909): "In this struggle the still larger issue is bound up with whether the White or Yellow Race shall gain final supremacy. Christian civilization cannot afford the loss of this Continent. FOR AUSTRALIA IS THE PRECIOUS FRONT BUCKLE IN THE WHITE GIRDLE OF POWER AND PROGRESS ENCIRCLING THE GLOBE."[47]

In Canada as well concern about racial struggle and competition pervaded discussion on immigration. Especially in British Columbia, hatred against the "Mongolian race" sparked brutality in the streets and attempts to exclude not only the Chinese but also the Japanese and those from India. Yet, to exclude these latter two groups was fraught with political and diplomatic difficulty. The Indians possessed, after all, the rights of British subjects, and after the signing of the Anglo-Japanese Treaty of 1902, Japan constituted a nation in close alliance with Britain and hence the British Empire. The intricacies and subtleties of foreign affairs are often lost upon those engaged in the passions and violence of race riots, however, and mounting protests from Victoria and Vancouver and the formulation of the Asiatic Exclusion League created serious domestic pressures upon the Canadian government. The result in the decade following 1900 took the form of a number of exclusion laws designed to create a "White Canada." Lest there be any loopholes, the Immigration Act of 1910 provided the all-encompassing authority to prohibit the entry "of immigrants belonging to any race deemed unsuited to the climate or requirements of Canada."[48] The lyrics of "White Canada Forever," expressed the prevailing opinion: "We welcome as brothers all white men still, but the shifty yellow race . . . must find another place."[49]

Although the pattern of exclusion based upon racial hatred and fear was unmistakable throughout South Africa, Australia, New Zealand, and Canada, these self-governing territories possessed no monopoly on prejudice of race. In Central and South America after the turn of the century a considerable number of writers expressed opinions about the biological superiority of whites, the inferiority of dark-skinned blacks and Indians, and the fear of more mixed blood resulting from unrestricted immigration.[50] Even though such opinions were not nearly so widespread as elsewhere, they nevertheless existed with sufficient force to influence policy. In Paraguay the Immigration Law of 1903 placed limitations on the entrance of "individuals of the yellow or black races." During the following year, Costa Rica restricted Asians and those of certain other races from entering the country. Uruguay passed similar contemporary legislation against "Asiatics and Africans."[51] Persecution of Asians occurred on several occasions in northern Mexico, and the 1911 massacre of Torreon cost three hundred Chinese their lives. Such examples as these, wrote Magnus Morner, one of the world's foremost authorities on racial attitudes in Latin America, demonstrate that racism "is not a phenomenon unique to Anglo-Saxons, Germans, and South Africans."[52]

Between the Canadians in the north and the Latin Americans to the south, the most striking case of racial exclusion in immigration policy occurred in the United States. Those same writers who preached about the importance of struggle among the races also raised their voices on the danger of the rising tide of color on the unprotected shores. Josiah Strong described unrestricted immigration as one of the great "perils" facing the United States and warned that unless stopped, this "gulfstream of humanity" would "flow on with a rising flood" to threaten the racial integrity of the nation.[53] "There is now being injected into the veins of the nation," he declared, "a large amount of inferior blood every day of every year."[54] Others, like Thomas Bailey Aldrich, echoed this theme; in his widely discussed poem, "Unguarded Gates," Aldrich lamented: "Wide open and unguarded stand our gates, and through them passes a wild motley throng. . . . O Liberty, white Goddess! Is it well to leave the gates unguarded?"[55]

Francis Walker, former commissioner of Indian affairs and superintendent of the celebrated 1890 census that focused so much on blacks, turned his attention to immigrants and warned in Social Darwinian terms that they "are beaten men from beaten races; representing the worst failures in the struggle for existence."[56] Some spoke in fear that the mixture of the races would lead to "racial retrogression" or "race suicide" and urged the country to "drive back the hordes of the dark and degenerate races . . . lest they may enter in to infect and degrade."[57] Others contemptuously wrote of the "Yellow Peril" from the Orient and those "whose skins are black, yellow, or red."[58] Always on the alert against possible racial degeneration, President Theodore Roosevelt also expressed concern over the need for exclusion and the determination to do something about it when he declared:

> We have got to build up our western country with our white civilization and we must retain the power to say who shall and who shall not come to our country. Now, it may be that Japan will adopt a different attitude, will demand that her people be permitted to go where they think fit, so I THOUGHT IT WISE TO SEND THAT FLEET AROUND THE PACIFIC TO BE READY TO MAINTAIN OUR RIGHTS. . . . The fleet is there in the [racial] interests of the whole Pacific Coast, the interests of British Columbia as well as those of California, and it is in the interests of Australia as well. . . . [For] self preservation is the first law of nature.[59]

The coercion exerted by battleships sent overseas to secure racial exclusion coincided with the efforts of pressure groups at home to achieve the same objective. On the East Coast the influential Immigration Restriction League devoted its considerable energies to tapping the roots of racial prejudice and U.S. nativism and campaigned for the exclusion of darker-skinned "new immigrants" of "non-Nordic" or "non-Aryan" stock.[60] On the West Coast the formation in 1905 of the Asiatic Exclusion League focused upon the "steady stream" of yellow "Japs" contaminating the racial purity of the nation and advocated a program to "Keep California White."[61] Both groups consistently used the ideology of racial struggle to support their arguments as well as presumed evidence from eugenics to bolster their claim that these immigrants were biologically inferior, and both sought federal legislation to stem the tide. Blue-blooded patricians like Republican Senator Henry Cabot Lodge, Populists like William Jennings Bryan, and Democrats like Woodrow Wilson could all find common ground on platforms of racial exclusion and the belief that assimilation in the U.S. melting pot should not cross the color line. Indeed, even some of the groups most vocal in expressing racist opinions were those supposedly dedicated to the principles of democracy such as labor unions, Progressives, and Socialists, whose worries were about job displacement and competition in the economic sphere.

Responding to this pressure (and in some cases leading it), Congress passed several immigration laws after the turn of the century and tried on other occasions to enact a "Natal formula" of its own, learning from South Africa how to use literacy tests as a legal means for excluding those not "pure Caucasians."[62] An executive order of 1907 debarred further Japanese immigration via Hawaii, Mexico, or Canada, and a subsequent "gentlemen's agreement" with Japan provided additional restrictions. New legislation created a U.S. Immigration Commission whose final report sought to prove the biological inferiority of non-white races.[63] Viewing even these actions as an indication of weak national resolve, California passed its own discriminatory regulations segregating Japanese children in public schools and the Alien Land Law of 1913, which limited land ownership for Japanese. One local periodical described the motivation for such measures and statutes simply enough: "race hatred and race prejudice."[64]

The creation of these unilateral immigration laws specifically excluding people and discriminating against them solely on the basis of race produced a situation described by an exclusionist as one in which "the rising tide of color finds itself walled in by white dikes debarring it from many a promised land which it would fain deluge with its dusky waves."[65] As such, wrote scholar Hugh Tinker, this policy marked "a clear demonstration of the division of the world along racial lines" and provided the source of great resentment by those of color.[66] Yet, in the politics and diplomacy of racial discrimination, the victims and their governments found that they could do little to halt or reverse the trend. Diplomatic protests and official complaints brought scant relief or sympathy. Humiliated by the deliberate exclusion of their own nationals abroad, the Chinese government formally protested to the Western powers but found itself simply dismissed. Indians vigorously objected to restrictions placed against them and steadily pressed the point about their rights as British subjects within the empire, but to no avail. In South Africa, for example, the inspirational Mohandas Gandhi became increasingly frustrated by the refusal of the authorities to take his complaints about discrimination seriously and actually began his public career of political protest in an effort to secure racial equality. Time and time again the protests of non-whites against limitations were quietly ignored, politely dismissed, or blatantly rejected. Those who had imposed such restrictions saw little reason to respond in any other way and preferred, in the words of British Prime Minister Joseph Chamberlain, "to let sleeping dogs lie."[67]

Only a single exception existed to this pattern of impotence in the face of racial exclusion: Japan. The difference certainly was not that the Japanese (who often excluded other Asians from their own territory) necessarily had a greater or lesser sensitivity than anyone else but that they alone among the discriminated possessed power. Relative treatment provided a good indication of relative weight carried on the international scene. China, with the strength of its empire withering and its national integrity emasculated by the powers of the West, could only plead for indulgence.[68] India, under the nearly total control of the British, could come with only a beggar's bowl in hand. Gandhi's diminutive stature and nearly naked appearance invited ridicule from those accustomed to view power in physical terms alone. In marked contrast with all of these stood the Japanese, whose strenuous efforts to "Westernize," to become a treaty partner with Britain, and to create a powerful military machine brought them surprising victory in the Russo-Japanese War of 1904–1905. This dramatic success with armed force, as we shall soon see, had momentous implications for international racial attitudes. It immediately brought heightened respect—and fear. There could be reason for concern when the *Mainichi Shimbun* threatened: "Stand up, Japanese nation! Our countrymen have been HUMILIATED on the other side of the Pacific. . . . Why do we not insist on sending [war] ships?"[69]

Consequently, those nations imposing immigration restrictions outwardly treated the Japanese differently than anyone else. Japan alone could demand and, in many cases, receive the opportunity to negotiate immigration arrangements rather than simply having them unilaterally imposed. Both the United States and Canada, for example, engaged in lengthy and intensive diplomatic negotiations with Tokyo over the sensitive issue of racial exclusion. In the end, the parties agreed upon several "gentlemen's agreements" whereby the Japanese pledged to restrict on their own the number of passports issued for direct travel to North America.[70] By stopping emigration at its source, the arrangement satisfied Washington and Ottawa; and by being the result of negotiation, satisfied Japan's amour propre and provisionally provided a face-saving solution to a difficult problem.

Despite the temporary success of these diplomatic negotiations, both sides resented having to negotiate in the first place. Japanese indignation stemmed from the original racial discrimination committed against them. U.S. and Canadian frustration came from having to spend considerable time, money, and effort on negotiations with a non-white people whom they regarded as racially inferior and "lesser breeds without the law."[71] Yet this swelling resentment, exacerbated by growing power, represented only the beginning. The racial attitudes that had created this problem and the power that had momentarily resolved it would each grow rather than diminish, for the rising tide of color first evident in immigration also would be seen in resistance to imperialism.

Imperialism and Racial War

The outward thrust of European imperialism and the wars necessary to conquer native peoples reached a dramatic climax in the years between 1890 and the outbreak of World War I. Propelled by a variety of motives, exploiting superior military technology, and employing attitudes that Davis described as "pervasive racism"[72] wherever they went, the powers of Europe ran at a fevered pace to control the inhabitants of Africa, Asia, and the Pacific. What had emerged as a general policy during the latter nineteenth century now exploded with unsurpassed violence and intensity, for no major nation wanted to be left out of this pursuit of imperial possessions.

Arguments of racial struggle based upon the Darwinian concepts of "survival of the fittest" and "natural selection" surrounded the entire process. Perhaps no one encapsulated the attitude better than the British eugenicist, Karl Pearson, in his classic essay of 1900 entitled *National Life From the Standpoint of Science*. "History shows me one way, and one way only," he wrote, "in which a state of civilization has been produced, namely, the struggle of race with race, and the survival of the physically and mentally fitter race. This dependence of progress upon the survival of the fitter race," he continued, "is the fiery crucible out of which comes the finer metal. You may hope for a time when the sword shall be turned into the plowshare. . . . But, believe me, when that day comes mankind will no longer progress; there will be nothing to check the fertility of inferior stock; the relentless law of heredity will not be controlled and guided by natural selection."[73] Imperialism, he and others believed, demonstrated the fulfillment of this unavoidable natural struggle and the necessity for the "inferior races" to submit in the face of white supremacy.

Such attitudes and their accompanying policies appeared most starkly on the African continent. Not satisfied with the imperial gains of the recent past, after 1890 Europeans launched their unprecedented "scramble for Africa" designed to conquer all remaining territory, rather than simply some. Moving inland from their coastal footholds, white Europeans set about to consolidate and enlarge existing empires. Britain secured recognition for expanded claims in Zanzibar, Kenya, Uganda, Northern Rhodesia (now Zambia), Bechuanaland, Nigeria, and Nyasaland (now Malawi). Britain took the Sudan and by defeating the Boers removed the last obstacle for creating the Union of South Africa. The French seized the Ivory Coast, occupied the ancient cities of Timbuktu and Say, consolidated their power in Niger and Chad, and welded several holdings together into a vast French West African empire. They then took Madagascar and Morocco. Portugal secured control of Mozambique, Spain grabbed Spanish Morocco, and Italy moved in to take Tripoli (now Libya). Germany strengthened its position in a variety of areas, expanded its territory in the Cameroons, and through the influential *Alldeutscher Verband*, or Pan-German League, aggressively sought more acquisitions.[74]

These many victories once again seemed to confirm in the minds of Europeans what they already believed and what they wanted to see, namely: the apparent biological superiority of whites over blacks. Writers such as British author Benjamin Kidd, the French naval officer Leopold de Saussure, and the German explorer and soldier Karl Peters all openly advocated imperial conquests on the basis of the racial inferiority of black Africans.[75] In the case of the Germans in South-West Africa (now Namibia), this attitude provided justification for the German refusal to negotiate with the Herero tribe and the order instead for its complete extermination (*Vernichtungsbefehl*).[76] Once secure in South Africa, Lord Milner, the British high commissioner, asserted that "a political equality of white and black is impossible. The white man must rule," he argued, "because he is elevated by many, many steps above the black man; steps which it will take the latter centuries to climb, and which it is quite possible that the vast bulk of the black population may never be able to climb at all."[77] Interestingly enough, even the socialist critics of imperialism and its concomitant capitalist exploitation maintained an outlook of intense racial superiority and rarely considered Africans as people in the white European sense of the word.[78]

Imperialism against blacks in Africa was accompanied by further attacks against non-whites in Asia and the Pacific. In this case, Kaiser Wilhelm II of Germany emerged as one of the leading spokesmen for modern racist thought. His close personal friendship with Houston Stewart Chamberlain and his own drive for *Weltpolitik* only encouraged his belief in global racial struggle and white superiority. The power demonstrated in Wilhelm's despatch of marines in 1897 to China amid slogans of race forced a lease arrangement on the port of Kiaochow, secured the province of Shantung as a German sphere of influence, and

The White Knight Guarding Against the "Yellow Peril"
(source: *Simplicissimus*, 1914)

helped to breed a growing racial prejudice against Asians. Cartoons eventually displayed images of a white knight courageously guarding against waves of the *gelbe Gefahr*, the "Yellow Peril"—subhumans from the Far East.[79] In similar fashion, Russia moved in to obtain a lease of Port Arthur for naval facilities, and France acquired one at Kwangchow. Not to be outdone by its rivals, Britain forced the Chinese to grant one lease on Weihaiwei, another for the Kowloon Peninsula opposite Hong Kong, and a sphere of influence in the rich Yangtze valley. The only European state whose demand for territory the Chinese empire ventured to deny was Italy, and that resulted not from a lack of racial attitudes in Italy but rather from a lack of power. Elsewhere the British extended their control in Tibet, as did the Russians in Persia and Manchuria, the French in Southeast Asia, and the Germans in the Samoan and Caroline islands of the Pacific.

These phenomenal successes by others and the opportunities for relatively easy conquest proved to be a temptation that the United States could not pass up. The prospects for enhanced economic gain, national prestige, and international power, when combined with the prevailing and pervasive Social Darwinist attitudes about race, propelled the United States out into the larger world to secure possessions in earnest.[80] The pivotal year was 1898. Congress disregarded the wishes of Hawaii's non-white inhabitants by annexing the island with a simple resolution and, more importantly, jettisoned more than fifty years of peace with other states by declaring war on Spain in an effort to seize its remaining holdings of empire. President William McKinley, pushed by enflamed public opinion, sent forces to the Caribbean and Manila Bay in the South China Sea.

With the sole exception of Britain, all the powers of Europe unanimously condemned the U.S. action as a war of aggression—not against the native populations living in these islands, but rather against the Spanish who occupied them. The Spanish-American War, or "The Splendid Little War," as the victors preferred to call it, brought in enormous acquisitions at very little cost. As a result of its decisive victories, the United States quickly took Cuba, Puerto Rico, Guam, and the Philippines. In the last case, there followed two years of bloody warfare against the Filipino leader Emilio Aguinaldo, contemptuously described in Washington as an inferior "Chinese half-breed."[81] Meanwhile, in rapid sequence the United States occupied Wake Island and part of Samoa, sent troops into China to extract concessions, and in 1904 President Theodore Roosevelt, practicing his particular brand of "big stick diplomacy," seized the Panama Canal; the following year he took control of the customs houses in the Dominican Republic. U.S. military intervention soon followed in Nicaragua. Thus, within a very short period of time, the United States burst beyond its own territorial confines, stepped upon the stage of empire, and joined with Europeans in subjugating the non-white world through imperialism.

These many imperial conquests created what John Hope Franklin called the U.S. "Empire of Darker Peoples": in the Pacific "an empire composed primarily of darker peoples—Polynesian, Japanese, Chinese, and others" and, in the Caribbean, control that "brought into its orbit millions of people of African or mixed descent."[82] Much of the impetus for this imperial drive and the eagerness to use armed force against natives, of course, sprang from the deep and widespread attitudes toward race developed over many years. Indeed, many observers believe that U.S. imperialism cannot be understood at all apart from U.S. racism.[83] Roosevelt, among others, certainly viewed imperialism as racial war. He lashed out at those who would apply the "rules of international morality" to "savages" and "beasts," asserting that such critics failed "to understand the race-importance of the work which is done by their . . . brethren in wild and distant lands. The most ultimately righteous of all wars," he argued,

> is a war with savages, though it is apt to be also the most terrible and inhuman. The rude, fierce settler who drives the savage from the land lays all civilized mankind under a debt to him. American and Indian, Boer and Zulu, Cossack and Tartar, New Zealander and Maori—in each case the victor, horrible though many of his deeds are, has laid deep the foundations for the future greatness of a mighty people. The consequences of struggles for territory between civilized [white] nations seem small by comparison.

Using global references, Roosevelt concluded that it "is of incalculable importance" that lands "should pass out of the hands of their red, black, and yellow aboriginal owners, and become the heritage of the dominant world races."[84]

This expression of imperialism and racial war differed not at all from those heard in Europe, as both Americans and Europeans imposed their control upon those of color. Yet, unlike the others with overseas empires, the United States possessed a major race problem within its own borders. Politically, this created serious difficulties, for an imperial policy toward race abroad could not be allowed to upset the racial arrangements at home. In fact, this was precisely the concern of many anti-imperialists who, ironically enough, used racist arguments as well. Both the imperialists and the anti-imperialists shared the common assumptions about the inequality of the races and the superiority of whites as facts of life but drew different conclusions. Whereas the advocates of empire employed theories of racial struggle to justify conquest, their opponents marshalled ideas of race prejudice to criticize the acquisition of territory.

Southern Democrats, for example, demonstrated near unanimity in condemning imperialism on the grounds that brown and yellow natives, like blacks, were innately inferior to white people, would "mongrelize" racial purity, and could never be assimilated into U.S. life. As Benjamin Tillman stated while speaking for the minority against the treaty with Spain to acquire the Philippines, "as a Senator from South Carolina, with 750,000 colored population and only 500,000 whites, I realize what you are doing, while you don't; and I would save this country from the injection into it of another race question which can only breed bloodshed and a costly war."[85] Failing to halt annexation, these opponents did what they considered the next best thing: to successfully ensure that the yellows and the browns in the Philippines and blacks in Puerto Rico would not be allowed to enjoy full liberties of self-government, lest they inspire people of color in the United States to seek greater political opportunities themselves.[86]

Not all Americans felt comfortable with these developments, and some worried about embarking on a career of international plunder and suppression of native peoples that might lead to the decadence and corruption associated with empires.[87] This concern, when combined with pangs of conscience, perhaps explains why popular opinion so readily seized upon a humanitarian explanation for the nation's brutal and aggressive behavior. The launching of U.S. imperialism produced one of those classic expressions that uniquely captures a mood, justifies a policy, and simultaneously captures the imagination. The U.S. seizure of the Philippines inspired British poet Rudyard Kipling to coin a phrase that gained instant fame and lasting immortality: "The White Man's Burden." His poem of that title contained a mixture of racial superiority, arrogance, responsibility, and humanitarianism expressing the nonexploitative ideal of imperialism toward native races that he described as "new-caught, sullen peoples, half-devil and half-child."[88] The idea of a civilizing mission for the weak, lesser breeds most certainly was nothing new and had been used for several centuries by Europeans with reference to the conversion of "heathens." But now the theme caught fire, and the apologists for empire in Europe and the United States found themselves wildly applauded when they spoke not of profits, strategic bases, or geopolitical advantages, but of "duty," "divinely-ordained mission," and the responsibility "to carry light and civilization into the dark places of the world."[89] At the peak of imperialism, the expression "White Man's Burden" served a need by providing a welcomed elevated justification for all those engaged in the Western conquest of the non-white world.

Whatever the explanation or motivation for imperialism, whether for greed or God, the fact remains that between 1890 and the outbreak of World War I, the imperial powers completed the "Europeanization of the world." Native peoples could see little, if any, distinction between the Europeans and the Americans and witnessed how Western technology, wealth, and organization created enormous power sufficient to carve out vast political and economic empires over the entire globe. Outside Antarctica and the Arctic, by 1914 there remained less than a fifth of the world's land surface that was not directly under a European flag or that of a country of European settlement. White imperialists thus could bask in their glory and accurately boast that "the sun never set" upon their possessions. Britain ruled 400 million people outside her own borders; France, 50 million; Germany and Italy, about 14 million each; and Russia and the United States exercised control over many millions more.[90]

It is critical to pause here and consider these phenomenal numbers and the staggering dimensions they convey. More than half a billion people throughout the world who happened to be dark skinned directly suffered at the hands of imperialists who happened to be white. No continent and no non-white race escaped. In the West there was—and continues to be—an overwhelming desire to pretend that the territories occupied by these people were somehow "vacant," "available," or hanging "like a ripe pear waiting to be plucked."[91] Historian William Appleman Williams was correct when he asserted the persistent existence of the "myth of empty continents dotted here and there with the mud huts, the lean-tos, and the tepees of unruly children playing at culture."[92] The elaborate construction of these mighty empires involved the taking of wealth, property, freedom, and in some cases, the lives of hundreds of millions of individual people. For them and for their descendants who vowed never to forget, the consequences of this imperialism proved to be of overwhelming importance for the global politics and diplomacy of racial discrimination in the twentieth century.

These victims, as we have seen, received no invitation to participate in any negotiations or assemble around diplomatic conference tables. Instead, they could only watch in seething anger as the Great Powers traded, sold, and divided peoples and properties like pawns in an international chess game of diplomacy. They could only listen as they heard themselves described as "semi-barbaric," the "rude Negroes in Africa," the "ignorant Pariahs in Asia," and the "half-savages from Oceania."[93] A few frustrated individuals attempted to hold the first embryonic Pan-African congress in London during 1900 to resist this, but they lacked power and could do no more than make observations about the future.[94] Among these, however, the most notable was the prediction of Du Bois, who used this occasion to make his celebrated statement: "The problem of the twentieth century [will be] the problem of the color line—the relation of the darker to the lighter races of men in Asia and Africa, in America and the islands of the sea."[95] Such prescient conclusions, no matter how correct, nevertheless made little impact on statesmen of the West. Consequently, for the victims of imperialism the only choices available were either to submit and collaborate in peace or to resist and fight in war.

History has shown precious few examples of people voluntarily surrendering what was theirs without a struggle. The campaigns of imperialism were no exception. Wherever they went, Europeans and Americans found themselves confronting bloody resistance. In Africa alone, the British encountered fierce fighting against the Xhosa and Zulu among southern African tribes, the Masai in the Kenya highlands, the Asante in Ghana, and the Bunyoro in Uganda. Extensive battles raged between French forces and the Mande in upper Senegal and lower Mali, and the Rabih in Niger and Chad. German troops fought costly campaigns against Swahili peoples in Tanzania, and the Nama and Herero in Namibia. Portuguese soldiers struggled with the Ovimbundu in Angola, and white Rhodesian settlers battled the Mashona and the Ndebele. These were not minor skirmishes but wars, some of which lasted for months or even years. Moreover, they were race wars between white and black and were viewed as such by the combatants.[96] Time and time again, however, in these wars and in those fought in Asia and the Pacific, the military superiority of the West proved triumphant.

Only gradually did this course begin to turn and the tide of color to rise. The first sign of this change appeared in the mountains of northern Ethiopia. Goaded into action by public opinion, anxious to expand their African empire like other Europeans, and contemptuous of their black opponents whom they regarded as racially inferior, the Italians in 1896 ordered the advance of twenty thousand troops into the Ethiopian interior toward the city of Adowa. There they confronted the astute and skillful Menelik II, *Negus Negast* (king of kings) of Ethiopia, and his determined forces. Once the Italians attacked they discovered their disastrous mistake. The Ethiopians sliced them to ribbons. In one day, Italy lost more men than had died in the wars of unification in 1859 and 1860. A total of nearly fourteen thousand soldiers lost their lives in this single battle, and in the end the Ethiopians won a decisive and significant victory over the invading Italians.

This success secured independence for Ethiopia and allowed it to stand almost alone among African countries in escaping the imposition of European imperialism.[97] More important for the politics and diplomacy in the global issue of race, the Battle of Adowa represented the first modern military struggle in which those of color were victorious over whites. Europeans understood this and described the result as a "disaster of the first magnitude."[98] "The defeat of the Italians by King Menelik," declared one observer in Paris, "is an event which you should keep in your memories. It is the waking up of Africa to meet what has been hitherto the distainful seizure by Europeans of these countries which we call barbarous." Menelik's victory, he maintained,

is that of all Africa; and this point of view will gradually become patent. In these countries, where news traverses the deserts as on the wings of the wind, you may be sure that from one end of Africa to the other it is already known, or will be tomorrow, that Africa has conquered Europe, and throughout those dusky myriads there will be a waking to life and to an attitude of defense. This is a reason why this whole business is so serious and why nothing could be more heedless than to rejoice at the defeat of the Italians. That defeat is also ours.[99]

This shocking blow to Western pride and prestige in Africa provoked alarm in Europe and the United States but inspired imitation in the Far East. If the seemingly invincible whites could be humiliated in the mountainous terrain of Ethiopia, then why not in the cities of China? Seething for years with hatred against the encroachments of the "foreign devils" in their country, thousands of Chinese now saw the opportunity to strike back. Outbreaks of violence against missionaries, traders, and diplomats occurred in 1898, and extra guards had to be brought to Peking to protect the legations. With the explosion of the Boxer Rebellion in 1900 and the deployment of imperial Chinese troops, however, China was at war with those powers that sought to carve it up. Several hundred white foreigners, including a number of people from the diplomatic corps, were killed in the struggle, and a siege against them lasted two months. Swift reprisals followed in a punative expedition that included British, German, French, Russian, Japanese, and U.S. troops. Nevertheless, a defiant attack had been made, and it demonstrated to those from faraway lands in Europe and North America that these "lesser breeds" would not remain passive and, if necessary, would kill.[100]

Among these conflicts between races, none was more psychologically momentous than the Russo-Japanese War. Fierce competition between these two imperialist nations greedy for territorial aggrandizement in China led to numerous clashes after the turn of the century. Growing tensions escalated, and by 1904 erupted into a major war. The Japanese attacked with speed and surprise, and the Russians found themselves being rolled back and badly beaten in a series of battles around Mukden in which more troops participated with heavier casualties suffered than in any other fighting since the Franco-Prussian War.[101] The Russians watched their armies expelled from Manchuria, their Far Eastern fleet rendered ineffective, and their base at Port Arthur forced to surrender after a long siege—all to troops whom they arrogantly regarded as racially inferior, yellow, slant-eyed "monkeys."[102] In desperation they sent from Reval another fleet around Europe, Africa, and Southeast Asia, only to be sunk to the bottom of the Tsushima Strait by the Japanese navy in 1905. The news of this defeat stunned the world. Alfred Zimmern, then a young lecturer at Oxford, walked into his class announcing that he was putting aside Greek history for the morning, "because I feel I must speak to you about the most important historical event which has happened, or is likely to happen, in our lifetime: the victory of a non-white people over a white people."[103]

Watching the landing in Japan of Russian prisoners taken during the war, French journalist René Pinon described the horrifying spectacle of "little Nippons" humiliating the "big splendid" white men "whom they so detest!" This scene, he wrote, of "whites, vanquished and captives, defiling before those free and triumphant yellows—this was not Russia beaten by Japan, not the defeat of one nation by another; it was something new, enormous, prodigious; it was the victory of one world over another; it was the revenge which effaced the centuries of humiliations . . . ; it was the awakening hope of the Oriental peoples, it was the first blow given to the other race, to that accursed race of the West."[104]

Far from being horrified, Du Bois and many other blacks in the United States found inspiration in this dramatic success of an Asian people against Caucasians and predicted that one day there would be a joint awakening of the black, brown, and yellow peoples who, unless whites changed their attitudes and policies, would launch a global race war.[105] Even those with strongly racist views about white superiority drew exactly the same conclusion and spoke of worldwide "racial wars" and the international "conflict of color."[106] "The echoes of that yellow triumph over one of the great white Powers," wrote the U.S. author Lothrop Stoddard with fear, "reverberated to the ends of the earth," for the Russo-Japanese War "dramatized and clarified ideas which had been germinating half-consciously in millions of colored minds, and both Asia and Africa thrilled with joy and hope. Above all, the legend of white invincibility lay, a fallen idol, in the dust." This, he declared, marked a terrifying indication of "the rising tide of color" and raised the prospect of future race wars around the world.[107]

These costly setbacks and the strong possibility of others in the future demonstrated that the height of imperialism had been reached. Few new acquisitions could be won, and those already held would become increasingly difficult to maintain in the face of determined resistance and emotional discussion about race wars. Moreover, the slow but steady emergence of Asia, Africa, and the United States with its own recently acquired empire, the rising pressures of non-white peoples to be heard, and the growing interracial features of international relations all began to place severe strains upon the European-centered diplomatic system of the past,[108] bringing to mind the earlier words of Queen Victoria, who had said, "We shall never really be liked . . . if we keep up this racial feeling, and some day real danger may result from it."[109] For this reason, diplomats now spoke of "a great turning point of world politics," the "logic of history," and the need to recognize "new tasks" for diplomacy.[110] Other observers of global affairs described these swelling changes as the "writing on the wall" for "the end of one immensely long age in the world's history and the beginning of another."[111] This seemed to be confirmed all the more when the Universal Races Congress held its first meeting in London during 1911. Lest there be any confusion about the major cause of these developments, the French socialist leader Jean Jaurès declared, "There are all these people of all races who have seemed inert . . . and sunk deep in an eternal sleep, who are now awakening, demanding their rights, and flexing their muscles."[112] "The world-wide struggle between the primary races of mankind—the 'conflict of color,' " wrote another with the same opinion, "bids fair to be the fundamental problem of the twentieth century" and "perhaps the gravest problem of the future."[113]

All the problems of imperialism and interracial international tension added dangerous fuel to an already-smoldering situation waiting to burst into flames. Rigid alliance systems, feverish military and naval arms races, unsettling domestic unrest, unrelenting diplomatic crises, extreme nationalism, strident leaders, predetermined war plans, and armed conflict all contributed their share in creating a volatile atmosphere in which an incident was capable of setting off a major conflagration. When the explosion came, it brought nothing short of a world war, the likes of which never had been seen in history.

World War I and Racial Tensions

A mere four or five bullets fired from an assassin's pistol in the hot summer of 1914 not only killed Austria's Archduke Franz Ferdinand and his wife but also sent shock waves rippling through Europe. These shock waves started troop trains moving on their way to a war that would convulse the world. When World War I began, it had little or nothing to do with race and few could anticipate what horrors and carnage lay ahead. Indeed, the nearly universal initial reaction of enthusiasm indicated little concern for the future and joyous confidence in a short and glorious armed conflict. Yet, when the war finally ground to an end in 1918 after years of the bloodiest fighting ever known to man, few could escape its staggering consequences.

Predictions on all sides of a lightning quick, mobile war rapidly vanished into clouds of artillery smoke on the horizon and clumps of mud in the trenches. The century's new scientific discoveries unleashed unimaginable forces of destruction that revolutionized modern warfare, obliterated the old distinctions between civilian and combatant, laid waste to entire provinces, and destroyed human lives in numbers without precedent. Europe and the world staggered in disbelief as more than four years of protracted total war killed two million young Germans, only slightly fewer Russians, more than one million French, and almost as many English and Austrians. The numbers wounded or maimed for the rest of their lives were even greater. Such tragic figures as these did not shorten the struggle, however. Survival required all the wealth, industrial capacity, personnel, and morale that entire societies could mobilize, and in some cases, even more than they possibly could provide. Convulsed in war and then torn by revolution, the empires of Germany, Austria-Hungary, and Russia crumbled apart. Watching this bloodbath of violence and chaos, non-whites around the world could not help but wonder how this war would affect them and what it might mean for racial tensions.

For Europeans concerned about race, the outbreak of World War I produced profound embarrassment. All the ideological slogans and statements about superior, "civilized," white culture used for generations to justify everything from slavery to imperialism seemed deathly hollow before this particular spectacle of slaughter. Thoughtful observers understood that their own battlefields might well record a barbarism far worse than any of the most exaggerated accounts of tribal warfare among "lesser breeds." As the war raged beyond all expectations, this embarrassment turned to genuine concern and even fear. With troops from the empire being recalled to protect the European homeland, imperial possessions would be much more difficult to hold. Moreover, with whites killing other whites by the millions (sometimes even accusing each other of "racial betrayal"), native races might well begin to view their plight—and their future—in a very different light. This is exactly the prospect that brought terror into the minds of many in the West. As one frightened author expressed the problem:

> The colored world suddenly saw the white peoples which, in racial matters had hitherto maintained something of a united front, locked in an internecine death-grapple of unparalleled ferocity; it saw those same peoples put one another furiously to the ban as irreconcilable foes; it saw white race-unity cleft by political and moral gulfs which white men themselves continuously iterated would never be filled. As colored men realized the significance of it all, they looked into each other's eyes and there saw the light of undreamed-of hopes. The white world was tearing itself to pieces. White solidarity was riven and shattered. And—fear of white power and respect for white civilization together dropped away like garments outworn.[114]

It took very little time for this dramatically changed attitude to become evident. In fact, within the first few weeks of the war, non-whites began to anticipate what might happen if the ruling nations of the world actually did exhaust themselves in a white civil war. Mohamed Duse, the influential and articulate editor of the first Afro-Asian journal, *African Times and Orient Review*, contemplated from London that the black, brown, and yellow races of the world might benefit enormously from this conflict among whites. Colored peoples, he wrote, even though unarmed and disunited, should carefully watch this war, for "all the combatants, the conquerors and the conquered alike, will be exhausted by the struggle, and will require years for their recovery." "Watch and wait!" he declared, for "it may be that the non-European races will profit by the European disaster."[115]

Other observers were not so content simply to watch and wait, and they seized this opportunity to inveigh publicly against "racial prejudice, that cowardly, wretched caste-mark of the European and American the world over," asserting, "You are deaf to the voice of reason and fairness, and so you must be taught with the whirring swish of the sword when it is red."[116] Du Bois emphasized this theme of struggle as well and saw World War I transforming global power relationships and thereby bringing new opportunities for the oppressed. "The colored peoples will not always submit to foreign domination," he wrote. "These nations and races," continued Du Bois with determination and growing confidence, "composing as they do the vast majority of humanity, are going to endure this treatment just as long as they must and not a moment longer. Then they are going to fight and the War of the Color Line will outdo in savage inhumanity any war this world has yet seen. For colored folk have much to remember and they will not forget."[117]

Even if the war appeared to hold out promise for people in Africa and Asia, many there believed that they would escape any direct involvement in the conflict. Europe, after all, was physically far removed from their own native lands. This illusion, like so many others during the war, did not last long. The same jealousies and rivalries that provoked World War I on European soil quickly descended on overseas possessions as well, and imperial competitors launched attacks in accordance with wartime alignments. Australian and New Zealand forces carried the war to German Samoa, German New Guinea, and German holdings on the Mariana, Caroline, and Marshall islands, among others. Japanese troops attacked Germans in Kiaochow and then moved along the Shantung Peninsula in China. Europeans fought throughout the Middle East during the war in order to complete the dissection of the Ottoman Empire, much of it at Arab expense. In Africa, the British without hesitation pressed blacks into military service to fight in the British wars, even though they refused to grant the blacks any rights in exchange. Black African soldiers helped British troops fight Germans (and blacks whom the Germans recruited from their own empire) in Togoland, the Cameroons, and German East Africa (now Tanzania).[118] South African forces moved against German-held possessions in South-West Africa and seized territory that they still claimed in the late 1980s in Namibia. For Africans, wrote noted authority Robert Cornevin, this carrying of the war to their continent left "unforgetable memories" of forced recruitment, flights of villagers, and death. "Two facts," he maintained, "especially left their imprint upon the African combatants: in battle a white bullet did the same job as a black bullet, and a dead white man was the same as a dead black." It was this experience more than any other that implanted the idea "in the African mind that the whites were not invincible."[119]

Not content with taking the war to Africa and Asia, white Europeans took Africans and Asians to the war. Desperate for manpower, the Europeans determined that they could use their vast reservoir of imperial subjects as soldiers in Europe. It is estimated, for example, that nearly two and one-half million colonials fought for Britain, and thousands more served as noncombatants.[120] They came from India, British East and West Africa, Egypt, the West Indies, South Africa, Mauritius, Fiji, and China. They battled alongside British troops in France and beside Australians at Gallipoli. All were regarded as equal when it came time to fight and die, but not for protection under the law, voting, or immigration. France similarly pressed into military service hundreds of thousands of Africans from Algeria, Morocco, Senegal, and Dahomey. These French African forces, along with others brought from Southeast Asia, fought in all of the major battles of the war, contributing heavily to the defense of France and causing enormous resentment among German soldiers, who despised having to fight against colored troops.[121]

This extensive participation of non-whites in the combat of World War I, wrote historian Immanuel Geiss, proved to be of "extraordinary importance" in the subsequent development of African and Asian nationalism.[122] It accelerated existing resentment against Europeans, struck blows that shook the imperial system, and greatly politicized those who survived. Soldiers from diverse parts of the world established contact for the first time with like-minded, politically conscious individuals also drawn unwittingly into this war. Together they witnessed European disasters and loss of confidence, and together they considered their common opportunities for the future. Indeed, several of those who would become leaders in the decolonization movement, including Ho Chi Minh, Chou En-lai, and Lamine Senghor, became politically active as a result of their experiences during World War I.[123] In 1916 the Congress party began to demand "Home Rule for India" in exchange for all the Indian sacrifices. With reference to the French empire, one colonial administrator declared that the thousands of African soldiers who fought in the trenches of France "dug the grave of the old Africa" of exploitation by whites.[124]

In addition to loosening the power of empire, many of those who fought in the war as "colored troops" sought to use their combat experience to fight prejudice and to gain racial equality. Service in the British and French armies expanded hitherto narrow horizons and convinced countless numbers of black, brown, and yellow combatants that their experience on the battlefield proved that they were every bit the equal of white men. With a growing sense of self-awareness, they therefore began to ask challenging questions about their treatment in the past and to express expectations that their many sacrifices would be rewarded when the war ended.[125] As Duse argued in the pages of the *African Times and Orient Review*:

> We are forced to observe that the once despised black man is coming to the front in the battle for freedom, and the freedom which he helps to win for the white man must also be meted out to him when the day of reckoning arrives. . . . In helping the British Empire and the French Republic in the hour of need you are helping yourselves to a freedom which cannot be denied to you and to a glory which shall be engraved upon the brazen tablets of fame which the rains of ages shall not wash away.[126]

Such hopes for social and political equality inspired not only those troops of color from European imperial possessions but also U.S. blacks who fought for the United States in the war.

The initial reaction of most Americans to the outbreak of World War I was a determination to do as much as possible to stay out of the conflict. Suspicions of diplomatic intrigues and "entangling alliances" encouraged isolationism and neutrality. On occasion, the war in Europe even afforded some benefits, as it did by offering a distraction when the United States—over the loud protests of the U.S. black community— occupied the black republic of Haiti in 1915, invaded the Dominican Republic the next year, and sent an expeditionary force into Mexico.[127] The war also provided the opportunity for further discussion about competition among the races and racial suicide, as evidenced by the popularity of a white supremacist film, *The Birth of a Nation*, and by the book by the New York patrician and follower of Gobineau, Madison Grant, entitled *The Passing of the Great Race*.[128] These several examples appeared as mere prelude, however, when the United States entered the war in 1917. Once it became a belligerent, the United States, like all others who participated in the war, faced a serious problem of manpower and to meet this need turned to its large black population for assistance.

When the war began for Americans, approximately 20,000 of the 750,000 men in the regular army and the National Guard were black. During the period of Selective Service enlistments after U.S. entry into the war, more than two million blacks registered for military service and nearly one-half million served. By the end of the war they constituted more than one-third of the entire U.S. force.[129] This massive influx of blacks into the armed services greatly exacerbated racial tensions, provoking strenuous opposition to any commissioning of black officers, integrated training camps, or equal consideration for promotion and assignment. Although the War Department issued numerous orders for fair and impartial treatment of black soldiers, these orders resulted in little discernible improvement, and in several southern cities racial riots were directed against blacks in uniform. In some cases, public lynchings with displays of appalling violence occurred, and within the army itself psychologists used intelligence tests to demonstrate "the intellectual inferiority of the Negro."[130] Nevertheless, many of these black soldiers believed that despite such serious problems, in the long run their sacrifices would pay dividends and that the "war to make the world safe for democracy" could not help but extend democratic principles to them as well. Even Du Bois subscribed to this belief and encouraged his readers to "close ranks shoulder to shoulder with our white citizens and the allied nations that are fighting for democracy."[131]

The vast discrepancies between black hopes for the future and actual practice at home in the United States made a ready target for German propaganda. In September 1918 Germans scattered circulars over the lines to demoralize these black troops, encouraging them not to be deluded into thinking that they were fighting for humanity and democracy. "Do you enjoy the same rights as the white people in America, the land of Freedom and Democracy," they asked, "or are you rather not treated over there as second-class citizens? Can you go into a restaurant where white people dine? Can you get a seat in the theatre where white people sit? . . . Is lynching and the most horrible crimes connected therewith a lawful proceeding in a democratic country?"[132] Although there were no reported cases of desertion, such propaganda, particularly when combined with the favorable French treatment of U.S. blacks during the war, could not help but foster a growing consciousness of racial inequality in the United States and a resolve to do something about it when the war ended.

In the midst of this ferment among non-white troops and increased awareness of racial tensions during World War I, the czarist regime of Russia collapsed under the might of the Bolshevik Revolution. Unable to meet the needs of its war-weary people, suffering from military defeat, and plagued by court intrigues and incompetence, the Russian government fell prey to the attacks of V. I. Lenin and the ruthless determination of the Bolshevik party to impose drastic changes on the country and on the world. Lenin declared to all who would listen that World War I was a conflict for imperialist gain rather than democratic principles. After seizing the documents of the czar, he revealed that although European governments publicly held out the promise of possibly relaxing control over their empires to those soldiers from abroad who were fighting for them, in private they had signed a number of secret treaties for "territorial desiderata" to carve up even more imperial possessions.[133] Shrewdly seeing the political advantages as well as the justice of appealing to racial inequalities, he sought to make Moscow the capital for colored emancipation. Lenin tried to convince soldiers from Africa and Asia, and black troops from the United States, to stop fighting for the "capitalistic imperialists" of the West and promised his support for national self-determination among non-white peoples of the world.[134] Such appeals and promises proved to be very attractive and highly seductive to many who had suffered from power and prejudice and, as we shall see, would remain so throughout the global politics and diplomacy of racial discrimination in the twentieth century. To the oppressed seeking freedom and equality, these promises offered hope and salvation. Yet, to many in the West they posed a threat instead and sparked fear. In "every quarter of the globe," cried Stoddard with fright, "in Asia, Africa, Latin America, and the United States, Bolshevik agitators whisper in the ears of discontented colored men their gospel of hatred and revenge."[135]

Alarm over what bolshevism and the revolutionary Soviet regime would mean for international racial relations was part and parcel of the immense upheaval and dislocation of World War I. By distorting and destroying so much of the past, these years of death and devastation seemed destined to make unrecognizable a great deal of the once known world. When the fighting finally ceased in November 1918, European self-confidence and global dominance, in the words of one French diplomat, "ceased to exist."[136] For some, this collapse brought deep anxiety and terror. But for others, particularly non-whites, it carried the possibility of exciting new opportunities for a more hopeful future.

*   *   *

All this discussion about democracy and racial emancipation during the war thus raised both fears and hopes around the world. Its coming on the crest of a rising tide of color, of racial consciousness, of immigration quotas, and of imperial conflicts with non-white victories between 1890 and World War I made its impact even greater. Black, brown, and yellow troops that fought in the war emerged with a new pride of race and anticipated that with the signing of the armistice they would be rewarded. They believed that whites would see the incongruity and the injustice of granting them equal opportunity to die but not to live. In looking back, they saw a past of oppression from slavery, racist ideology, immigration restrictions, and imperialism. In looking forward, they saw a future with the prospect for freedom. "As this hath been no white man's war," said one veteran of color with determination, "neither shall it be a white man's peace."[137] Consequently, with excitement they anticipated approaching the Paris Peace Conference to request international recognition of the principle of racial equality.

3
Racial Equality
Requested—and Rejected

THE POPULATION OF THE WHITE PEOPLE in different quarters of the world is calculated at seven hundred millions, while the non-whites number eleven hundred millions. The fact that these two groups are now sharply divided on account of the white people formally refusing to admit the other races on a footing of equality can only tend to accentuate racial prejudices which will far from realize President Wilson's ideal of lasting peace for the world.
—Japan Times

Prelude of Anticipation

The great and the small who assembled at Paris in 1919 were, for a short period of time, the arbiters of the world. Their decisions influenced the globe, and observers appropriately described their peace conference as "the clearing house of the Fates."[1] Added to the silent influences of the dead from World War I were the tumultuous demands of the living, who had survived. Individuals, pressure groups, political parties, states, empires, and races met to vie with each other over both spoils and principles. Although some saw themselves as only cleaning up the folly of an exhausted civilization gone mad, others sincerely believed that they could create an entirely new era in which respect for basic human rights and equality would rule supreme. As one diplomat recorded the mood: "We were journeying to Paris not merely to liquidate the war, but to found a new order. . . . We were preparing not Peace only, but Eternal Peace."[2]

To the hopeful, this was to be a world of a "new" diplomacy different in its origins, objectives, and methods from those of the past.[3] The optimists believed that respect for individuals and countries could be guaranteed in large measure by the participation of states and peoples heretofore excluded from that "inner sanctum" of high international politics. This development had been foreseen shortly before and during the war when many people throughout the globe spoke of the necessity for emancipation and equality.[4] Activists stressed this point even further at Paris. Indeed, the peace conference itself struck many contemporaries as a dramatic visual representation of the new age. W.E.B. Du Bois, the black leader from the United States, excitedly described the gathering as "THIRTY-TWO NATIONS, PEOPLES, AND RACES. . . . Not simply England, Italy, and the Great Powers are there, but all the little nations. . . . Not only groups, but races have come—Jews, Indians, Arabs, and All-Asia."[5] Another observer in Paris described the conference in the following words: "Chinamen, Japanese, Koreans, Hindus, Kirghizes, Lesghiens, Circassians, Mingrelians, Buryats, Malays, and Negroes and Negroids from Africa and America were among the tribes and tongues forgathered in Paris to watch the rebuilding of the political world system and to see where they 'came in.'"[6] This was something unknown in the annals of diplomacy, and to those who had been discriminated against for so long, the time appeared particularly ripe to request that all nations now support the principle of racial equality.

Hoping to seize this unique opportunity to place the cause of racial justice before the world, Du Bois set about to organize a Pan-African congress to meet in Paris in conjunction with the peace conference. He believed that the discussion of a new kind of diplomacy, the loosened ties of empire resulting from European weakness and loss of confidence, promises of national self-determination, and the rewards due those who served in the war created a special climate for exciting changes. In this extraordinary context, he wrote, "it would be a calamity for the two hundred million black people to be absolutely without voice or representation at this great transformation of the world."[7] Du Bois wanted to bring together not only Africans but also delegates from all countries in which there had been racial discrimination, including China, Japan, and India, and from racial minorities in North and South America and Europe. Representatives from private philanthropic and humanitarian groups concerned about racial prejudice received invitations as well. On the agenda was the discussion of the history of racial discrimination, the ways to eliminate this discrimination, the prospects of its elimination on a global scale, and most immediately ways to bring "all pressure possible on the delegates at the Peace Table in the interest of the colored peoples of the United States and the world."[8]

Although enthusiastically supported by many people, most governments did not appreciate this rather unorthodox effort to publicize the international problem of race. The U.S. government considered it embarrassing and dangerous and therefore opposed the meeting, denied passports to those Americans (black or white) who wanted to attend, and in the words of one observer, "tried, as best it could, to prevent the congress from taking place."[9] The Foreign Office in London similarly refused to allow Africans from British colonies to travel to Paris for the congress, and British military authorities would not permit a representative of the Anti-Slavery and Aborigines Protection Society to attend. Among the powerful white nations, only France considered the proposal. Through the efforts of Blaise Diagne, a black Senegalese member of the French Chamber of Deputies who had successfully brought thousands of native troops from Africa to help during the war, French Premier Georges Clemenceau agreed that the congress could be held. Yet, even in granting permission, he warned, "Don't advertise it."[10]

Despite these obstacles, when the First Pan-African Congress opened at the Grand Hotel in Paris during February 1919, it could boast of being "the first assembly of its kind in history."[11] Fifty-seven delegates attended, with thirteen from the French West Indies, seven each from Haiti and France, three from Liberia, two from the Spanish colonies and one each from the Portuguese colonies, San Domingo, Britain, British territories in Africa, French possessions in Africa, Algeria, Egypt, the Belgian Congo, and Abyssinia. Sixteen were from the United States, most of whom, like Du Bois, already had been in France and thus escaped passport control. The participants immediately put themselves on record as being vitally interested in the deliberations of the Paris Peace Conference concerning race, especially with respect to the proposals for racial equality and self-determination. Solemn and impassioned speeches alike called the attention of the world to the problem of racial discrimination and indicated a firm resolution among colored peoples around the globe to seek for themselves the liberation and democratic treatment for which they had sacrificed during the war. Years later, Du Bois would be praised for his foresight and as the "Father of Pan-Africanism" for this effort and the congress hailed by African nationalists as the historic signal for the emancipation of their continent.[12]

Such praises and accolades belonged to the future, however, for in 1919 the First Pan-African Congress could produce only speeches and resolutions begging for attention and sympathy. Considering the opposition and obstacles thrown in their way, it is surprising that the participants even came together at all. But their greatest limitation by far resided in the fact that they possessed no power. Those who attended the congress had not been officially delegated by anyone or any government. Instead, they came on their own accord as private individuals and as victims of prejudice. In these days before nongovernment organizations (NGOs) had any opportunity to influence diplomatic negotiations, all the participants could do was speak about the global issue of race, distribute their proclamation to official delegations, and hope that someone would listen with concern. As Du Bois himself recognized, "We were, of course, but weak and ineffective amateurs chipping at a hard conglomerate of problems about to explode in chaos."[13] Within the arena of politics and diplomacy, only those with power could participate in the deliberations. People desperately seeking to combat racial discrimination in the world needed a powerful and officially recognized voice at the peace conference itself, some government that would not be afraid to speak for them and would champion the cause of racial equality. They found such an advocate in Japan.

It is hardly surprising that the Japanese should have been concerned about the issue of equality among races in international relations. As we have seen, in the years before and during World War I racial discrimination reached new intensity, and for Japan the foreign policy manifestations of racial prejudice had been serious.[14] Severe immigration restrictions greatly intensified hostilities and embittered diplomatic relations with the United States, Canada, and Australia. Various laws in California segregated Japanese children from public schools and prohibited their parents from ownership of real property. Discriminatory judgments at the Hague Permanent Court of Arbitration against Japanese nationals grated against their sensitivities even further.[15] Businessmen and professionals from Japan complained of maltreatment and humiliation when they traveled abroad. They conveniently ignored the discrimination they practiced against others, such as the Koreans and Chinese in Japan, and drew attention only to the discrimination practiced against themselves.

The most offensive feature of all these practices of which they were victims, as expressed by the Japanese Foreign Ministry, was that the citizens of Japan suffered from discrimination while those aliens of white origin did not.[16] During World War I, they watched themselves portrayed by allies and enemies alike as threatening, scheming, slant-eyed, racially inferior creatures, constituting the most dangerous element of the "Yellow Peril."[17] They heard commentators openly assert that the world would be safe only if the Japanese would "stay in their place"—"one in which they do not greatly intensify and so embitter the struggle for existence of the white man."[18] Complaints from Japan went unheeded—particularly those to the United States. Indeed, according to Asian specialist Akira Iriye, "The self-conscious antagonism between Japanese and Americans came to a climax during World War I."[19]

One of the reasons for this intensified antagonism could be seen in the continuous and vocal insistence by Japan that action be taken to end these violations of human rights. A great deal of negative publicity was given, for example, to a speech made by Premier Shigenobu Okuma in which he condemned the treatment accorded to those of color by whites. He made his opinion clear that such discrimination was not simply a problem between Japan and the United States. "It is of far deeper meaning and wider scope," he said, "being an expression of the racial prejudice lying at the bottom of the affair." Okuma continued: "It is, in fact, no exaggeration to say that from its satisfactory solution will date the harmonization of different civilizations of the east and the west, thus marking an epoch in the history of human civilizations. If, on the other hand, the solution be proved unattainable, one must then forever despair of the possibility of harmonizing the different thoughts and systems of cultures of different races. In this sense the importance of the problem is universal." The premier concluded his speech by saying that "inferiority must end" and declaring that Japan "plans to gain equality."[20]

The opportunity to gain such equality appeared after World War I when Japan emerged on the side of the victors. Long resentful that their country's stunning action in the Russo-Japanese War had never received the recognition in international politics that it deserved, Japanese leaders now determined that their recent military victories would never be ignored or pushed aside. Startling successes against German possessions in the Far East, occupation of Russian maritime provinces, burgeoning industrial strength, and loyalty to treaty obligations with the Entente would guarantee them a place among the Great Powers at the peace conference. Now they could speak in international relations with a voice heretofore only imagined in dreams. Here they also could press for their demands: transfer to Japan of German rights in Shantung; possession of the islands in the South Seas occupied by Japanese naval forces during the war; and, of particular importance, recognition of the principle of racial equality—at least among the influential nations of the world.[21]

Japanese press opinion appeared to be absolutely unanimous in stressing the necessity for their representatives to insist on this matter of human rights. The *Hochi* declared that "discrimination is humiliation and therefore an injustice to the people discriminated against,"[22] and demanded that the Japanese delegates "not fail to have the matter brought up" at the conference—"and solved properly."[23] The *Yorozu* announced that "now is the time to fight against international racial discrimination."[24] "Barring all else," stated the *Nichinichi*, "Japan must carry through her point on this score [of racial discrimination]."[25] "As to the terms of peace," said the particularly outspoken *Asahi*, "Japan should insist on the equal international treatment of all races . . . not only for Japan but for all the countries of Asia."[26] "No other question," it continued, "is so inseparably and materially interwoven with the permanency of the world's peace as that of unfair and unjust treatment of a large majority of the world's population." The Japanese mission, therefore, should be the vindication of "the wrong suffered by other races than the white."[27]

The prospects of achieving this mission and the other objectives at the peace conference seemed excellent to the Japanese. All the leading victorious powers already had recognized Japan's special interests in Shantung—the British, French, and Italians with the London Declaration of 1915 and later in an exchange of notes in 1917; the Americans with the Lansing-Ishii Agreement of 1917; and even the Chinese with the Peking Treaty of 1915 and an exchange of notes as late as September 1918.[28] For the Japanese, the acceptance of this demand appeared as "a foregone conclusion."[29] On the racial equality issue, they were also confident. The Japanese Foreign Ministry had discussed its concern with race well in advance of the conference.[30]

In addition, President Woodrow Wilson's many inspiring speeches had created beautiful images of a future world. One war message, in the words of a careful contemporary observer, "went most forcibly home to the Japanese mind."[31] In this particular speech Wilson announced: "Only a peace between equals can last. Only a peace the very principle of which is equality and a common participation in a common benefit. The right state of mind, the right feeling between nations, is as necessary for a lasting peace as is the just settlement of vexed questions of territory or of racial and national allegiance. The equality of nations upon which peace must be founded, if it is to last, must be an equality of rights."[32] Since the same man who had said this was now about to lead much of the peace conference, there seemed to be little to fear. As one paper stated, "If the discrimination wall is to remain standing, then President Wilson will have spoken of peace, justice, and humanity in vain, and he would have proved after all only a hypocrite."[33]

The confidence of the Japanese was heightened even further by the quality of their delegation: Marquis Kimmochi Saionji had been Japanese premier and now served as a leading statesman with unparalled prestige; Baron Nobuaki Makino, who had once occupied the position of minister for foreign affairs and actively participated as a leading member of the *Gaiko Chosaki*, or Foreign Affairs Advisory Council, also carried great respect. To assist them, the Japanese government appointed Viscount Sutemi Chinda, His Imperial Majesty's ambassador at London. The public enthusiastically welcomed these choices and hailed these men as simply ideal, unequaled in prestige, and highly qualified to achieve Japan's objectives.[34] The *Asahi* looked forward "with great expectations" and declared, "The country cannot have a better set of men to represent it on so momentous an occasion as the great peace conclave, and it would expect that its success at the conference will be proportionately great."[35]

Some observers described them as "one of the most perfectly organized delegations in Paris."[36]

For all these reasons, the Japanese delegates set sail "amid banzais" and "deafening cheers" from the public, which completely expected them to achieve great success.[37] Lest they forget their mission, however, the leading Tokyo newspaper, *Asahi*, issued one last piece of advice to the delegation on their way to the Paris Peace Conference: "Above all our Peace Envoy must not forget to persuade the Conference to agree to the relinquishment of the principle of racial discrimination, which if allowed to exist would continue to be a menace to the future peace of the world. Fairness and equality must be secured for the colored races who form 62 percent of the whole of mankind."[38]

"This Great Question of World Policy"

Upon arrival at Paris, the Japanese delegates immediately, carefully, and methodically began to push for the principle of racial equality. They quickly determined that the best opportunity for success lay in the League of Nations Commission. This was the body charged with the special tasks of creating a new organization to promote international reconciliation and of delineating the fundamental principles on which it would operate. They knew that Wilson personally attached overwhelming importance to the work of this commission and to the drafting of the Covenant for the League. He had specifically expressed concern about the rights of religious, national, and racial minorities in this context.[39] It was with great confidence, therefore, that the Japanese approached the U.S. delegation to solicit support for their plan to include an explicit statement on racial equality in the Covenant of the League.

Makino and Chinda were received on 4 February by Wilson's close friend and advisor, Colonel Edward House. After the usual pleasant preliminaries, the conversation became serious as the Japanese asked for U.S. support for the principle of racial equality. Rather than provide immediate and unconditional assurances of support, however, House hesitated. He stated that he, of course, personally deplored any prejudice of race and described it as "one of the serious causes of international trouble" and a problem that someday "should in some way be met."[40] Nevertheless, at this particular time and place he would advise caution. The Japanese, House suggested, should prepare two resolutions: one that would state what they desired and the other consisting of the minimum they would accept. This the Japanese agreed to do. Yet, when they came back with the first text, it was, according to House, "discarded at once."[41] Wilson modified the second proposal and returned it to Chinda for consideration. From the Japanese viewpoint, Wilson's amended suggestion for the equal treatment of races "was practically meaningless."[42]

This conflict opened the first round of a tremendous controversy over the principle of racial equality at the Paris Peace Conference. The Japanese had expected that for reasons of both pragmatism and principle their proposal on basic human rights could not be rejected. They quickly discovered, however, that when they dealt principally with the Americans, British, and Australians, domestic politics and prejudicial attitudes of those people about race stood in the way of human rights.

The Japanese accurately determined that Woodrow Wilson held in his hands much of their fate on this issue of race. They knew that he faced strong political pressures at home on the matter of immigration, but his many wartime speeches on democratic principles and equality of rights had convinced them that this president could transcend domestic politics. Had they known about his specific opinions concerning racial superiority, they would have been less optimistic. Several years earlier, for example, Wilson had written that on the question of Asian immigration, "I stand for the national policy of exclusion. We cannot make a homogeneous population out of a people who do not blend with the Caucasian race. Oriental coolieism," he concluded, "will give us another race problem to solve and surely we have had our lesson."[43] This statement indicated his attitude not only about those with yellow skin but about blacks as well. Although approached on numerous occasions by blacks for assistance in fighting discrimination and enacting antilynching laws, Wilson did little to help. In fact, it was Wilson, a southerner, who first introduced segregation into departments of the federal government itself. When a group of black representatives came to him in protest, he condescendingly responded, "Segregation is not humiliating but a benefit, and ought to be so regarded by you [colored] gentlemen."[44]

Wilson strongly disliked these encounters with petitioners raising the sensitive and volatile issue of race, but try as he might, he could not avoid them. The large number of blacks in the U.S. forces during World War I created many domestic and foreign problems, which he tried desperately to sidestep. Blacks accused him of maintaining a "lukewarm aloofness" toward racial questions and of "cautious and calculated neglect."[45] The activities of the National Association for the Advancement of Colored People in drawing public attention to racial discrimination and particularly to the practice of lynching embarrassed and troubled him even further, especially when the NAACP leaders publicly asked, "Mr. President, why not make America safe for democracy?"[46] When the war ended and it appeared that Du Bois would bring the issue before an international forum, Wilson attempted to prevent the Pan-African congress from meeting, and as we have seen, the U.S. government refused to issue passports to those who wanted to attend. In addition, Wilson even sent Robert R. Moton, the successor to the distinguished Booker T. Washington at the Tuskegee Institute, as a special emissary to France after the war "to prevent the returning black veterans from demanding equality."[47]

Not only did Wilson possess his own prejudices about race, but he also faced the consequences of racial discrimination in U.S. politics. As Harold Nicolson, a British diplomat sent to the Paris Peace Conference and later a distinguished historian, viewed the situation, Wilson "found himself in a grave difficulty." Any statement about racial equality as proposed by the Japanese in the Covenant of the League, he wrote, "implied the equality of the yellow man with the white man" and this, in turn, "might even imply the terrific theory of the equality of the white man with the black." If this occurred, suggested Nicolson, "no American Senate would ever dream of ratifying any Covenant which enshrined so dangerous a principle."[48] Wilson and his advisors understood this very well.

Delegates from Australia and Britain shared the same attitudes about racial distinction, exclusion, and separation. The tenacious Australian prime minister, William Hughes, long had supported immigration quotas in his country, refused to compromise with Asians in diplomatic negotiations, and unashamedly proclaimed his belief in white superiority.[49] Further expressions of his fear of "the advance guard of the great army of colored men" did little to change this assessment, nor did his strident campaign platform that included the statement: "Our chief plank is, of course, a White Australia. There's no compromise about *that*. The industrious coloured brother has to go—and remain away!"[50] The official attitude of the British did not differ at all in substance. Lord Robert Cecil, who represented the empire on the League of Nations Commission, stated that with reference to *any* Japanese clause on racial equality, "the British would not agree to it at all, probably not in any form."[51] His colleague, Foreign Secretary Arthur Balfour, expressed to House the reason for this attitude in a conversation recorded by another member of the U.S. delegation: "Colonel House handed me a pencil memorandum which he showed to Mr. Balfour, commencing with the proposition taken from the Declaration of Independence, that all men are created equal. Mr. Balfour said this was an eighteenth century proposition which he did not believe was true. He believed it was true in a certain sense that all men of a particular nation were created equal, but not that a man in Central Africa was created equal to a European."[52]

Such attitudes about race held by their "close allies" confounded the Japanese expectation that a proposal on human rights would be accepted. Their partners in the recent war emerged victorious but wanted nothing to do with racial equality. To make matters more complicated, opinion in Japan became even more insistent. A mass meeting in Tokyo sponsored by twenty-seven different organizations was convened to place more pressure upon the peacemakers in Paris. Collectively the organizations created the Association for the Equality of Races and passed a resolution declaring that racial discrimination not only struck against the great principles of liberty and equality but if continued, would be a major cause of future international conflict. "If it is allowed to remain," stated the text, "all the alliances and treaties will only be castles of sand, and the general peace of the world will not be secured."[53] To avoid this possibility, continued the resolution, "the Japanese nation should do its utmost to see that discriminatory treatment based on racial difference, which has hitherto prevailed in international relations, be removed by the Peace Conference."[54] Leaders of the rally then cabled this text to their delegation, sending copies to Georges Clemenceau and Woodrow Wilson as well.

Faced with resistance among presumed friends from abroad and pressure from home, the Japanese decided to appeal to the League of Nations Commission as a whole. On the evening of 13 February, Baron Makino defied House's stereotype that "the Japs never speak,"[55] and rose to make a formal statement. He began by saying that prejudices had been a teeming source of troubles and wars throughout history and that they might become even more acute in the future. The problem, he recognized, possessed "a very delicate and complicated nature, involving the play of deep human passions," but he argued that human rights could not be denied simply because of one's race. Shared struggles during the war, noted Makino, demonstrated that different races worked with each other, saving lives "irrespective of racial differences, and a common bond of sympathy and gratitude has been established to an extent never before experienced. I think it only just that after this common suffering and deliverance the principle at least of equality among men should be admitted and be made the basis of future intercourse." People throughout the world were demanding that they be treated on an equal footing, particularly now that under the proposed League of Nations they might be required to lay down their lives to protect those of another race or nationality. For these several reasons, said Makino, political and moral integrity required that all delegates use the golden opportunity offered by the new League to go on record supporting the following amendment: "The equality of nations being a basic principle of the League of Nations, the High Contracting Parties agree to accord, as soon as possible, to all alien nationals of States members of the League equal and just treatment in every respect, making no distinction, either in law or in fact, on account of their race or nationality."[56] This statement presented the Japanese position on racial equality. In the words of one observer, "it struck fire at once."[57]

The response of the British delegation to this speech was quick. Lord Robert Cecil stated that there already had been "long and difficult discussions" about this matter. He expressed sympathy and hope for future toleration, but said that in this case, the issue was "highly controversial" and would create "extremely serious problems" that he wished to avoid. Cecil therefore thought it wiser to postpone discussion altogether. The delegates from Greece and Belgium expressed similar opinions, whereas those of Brazil, Romania, and Czechoslovakia indicated that they might be willing to support a statement on racial equality. Wellington Koo, representing China, considered the response of those voicing their opposition offensive and announced that he was "profoundly interested" in the question and "in full sympathy" with the spirit of the proposed amendment.[58] The importance of this move was not lost as the lines began to be drawn in this controversy. A member of the U.S. delegation wrote, "In this great question of world policy, it is highly significant that the Chinese, though suspicious of the Japanese in every other way, came here to their support."[59] The response of the Australian Hughes to the Japanese proposal for racial equality, as described by one official, was "instant and desperate opposition."[60]

Seeing the intensity and tension rapidly rising and seeking to avoid a headlong clash, Colonel House proposed a delay in discussion.[61] Additional time, suggested the U.S. delegation, could be used productively for further reflection and negotiation. Others accepted this proposal with the clear understanding that additional conversations and deliberations would follow. Nevertheless, after the meeting President Wilson instructed that the Covenant be printed and distributed as it stood, deliberately omitting any mention of the racial equality clause. When he read the text before the plenary meeting of the peace conference on the next day, nothing at all appeared about race.[62] Those hearing the words for the first time thus had no idea that the issue of race even had been discussed. That evening Wilson left Paris for Washington, in part to avoid the reaction bound to follow this move. The Japanese and their supporters were furious at this attempt to trick them by creating a fait accompli and avoiding open, serious debate. Controlling his anger but refusing to be silenced, Baron Makino announced that Japan regarded this matter of racial equality as being of fundamental importance to the world and therefore would resubmit its proposed amendment at the earliest opportunity.[63]

During the month of Wilson's absence from the Paris Peace Conference, the question of racial equality did not sleep.[64] Indeed, after the plenary session meeting, the issue went public. No longer would the matter of discrimination be confined to private conversations and secret commission meetings. Now all of the delegates became aware of the Japanese proposal, and as a consequence that was even more disruptive, so did their respective citizens at home. At a time when public opinion began to make its influence felt in diplomacy, such a change carried great significance. The matter of discrimination aroused passions on both sides of the controversy and directly affected the outcome of the negotiations. To reach a just and equitable resolution in this emotion-filled context, said Baron Makino to the correspondent of the *New York Herald*, "all people must be prepared to do a little hard thinking, and to have enough courage to part with many prejudices we have inherited from our ancestors, among which are racial prejudices."[65]

The Japanese pushed hard on this matter. Pressure mounted from legislative and public meetings protesting "the badge of shame" imposed by the white race against the colored races of the world.[66] Private citizens worked in organizations to eliminate racial discrimination, and individuals wrote articles in several languages stressing the importance of human rights in international relations.[67] The Japanese press went even further: A significant article in *Asahi*, for example, compared the mission of Japan with that of Britain at the 1815 Congress of Vienna and noted that then the British were the only ones courageous enough to face strong opposition and fight for humanity and justice by opposing the practice of slavery. The paper continued:

> Now the question of racial discrimination occupied today precisely the position which that of slavery did then. . . . Japan being the leading colored Power, it falls on her to go forward to fight for the cause of two-thirds of the population of the world. Japan could not fight for a nobler cause. . . . Japan must endeavor to make the Peace Conference leave behind a glorious record of putting an end to an inhuman and anti-civilization practice as did the Vienna Conference a hundred years ago.[68]

"The contention against racial discrimination," wrote *Nichinichi* bluntly, "must be insisted upon to the last."[69]

The Controversy Intensifies

The Japanese delegates understood perfectly well, however, that any successful resolution on human rights would come not from words in the press but rather from careful and exacting negotiations with the other representatives in Paris. There the key still rested with the Americans, British, and Australians. Time after time Makino and Chinda arranged private meetings with individuals and with groups and "drafted amendment after amendment in the hope of finding one that would satisfy the other Allies."[70] Nevertheless, they met with continued opposition. Britain, for its part, submitted to the other delegations legal arguments explaining why different states and races could not be considered equal.[71] At home, English publications continued to reinforce existing stereotypes of external differences with statements such as "the Japanese are five feet high, brown in color, they have swivel-shaped eyes, and they eat raw fish."[72]

These indignities and insults appeared mild, however, when compared to the statements of Hughes. With his policy of "Slap the Jap,"[73] he publicly insisted that he would "not deviate an inch" from his position.[74] "Hughes insists that nothing shall go in, no matter how mild and inoffensive," recorded House in his diary; House noted that Hughes even threatened to appeal deliberately to racial prejudices and "raise a storm of protest not only in the Dominions but in the western part of the United States."[75] In secret conversations with the British delegation, Hughes warned that Australia would oppose the entire League of Nations if a clause on racial equality were included in the Covenant.[76] Surprisingly enough, he unabashedly said the same thing in public as he raised the issue that had complicated—and would continue to complicate—all international efforts to eliminate racial discrimination: domestic jurisdiction. "No matter how innocuous it may seem in form," Hughes declared in explaining his opposition, "it is certainly aimed at giving the League control of questions relating to immigration and nationalization, a matter which cannot be surrendered by any State with such impairment of its sovereignty as to make it in effect a subject State. Australia would not sign the Covenant," he asserted, "if it contained any such amendment" about racial equality. "It would be unacceptable, no matter how drafted," Hughes concluded, "for it strikes at the root of a policy vital to the existence and ideals of Australia."[77]

Frustrated in their negotiations with the Australians and British, the Japanese turned increasingly to the U.S. delegation where they continued to believe they might find sympathy. Indeed, according to House's former secretary Stephen Bonsal, the representatives of Japan called "almost every day."[78] Each time the colonel was kind but firmly refused to make any concessions at all.[79] Anticipating that such discussions might prove to be fruitless, the Japanese determined to appeal directly to Wilson himself. On 4 March, the day the president left Washington to return to the peace conference, Viscount Kikujiro Ishii, the ambassador of Japan to the United States, handed him a memorandum concerning racial equality.[80] Ishii politely thanked Wilson for his "sympathy and support" in the past but nevertheless cautioned that should this provision "fail of general recognition the Japanese Government do not see how a perpetual friction and discontent among nations and races could possibly be eliminated." Ishii informed the president that Japan would not deviate from this objective. He concluded that any support or positive suggestions on this matter would be received "with great pleasure."[81]

Not satisfied with this personal appeal to President Wilson for assistance on the racial equality principle, Ishii made a public address before the Japan Society in New York on 14 March. Hoping to generate public support and perhaps put pressure on Wilson, the Japanese ambassador stressed that a great war for international justice had just been fought with races fighting "side by side," and he asked, "Why should this question of race prejudice, of race discrimination, of race humiliation be left unremedied?" Ishii stated that the injustice of denying human rights should be considered independently of the politically sensitive issue of labor and immigration. The one, he said, resulted principally from economic factors, whereas the other entailed a deep matter "of sentiment, of legitimate pride, and of self-respect." The Japanese government, announced Ishii explicitly, would not use this principle of racial equality as a wedge to insert more immigrants into the United States.[82] On the following day, the *New York Times* noted that "not only the remarks of the Ambassador but also the earnestness with which he uttered his plea developed immediate interest among statesmen and diplomats." It seemed clear, announced the paper, that Japan intended to make "a definite stand on the race discrimination issue."[83]

Ishii's well-publicized speech provoked quick reaction. Western senators in the Capitol expressed fear over Japanese intentions.[84] A movement started in the California legislature to pressure Wilson through statements like those of Senator J. D. Phelan, who declared that "equal rights cannot be accorded to Oriental peoples without imperilling our own national existence and destroying western civilization."[85] Fearing that a racial equality clause might be written into the Covenant, the San Francisco Board of Supervisors even sent a resolution to Washington and Paris strongly opposing such actions.[86] On the other side, Japanese residents from Hawaii sent telegrams to the U.S. delegation urging support for this principle of human rights.[87] Americans were "very sensitive of race problems," editorialized the *Asahi*, but must be reminded of their own Declaration of Independence, which contained "unmistakable guarantees of justice and equality like to all mankind."[88] In addition, private petitioners in Japan banded together and explicitly warned the council at Paris that unless it abolished every racial hindrance and disqualification, "all conferences of peace, alliances, and leagues of nations can build only on sand."[89]

Sensing this strong reaction and meeting continued resistance in the negotiations, Makino and Chinda decided to reassess their position. The Japanese Foreign Ministry archives reveal that they had no success in dealing with Cecil, no straight answer in discussions with House, and no fruitful meeting with Hughes, who deliberately avoided conversation on the pretext of illness or travel.[90] Consequently, they determined that their best chance rested with a revised amendment. In order to facilitate approval they pared down their initial proposal to a less offensive statement merely asking support for "the principle of equality of nations and just treatment of their nationals."[91] It was obvious, in the phrase of one scholar, that the "word 'race' was studiously avoided."[92] A bitter debate opened within the Japanese delegation when several members deplored this omission as "a miserable compromise." "It is absolutely meaningless," said one angry delegate. "Stick to equality [of race] or no. Let us be honest with those who oppose us, even if they fear to be honest with us."[93] The reasonableness of this milder amendment, they thought, would guarantee approval.[94]

Makino and Chinda once again approached Colonel House, this time with their watered-down amendment leaving out the word *race* altogether. After examining the proposal, House announced that he would support it subject to two conditions: first, that the word *equality* be deleted from the text; second, that the proposal be inserted into the preamble of the Covenant and not be an independent operative clause that would imply enforcement.[95] This, of course, would completely gut any meaning for human rights at all. A subsequent meeting with Cecil, General Jan Smuts of South Africa, and the prime ministers of Canada, Australia, and New Zealand in an attempt to reach a compromise yielded no results. Indeed, Hughes declared that he would oppose the Japanese proposal "absolutely," announced that "ninety-five out of one hundred Australians" rejected the very idea of equality, and then walked out of the discussion.[96] Angered and frustrated, Makino announced at a press conference that if Japan lost on this matter it might refuse to join the League of Nations itself. "We are not too proud to fight but we are too proud to accept a place of admitted inferiority in dealing with one or more of the associated nations," he said. "We want nothing but simple justice."[97]

The final decision on the racial equality and "simple justice" issue came swiftly on 11 April. In the words of one of the participants, this "was indeed a day of battle!"[98] On this date the League of Nations Commission met under the chairmanship of Wilson in final session, which lasted until nearly one o'clock in the morning. The president had just finished a vigorous fight for a special reservation clause stating that nothing in the Covenant would affect the validity of the Monroe Doctrine. (The Americans had been so adamant on this point that House threatened "to ride over" any opponents, saying that "they could go to Hell seven thousand feet deep" because the clause "was going to be put through the way it was."[99]) Although strongly opposed by the French, who protested against this special privilege, the U.S. reservation had been passed with the support of the Japanese. Now it was their turn. All of the delegates knew of the new amendment from Japan. Moreover, they already had prepared their fixed positions on what was described as "the burning question"[100] and one "so filled with explosives."[101] Makino restated his insistence that the Japanese were "not too proud to fight."[102] Hughes stated to the Associated Press that he remained unalterably opposed to the proposal "in any form."[103] Cecil received instructions to support the Dominions and to place the British vote squarely against Japan.[104] Among the principal actors, only Wilson refused to reveal his decision in advance.

In the midst of this atmosphere of extreme hostility and predetermined positions, Makino rose to make his speech. This time, as he had done on so many other occasions, he calmly but firmly renewed the Japanese plea for human rights and racial equality—a matter he described as "of great moment and concern for a large part of mankind." The whole purpose of the League, began Makino, was "to regulate the conduct of nations and peoples toward one another, according to a higher moral standard than has reigned in the past, and to administer justice throughout the world." In this regard, the wrongs of racial discrimination have been, and continue to be, the source of "profound resentment on the part of large numbers of the human race," directly affecting their rights and their pride. Many nations had fought in the recent war to create a new international order, he said, and the hopes of their nationals now have risen to new heights with victory. Given the noble objectives of the League, the considerable wrongs of the past, and the great aspirations of the future, stated Makino, the leaders of the world presently gathered in Paris should openly declare their support for at least "the principle of equality of nations and just treatment of their nationals."[105] Upon concluding his speech, Makino sat down before a stunned, silent audience. The presentation "was admirably done," recorded one member of the U.S. delegation, "and it seemed to me that they had the support of the entire room."[106] Others described the speech as "cogent" and "impressive," "dignified," "strong," "admirable" and "most embarrassing" to those who opposed the Japanese position.[107] By all accounts, Makino presented a most persuasive and moving performance.

After the initial shock had passed, Cecil spoke for the British Empire and addressed the assembled delegates, delivering what one observer described as a "pathetic speech" and "a deliberate evasion of the issue."[108] Cecil announced that he personally agreed with the Japanese proposal and position on human rights but regretted that he was "not in a position to vote for this amendment." The words, he claimed, were not precise and he feared that if approved they would "open the doors to an immense controversy and to an intrusion into the domestic legislation of states."[109] The rest of Cecil's speech betrayed his own perplexity and embarrassment. When finished, in the words of one listener, Cecil "sat silent with eyes fixed on the table, and took no part in the subsequent debate."[110]

Chinda replied immediately to the objections raised by Cecil "in the strongest public language yet used by Japan on the issue."[111] Japan, he stated, had not explicitly raised the issue of race and immigration. The now-modified amendment asked for nothing more than a formal recognition of the principle of equality of nations and the just treatment of their nationals. Support of this simply would "signify that all the members of the League should be treated with equality and justice." Rejection, however, clearly would indicate "that the equality of members of the League is not recognized." This principle, he concluded, was of great importance and the national aspirations of the people of Japan were depending upon its adoption.[112] Prime Minister Vittorio Orlando of Italy also spoke in favor of the statement on human rights. Equality was a question that perhaps ought not to have been raised, he said, but once raised, there was no other solution except that of adopting the amendment. Senator Léon Bourgeois of France urged adoption and argued that it would be impossible to reject this proposal that embodied "an indisputable principle of justice."[113] Further statements of strong support came from China as well as from the representatives of Greece and Czechoslovakia, who had been persuaded to change their minds. It appeared that a majority would vote for the Japanese proposal and that it would pass.

Then Wilson, as chairman of the session, decided to act. He had just been handed a note from House that warned bluntly, "The trouble is that if this Commission should pass it, it would surely raise the race issue throughout the world."[114] In the words of Birdsall, "Wilson took the hint."[115] The president launched into a lengthy statement that began, "Gentlemen, it seems to me that it is wisest that we should be perfectly candid with one another in a matter of deep importance like this." He stated his hope that "national differences and racial prejudices" would be "forced as much as possible into the background" at this juncture in history, for "the burning flames of prejudice" surely would "flare out in the public view." This, said Wilson, he wanted to avoid at all costs. The principle of the equality of nations was already an implicit, fundamental feature of the League, he declared, and it was not necessary to state it explicitly in the preamble of the Covenant and thus cause controversy. "I offer these suggestions with the utmost friendship, as I need not assure my Japanese colleagues," Wilson concluded, "and with a view to the eventual discussion of these articles."[116] He hoped these words would suffice to defuse the situation.

The delegates from Japan, however, were swayed neither by these assurances of friendship nor by promises of "eventual discussion." Makino said that he did not wish to continue an unprofitable discussion, but on this matter of principle he was representing the unqualified opinion of his country. Therefore, he could not avoid the necessity of asking the commission to make a definite decision, and toward this end, he had the honor of asking his fellow members to vote upon the amendment as stated. Wilson desperately wanted to avoid taking an official vote, but this explicit request forced his hand. He therefore reluctantly and nervously called for a vote. The final tabulation confirmed his worst fears, for the result indicated eleven out of seventeen in favor of the Japanese proposal—a clear majority.[117]

Confronted with this result, Wilson suddenly declared from the chair that the amendment had failed. It could not be adopted, he announced, for it had been unable to secure the unanimous approval of the entire commission. This announcement shocked the majority of the delegates, for they knew perfectly well that on two other occasions (both of which greatly concerned Wilson), the unanimity "rule" had not applied at all.[118] F. Larnaude, the French legal expert, quickly brought this to the attention of the commission and stated that a majority had voted for the amendment.[119] When questioned, Wilson admitted this fact but said that in this particular case there simply were "too serious objections on the part of some of us" to have it inserted in the Covenant. "I am obliged to say," he concluded, "that it is not adopted."[120] Wilson wanted to move on quickly, but Makino briefly stopped him. In great disappointment, he stated that the Japanese delegation wanted the transcripts of this meeting to clearly indicate that a majority vote had been secured—"for the record."[121]

Rejection and Reaction

The decision on the Japanese amendment in Paris quickly made headlines. In the United States the *Sacramento Union* announced in bold letters on the front page, "PEACE DELEGATES BEAT JAPAN'S PROPOSAL FOR RACIAL EQUALITY,"[122] and the *San Francisco Chronicle* declared, "JAPAN DENIED RACE EQUALITY."[123] Those who supported the proposal, however, were shocked. They described the decision as "outrageous,"[124] "a snub and humiliation,"[125] and "deplorable."[126] Among the Japanese press, the *Nichinichi* stated its belief that with this failure of the human rights provision, the League now would be made a "medium for provoking racial hatred and jealousy that will lead to friction and hostilities" throughout the world.[127] The *Kokumin* observed that the delegates "have dared to invite the ill feeling of 1,000,000,000 colored people, and have made their countries the living exponents of a way to destroy the League of Nations."[128] Even the moderate *Japan Times*, which catered mostly to white Europeans and Americans, editorialized in the following words: "A historic and august congress of the representative white peoples has now formally refused to admit and accept the principle of equality of the non-white people with themselves. It is sincerely to be lamented that this action of the League of Nations Commission will most probably result in erecting a perpetual barrier against a harmonious comingling of the races toward which the world tendency has been thought to have been moving."[129]

After Wilson's ruling, but before the Covenant was printed in its final form, in the words of one observer, "the Japanese did all that was humanly possible to secure correction of this injustice."[130] In this effort they failed. Nevertheless, Makino refused to be silenced and rose again to speak at the final plenary session of the League of Nations Commission. There he reaffirmed his deep conviction that the race question still remained "a standing grievance which might become active at any moment." He explicitly stated that Japan wanted nothing more than to set forth a guiding principle for future international relations, not to encroach on the internal affairs of any nation. Makino then reviewed the whole history of the proposed Japanese amendment: how it had been introduced, how it had met with resistance, how it had been modified in order "to conciliate the viewpoints of different nations," and how even the mild amendment had been rejected "although it obtained, may I be permitted to say, a clear majority in its favor." He announced that as a result of this, Japan now wanted to return to the original proposal and to declare itself in favor of the principle toward all alien nationals of "equal and just treatment in every respect, making no distinction, either in law or in fact, on account of their race or nationality." Makino declared that since the opposition was so strong he would not press for the adoption of his proposal at this moment. Nevertheless, he concluded, "I feel it my duty to declare clearly on this occasion that the Japanese Government and people feel poignant regret at the failure of the Commission to approve of their just demand for laying down a principle aiming at the adjustment of this longstanding grievance, the demand that is based upon a deep-rooted national conviction. The Japanese Government and people will continue in their insistence for the adoption of this principle by the League in the future."[131]

As one correspondent described it, "The League of Nations was being born without a racial or national equality hair on its head."[132]

The weeks and months following the historic decision on the principle of equality at the Paris Peace Conference were filled with emotional recriminations, hostile warnings, and a few solemn reflections. Some in Japan blamed "the indolence, timidity, and incompetence" of their once-praised delegates[133] and argued that had they been firm, "they would have never brought on themselves the failures which now darken their record."[134] Others accused the prejudices and "paralyzed conscience" of the "so-called civilized world" of the Anglo-Saxons.[135] Still others placed the blame squarely on the shoulders of specific individuals—Cecil,[136] Hughes,[137] and particularly Wilson, who used one voting arrangement for his own positions and another for those of everyone else.[138] Warned one paper, "The majority of mankind will yet have occasion to make President Wilson regret his mistake in the unfair decision he made in adopting the minority opinion in rejecting the [equality] principle."[139] Anger was expressed as well in other editorials that threatened an "awakening of the colored peoples of the world against the white."[140] The failure to support the principle of equality at Paris, stated the *Yorozu*, was like "wrapping explosives in a wet rag."[141]

Several critics of the Japanese tried to ignore these expressions of indignation and anger by claiming that Japan had not been serious about the racial equality issue at Paris. That is, that the human rights issue simply had been a bluff at best or a camouflaged bargaining counter at worst. The argument was made that Japan neither expected nor intended to win on the matter of equality and that it therefore had tried to use a problem that it knew to be embarrassing to the Anglo-Saxons in order to extract concessions on the Shantung Peninsula.[142]

The Japanese responded to these charges immediately. A spokesman for the delegation firmly asserted that there was "absolutely no truth in this allegation." He accurately stated that the introduction of the racial equality clause had been decided upon well before the delegates left for Paris, when no one in Japan entertained any serious anxiety or foresaw difficulty on the Shantung question. In addition, the fate of the equality clause had been decided during the 11 April meeting, long before the Council of Four even considered the issue of Shantung. And finally, despite the failure of the commission to support the principle of equality, the Japanese had declared their support of the League publicly two days before the final decision on the Shantung Peninsula. For these reasons, the spokesman concluded, "In the minds of the Japanese delegates, the justice of their contention on these two questions was so patent that never for a moment did it enter their mind that such tactics as insinuated were necessary."[143] Confidential Western sources confirmed this opinion as well,[144] and in the words of one observer, the force of the Japanese argument "pulverized" the critics.[145]

The factor that seemed to hurt the Japanese most, however, was not the criticism of supposed motives or tactics but rather the failure on the part of those from the West even to appreciate the importance of their efforts to secure agreement on the principle of racial equality.[146] As one contemporary described it, they "had neither time nor thought" for this matter.[147] The peacemakers not only refused to adopt the principle of racial equality but—perhaps even more telling—also refused to recognize that this issue might be of intense concern to millions of people throughout the world. There were, without question, many immediate and monumental problems competing for attention at Paris and demanding solutions. Nevertheless, at the peace conference, Japan was regarded by friends and critics alike as "the standard-bearer of the colored cause"[148] and as the leader of a great historic mission to advance human rights.[149] Spokesmen described the racial equality issue as being "of absolute importance"[150] and as "one of the most, if not the most, important international problems confronting us today."[151] This matter, however, was seldom reported in the Western press,[152] not followed carefully in official transactions,[153] and largely dismissed by those responsible for negotiations.[154]

This prevailing attitude toward racial equality among the powerful at the Paris Peace Conference also pervaded the important issue of imperialism. During the war a number of treaties secretly signed between the allies sought to redistribute the imperial possessions of their adversaries. The entry of the United States into the war as a belligerent greatly complicated these private real estate arrangements, however, as Wilson declared his support for the national self-determination of peoples. His Fourteen Points promised a "free, open-minded, and absolutely impartial adjustment of all colonial claims" with "strict observance of the principle that in determining all such questions . . . the interests of the populations concerned must have equal weight" with claims listed by those seeking title.[155] This promise, as could be expected, generated enormous hopes among the hundreds of thousands of colored troops who fought in the war. Yet, such inspiring words and dreams of principle quickly vanished in the politics and diplomacy of the victorious. Despite the promises, no country was prepared to surrender its overseas possessions voluntarily, much less grant natives a voice in their fate. In fact, the defeat of Germany and Turkey dangled the prospect of gaining control of even more. "If, when all of this is over," wrote one British advisor, our empire "emerges greater in area and resources . . . who has the right to complain?"[156]

Britain, France, Belgium, Australia, New Zealand, South Africa, and Italy all stood in a queue demanding the right to occupy former German or Turkish territory and subject additional native populations to their rule. Because their proposal for racial equality had been rejected, the Japanese threw principle to the winds and destroyed much of their subsequent credibility by succumbing to the desire for territorial acquisition and participating in this massive land grab as well.[157] Attempting to present pious justifications, the gathered powers collectively argued that the German "Huns" had betrayed their sacred trust to civilization and the "White Man's Burden" and ruthlessly exploited their colonies "without thought of the interest or even the ordinary human rights of their inhabitants."[158] Briefing papers for the negotiators accused Germany of being hopelessly "indoctrinated with the creed of racial superiority" and shamefully regarding the native "as an inferior being, whose purpose was to serve the ends of the white man."[159] By contrast, the negotiators portrayed themselves and their colonial policies as models of enlightened administration with little discrimination on the basis of race, thus entitling them to rule.

These arguments, meant for public consumption, were supplemented by more candid explanations in private, as the peacemakers referred to those about to be swallowed as "primitive peoples," "savage tribes," racially inferior "niggers," and too "backward" for self-government.[160] When Wilson questioned Hughes about his blunt and uncompromising demand for all of New Guinea, the Australian prime minister replied with his usual declarations of white superiority and then said, "Do you know, Mr. President, that these natives eat one another?"[161]

Using arguments and power that had worked so well in the past, the diplomats and politicians at Paris set about to redistribute the land and people of others. In Africa the British took Tanganyika Territory (now Tanzania) and, with the French, adjoining parts of Cameroon and Togo. The Belgians extended their control into Ruanda-Urundi (now Rwanda and Burundi), while South Africa moved into South-West Africa (now Namibia), where it has remained. In the Middle East Britain grabbed Palestine, Transjordan, the Persian Gulf states, and Iraq. France obtained Syria, including present-day Lebanon, and a sphere of influence over the Turkish region of Cilicia, while the Italians got the same in western Turkey. In the South Pacific the spoils were divided between Australia and New Zealand, while Japan took Shantung and former German islands north of the equator. In the event that all this taking and trading appear too crass, the powers agreed not to call their new acquisitions colonial possessions, but rather *mandates*. They solemnly promised to govern these territories as a "sacred trust of Civilization" until such time as these "backward" peoples not yet ready for self-government were "able to stand on their own feet in the strenuous conditions of the modern world."[162]

To some observers, these solemn promises and declarations of noble intent indicated a shifting climate of opinion away from the blatant imperial conquest of the past. They appeared to indicate an emerging sense of guilt, an uneasiness with theft, and a need to speak of obligations.[163] The attitude of George Louis Beer, the U.S. Colonial Delegate to the Peace Conference, for example, clearly revealed a genuine concern for native interests and a sense of responsibility to treat the natives with dignity and respect.[164] Others remained skeptical and completely unconvinced, sharply criticizing the creation of a mandate system as old-fashioned imperialism packaged in a new guise of platitudes. Critics saw little, if any, difference between how the imperial powers ruled colored peoples in their "mandated" territories and colored peoples in their existing colonies. They described such a ploy as "the crudity of conquest draped in the veil of morality," "moral wrapping paper," and mere fig leaves designed to conceal the nakedness of their aggression.[165]

This blatant disregard for the promises of self-determination during the war, and the intensified racial consciousness and nationalism generated by that conflict, produced serious reactions immediately. The May Fourth Movement of 1919 in China, for example, which exploded initially in response to these peace terms, was actively led by those who wanted to drastically transform Chinese society, including a young library assistant named Mao Tse-tung. "It was the most important evidence yet to be seen," wrote one historian, "of the mounting rejection of Europe by Asia."[166] The same year witnessed the birth in Tunisia of the Destour party, which called for freedom from France, and the growth (to two and one-half million people) of the Indonesian nationalist party, which demanded complete independence from the Dutch.[167] The British Empire similarly found itself challenged as never before. In March of 1919, Egyptian nationalists, inflamed by London's refusal to allow them to place their case before the peace conference and by the arrest of their leaders, began demonstrating, rioting, and assassinating British army officers. In April a rash of rebellions broke out in the Punjab that were serious enough to convince one British general to open fire on a crowd of unarmed Indians in a public square in Amritsar, firing into their backs until the ammunition ran out, killing nearly four hundred and wounding more than one thousand. The same month saw a bloody clash in Palestine. In May, Britain was at war with Afghanistan and about to be, it seemed, with Turkey. To many, it appeared as though the British and the other imperial powers had "overgorged" themselves on imperial possessions[168] and that imperialism in the twentieth century would not be so easy as it had been in the past.

Violent reactions also occurred in the United States. Frustrated by the refusal of the peace conference to support the principle of racial equality or self-determination and angered by their own government's deliberate inaction in the face of blatantly illegal and discriminatory policies, many U.S. blacks resolved to demand their full rights of citizenship. This determination was especially strong among returning black soldiers, whose participation in the war as a crusade for democracy had raised the not unnatural dream of a little more democracy at home. "We stand again to look America squarely in the face and call a spade a spade," wrote Du Bois in May 1919. "We *return*. We *return from fighting*. We *return fighting*. Make way for Democracy! We saved it in France, and by the Great Jehovah, we will save it in the U.S.A. or know the reason why."[169] Others, like members of the revived Ku Klux Klan, fully determined that they would never allow these demands for equality to be met and openly proclaimed their program of "uniting native-born white Christians for concerted action in the preservation of American institutions and the supremacy of the white race."[170]

These clashing attitudes exploded into open violence during the long, hot summer of 1919. From June to October, the United States witnessed major race riots in Chicago, Knoxville, Omaha, and the nation's own capital, Washington, D.C., among other cities. Lynchings, burnings, floggings, shocking terror, and destruction accompanied what some called nothing short of a "race war."[171] Authorities called out police, troops from the army, and members of the National Guard to restore order. When it was over, more than one hundred people had been killed, thousands injured, and millions of dollars of property damage incurred.[172] This "Red Summer" that followed the politics and diplomacy of discrimination at the Paris Peace Conference, wrote John Hope Franklin, "ushered in the greatest period of interracial strife the nation had ever witnessed." The violence, he observed, was not confined to any particular section of the country, but occurred in the North, South, East, and West—"wherever whites and blacks undertook the task of living together."[173]

International press coverage focused upon these race riots in the United States and carried the news around the world. To many in Japan, stung by Wilson's deception on racial equality, this presented a temptation too great to resist. "It is ironical," remarked the *Mainichi*, "and at the same time regretable that while Americans are indulging in vituperations of Japan as a 'Yellow Peril,' a 'Black Peril' should have arisen within the borders of the United States themselves. These troubles may be taken as evidence of the tensions existing between black and white races. It is not surprising that the former should be despised, hated, and excluded by the English-speaking peoples, who are by nature arrogant, domineering, and disposed to think of themselves as a superior race."[174] The *Asahi* used similar language when proclaiming, "What an irony it is that such disturbances should have occurred in the United States, the protagonist of the League of Nations! Is it not most urgently necessary to rectify the arrogant attitude of the whites not only towards the blacks but also the other colored races?"[175] "The racial strife in America," concluded the *Hochi*, "is a disgrace to the civilized world, and if the United States wishes to preach the principle of justice and humanity to others they must first solve the race problem within their own borders."[176]

*   *   *

These violent race riots, rejections of racial equality, and dashed hopes for self-determination all emerged anew from the Paris Peace Conference. The contrast between the initial, extraordinary expectations and the final, insulting results could not have been more acute, and this made it worse. Perhaps the hopes of millions of people around the world for an end to racial discrimination far exceeded what was possible for politics and diplomacy in 1919. An effort had been made to seize an absolutely unique opportunity and promote human rights in international relations, but power and prejudice proved to be stronger.

All this prompted Okuma, the "Grand Old Man" of Japan, to reflect that the racial issue would continue to be an extremely serious problem. "The root of it lies in the perverted feeling of racial superiority entertained by the whites," he wrote. "If things are allowed to proceed in the present way, there is every likelihood that the peace of the world will be endangered. It, therefore, behooves all well-wishers of mankind to exert their utmost to remove their gross injustice immediately."[177] Ambassador Ishii expanded on these thoughts and concluded:

The problems of population and race will in the future form the hardest and most important issues between nations. These problems have failed of solution by the old methods of agression and diplomatic intrigue and the world is expecting a new style of diplomacy to solve them. . . . The advanced nations must be generous enough to appreciate the awakening of the backward races and take measures to satisfy their longings, while on their part the backward races must guard against hastiness and rash conduct and understand their duty to exercise moderation and march toward their objectives in an orderly manner. . . . It must be remembered that these problems do not concern Japan and the United States alone, but are common to most countries of the world. The satisfactory solution of these baffling problems is the responsibility of twentieth century diplomacy.[178]

The accuracy of his prophecy soon would be seen, as the world moved from one war into another via the Third Reich.

4

From One War to Another

THE "RACIAL EQUALITY" QUESTION IS A HIGHLY combustible
one. . . . The white and the colored races cannot and will not
amalgamate. One or the other must be the ruling caste. . . . There
is, therefore, at present in practical politics no solution to the racial
question.

—British Foreign Office

The "Highly Combustible" Question

By raising the racial equality question at the Paris Peace Conference, the Japanese and their supporters served notice to the international community that they intended to make the discussion of race part of the politics and diplomacy of the twentieth century. They indicated their firm determination to focus global attention upon the heavy burden of discrimination in the past and to bring about change for the future. Their attempt to secure a provision for "equal and just treatment in every respect, making no distinction, either in law or in fact, on account of race or nationality"[1] attracted the attention of millions but failed in the end at the hands of President Woodrow Wilson and others representing the white, Western nations of the world. Such a rejection of the principle of racial equality, when coupled with the new mandate system for increased imperial control, led to dashed hopes, extreme bitterness, fierce hostility, and accentuated prejudices for the decade of the 1920s. Rather than creating a dialogue for constructive discussion, this forcing of the issue of race into the open made all parties more conscious than ever before of their racial differences.

The heightened international awareness of race prompted several nations and individuals to assess the nature of this highly combustible question that was not likely to go away. One of the most remarkable and unrestrained of these assessments came from the British Foreign Office. Greatly worried about the rising tide of color around the world,

the growing assertiveness of colonial peoples, and the implacable resistance among the peoples of the Dominions and the United States to
accept the principle of equality, staff officials prepared a lengthy study
on the role of race in global politics and diplomacy. The result of their
labors emerged as a highly confidential and candid report, "Racial
Discrimination and Immigration," tracing the history of the problem,
discussing its fate at the Paris Peace Conference, offering analysis, and
providing conclusions, not the least of which read, "Great Britain, the
Dominions, and the United States all are equally interested in avoiding
a discussion of this subject." Yet, since the question of racial equality
now could no longer be avoided, advised the report, then the practical
task was to deal with it in such a way as not "to burn our fingers."[2]

The Foreign Office believed the problem of race to be extremely
serious and considered its emergence at Paris as a most dangerous sign.
Any effort "to brush this subject aside as irrelevant," it warned, would
be a serious mistake, for racial matters would increase rather than
decrease in intensity, especially those concerning immigration. In its
analysis, the Foreign Office report focused on Japan, declaring that for
political reasons the Japanese were feared and for "racial reasons" they
"are not wanted. . . . In the United States of America the racial antagonism
to the Japanese appears to be a corollary to the Negro question. It is
a manifestation of the American's instinctive hatred of 'color' in any
shade." Yet, the problem encircled the globe. "The 'racial equality'
question in its present stage," stated the confidential memorandum,

> primarily concerns the following countries: Japan, China, British India,
> United States of America (especially California and the Pacific States),
> Canada, Australia, New Zealand, South Africa. The first three countries
> demand the right of free immigration and freedom from discrimination
> disabilities for their nationals in the territories of the last five countries.
> *The question can be regarded from an economic or from a political point of
> view, but in its essence it is a racial one.*[3]

White and colored races will not amalgamate, continued the Foreign
Office report, and "countries where the white population is in power
have determined from a sure instinct for self-preservation that they will
never open their doors to the influx of the colored race, which might
eventually become dominant." In this policy of racial exclusion, stated
the assessment, the United States, "taught by the Negro trouble, . . .
have taken the lead," closely followed by the British Dominions of
Canada, Australia, New Zealand, and South Africa. Among those being
discriminated against, it stated, "only one of the aggrieved colored races
has acquired sufficient material strength to demand a hearing, and that is

Japan." "Japan," stated the Foreign Office in a passage that deserves careful attention and quotation, "is the only non-white first-class Power. In every respect, except the racial one, Japan stands on a par with the great governing nations of the world. But, however powerful Japan may eventually become, the white races will never be able to admit her equality. If she can enforce her claim she will become our superior; if she cannot enforce it she remains our inferior; *but equal she can never be.*"[4] For the Foreign Office, there appeared only one conclusion to reach from all this: In practical international politics, the highly combustible racial question had "no solution" and "no cure."

This fixed resolution of the British, their Dominions, and the Americans to reject racial equality was matched by the opposing determination of the Japanese and their supporters to gain it. By leading the crusade for race during the Paris Peace Conference, Japan demonstrated an unprecedented commitment and staked out a strong public position as the standard-bearer of the "colored cause."[5] The humiliating defeat, despite a majority of votes for a nondiscrimination statement in the League of Nations Covenant, seemed to strengthen the Japanese resolve even further. As Makino already had warned after the unsuccessful negotiations, "The Japanese Government and people will continue in their insistence for the adoption of this principle by the League in the future."[6] To confirm this point, the Japanese minister for foreign affairs announced before the spring session of the Diet in 1920 that the proposal for racial equality would "be presented again at every possible opportunity."[7] It was precisely this prospect of constantly having the racial question raised that worried the British Foreign Office so greatly. Officials there recognized the vulnerability of their position throughout the empire and realized that "Japan's championship of 'racial equality' especially in the matter of immigration, is bound to gain much sympathy," particularly among Indians with "considerable interest" in this issue. They feared that the Japanese would use racial equality as a "trump card" and a "weapon" to "stir up trouble" in the world.[8]

Such troubles, in fact, did begin to multiply as others also added their voices and energies to this global controversy. In both Asia and Africa, World War I and the Paris Peace Conference had enormously accelerated racial consciousness and nationalism, frequently joined in explosive combination. The extraordinary politicizing effect of these monumental events encouraged many to organize themselves and strike blows against racial discrimination and its manifestations in immigration restrictions and imperialism. In China the Pan-Asian Society, for example, increasingly focused upon the racial issue. Its publication, entitled *Ta Ya*, explicitly addressed itself to the "1,000 million souls of Asia" who suffered "from the oppression of the white races of Europe and America."[9]

In 1920 representatives from Nigeria, Sierra Leone, Gambia, and the Gold Coast (now Ghana) met in Accra and founded the National Congress of British West Africa to promote self-determination and the elimination of racial discrimination. The following year, intellectuals from the French colonies formed the Union Intercoloniale for the same purposes, whereas others soon created the Ligue Universelle pour la Défense de la Race Noire. Shortly thereafter the West African Students' Union (WASU) was formed in London to work toward the same basic goal.[10] Others organized a conference for the "Colored International," composed of representatives from Japan, China, India, the Philippines, East Indies, the Malay states, Egypt, and Turkey, to support "the abolition of racial discrimination in the immigration policies of certain white nations, and to combat the assumption of social and ethnological superiority by the white races."[11] Then, two Pan-Asiatic conferences added still more voices to the growing protest by non-whites against domination and discrimination.[12]

As could be expected, such conscious efforts to confront racial discrimination provoked fear and deep concern among many whites. Writing from the United States, Lothrop Stoddard saw imminent catastrophe resulting from the aftermath of World War I—"a Nordic civil war" in which "the best of all human breeds" suffered and died while "the little dark man" emerged as "the final winner." The "colored races have been drawn out of their traditional isolation and have been quickened by white ideas," he declared, creating "a wide-spread ferment which has been clearly visible for the past two decades, and which is destined to grow more acute in the near future." This turmoil caused by the "white world's weakening," he continued to warn, "has opened up the possibility of violent 'short cuts' which would have mutually disastrous consequences. Especially has it evoked in bellicose and fanatical minds the vision of a 'Pan-Colored' alliance for the universal overthrow of white hegemony at a single stroke—a dream which would turn into a nightmare of race-war beside which the late struggle in Europe would seem the veriest child's play."[13]

Speaking before the House of Commons in London, Ramsay MacDonald also cautioned about the acute danger for the world that would result if intense racial struggles exploded.[14] The former French minister of colonies, Albert Sarraut, openly renewed a discussion of the "Yellow Peril" and declared that "a race conflict would mean the utter destruction of our civilization."[15] When several non-white nations later sent representatives to an international conference on racial discrimination in Shanghai, one official in Australia wrote that the participants reached "the inescapable conviction that the white man will never voluntarily accept the colored man as an equal and that only by force, if ever, will the hated stigma of racial inferiority ever be removed." The results of this realization, he warned, "present the potentialities of world-wide trouble, and may ultimately bring about the gravest consequences to the Western nations."[16]

For some, this problem of race in diplomacy came much sooner and much closer to home than expected. When questions arose after the war about German compliance with the Treaty of Versailles, France began to send occupation forces into the Rhineland. A relatively large percentage of these were black soldiers from Senegal, Morocco, Algeria, and other colonial possessions. This action immediately provoked a storm of protest. The French government (which had been warned by British Prime Minister David Lloyd George at the Paris Peace Conference not to "train big nigger armies")[17] quickly made efforts to justify the use of their so-called *Troupes de Couleur*, but many Europeans who sympathized with the French desire for security believed that the utilization of blacks against Caucasians breached the acceptable norms of behavior.[18] Germans regarded this treatment as particularly insulting and degrading and vociferously objected in both diplomatic protests and in the press. They called it the "Black Shame" and the "Black Blemish," referring to these black troops as beasts and inferior beings from the "low and lowest tribes" of humanity.[19] They appealed to the international community to remove these black forces, not only for their own country, but also "for civilization and the white race."[20]

Constantly confronting attitudes such as these at home and abroad after the war, the indefatigable Du Bois set about to organize a series of Pan-African conferences. Refusing to be deterred by the failure of his first effort to help secure racial equality at the Paris Peace Conference, he initiated correspondence with a number of black leaders around the world encouraging them to participate in further international meetings. He received generally favorable responses to his invitations, including one from Casely Hayford of the Gold Coast who wrote, "I have always looked forward to the time when representative and other responsible members of our race could meet together upon a common platform for the discussion of common problems affecting us all, and I am sure I am not alone in this wish."[21] Inspired by the vision of working with others to combat the global problem of racial discrimination, more than one hundred agreed to participate in the proposed conference, including Diagne from France, a large group from the United States, and others from Haiti, Dahomey, French Antilles, Sierra Leone, Grenada, Britain, and South Africa.

The Second Pan-African Congress of 1921 met in several sessions, beginning in London and then continuing in Brussels and Paris. Excited about the task before them, the participants eagerly threw themselves into discussion and debate. Their deliberations quickly revealed that there existed among them many tensions and divisions, generated by differing national perspectives, contrasting political ideologies, and conflicting personalities, not the least being the often inflexible and abrasive Du Bois himself. Nevertheless, the common denominator of vehement opposition to attitudes of racial superiority among whites and manifestations of racial discrimination overcame immediate differences and kept them together to pass a major resolution entitled "Declaration to the World." Its text began with a ringing cry: "The absolute equality of races, physical, political and social is the founding stone of the world and human advancement. No one denies great differences of gift, capacity, and attainment among individuals of all races, but the voice of Science, Religion, and practical Politics is one in denying the God-appointed existence of super-races or of races naturally and inevitably and eternally inferior." Looking back toward the past, the resolution asserted:

> That in the vast range of time, one group should in its industrial technique, or social organization, or spiritual vision, lag a few hundred years behind another, or forge fitfully ahead, or come to differ decidedly in thought, deed, and ideal, is proof of the essential richness and variety in human nature, rather than proof of the co-existence of demi-gods and apes in human form. The doctrine of racial equality does not interfere with individual liberty; rather it fulfills it. And of all the various criteria of which masses of men have in the past been pre-judged and classified, that of color of the skin and texture of the hair, is surely the most adventitious and idiotic.

Describing themselves as "those who see these evils of the color line and racial discrimination," the participants declared that "the habit of democracy must be made to encircle the earth. . . . Local self-government with a minimum of help and oversight can be established tomorrow in Asia, in Africa, America, and the isles of the sea."[22]

The hope generated by this resolution and the momentum created by such an international gathering led to the creation of the Pan-African Association and subsequent Third Pan-African Congress in London and Lisbon during 1923 and the Fourth Pan-African Congress in New York during 1927. Du Bois frequently took the initiative for organizing these meetings and providing major inspirational speeches like "The Black World at Present" and "The Future of Pan-Africa." Inspired visions and eloquent words, however, do not always produce immediate results. The differences among the Pan-African participants, in addition to the lack of financial resources and opposition of several governments, continued to plague the movement and deny it the critical acquisition of power. Even Du Bois recognized the sparse achievements in the realm of practical politics and diplomacy. "What has been accomplished?" he asked in a moment of reflection. "This: we have kept an idea alive; we have held to a great ideal, we have established a continuity, and some day when unity and cooperation come, the importance of these early steps will be recognized."[23]

Not all of those concerned with global racial discrimination were content with merely keeping an idea alive or holding to a great ideal. Many found Du Bois and his intellectual friends too abstract, too slow, too ineffective, and sometimes too fair-skinned. They turned instead to a radical and angry movement known as Garveyism. Its name came from its flamboyant leader, Marcus Garvey, a native of Jamaica who had worked on the *African Times and Orient Review* in London, founded the Universal Negro Improvement Association, and then moved to Harlem in New York City where he began public agitation. Although Garvey was attacked by contemporary and subsequent critics as "messianic," "racist," "pseudo-fascist," and "Black Zionist,"[24] his magnetic eloquence and abundance of ideas attracted a mass of followers for his dream of leading all blacks "Back to Africa" and of liberating that continent from white control. "What is the barrier," he asked, "to achieve this goal? The barrier is the white man," he shouted to his audience, "and we say to the white man who now dominates Africa that it is to his interest to clear out of Africa now, because we are coming not as in the time of Father Abraham, 200,000 strong, but we are coming 400,000,000 strong and we mean to retake every square inch of the 12,000,000 square miles of African territory belonging to us by right Divine."[25]

Garvey's persuasive words and emotional appeal inspired thousands of blacks from the Americas to Europe and Africa. Indeed, one authority described his influence as nothing short of "world-wide in scope" and one that "attracted the attention of the colored world to a degree never before achieved by a Negro organization."[26] His International Conventions of the Negro Peoples of the World, beginning in 1920, brought delegates from around the globe. His newspaper, the *Negro World*, was disseminated over several continents until banned by many colonial governments as dangerous sedition. Garvey told his audience what they wanted to hear: The heavy burden of racial discrimination could be changed, and black skin should be seen as a symbol of greatness rather than a badge of shame. "Up, you mighty Race!" he exhorted his followers. "Now we have started to speak and I am only the forerunner of an awakened Africa that shall never go back to sleep."[27] These words directly influenced many of the subsequent African nationalist leaders who credited him as their inspiration, including Jomo Kenyatta of Kenya, Nnamdi Azikiwe of Nigeria, Kenneth Kaunda of Zambia, and Kwame Nkrumah of Ghana. As one writer from South Africa observed, "Marcus Garvey gave to the

Negroes of the twentieth century a sense of self-awareness, a sense of pride and dignity that largely overcame the inferiority complex bred by centuries of racial and color oppression."[28]

This emerging awareness of race as a source of esteem and respect among blacks stimulated other movements as well. Blacks in French-speaking territories also found inspiration from Du Bois and Garvey and began to express their newly found racial pride under the banner of "Negritude." Jean Price-Mars from Haiti started to publish *La Revue du Monde Noir,* whereas his compatriot Aimé Césaire, together with Léopold Senghor from Senegal, founded another journal, *L'Etudiant Noir.* Together they reached out to the black world, stressing their common African roots, unique cultural contributions, and the historic achievements of blacks. They encouraged their followers to recognize objectively these special accomplishments and to feel subjectively the "soul" of their race. The Negritude movement grew steadily, inspiring pride among blacks and a determination no longer to submit passively to being oppressed by the Great Powers, whom they described as "the Great Whites."[29]

What brought inspiration to the oppressed, however, brought fear to others. It was not difficult to see a relationship between color and class.[30] Consequently, a theme and a question came to the fore that would echo again and again in the politics and diplomacy of racial discrimination in the twentieth century: What connection, if any, existed between the struggle for racial equality on the one hand and communism on the other? Garvey, for example, publicly rejected communism as a political ideology that used the idea of helping blacks only as a pretext for its own purposes and that remained under the control of racially prejudiced whites.[31] Nevertheless, in Europe people referred to him as "the black man with red ideas,"[32] while in the United States security agents maintained that Garvey's Universal Negro Improvement Association represented "the Communist party which is affiliated with the Russian Soviet Government."[33] Critics similarly scoffed at Du Bois and his Pan-African movement as no more than a front organization for bolshevism that possessed ties with the Third (Communist) International.[34] The shrewd efforts of the Comintern to exploit this rising racial conciousness as a powerful force of change in world history and to draw attention to the relationship between capitalism and racial discrimination accentuated the connection in people's minds between Pan-Africanism and Garveyism, on the one hand, and communism, on the other, even further.[35] Those who believed in racial discrimination, like Lothrop Stoddard, saw an intimate relationship between these two forces, arguing that "every nationalist aspiration, every political grievance, every social discrimination is fuel for Bolshevism's hellish incitement to racial as well as to class war."[36] Others as well made this connection, claiming that one advocate of global racial equality was no more than "a Communist of the 'reddish' type, an apostle of destruction who looks forward to the time when the new 'terror' shall become universal."[37]

These fears of upheaval and revolution caused by racial agitators renewed efforts to tighten control over native populations in colonial territories and to exclude further the unwanted by immigration restrictions. Spokesmen increasingly called upon "the white world" to band together for self-defense and to protect its racial purity by means of stopping "undesirables" at the border.[38] They fanned the flames of antibolshevism against "Reds," anti-Semitism against Jews, and especially "colorphobia" against those with black, brown, or yellow skins.[39] France, Belgium, Portugal, Italy, and Britain all strengthened the power of white settlers in their colonies, and in 1923 internal autonomy in Southern Rhodesia passed into the hands of a minority government on its way to becoming "The Great White Dominion."[40] South Africa, Australia, New Zealand, Canada, and the United States all tightened their immigration restrictions during the same period.[41] The United States, for example, passed its comprehensive immigration bill in 1924 to guarantee, as described by its chief sponsor in the Senate, "that our incoming immigrants should hereafter be of the same [Nordic] races as those of us who are already here."[42] These several policies of prejudice provoked immediate and intense resentment around the world. Speaking on behalf of non-white peoples everywhere, Shigenobu Okuma forcefully declared, "If you ask me what we want, then I must say frankly that we want equal treatment. . . . We want you to cease racial discrimination."[43]

Rather than ceasing, however, the attitudes of whites against those of other races actually intensified as never before during this period. Added to the explicit ideology of race emerging among the early Nazis in Germany and the Fascists in Italy,[44] were voluminous works of others in Europe and the United States. Numerous French authors devoted much time discussing the growing global tensions of race and developing various theories of racial superiority.[45] Respected British writers similarly extolled the virtues of their own Caucasian race and defended their colonial rule on racial grounds, all the while describing those with darker skin color as belonging to the "backward," "inferior," "uncivilized," and "primitive" races of mankind in the twentieth century.[46]

Americans also added their voices to this discussion. Indeed, one authority described this period of the 1920s as the very "flowering of racism" in the United States.[47] It would be a misinterpretation of the strength of attitudes of racial superiority to imagine that these attitudes were confined to the extremists in the Ku Klux Klan. Many eminent scientists and social scientists deplored the excesses of violence and emotion but at the same time wrote scholarly books describing the inferiority of other races. As one observer wrote, "it was mainly the academic writers on racial differences who made racism respectable."[48] These included, among many others, Lothrop Stoddard's *The Rising Tide of Color Against White World Supremacy* (1920), Clinton Burr's *America's Racial Heritage* (1922), Charles Josey's *Race and National Solidarity* (1923), and Stoddard's subsequent book that popularized the English equivalent of *Untermensch* or subhuman before the Nazis ever used it, *The Revolt Against Civilization: The Menace of the Under Man* (1922). Stoddard warned of the danger that racial intermixture would create a new "Dark Age," wrote of the prospects of "racial war," and called upon "the white world" to unite in confronting the dangers arising from the increased political aspirations of the colored peoples in Asia, Africa, and Latin America.[49]

Such outspoken writings aggravated global racial tensions even further. When combined with more restrictive immigration obstacles, heightened consciousness of race, and a growing determination among many to combat racial discrimination, they greatly inflamed politics and diplomacy around the world. Discussions of racial wars, racial alliances, and the necessity for racial purity in relation to other races emphasized that international relations increasingly were becoming interracial relations as well. As Alfred Zimmern of Oxford wrote then, "The race question, stirring as it does some of the most elemental of human passions, is the most urgent problem of our time."[50] Some responded to the race question by intensifying their prejudice and erecting still additional barriers. Others sought a way out of the viciousness by placing their hopes in the new League of Nations.

The League and Racial Issues

Millions of people heralded the creation of the League of Nations at the end of World War I as a grand new beginning in international relations. If diplomats only had an organization to facilitate open and rational discourse, the League supporters believed, the intrigues and misunderstandings from "secret diplomacy" in the past could be eliminated, the sacrifices made in "the war to end all wars" justified, and the dream of "making the world safe for democracy" realized. Woodrow Wilson, for example, firmly believed that such a body could promote international cooperation and achieve peace and security for the world. In response to his dream and challenge for a bold experiment, and in deference to the power that he represented, the Paris Peace Conference incorporated the Covenant of the League of Nations into the text of the postwar treaties themselves. Full of hope for the future, delegates first assembled in the beautiful setting of Geneva in 1920 and described the event as "unprecedented greatness," a "unique opportunity," one that "will have a permanent influence on the evolution of the nations," and "the divine seed of future harvests, the witness of the world to be."[51] "Let us dedicate ourselves to humanity," declared another. "Working together, let us seek to prepare and step by step to achieve the reign, so long awaited, of international morality and human rights."[52]

Despite these solemn declarations, heartfelt hopes, and pledges to respect "diverse civilizations, races, and tongues,"[53] serious questions about the true intentions of the League surfaced immediately. As we have seen, the politics and diplomacy of discrimination already had determined that the Covenant would contain no provision supporting the principle of racial equality. In addition, rather than supporting the self-determination of native peoples, the League set about to administer a mandate system of control over colonial areas. Moreover, despite the inclusion of a few scattered representatives from such countries as Japan, China, Haiti, Liberia, and Ethiopia that had never before been allowed by the Western powers to participate in this kind of setting, the League remained essentially "an all-white and predominantly European affair."[54]

Nevertheless, among the various instrumentalities of diplomacy during the interwar years, the League of Nations, its allied organs, the International Court of Justice and International Labor Organization, and its special bodies, such as the Temporary Slavery Commission and subsequent Committee of Experts on Slavery, were the only ones to provide even a semblance of concern about equality under the law. The League's noble statements of principle, the protection of minorities, and the dream of eventual independence for mandated territories held out the only hope available for those seeking to eliminate racial discrimination on a global scale. Consequently, those prepared to fight this struggle turned to the League for assistance.

One of the initial hopeful signs in this regard came from a series of unique obligations known as the Minority Treaties. The victorious powers of World War I decided that the states constituted or enlarged as a result of the peace settlement should be bound to protect minority groups living within their new borders. Through treaty stipulations the powers therefore imposed upon Poland, Czechoslovakia, Yugoslavia, Romania, Greece, Austria, Bulgaria, Hungary, and Turkey special obligations. These states undertook to "assure full and complete protection of life and liberty" to all their inhabitants "without distinction of birth, nationality, language, race, or religion." Albania, Estonia, Latvia, Lithuania, and Iraq all assumed similar responsibilities as a condition of their admission into the League of Nations. To ensure fulfillment, the provisions affecting "persons belonging to racial, religious, or linguistic minorities" for the first time were made "obligations of international concern" and placed under the guarantee and supervision of the League.[55]

Minorities enthusiastically endorsed these provisions, viewing them as a new and courageous international effort to protect human rights. It is estimated that during its existence, the League received nearly nine hundred petitions from minority groups protected by the treaties.[56] Nevertheless, it quickly became apparent that this arrangement suffered from a number of serious problems. Some of the difficulties, as one diplomat candidly admitted, stemmed from the fact that the obligations to protect minorities resulted not from negotiations among equals, but only by unanimous Great Power pressure exerted on the smaller states concerned. Powerful states were not willing to apply the same standards to themselves or their colonies or allow the League to impose such obligations upon all of its members. Thus prevented from any universal or effective enforcement, the League became accused of being dilatory, ineffective, secretive, selective in its application of standards, geographically confined only to parts of Europe rather than other areas of acute racial tensions, and politically motivated.[57]

Moreover, the League found itself directly confronting the issue that would constantly plague all future international efforts to deal with the sensitive subject of racial discrimination: national sovereignty and domestic jurisdiction. Solemn declarations of principle were one thing, but intervention by others into domestic matters something quite different. In its experience with minority protection, the League of Nations discovered, as would the United Nations later, that governments regard such attempts to influence treatment of their own citizens as "unwarrantable interference with their internal affairs."[58] Indeed, it was precisely this issue of the relationship between national sovereignty and racial prejudice that provided one of the major reasons why the United States refused to join the League of Nations in the first place. As Senator James Reed of Missouri asserted: "Think of submitting questions involving the very life of the United States to a tribunal on which a nigger from Liberia, a nigger from Honduras, a nigger from India . . . each have votes equal to that of the great United States."[59]

The implications of this doctrine of the supremacy of sovereignty could be seen in the way that the League handled—or did not handle—individual petitions. Hopeful that the principles embodied in the Minority Treaties might be applied to them, for instance, a number of black organizations petitioned for an extension of protection and prohibition of discrimination. Indeed, before the League even fully began its operations, a group from the National Colored World Democracy Congress renewed an appeal for a racial equality clause in the Covenant. Its petition to the Council argued that it was "monstrously unfair" to accord guarantees to minorities in Czechoslovakia and Poland while at the same time refusing to extend identical protection to blacks in the United States. "The peace of the world has not been made secure," they declared, "unless and until the union of the civilized governments declare for . . . rights and protection of life without distinction of race and color. Colored America, as yet confident in the ultimate ascendency of the Right over Might, calmly waits upon the League of Nations."[60]

This petition surprised and embarrassed the League, which initially had little idea of the implications that the Minority Treaties for Europe would have upon the dream of nondiscrimination elsewhere or the political and diplomatic difficulties that they would cause. But it was only one of the first among many petitions: Others similarly and quickly appealed for the "equality of race treatment by all nations in the League."[61] Du Bois and the Pan-African congresses called upon the League to "turn its attention to the great racial problem as it today affects persons of Negro descent," to "promote Peace and Justice among men," and to "take a firm stand on the absolute equality of races."[62] Stronger petitions came from Marcus Garvey and his Universal Negro Improvement Association and African Communities League that claimed to consist collectively of "six million members scattered in Africa, the West Indies, South and Central America, North America, Europe, and Asia" and that asserted in their "Petition of the Negro Race":

> Your Petitioners were told, as a race, that all peoples who contributed to the war would be considered at its conclusion. . . . [But] absolutely no consideration has been given us as a people for the splendid service we rendered during the war. Our men have died by the thousands to uphold the principles of the war. . . . Your Petitioners desire to impress upon you the fact that the four hundred million Negroes of the world are no longer disposed to hold themselves as serfs, peons, and slaves, but that it is their intention to look forward to the higher benefits of human liberty, human rights, and true democracy.[63]

Still more letters poured into the League of Nations from South Africa, Australia and New Zealand, India, France, Cuba, and the United States, among many other countries. Some were typed and eloquent in their use of language, while others arrived handwritten on notepaper, like the one, making up in passion what it lacked in grammar and spelling, that asked, "How many time have the league give the land that belong two the african people two white pepole? So what have the league give the wright two jews and withold the wright from the black?"[64]

These many petitions and pleas clearly placed the League of Nations in a most awkward position. As one internal staff note observed, "They have a real case which we cannot totally ignore and should not greatly encourage."[65] If the League responded adequately to the petitioners, it would alienate powerful states and vested interests in the world. To deal with these private letters from the United States, for example, warned one official confidentially, "might antagonize many of our friends in America, who might think that the League was meddling in the Negro question in the States, where this question is a very burning one."[66] Yet, if it did not respond, it would violate its own basic principles. When faced with this dilemma, the League chose power over principle and, in the end, lost them both.

Consequently, those who submitted pleas to the League of Nations concerning racial discrimination received little, if any, assistance. Du Bois traveled to Geneva to deliver personally his Pan-African congress petition but obtained only a cold reception. The secretary-general responded to the many letters from Garvey by saying that "the rules of procedure" did not allow for a consideration of his repeated requests and refused to meet with the delegation from Garvey's Universal Negro Improvement Association, saying that previous commitments "make it unfortunately impossible for me to foresee any moment in the near future when I shall have the necessary time at my disposal."[67] Other petitioners were told simply that "it is not possible for the Secretariat to take up this question."[68] This flood of appeals about race proved to be highly embarrassing to the League's member states, which by 1928 found it necessary to reaffirm their commitment to the principle of sovereignty and their determination "to insure that states with a minority within their borders should be protected from the danger of interference by other powers in their internal affairs."[69]

This explicit emphasis upon "domestic jurisdiction" confronted not only these outside petitioners who possessed little power, but even members of the League itself who attempted to raise the issue of discrimination on the basis of race. As has been pointed out, when Japan failed to obtain a racial equality clause in the Covenant at the Paris Peace Conference, its delegates vowed that "the Japanese Government and people will continue in their insistence for the adoption of this principle by the League in the future."[70] True to this pledge, the representatives of Japan at the League of Nations continued to pose the racial equality question, especially as it arose with reference to immigration problems.[71] Nevertheless, their protests and requests, each time they were raised, foundered upon racial prejudice and the rock of national sovereignty. The Japanese delegate in Geneva, Mineichiro Adatci, said during one debate that unless the assembled members fulfilled their "moral and political duties" and resolved this issue of discrimination, "the League of Nations will remain quite indifferent to the fact that the most flagrant acts of injustice are being committed under the purely technical and juridical cover of the alleged domestic jurisdiction of a State which is a Member of the League."[72] His colleagues remained unmoved by this argument. They also appeared to be absolutely unaffected by the magnificent mural painted by José-Maria Sert on the very wall above them in the Palais des Nations depicting the tragic plight of enslaved black men bound by chains around their necks and legs and longing to be free. These delegates, and the states they represented, thus refused to empower the League to address this delicate and combustible issue of race.

The handling of mandates by the League of Nations revealed yet another aspect of this same pattern. As we have seen, despite solemn wartime promises about possible self-determination, the victorious powers attempted to continue their control of colonial territories by means of a mandate system supervised by the League. The powers hardly needed to be reminded that these areas were populated largely by those of black, brown, and yellow skin color.[73] After dividing the spoils from the war, the victors refused to commit themselves on eventual independence for the mandated territories and used their position to consolidate control. Although the establishment of the League's Permanent Mandates Commission introduced the concept of an international check upon the worst abuses of imperialism and provided both an opportunity for a liberalization of colonial policies and a forum for conscientious discussion among delegates of such important topics as slavery and health care,[74] some states remained steadfastly unaffected by these innovations. They consistently refused to grant the native authorities sovereignty or representation in the League.[75] Some even referred openly in the Assembly of the League itself to the inhabitants under its charge as "the savage races," "the uncivilized races," and "the savage hordes of Africa."[76] Lord Cecil of Great Britain went as far as to include in the official records of the Mandates Commission a copy of a suggestion made to impose a system of segregation upon natives and "to prevent equality between white and black, to uphold the status of the white men."[77]

This general attitude and approach of members of the League toward the problem of race could be seen in striking detail when the League dealt with the specific case of Ethiopia. This African state's application for admission to the League of Nations provoked much debate among the delegates. Sir Joseph Cook of Australia warned in dire tones that if admitted, Ethiopia "might examine and criticize countries whose civilization was more advanced than her own," thus raising the issue of racial discrimination in the international forum.[78] This prompted Henry de Jouvenel of France to rise and declare that the time had come to end such classifications of race and color, arguing that surely one of the tasks of the League was "to eliminate these very prejudices as far as possible and to realize the equality of nations."[79]

Ethiopia eventually obtained admission, but only after considerable discussion and the signing of a special declaration on slavery not required of other states members of the League. Even then, however, the British and Italians, in violation of their own obligations under the Covenant, attempted to carve out special spheres of influence within that country, forcing the Ethiopians to shame their fellow members by publicly reminding them that "we were told that all nations were to be on a footing of equality within the League and that their independence was to be universally respected."[80] As we shall see, the inaction and excuses of the League upon the actual invasion and conquest of Ethiopia by Italy in 1935–1936, and its accompanying arguments about racial differences between whites and blacks, simply confirmed the traditional pattern of prejudice even further. One black petitioner asked the League in frustration, "What good have you done in the world?"[81]

As a consequence of this record, criticisms against the League of Nations in its approach to racial questions have been harsh. One scholar, for example, concluded that the organization demonstrated itself to be "an instrument for perpetuating international white racialism rather than a move against racialism and colonialism."[82] Such judgments are likely to continue. Yet, in considering this criticism, it is important to remember that the League, like any other international organization today, could do no more than its sovereign members were willing to let it do. Its majority of Western members simply remained unalterably opposed to letting the organization take any decisive action to combat racial discrimination, and the power was theirs to wield. Once this realization became apparent to many of those who advocated equality among races, they removed their hopes from the League of Nations and transferred them to two new and more radical organizations designed to challenge the status quo rather than protect it.

To indict almost deliberately the League of Nations for its failures in this matter, the founders of these organizations specifically chose the word *league* as a part of their official titles. The League Against Imperialism, for example, emerged in 1927 out of an international conference of participants from Europe, the United States, Central and South America, the Caribbean, Africa, and Asia. Among its founders could be seen such notables as Henri Barbusse and Romain Rolland from France, Albert Einstein from Germany, Mme. Sun Yat-sen from China, Paul-Henri Spaak from Belgium, Lamine Senghor from Senegal, Richard

Moore and Upton Sinclair from the United States, J. T. Gumede from
South Africa, Mohammad Hatta from Indonesia, Messali Hadj from
Algeria, Victor R. Haya della Torre from Peru, Jawaharlal Nehru from
India, and Ho Chi Minh from Indochina.[83] It explicitly sought to achieve
the abolition of racial discrimination on a global scale and, in this regard,
was seen by some as "a non-white counterforce to the League of
Nations."[84] Another organization, the League of Colored Peoples, was
formed in 1931 similarly to promote the idea "that all races, creeds,
and colors have their part to play in evolving a new order and system"
for the world.[85] Its journal, *Keys*, symbolically portrayed the racial problem
as a piano with keys that one could not play by striking only the white
or only the black keys, but to obtain a harmonious melody one had to
play both. Together these two leagues sought to advance international
racial equality by struggling against imperialism, immigration restrictions,
segregation and discrimination, and ideologies of racial superiority wherever they occurred. Among the latter, the leagues discovered shortly
after their founding that they faced not only their old, familiar adversaries
but a new, growing, and perhaps even more terrifying threat: fascism.

Fascism and National Socialism

Among the many forces arising from the confusion between the two
world wars, perhaps none possessed more catastrophic consequences
than the rise of fascism. The political, economic, and social dislocations
as well as the spiritual disillusionment following World War I provided
a breeding ground for those with contempt for representative government,
rational discourse, and respect for individual rights. Such people rejected
what they called the liberal, bourgeois system of values, advocating
instead authoritarianism, anti-Marxism, an organic state, and a belief in
the importance of discipline, determined action, and, in many cases,
racial superiority. They sought security through national myths and
symbols that left little or no room for those who were different.[86] The
widespread appeal of such ideas could be seen in the fact that by the
1930s no European country remained without its own native fascist
movement. Despite their national differences, individually and collectively
the Fascists looked with admiration upon the two Fascist parties able
to achieve power and directly influence politics and diplomacy: the
Fascists of Benito Mussolini in Italy and the National Socialists of Adolf
Hitler in Germany.

The racial doctrines of the Italian Fascists, compared to those of the
Nazis, evolved more slowly and in a less determined manner. Although
inclined toward anti-Semitism, Mussolini initially thought it unwise to
provoke Jews in Europe (particularly those active in his own party)[87]

and naturally questioned the validity of any dogma of race that left out Italians in favor of blond, blue-eyed northerners.[88] In fact, he criticized Hitler's racial fanaticism against Jews and openly ridiculed the "Aryan" myth, contending that the pretentious racial purity of the Germans would lead only to congenital idiocy.[89] This moderation did not apply to people of color, however, with respect to whom his emphasis was on imperialism, conquest, and domination. From the very beginning, wrote Mussolini's biographer, Denis Mack Smith, the Duce regarded Africans as "inferior beings" and saw himself as defending "western civilization against the colored races."[90]

Mussolini's particular attitude in this regard is fundamental to any understanding of his invasion of Ethiopia and its subsequent designation as a turning point in his racial policies. Long anxious both to avenge the humiliation of Italy by black troops at Adowa and to demonstrate the strength of fascism by extending colonial possessions, Mussolini assembled considerable forces and launched an attack on Ethiopia in October 1935. Ignoring the rules of war, the Italian army deliberately bombed hospitals marked with the Red Cross insignia, shamelessly employed outlawed mustard gas, and attacked defenseless women and children. When criticized for this appalling brutality, Mussolini responded that the Ethiopians were a barbaric, inferior race that practiced slavery and remained "unworthy to stand side by side with civilized nations," and he said that he would treat these black African people as he saw fit.[91] Consequently, the contest between one force using these methods and equipped with the best technology the leaders could find and another armed with only spears and staves left little doubt about the outcome.

In desperation, the Ethiopian emperor, Haile Selassie, personally appealed to the League of Nations for assistance. Not only did he deeply believe in its principles, but he also realized that for small states like his, the League offered the only hope for collective security. As, swathed in a dark cape, he slowly mounted the rostrum in Geneva, a hush of expectation fell upon the delegates. For the first time in history, an African leader was about to protest a European invasion before an international tribunal. Before the eyes of the assembled diplomats and film of new movie cameras recording the event for posterity, he delivered the plea of his people to the world, calling on the League to have the courage of its convictions and be true to its principles, to uphold treaty obligations and commitments, to defend the equality of states and peoples, and to protect the victims of aggression. "In a word," he concluded, "it is international morality that is at stake. . . . God and history will remember your judgment."[92]

Haile Selassie's powerful and moving speech produced genuine emotions, but not meaningful actions. Like diplomats at other times, the

delegates found themselves facing an extremely complex international problem and being simultaneously pulled in different directions. They wanted to honor their pledges, protect recognized borders, support the integrity of the League of Nations, and maintain the peace. But they also wanted to avoid endangering their security and trade, antagonizing Mussolini or Hitler, or threatening their own empires of subject peoples and racial attitudes. As two scholars concluded, with specific reference to this last factor, "The assumption of white, western superiority was the biggest obstacle the Ethiopians had to overcome."[93] In the end, these League members decided to "note" and "deplore" Italian aggression against Ethiopia but to risk no action that might effectively deter or punish Mussolini's government. This decision resulted in part from a variety of strategic, political, and economic considerations and in part from racial prejudice. One journalist reflected the opinion of many when he confessed: "I admired [Haile Selassie] immensely and wished him good luck and wise counsel in the conflict. . . . Nevertheless, I believed firmly that it was not right that Whites should be defeated in Africa.
. . . I believed firmly that if any advance—political, industrial, or agricultural—was to be made in Africa, it must be under the leadership and the domination of the white race."[94]

The delegates' attitude toward race, the abject inaction by the League of Nations, and the aggression by Italy against Ethiopia provoked a storm of protest. The events seemed to indicate, in the words of one observer, "a complete demonstration of how much stronger white solidarity was than Western protestations of democratic belief in freedom and justice."[95] A surge of black anger and frustration arose in reply, particularly among those in the United States, the Caribbean, and the British colonies in Africa. For them, Ethiopia held a special, almost mythical, place as the only African nation that alone had inflicted a major defeat upon a white European power and alone had preserved its independence from white rule. Some viewed Ethiopia as a "Black Zion," while the more extreme among them frequently took to calling their movement "Ethiopianism" and themselves "Rastafarians" after Haile Selassie's given name, Ras Tafari.[96] They immediately joined with many in the Pan-African movement, the League of Colored Peoples, and the newly formed American Committee for Ethiopia and International African Friends of Ethiopia to vehemently condemn the Italian attack.[97] Marcus Garvey declared Mussolini to be "the arch barbarian of our times."[98]

Stinging criticisms such as these, when combined with the whole experience of the Italian-Ethiopian War, helped push the touchy and volatile Mussolini toward a new articulation and intensification of racial policies. His first efforts focused upon blacks in conquered Ethiopia. As early as 1936 the *Gazzetta del Popolo* declared in bold print that "THE

FASCIST EMPIRE MUST NEVER BECOME AN EMPIRE OF MULAT-TOS" and soon asserted, "It is unthinkable that Fascist Italy would ever allow . . . the finest, the best-balanced nation in the world to mix its blood with that of a negroid or semi-negroid race, a primitive race fundamentally separated from the white race because of its biopsychological characteristics."[99] The government flatly rejected the requests of the Italians who wanted to make what reparations they could by adopting Ethiopian orphans. Within the next two years Mussolini promulgated laws explicitly designed to segregate the races by means of a color bar and to prevent Italian blood from being mixed with that of black Africans. As Angelo Piccioli of the Italian Ministry for Africa proudly announced in an official document: "Italy is the first European nation to uphold the universal principle of the superiority of the white race and take the appropriate steps to ensure that the purity of its blood is not polluted by miscegenation. Once again, Italy has shown the nations the way."[100]

With these policies toward blacks leading the way, Mussolini's government then turned its attention toward Jews. The war of imperialism against Ethiopia not only had alienated those of color in the world but had also provoked similar criticism from Jewish leaders from many countries and driven a wedge between Italy and the Western democracies. This, in turn, restricted Mussolini's diplomatic options and drew him closer both to Germany and to its Nazi philosophy. In the face of these several developments and with a desire to buttress fascism with ideological doctrines stressing national strength and unity, Mussolini dropped his earlier contempt for biological racial theories and in 1938 issued his famous Manifesto of Fascist Racism. In it he openly declared, "It is time that the Italians proclaimed themselves frankly racist" and recognized that the Fascist regime "has been based upon racism." The manifesto deliberately considered those of the Jewish faith as a physiological "race" rather than a religious or historic group and announced that "the question of racism in Italy should be treated from the purely biological point of view." It then sought to strike against Jews and blacks with the same blow by asserting the need for a strict distinction between the "Mediterranean race" on the one hand and the "Semitic [Jewish] and Hamitic [black]" on the other, declaring that any theories to the contrary were "absolutely inadmissible."[101] After this official statement, the issue of race increasingly occupied an important place in Fascist literature and policy in the form of racial laws of discrimination,[102] and Mussolini's foreign minister, Galeazzo Ciano, proudly announced that henceforth "the racial question" would be "fundamental" to Italian diplomacy.[103]

By the late 1930s the diplomacy of Italy, like that of most other states, focused attention upon the growing strength of Nazi Germany and its powerful leader Adolf Hitler. Within only a few years, this mesmerizing orator and skillful political opportunist had risen from obscurity to become the führer of the feared Third Reich. Once in power, he immediately began to place the National Socialist program into devastating practice at home and abroad, including its dogma of extreme racial superiority. The results of unparalleled brutality stunned the world and created what has been called "the most murderous racist policy in history."[104]

Hitler, in contrast to Mussolini, did not adopt the issue of race after assuming power or conquering foreign territory. For him it formed an integral part of his entire program from the very beginning. Building upon the earlier theories of Gobineau, Lapouge, and Chamberlain,[105] Hitler became nothing short of obsessed with the concept of race. At an early stage, he wrote in the autobiographical *Mein Kampf* (1925 and 1927), insight and experience convinced him that "the racial question gives the key not only to world history, but to all human culture."[106] Throughout the pages of this shockingly frank book Hitler told his readers about the importance of racial struggle within nature, the superiority of the "master race" or "genius race" of "Aryans," and the necessity to avoid "racial contamination" with inferiors that would "deprive the white race of the foundations for a sovereign existence through infection with lower humanity." He vehemently attacked the very concept of racial equality as the invention of weaklings and cowards and warned that those with black, yellow, red, and brown skins could easily create a "bastardized and niggerized world." Hitler poured out his most intense venom upon the Jews, whom he insisted upon calling a biological "race" that destroyed civilization by spreading decadence, supporting bolshevism, and crawling "like a maggot in a rotting body." When faced with this extreme danger, declared Hitler, the state "must set race in the center of all life" and "must take care to keep it pure," boldly recognizing that racial preservation will succeed only when the inferior races are "exterminated."[107]

These ideas, and the force with which they were presented, attracted like-minded followers to the magnetic Hitler and the emotionally appealing National Socialist party. Race provided an explanation to history and nature, a source of pride to unite the nation, a focal point for hatred of common enemies, a scapegoat for problems, a clarion call for determined action, and a justification for brutal policies, including war. Not surprisingly, the Nazi party's first platform (which remained unaltered during Hitler's life) endorsed the principle of racial inequality. When the party leaders wanted "scientific" proof of the superiority of their own race, they turned to academicians like Professor Hans F.K. Gunther and his *Rassenkunde des deutschen Volks* (1922). When they wanted discussions on the "mystery" and "soul" of race, they turned to their own party members. The Nazi's ideologist, Alfred Rosenberg, for example, added further fuel to the racial fire with his *Der Zukunftsweg einer deutschen Aussenpolitik* (1927) on the future of race and German foreign policy, accusing liberals of serving "the black, the red, and the yellow internationals"; pledging that Germany would join Britain, the United States, and Italy in protecting the threatened white race; and proclaiming, "Aryans of all lands, unite!"[108] His subsequent *Der Mythus des 20. Jahrhunderts* (1930) emphasized the critical importance of race purity, the sacredness of blood, and the unavoidable struggle for racial supremacy.[109] As Hitler himself reiterated, the superior race "has a right to rule the world and we must take this racial right as the guiding star of our foreign policy."[110]

As the Nazis hoped, and as the potential victims feared, when Hitler became chancellor of Germany in January 1933 the door was opened for him to transform these various theories of race into actual practice. From this position, he could make racial discrimination state policy, and he did. Hitler began cautiously, but immediately. Now with the authority of the government in power, he purged the civil service of anyone not considered "Aryan," closed the German office of the League Against Imperialism, which sought to attain racial equality for blacks, and removed Jewish judges and lawyers from the courts. He soon revoked the citizenship of all "undesirables" who had been naturalized during the Weimar period and issued a decree on 11 April authorizing further discrimination against anyone descending from a "non-Aryan," especially Jews.[111] With state approval, the Nazi's Rassenpolitisches Amt (office for racial policy) began to publish a journal entitled *Neues Volk* that emphasized racial purity and genetic breeding, the subhuman nature of Jews, and the danger to the white race presented by blacks and Asiatics.[112]

Such a blatant emphasis upon race, particularly when accompanied by violence and even murder in the streets, provoked a storm of criticism from around the world. Various governments and groups in Africa, Asia, Latin America, the United States, and Europe voiced their concern about this racial legislation and its meaning.[113] Their protests thereby began to move the issue out of the purely domestic context and into the area of diplomacy. Hitler reacted sharply to this and quickly had his minister of the interior, Wilhelm Frick, call a special meeting of the diplomatic corps and foreign press to set the record straight. How a great nation like Germany treated its own people, he declared, was its own business and not a subject to concern the international community. In order to place the matter in perspective, Frick reminded his listeners that the Nazis were hardly unique in this regard, for "the race question plays an important part in the legal codes of a number of states." He singled out the United States and Australia for special attention, noting that their immigration restrictions represented legislation created "from a racial point of view" designed deliberately to exclude "members of certain races." He could have used many other examples as well. Frick therefore announced that Germany had no intention of changing its policy and that the Nazi state would continue to do what it must to keep the "racial composition as undefiled and unmixed as possible" and to require "racial legislation to remind us once more of our most sacred values."[114]

Growing in boldness with the consolidation of their dictatorial regime, Hitler and the Nazis felt secure enough to go even further. They therefore issued the Law for the Protection of German Blood and Honor and the Reich Citizenship Law (known as the Nuremberg Laws of 1935), announcing that "the purity of German blood is the necessary prerequisite for the existence of the German nation," declaring that "a citizen of the Reich may be only that subject who is of German or kindred blood," and outlawing any mixed marriages to prevent racial contamination.[115] Hitler's discourteous treatment of the black U.S. athletes, Jesse Owens and Ralph Metcalf, during the 1936 Olympic Games sparked a quick reaction in the black press of the world, and his continuous statements about "inferior" Asiatics prompted strong protests from India and Japan.[116] The Nazi publication, *Neues Volk*, poured out venomous articles praising Mussolini's racial policies in Ethiopia, U.S. segregation practices and lynchings against blacks, and British and French imperialism against native colored populations, while warning all the time of the dangers inherent in the growing political consciousness among blacks in Africa and the United States, the large number of Asians, and the ever-hated Jew.[117] State-supported anti-Semitism escalated, the "Aryanization" of the economy by plunder increased, and the systematic abuse of Jews intensified. The prejudice exploded as never before in the ferocity and brutality of *Kristallnacht* (the night of broken glass) in November 1938 when Nazis and their supporters burned synagogues, looted Jewish businesses, and rampaging through the streets in an orgy of violence, beat and killed Jews. All this was a sign of things to come, including the shipment of several thousand Jews off to the newly constructed concentration camps of Dachau, Sachsenhausen, and Buchenwald.

The international reaction to this violence provided Hitler with a very good indication of how he might proceed in the future. The Fascists in Italy and the authoritarian regimes in Romania, Hungary, and Poland openly approved of *Kristallnacht*. Most other countries deplored and condemned such repulsive behavior but carefully confined their criticism to words rather than action. They expressed great sympathy to the victims yet argued that diplomatic practice long had agreed that how a nation treats its own citizens was a matter of domestic jurisdiction. In the one area where other countries legitimately could have helped—namely, the acceptance of refugees through immigration—they largely refused. Foreign consulates in Germany found themselves flooded with urgent and tragic pleas for visas from those seeking to escape Hitler's persecution. But Switzerland and most of the Latin American countries closed their doors by actually making their existing laws on entry for refugees more restrictive. None of the major powers, including Britain, France, the United States, and the Soviet Union, would permit any large-scale Jewish immigration into its borders. A spokesman from Australia announced that his country had no racial problems and was not eager to import any.[118] In some cases diplomats proposed that these victims of the Nazis be settled among blacks somewhere in Tanzania, Northern Rhodesia, Uganda, or Madagascar.[119]

In the setting of global politics and diplomacy in 1938 and 1939, of course, immigration policy appeared as perhaps the least among many extremely serious problems. Unchecked Japanese aggression in Manchuria, successful Italian conquest in Ethiopia, and outside intervention in the Spanish Civil War all had caused justifiable alarm and concern about the failures of collective security. Viewing this weakness as a lack of will among those who desired peace, Hitler withdrew Germany from the League of Nations, terminated disarmament talks, rearmed his country, occupied the demilitarized Rhineland in direct violation of the Treaty of Versailles, and formed the Axis alliance with Mussolini. Meeting no effective resistance against these acts, he decided to push ahead with his plans and explicitly outlined his next objectives to his foreign minister and leading generals. In the confines of this intimate group where he could reveal his inmost thoughts, Hitler repeated what he had stated so often before massive and emotional audiences, declaring that "the aim of German policy was to make secure and to preserve the racial community and to enlarge it." He insisted that this "could only be solved by means of force" and the willingness to risk war.[120] Precisely to avoid the prospects of such a war, Britain and France did all they could to appease Hitler, presenting no opposition when he annexed Austria and actually assisting him in the dismemberment of Czechoslovakia with the Munich Agreement.

These stunning diplomatic successes and conquests of territory without the use of armed force simply convinced Hitler of the infallibility of himself and his ideas. They also whetted his appetite for more. Years before, in *Mein Kampf*, he had stated that the survival of the superior racial composition of the Aryans depended upon an expansion of the territorial base and "racial core" of Germany and its ability to secure *Lebensraum*, or living space. This would be done, he wrote, at the expense of the inferior racial stocks to the east who would not be absorbed but enslaved and annihilated. Hitler declared that in this policy he had no intention of repeating the mistakes of the Spanish conquerors of Central and South America, who by intermarriage and their toleration of many peoples had caused racial degradation. Instead, he stated, his model would be those who conquered North America by ruthlessly sweeping aside "lower colored peoples" to ensure their own future and racial purity. Such a policy, he asserted, would be "a bloody one" but necessary, "especially when not some little nigger nation or other is involved, but the Germanic mother of life. A state which in this age of racial poisoning," he concluded, "dedicates itself to the care of its best racial elements must some day become lord of the earth."[121] Hitler now prepared to put this constant and consistent theme into devastating practice by issuing orders to his generals to lead an attack for *Lebensraum* and predicting "the destruction of the Jewish race."[122] This plunged the world into the abyss of yet another war and the horrors of the "Final Solution."

Into the Abyss of War and the "Final Solution"

Before its fires burned out, the war that Hitler unleashed with his attack on Poland in September 1939 made even World War I appear as a mere prelude. No war in human history ever caused so much disruption, devastation, or death. It killed seventeen million soldiers and, even more telling in an age of "total" war, eighteen million noncombatants. It cost trillions of dollars in military expenses and property losses. It generated a frantic search for modern weapons of mass destruction and introduced the world to the nuclear age. It encircled the globe, engulfing continents and peoples of different races far from the shores of Europe. Moreover, it gave fateful, new meaning to a word that would be used to describe the systematic extermination of whole populations: genocide.

Within four weeks of the invasion, Polish resistance collapsed before the might of the mechanized German forces and Poland fell as the first military victim of World War II. If any doubts remained about the seriousness with which Hitler held his views about race, they should have been dispelled immediately. "Close your hearts to pity. Act brutally," Hitler had told his commanders on the eve of war. "Eighty million people must obtain what is their right. Their existence must be made secure."[123] Now, with the conquest of Poland completed, he possessed the first opportunity to set the foreign aspects of his racial program into action. As early as 21 September 1939, Reinhard Heydrich, the tall, blond, blue-eyed chief of his elite security service (*Sicherheitsdienst*, or SD), issued to the *Einsatzgruppen* ("special tasks" groups) orders regarding "The Jewish Question in Occupied Territories." He began by warning his lieutenants that the measures they were about to undertake for "the ultimate goal" must be kept "strictly secret." These included the expulsion of Jews from certain areas, the "immediate Aryanization" of essential businesses, and the gathering of Jews together in "concentration points . . . so that future measures may be accomplished more easily."[124] Hitler personally reiterated these same points to his head of the High Command of the Armed Forces, General Wilhelm Keitel, stating that Poland had to be "cleansed" of racial inferiors and instructing him to remember that "shrewdness and severity must be the maxims in this racial struggle."[125]

To thus extend and intensify his racial policies beyond the confines of German borders and into foreign countries, Hitler understood that he needed to make a more determined commitment of resources. Consequently, at exactly this time of assured German victory over Poland, he created a supreme supervisory office for all racial questions and placed it under the direction of the powerful Reichsführer SS, Heinrich Himmler. The task of this organization, declared Hitler in his secret decree, was to "eliminate" the harmful influence of alien races.[126] For this purpose, Himmler received authority over all Reich offices and all administration in the newly occupied territories. These soon included an immense and complicated bureaucratic apparatus to carry out Nazi racial policies. Collectively, these offices investigated racial credentials, passed judgment on immigration and emigration questions, sponsored orphanages for "racially valuable" children, compiled racial registers, studied "positive eugenics," spread racial propaganda abroad, conducted euthanasia and forced sterilization, and carried out other assignments under the category of "special treatment" against "racial inferiors."[127]

Hitler's pursuit of racial programs in other countries, by necessity, followed the course of the war. Once Poland capitulated and the vast machinery to secure purity of the race was set into motion, he could prepare for an attack westward. The hammer fell in April 1940 as the German armies invaded Denmark and Norway, and again in May when they attacked the Netherlands, Belgium, and Luxembourg. Seemingly invincible, they then smashed into France and by June marched unopposed under the Arc de Triomphe in Paris. In each of these countries the Nazis confronted peoples whom they considered basically Nordic or Aryan like themselves and whom they wanted to assume somehow a position befitting their race within the New Order.[128] But this attitude absolutely did not apply to Jews or any others regarded by Hitler as inferior, who immediately found themselves being subjected to segregation, expropriation, internment, forced labor, and eventual deportation. Throughout occupied Europe their fate hinged upon each individual country's status vis-à-vis Germany, the strength of its respect for equal rights, and the willingness of collaborators to cooperate with the Nazi racial program. Those in Denmark received considerable protection, for example, whereas others were much less fortunate. The Vichy government of France, to illustrate, quickly annulled an earlier decree that punished slander and libel "toward a group of people who belong by origin to a particular race or a particular religion," thereby allowing a legal basis for subsequent discrimination and persecution.[129]

If the connection between the war and racial policies varied in accordance with circumstances in Western Europe, the same could not be said of the Eastern sector. As one high-ranking Nazi official described it, in the west they had a security "function" and in the east a "National Socialist mission." "Therein," he concluded, "lies something of a difference!"[130] Toward the east lay the land of traditional German dreams for territorial expansion (now emphasized under the theme of *Lebensraum* rather than the earlier *Drang nach Osten,* or eastward expansion). But according to Hitler, added to this long-standing objective was a new and more important factor: the "ideological and biological" struggle of race. Toward the east lived the Slavs, only slightly higher on Hitler's racial scale than Jews or blacks. Hitler declared, in an analogy that he believed others in the West would understand, "Russia is our Africa and the Russians are our Negroes."[131] There, said Nazi ideology, lived a race of inferior subhumans, born to be slaves, weakened by the blood of yellow "Mongoloid elements," corrupted by "barbaric" Asiatics, and poisoned by "Jew-Bolsheviks."[132] Military action taken against Poland and then southeastern Europe, declared Hitler, provided a mere taste of what was about to be served; for the real test—the "final struggle"— would take place when he invaded Russia.[133]

Hitler's decision to attack Russia in June 1941 proved to be one of his most fateful acts of the entire war. He regarded this campaign among his most essential and spent considerable time planning the details of the operation and setting policy for conquest and occupation. Hitler gave explicit warnings to his military commanders that this would be no ordinary conflict but a war of extermination that would require unmerciful, unrelenting harshness. He entrusted Rosenberg, the chief Nazi ideologist on race, to coordinate plans for the administration of occupied territory and to do whatever was necessary to eliminate the vermin from the east. He even issued advance immunity to soldiers ordered to conduct acts of savage brutality outside the boundaries of the laws of war.[134] In case his generals lacked the passion for racism, the determination for ruthlessness, or the stomach for mass exterminations, he entrusted "special tasks" to the *Einsatzgruppen.* As the army smashed its way through Russia, these elite death units followed in its wake, rounding up those whom they considered racially inferior, marching them naked toward open ditches, and then killing them by the hundreds of thousands. "No writer of murder fiction, no dramatist steeped in macabre lore, can ever expect to conjure up from his imagination a plot which will shock sensibilities as much as will the stark drama of these sinister bands," wrote the International Military Tribunal after the war. The tribunal estimated that perhaps two million defenseless human beings were murdered in this fashion described as "a crime of such unprecedented brutality and such inconceivable savagery that the mind rebels against its own thought image and the imagination staggers in the contemplation of a human degradation beyond the power of language to adequately portray."[135]

This grotesque "liquidation" and "depopulation," of course, stemmed from the Nazi fanaticism over race. But the practice (as we have seen in other times and places with slavery and imperialism) also helped to reinforce the ideology. German forces saw in the subjected state of the masses of Russian captives walking to their deaths confirmation of their theories of "degenerate-looking Orientals," the "Asian-Mongol virus," and inferior Slavs.[136] Military success appeared to prove the Germans' own superiority as a master race and the subhuman nature of the vanquished. One of Himmler's earliest postinvasion publications, for example, circulated under the title *Der Untermensch* (The subhuman). In graphic and perverse illustrations, it sought to demonstrate a sharp contrast between pure, clean, white "Aryans" of the West on the one hand and degenerate, filthy, subhuman, darker colored Slavs, Orientals, and Jews to the east on the other (the accompanying illustration, in which the Aryans are shown on the right and the subhumans on the left, is typical of those in *Der Untermensch*). The publication portrayed the struggle as one of superior biological race and blood against primitive, bestial "creatures" and concluded by sounding the alarm: "The *Untermensch* has risen to conquer the world. . . . Defend yourself, Europe!"[137]

Although they existed in Europe in their most extreme form, it would be a mistake to assume that the racial aspects of World War II remained only within European confines. This war was global in extent, even insofar as its racial component. Indeed, in terms of the world events that would follow the war, this component proved to be one of its most significant features. The sheer international dimensions of the war, by definition, raised intense interracial issues that unleashed powerful forces of change for the postwar world. Stunning German victories against Russia, for example, encouraged the Japanese to attack the U.S. base at Pearl Harbor and, in so doing, brought the combustible question of race to the Pacific as well.

In its immediate origins, strategic, political, and economic factors relating to East and Southeast Asia and the western Pacific far outweighed any consideration of the race of those involved. It would be an exaggeration

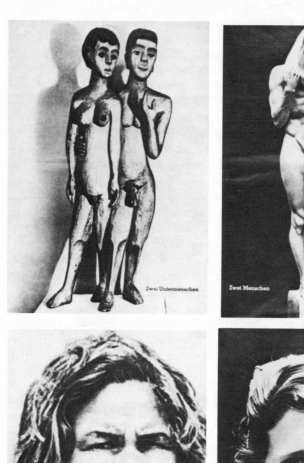

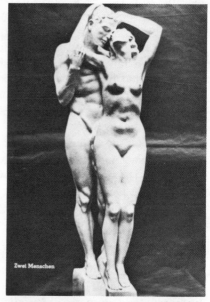

Nazi Racial Contrasts
(source: *Der Untermensch*)

to argue otherwise, especially when one considers that the first Japanese attack occurred in Manchuria. But once the Japanese, with their dramatic military operations, defeated Europeans and Americans in their imperial possessions, the struggle changed complexion. Both among the belligerents in Asia, Europe, North America, and Australasia, and the observers in Africa and Latin America, the war greatly heightened racial consciousness and antagonisms. Even as early as the attack upon Pearl Harbor, for example, numerous U.S. blacks saw the Japanese as an important standard bearer in the fight against racial discrimination, and one black reflected an attitude not at all atypical of many non-white peoples around the world when he wrote: "Although I genuinely participated . . . in the upsurge of anti-Japanese feeling which my patriotism demanded, it was not without an undercurrent of satisfaction that a non-White people had at long last slapped the face of the arrogant Whites. . . . The old master-servant relationship between the White and the non-White people had been dealt a staggering blow."[138] Not long thereafter, the U.S. government imprisoned Elijah Muhammad, the future leader of the Black Muslims, for favoring a Japanese victory over the United States in order for the black minority to be liberated by a colored nation.[139]

Once the Pacific battles began, of course, they brought into sharp focus tensions of race that long had existed and encouraged those who viewed the contest as "the Yellow Race against the White Race."[140] The Western Allies, for example, portrayed the Japanese as scheming, "murderous little ape men" and as savage, slant-eyed, "subhuman" creatures with a skull pattern and skin color grossly inferior to Caucasians.[141] In this context, it was not at all difficult for the press to invoke "the spirit of our race" against Asians.[142] Japan, for its part, depicted white opponents as decadent, selfish, and hypocritical enemies who practiced cruelties on a racial basis. They pointed to the traditional racial discrimination against Asiatics and blacks, arguing that this provided proof of what colored peoples of the Far East might expect in the event of a Western victory.[143]

These arguments of race proved to be particularly explosive in dependent areas under white domination. To many Asians who had suffered from racial discrimination and imperialism for years, the initial victories of Japan provided hope and a sense of pride in addition to the danger of a new conqueror. The appeal of fellow-Asians to throw off the domination of the alien whites tapped deep emotional roots. As one nationalist admitted, "Although my reason utterly rebelled against it, my sympathies instinctively ranged themselves with the Japanese in their fight against the Anglo-Saxons."[144] Others reported their satisfaction in seeing this "great disgrace on the white race."[145] Such reactions were taken very seriously in the West, for as the chief of the State Department's

Far Eastern Division predicted, the fall of Singapore, coming on the heels of the attack against Pearl Harbor, would "lower immeasurably . . . the prestige of the white race and particularly of the British Empire and the United States in the eyes of the natives of the Netherlands East Indies, of the Philippines, of Burma, and of India."[146] They worried, as well they might, what this demonstration of fallibility and loss of face would mean for the future of their empires.

The intensified sense of racial differences and hatreds brought out by the war made itself felt in other ways as well. Despite their propaganda on the theme of Asian brotherhood and unity against whites in the West, the Japanese frequently treated racial minorities in conquered territories in Asia and the Pacific with terrible harshness and brutality.[147] But just as the Japanese actions revealed more about their prejudice than their professed aims, so did the actions of the Western Allies. Despite their boasts of fighting for democratic principles, the Allies did little to change their practices of colonial rule during the course of World War II. The prejudices revealed here were evident much closer to home as well. In North America, for example, those of Japanese ancestry found themselves uniquely singled out for discrimination. In Canada more than twenty thousand of them were deported from the coastal regions of British Columbia and interned.[148] In the United States, the situation was even worse.

As early as February 1942, President Franklin Roosevelt signed Executive Order 9066, which gave to the secretary of war the power to exclude, remove, and then detain U.S. citizens of Japanese descent and their alien parents. Drawing upon a long history of racial prejudice on the West Coast and the fear of possible sabotage after the Pearl Harbor attack, the order quickly received the support of Congress, the Supreme Court, and the public at large. The U.S. government consequently rounded up more than one hundred thousand Japanese-Americans and resident aliens of Japanese descent, forcing them out of their jobs and homes and into confinement for two-and-one-half years. With no legal charges being made, these people were herded into what were publicly called "assembly centers" and "relocation centers," but what government documents of the time described as "concentration camps."[149] The camps were surrounded by barbed wire, armed guards, and dogs; and many were located on or near Indian reservations because of the outcry from white citizens that they might be faced with "yellow" Asians too close to them.

The internment of Japanese-Americans in the United States during World War II clearly provided yet another manifestation of racial prejudice. "This is our time to get things done," confessed one immigration official long supportive of exclusion in the name of racial purity, "that we have been trying to get done for a quarter of a century."[150] By way of sharp contrast, no mass exclusion or detention, in any part of the country, was ordered against citizens of white German or Italian descent. The difference in treatment, as almost all observers agree, stemmed from racial prejudice.[151] General John DeWitt, who recommended this action in the first place for "stern military necessity," wrote that the discrimination had to do with "racial affinities" and the widespread belief that the country faced "an enemy race."[152]

Among the various camps constructed during World War II to deal with those identified by race, however, absolutely nothing could match those of the Nazis. Temporary internment, no matter how cruel or dehumanizing, did not entail murder. Yet, as the war intensified and as the German campaign against the presumed *Untermensch* continued, the Nazis eliminated the distinction between detainment and death. Under the Nazis, concentration camps initially intended to confine were transformed into camps designed to exterminate. Consequently, with the evolution of the war, the most important differentiation between all the inhabitants of occupied Europe increasingly became that between those whom the Nazis and their collaborators considered racially superior and those whom they regarded as racially inferior. The former were permitted to live, and the latter condemned to die.[153]

As Hitler watched the distraction of the United States in the Pacific, the collapse of his neighbors in Europe, and the effectiveness of his death squads in areas of German occupation to the east, he no longer felt any need for caution or restraint. Now the once-heralded power of others appeared to be as incapable as law or ethics in imposing limits on behavior. The Nazi leadership consequently determined that the mass shootings, gas vans, and carbon monoxide asphyxiations in abandoned farmhouses used thus far in the war would no longer suffice for the task that lay ahead. The leaders wanted special annihilation centers out of sight where large numbers of men, women, and children could be killed as quickly and efficiently as possible. For this reason they constructed the camps of Auschwitz, Chelmno, Belzec, Sobibor, Majdanek, and Treblinka. If any question lingered about their ultimate purpose, Heydrich answered it during the Wannsee Conference of January 1942. Before the assembled representatives of all the leading offices of party and state, including the Foreign Ministry, he stressed the critical importance of "racial principles" and announced that henceforth he would coordinate a program of mass extermination. Its name: the "Final Solution."[154]

"In the course of the practical implementation of the Final Solution," asserted Heydrich, "Europe will be combed from west to east" to find racial inferiors.[155] Under the Third Reich, this was no idle boast. In

March the first group of Slovakian Jews began to arrive at Auschwitz, followed by others from the ghetto of Lublin sent to Belzec. Although even the minister for propaganda, Joseph Goebbels, described this procedure as "pretty barbaric,"[156] it continued and gathered frightful momentum. Indeed, now the killing began in earnest. The Nazis and their collaborators rounded up those whom they regarded as racially inferior in France, Belgium, the Netherlands, Luxembourg, and Norway and sent them to their death in the camps. The Nazis gathered others from Germany, Austria, Italy, Poland, Russia, Latvia, Estonia, Lithuania, Czechoslovakia, Hungary, Romania, Bulgaria, and Greece. Having transported their human cargo in crowded cattle cars, the Nazis unloaded the terrified people, made them undress, sorted out some for slave labor or unspeakable medical experiments in the name of "race science," and marched the rest to disguised shower houses where they would be gassed to death like insects. The bodies quickly were relieved of their gold fillings, hair, or anything else that might be useful and then burned in the open air or crematoria to make room for the next load. This, in the words of historian George Mosse, represented nothing short of the ultimate "triumph of racism in practice."[157]

Racial policies like these seem so grotesque, so perverse, so inhuman, and so self-defeating that they defy credulity. But tragically, the horrors of this Holocaust were all too real. Hitler and his followers pursued their goal of racial purity with such savage extremism that they often completely disregarded critical political, diplomatic, military, and economic consequences.[158] For example, even when the war was irretrievably lost, many diplomats in the Foreign Ministry still concentrated their efforts upon spreading doctrines of racial superiority to other countries. When Germany desperately needed manpower to produce armaments and provide essential services for the army, orders still insisted that thousands of able-bodied men spend their time determining the racial background of conquered peoples, compiling heredity charts, and rounding up civilians for racial resettlement schemes. The extermination camps received priority above the *Wehrmacht*, itself scarce on supplies, railroad deliveries, and other vital necessities of war. Moreover, in sheer fanaticism and desperation, as the Allies tightened their hold around German positions, orders instructed the commandants actually to intensify their rate of mass exterminations.[159] To his dying day, Hitler argued as he had years before in *Mein Kampf* that nothing could approach the importance of racial struggle.[160] As for Himmler, he sought to glorify these actions, and told his chief subordinates:

> I want to speak here before you in all openness about a very delicate subject. Among us it should be talked about quite openly, but despite

this we shall never talk about it in public. . . . I mean . . . the exterminations. . . . Most of you know what it means when a hundred corpses are lying together, when five hundred are lying together, or when one thousand are lying together. To have seen that through and while doing so . . . to have maintained our integrity, that has made us hard. This is an unwritten and never-to-be written page of glory in our history.[161]

*   *   *

This Holocaust of racial extermination, despite Himmler's proud boast, could be neither glorious nor unwritten. Genocide on a scale that eventually took the lives of an estimated six million human beings could never remain secret for long. As the war raged on, word of these shocking horrors of unrestrained power and prejudice began to leak out. In some cases, the horrifying news produced only international silence.[162] Among others, however, it spurred even greater efforts to eliminate such cruelty from the earth and forced many as nothing else ever had before to a turning point in their own attitudes toward the highly combustible question of racial prejudice.

5
The Turning Point

THE CANCEROUS NEGRO SITUATION IN OUR COUNTRY gives fodder to enemy propaganda and makes our ideals stick like dry bread in the throat. In anti-Semitism we are a mirror of Nazi grimaces. These motes in our own eye are not to be passed over. . . . Through revulsion against Nazi doctrines, we may, however, hope to speed up the process of bringing our own practices in each nation more in conformity with our professed ideals.
— Commission to Study the Organization of Peace

The War as a Mirror

Repulsed and horrified by the unimagined slaughter of millions of helpless human beings before their eyes, people around the globe desperately looked for answers that might explain how such atrocities possibly could occur. Immediately after the war, therefore, they sent their representatives to gather together, reflect upon the conflict, and determine the major cause of the catastrophe they all had just experienced. These delegates easily could have decided that this war resulted from any of the traditional explanations of armed conflict, such as territorial ambition, economic greed, human aggressiveness, armaments, appeasement, absence of collective security, or lack of wise statecraft, but did not. Instead, these diplomats felt compelled to focus upon only one. "The great and terrible war which has now ended," they poignantly concluded in a most remarkable statement, "was a war made possible by the denial of democratic principles of the dignity, equality, and mutual respect for men, and by the propagation in their place, through ignorance and prejudice, of the doctrine of the inequality of men and races."[1]

The horrors of this war and their relation to doctrines of racial superiority, as we have seen, certainly did not represent the first case of blatant discrimination in the world. But their extreme and abhorrent nature in this conflict, and the overwhelming magnitude of the persecution, raised the issue of race in a way that nothing else in history had ever done before. The experience convinced many that international relations never again could be considered apart from interracial relations and moved the famous anthropologist, Ruth Benedict, to write at the time that racism had reached "epidemic" proportions and become "the burning question" for the world.[2] Race, in fact, became such a powerful and pronounced factor of World War II that it profoundly shook power relationships, empires, and attitudes. Of particular importance, the war, in focusing attention upon the racial policies of others, provided a mirror that forced countless numbers of people to look at themselves and to see the contradictions between their declared principles on the one hand and their actual practices on the other.

The Allies had proudly and publicly enunciated their principles against nazism and its racial doctrines early in the war. Drawing upon great democratic values, President Franklin Roosevelt gave quick expression to the relationship between domestic liberties and international peace.[3] In an important message to Congress in January 1941 he stated: "Freedom means the supremacy of human rights everywhere. Our support goes to those who struggle to gain those rights and keep them."[4] Eight months later Roosevelt, together with Prime Minister Winston Churchill, elaborated this theme in the Atlantic Charter. This, in turn, served as the basis for the Declaration of the United Nations, signed in January 1942, in which twenty-six countries (and, subsequently a total of forty-six) proclaimed their commitment "to preserve human rights and justice in their own lands as well as in other lands."[5]

A declaration of principle like this provided tremendous inspiration for those fighting against the Axis and elicited enormous sacrifices for the cause of freedom. Yet, such a staggering proclamation, as one can well imagine, raised a series of fundamental questions with the potential for revolutionary consequences on global politics and diplomacy. Would this announced preservation of human rights and justice, for instance, end racial discrimination in Asia, Africa, and Latin America? Would it apply to colored native populations in the colonial possessions of Britain, France, the Netherlands, Portugal, Spain, or the United States? Would it prohibit imperialism or immigration quotas based upon race? Would it apply to racial minorities in the United States, Canada, Europe, Australia, New Zealand, or South Africa?

The explosive nature of these questions did not escape policymakers as they struggled to find answers. In London, for example, the Foreign Office carefully considered issuing a statement on the need to relax global racial tensions. "It is impossible for discrimination to be allowed to exist in the world as it stands today," wrote officials, and they agreed that they "ought certainly to grope for an eventual solution." Yet, they determined that at this time "it would be unwise for us to raise this matter," in part because the "Americans also *are far from any real belief in racial equality.*" To press the question of race, they confidentially concluded, would provoke "very acute problems for others such as the U.S. where any premature injection of the racial issue into existing controversies might have unfortunate results on the cause of aid for Britain."[6]

The Ministry of Information independently reached the same conclusion. Officials there knew that for propaganda purposes among Asians it would be highly advantageous to declare the beginning of a "new attitude toward them based no longer on the idea of exploitation and racial superiority but on equality, mutual respect, and friendship in a common struggle." But the officials recognized that this would require the government to make "a major declaration of policy and some statement further interpreting the Atlantic Charter" and that such an action would never be taken with Churchill at the helm.[7] Similarly, in a later internal study examining attitudes toward race and immigration, the Foreign Office warned that only restricted distribution be made of the report and advised simply: "It would be highly undesirable to start any discussion of this subject."[8] Australia and New Zealand also agreed among themselves to approach the issue of racial discrimination during the war with, in their words, "masterly evasion."[9]

In the United States as well governmental leaders knew that any widespread discussion about the principles of the Atlantic Charter and Declaration of the United Nations concerning racial equality would cause serious problems. The internment of citizens of Japanese descent on the basis of race flagrantly violated any proclamation about nondiscrimination.[10] Official resistance to accepting immigrants from China and India, despite their much praised status as Allies, similarly indicated that little had changed. When passing through Allied Africa, General Joseph Stilwell privately continued to refer to the people as "fuzzy wuzzies" and "niggers."[11] The greatest potential for explosion, however, came from U.S. blacks who faced not only a long tradition of racial discrimination in general but now specific segregation within war industries and the armed services in violation of recommendations to the contrary. As in World War I, the United States wanted blacks as soldiers, but not as full citizens with equality. Even the secretary of war himself, Henry Stimson, confided that in his mind whites and blacks could never be equal.[12] Frustrated and angry over this continued prejudice, many blacks actively supported the "Double V Campaign"—"victory over the Axis abroad and victory over racial discrimination at home."[13] Always fearful about the potential consequences of such activities, the Office of War Information secretly reported to Roosevelt on the mood of the "colored troops," special agents watched black organizations in Harlem that might try to unite all colored peoples into a common cause, and administration officials desperately worked behind the scenes to prevent a wartime march on Washington protesting racial discrimination.[14]

Similarly, among the Allies as a whole there remained a steadfast unwillingness to do much of practical value to assist Jews trapped in Hitler's inferno. Like the Nazis and others, the Allies continued to view those of the Jewish faith as a biological "race."[15] Although they might be willing publicly to condemn in the strongest possible language the Third Reich's policy of genocide,[16] none of the major Allies, including the United States, Britain, and the Soviet Union, would take specific measures to provide relief. Until they achieved military victory, of course, they could not completely stop the Holocaust; but as recent scholarship reveals, even when dealing with those things within their power, these countries still refused to grant asylum to people who might successfully escape, to consider possible rescue attempts, to provide emergency aid through neutral countries, or to loosen their immigration restrictions, and they agreed to prosecute anyone engaged in the purchase of exit visas to ransom Jews as guilty of trading with the enemy. As one observer bitterly noted, "the world is divided into countries in which the Jews cannot live and countries which they must not enter."[17] The International Committee of the Red Cross insisted upon maintaining neutrality in this situation, and the Vatican piously refused to make any comment (let alone take any action) at all. In private, the leaders of the countries fighting the Axis spoke of "serious complications," "anti-Semitic agitation," "a racial problem," and "these useless people."[18]

Surprisingly enough, public statements confirmed the message of these confidential decisions and documents. After signing the Atlantic Charter and the Declaration of the United Nations, Churchill quickly made it clear that these principles did not apply to British colonial territories.[19] He frequently and quite candidly spoke about the presumed inferiority of those around the world with non-white skin color and on one occasion even went so far as to declare: "Why be apologetic about Anglo-Saxon superiority [to other races]? We are superior."[20] Although South Africa joined in the war against Germany, a substantial proportion of the white Afrikaners remained highly sympathetic to the racial doctrines of the Nazis and openly said so through their own organization, the *Ossewa Brandwag*.[21] Officials from Australia and New Zealand similarly made no secret of their attitudes toward race. In the United States, even though Roosevelt was prepared to sign an executive order prohibiting discrimination by firms with defense contracts, his concern did not extend to enforcement. In fact, one of his own appointees on the Committee on Fair Employment Practices rather proudly stated, "All the armies of the world, both of the United Nations and the Axis, cannot force upon the

South the abandonment of racial segregation."[22] One group even organized a new association called the League to Maintain White Supremacy. As one scholar wrote in light of all this, "It is not easy to discover how these racial ideas . . . differed essentially from Hitler's ideology of a master race in Europe."[23]

Indeed, it was precisely this kind of comparison that provided a mirror. World War II, both overtly and by implication, placed ideas of race in a new and harsher light. In looking at the racial attitudes of others, many among the Western Allies saw a reflection of themselves. They examined the stated principles of the Atlantic Charter and Declaration of the United Nations and then the actual practice of their governments and concluded that a wide chasm separated the two. Some officials in the Foreign Office clearly admitted that in terms of the racial issue in British imperial policy, there existed genuine justification for criticism.[24] In South Africa, General Jan Smuts had to admit: "I have heard natives saying, 'Why fight against Japan? We are oppressed by the whites and we shall not fare worse under the Japanese.'"[25] Some members of the Australian public similarly noted the sharp contrast between their government's statements and practices and wrote to their prime minister that lasting peace never could be achieved if racial hatred and discrimination continued to be sanctioned.[26] The Dutch prime minister, P. S. Gerbrandy, also publicly acknowledged the deep international tensions caused by prejudice of skin color.[27]

In the United States the reflection became particularly difficult to avoid. Eleanor Roosevelt, wife of the president and a determined supporter of human rights, publicly criticized the country's racial discrimination and openly expressed her opinion that "the nation cannot expect colored people to feel that the United States is worth defending if the Negro continues to be treated as he is now."[28] Race riots in U.S. cities and on military bases during the war emphasized this contrast even further. "Write on my tomb," one draftee was said to have declared, "Here lies a black man, killed fighting a yellow man for the protection of a white man."[29] "This is not a war for freedom," asserted A. Philip Randolph, the militant organizer of the Brotherhood of Sleeping Car Porters. "It is a war to continue 'white supremacy' and the . . . exploitation of people of color."[30]

The more moderate Walter White, executive secretary of the National Association for the Advancement of Colored People, wrote Roosevelt directly, warning him of the hypocrisy of the Atlantic Charter and Declaration of the United Nations if confined only to those of the white race. "This could be treated from the world as well as the national point of view on the importance of the problem of color," he wrote. "Not only would this have its effect upon the colored peoples of the world, who constitute four-fifths of the world's population, through its demonstration that no longer will black, brown, and yellow peoples be treated as inferior or exploited by white peoples, but it would also have profoundly salutory effect upon the very serious domestic situation with respect to Negro-white relations."[31] His concern about prejudice was echoed by numerous Jewish organizations as well.[32] In addition, the factor of race received particular attention when respected Supreme Court Justice Frank Murphy, in a strongly worded dissent about the internment of citizens of Japanese descent, argued that the United States should look at itself carefully and see that it had become no better than its enemies by falling into "the ugly abyss of racism."[33]

If Western leaders or their citizens did not sufficiently turn that mirror toward themselves voluntarily, then outsiders did it for them. German, Italian, and Japanese propagandists during the war, of course, readily exploited these practices of intense racial prejudice and portrayed the emptiness of the declared principles about equality.[34] But others who firmly believed in democracy and freedom did so as well. Mohandas Gandhi of India proved to be one of the most direct in this regard. In a personal letter to Roosevelt, he urged that the Allies place their cause on an unassailable basis by firmly renouncing racial discrimination. "I venture to think," he stated, "that the Allied declaration that [they] are fighting to make the world safe for freedom of the individual and for democracy sounds hollow, so long as India and, for that matter, Africa are exploited by Great Britain, and America has the Negro problem in her own home."[35] "Where," cried black-bordered placards posted by Jewish organizations, "are the democratic governments?"[36]

As the war continued and as the evidence of wartime brutality and genocide mounted, discussions about human rights and race increased in frequency and intensity. Individual citizens, private groups, nongovernmental organizations, officials within bureaucracies, diplomats, foreign ministers, and heads of state increasingly pressed for some kind of response. By spring 1944 Roosevelt himself felt that he could no longer fail to combine publicly the general notion of human rights with the specific principle of racial equality. For this reason he finally announced, "The United Nations are fighting to make a world in which tyranny and aggression cannot exist; a world based upon freedom, equality, and justice; a world in which all persons regardless of race, color, or creed may live in peace, honor, and dignity."[37]

Encouraged by such an announcement, the influential Commission to Study the Organization of Peace, composed of distinguished scholars and prominent foreign policy experts, released its special report entitled *International Safeguard of Human Rights*. This study emphasized the existence of an intimate connection between human rights in domestic policy and human rights in foreign affairs. It stated that if basic rights and liberties for individuals were protected within each country, they were likely to be respected across national borders as well. Consequently, declared the report, "the relation between human rights and a just peace is close and interlocking." This connection, maintained the Commission, was never more evident or more intimate than in the area of racial discrimination, where "Hitler's gospel of Aryan superiority" generated "hatred and planted the seeds of war," and where in the future it would remain unless nations now took action to eliminate it.[38]

In order to make necessary changes, emphasized the Commission, the United States would have to begin by looking at itself in a mirror and seeing the motes in its own eye before viewing the beams in those of others. It pointed to the long-standing history of racial discrimination against blacks and to the widespread attitudes of anti-Semitism, contrasting these with the declared principles of the war. It recalled the country's behavior in this regard at the end of an earlier global conflict and warned, "We may be chastened by Wilson's rejection at Paris of the principle of racial equality—a rejection which embittered the Oriental world." The best way to avoid this problem again, argued the Commission, could be found in recognizing the mistakes of the past and to look toward the future. "We cannot postpone international leadership until our own house is completely in order," it declared. "Nor can we expect nations to agree that their own houses should be brought into order by the direct intervention of international agencies. We have only to consider the difficulties which any such course would encounter in our own or other countries."[39] But, hoped the Commission, through the experience of the war and a revulsion against Nazi doctrines of race, the world might speed up the process of bringing its own practices both at home and abroad more in conformity with its professed ideals.

This widely read report thus maintained that the world faced an unpredecented opportunity to take international action in the area of human rights and racial discrimination. But it also clearly recognized that the task would be enormously difficult. Traditions inhibit innovation, prejudices run deep, and diplomatic agreement is always hard to achieve. Among all of the problems to be faced ahead, however, the Commission singled out one for special attention: "the bogey of national sovereignty," which led to states' claiming a unique privilege of domestic jurisdiction and their viewing expressions of foreign interest in the welfare of their citizens as interference in the states' own affairs. "In the past," observed the report, "the protection of human rights has, in general, been the separate and independent responsibility of each nation. The individual person had to look to his own state's constitution and legal procedures. He could not look beyond." Now was the time for a dramatic and drastic new departure, the time for a turning point in the history of the world. The Commission declared with all the intensity it could command, "We are determined that hereafter no nation may be insulated and wholly a law unto itself in the treatment of its people."[40]

Wartime Proposals for International Action

This idea that nations could no longer claim an exclusive right to treat their citizens or subjects as the nations wished emerged out of a series of wartime proposals for international action to combat racial discrimination. A growing global awareness of the problems of the past, of Hitler's horrendous atrocities, and of the emerging opportunities for change in the future convinced many that the world had arrived at a turning point. It seemed to be the perfect time to take international action. Consequently, during the course of World War II, there emerged a number of plans and ideas for solutions to protect human rights in general and to prevent racial discrimination in particular.

Early in the war these proposals spoke only in general terms, indicating a recognition that something had to be done to relieve global racial tensions but lacking specificity. Foreign Office officials in London, for instance, acknowledged that discrimination on the basis of race clearly preoccupied the minds of many around the world suppressed by imperialism and excluded by immigration barriers, which no longer should be allowed to continue. They recognized that the problem had to be resolved but lacked the desire to pursue it more fully at that time and had little idea as to how it might be achieved.[41] British cabinet member Duff Cooper similarly warned his colleagues in 1941 that as a result of the war they would face non-white peoples "who are unwilling to acknowledge the superiority of Europeans or their right to special privileges" and proposed that they begin to consider a new basis for the future relationships with those of other races.[42] Later the lieutenant governor-general of the East Indies wrote to his superiors at The Hague, urging that they recognize that "a very important—if not the most important—point is the abolition of all racial discrimination."[43]

During 1942 the Congress of Racial Equality (CORE) organized its first campaigns for political action in the United States. Roosevelt's advisors likewise called to his attention the growing "color consciousness" emerging in the world out of the war and proposed that he consider taking some action.[44] Walter White wrote directly to the president, warning him that unless he provided some kind of response, disaster would follow: "If this war should end with the continuation of white overlordship over brown, yellow, and black peoples of the world, there will inevitably be another war and continued misery for the colored peoples of the United States, the West Indies, South America, Africa, and the Pacific."[45]

As the war progressed, these proposals for international action became more specific and focused upon particular aspects of the larger problem of discrimination and persecution. With the evidence of Hitler's massive genocide finding its painful way out of occupied Europe, for example, the Allies could not simply ignore what was being done in the name of racial superiority. Continued silence in the face of overwhelming evidence confirming the Holocaust suggested either gross callousness, stark apathy, or even worse, quiet approval. Particularly in the United States and Britain, where the opportunities for freedom of expression produced the greatest self-examination in that mirror of racial reflection, various groups continually pushed for some kind of official statement. When the government-in-exile of Poland added diplomatic pressure to that deriving from domestic politics, the issue could no longer be dismissed. Consequently, after considerable negotiations, the governments of Belgium, Czechoslovakia, Greece, Luxembourg, the Netherlands, Norway, Poland, Yugoslavia, and the French National Committee joined with the United States, Britain, and the Soviet Union to issue the United Nations Declaration on Jewish Massacres. In it they publicly spoke of racial discrimination, denial of human rights, and the appalling horror and brutality of mass extermination. In addition, they resolved to ensure that those responsible for these crimes would be punished by the international community.[46] Although this declaration did not promise an immediate response, it did provide through diplomacy recognition by several important states of the problem of race and proposed to take action in the future.

This declaration, in turn, inspired additional groups to draw attention to still other aspects of racial discrimination, including imperialism. Like its predecessor several years before, World War II weakened the ties of colonial empires and greatly accelerated the development of Asian and African nationalism. The principles enunciated in the Atlantic Charter and Declaration of the United Nations, and the declared struggle against Nazi racial doctrines, accentuated this development even further. In the Far East, the Indian subcontinent, and the Pacific, the war generated extensive discussions about race, the "white-versus-colored" conflict around the globe, and a considerable number of proposals for ending imperial domination in Asia.[47] The war similarly gave great stimulus to the Pan-African movement. Black leaders around the world like Du Bois, Nkrumah, Harold Moody, Nnamdi Azikiwe, George Padmore, and Amy Jacques Garvey, among others, all called on the Allies to honor their proclaimed principles and promote the independence of Africa.[48] Moody, who led the League of Colored Peoples, drew attention to the analogy of a mirror reflecting a nation's racial attitudes and wrote that people "are now beginning to see something of the evil of race discrimination and how incongruous it is to be fighting ostensibly against the [Nazi] *Herrenvolk* idea and then to be supporting it within their own communities."[49] He and his group drew up the "Charter for Colored Peoples" demanding racial equality and proposing that the colonial powers assume the obligation to render account to an international body about their administration of Africa and about steps they would take to transfer sovereignty for African self-government.[50]

These many proposals during the war to deal with the global problem of racial discrimination in its various dimensions, stimulated still others. Imperialism, immigration restrictions, racial segregation, and anti-Semitism all received further attention. Some proposals focused on inserting human rights provisions into treaties with former enemies, sponsoring international conferences dealing with racial discrimination, and creating special commissions on human rights with investigatory and quasi-judicial authority over individual states. The proposals that received the greatest attention, however, were those advocating an international declaration of human rights and the inclusion of articles prohibiting racial discrimination in the charter of a postwar international organization.

One of the first—if not the first—of all governmental proposals for an international document on human rights to emerge from the war came from within the U.S. Department of State. As early as 1942 a special legal subcommittee was created to deal with work in the field of postwar international organization. For months this group[51] held regular weekly meetings to prepare a draft international bill of human rights. According to one of its major participants, "the Legal Subcommittee assumed that the recognition and guarantee of basic human rights would be conducive to the development of conditions favorable to the maintenance of international peace."[52] The subcommittee consulted the texts of the English Bill of Rights, the U.S. Bill of Rights, the French Declaration of the Rights of Man and of the Citizen, the Declaration of the International Rights of Man as adopted by L'Institut de Droit International, a declaration proposed in 1936 by the Ligue des Droits de l'Homme, various suggestions from the American Law Institute and the Commission to Study the Organization of Peace, and the opinions of outside consultants.

Based upon the letter of these documents, the spirit of these proposals, and their own vision of the future, the members of this State Department group produced a number of drafts, all of which contained a nondiscrimination clause. "The necessity of prohibiting any discrimination," they wrote, " . . . requires no comment. It is the heart of any modern bill of rights, national or international."[53] Consequently, their final draft concluded with these words, "These human rights shall be guaranteed by and constitute a part of the supreme law of each state and shall be observed and enforced by its administrative and judicial authorities, without discrimination on the basis of nationality, language, race, political opinion, or religious belief, any law or constitutional provision notwithstanding."[54]

The critical difficulty with this draft article, of course, came from the words, "shall be observed and enforced . . . any law or constitutional provision notwithstanding." "It becomes immediately apparent," wrote Durward Sandifer, a specialist in legal matters assisting the subcommittee, " . . . that the principal problem is that of implementing the guarantees contained in any bill of rights."[55] He observed that phrases and words were one thing, but that implementation and enforcement were something quite different. Guarantees of human rights by their very nature impinged upon domestic jurisdiction and thus immediately brought the tenets of international law into conflict with the prerogatives of national law. Confronted with this issue, Sandifer outlined the available alternatives: promulgate a bill of rights as an international declaration without establishing any rules of enforcement or provide for sanctions through (1) the executive organ of an international organization, (2) an international commission, or (3) international judicial review of any violations of human rights. He cited the confidential assessment of Quincy Wright, the highly respected legal scholar, who perceptively argued that *any* of these solutions "would inject an element of international politics into the preservation of human rights, and would seriously hamper world institutions in maintaining rights in cases of serious abuse by a government of its own population."[56]

Sandifer continued to stress the tension that would exist between international and national law if enforcement provisions were included in a bill of human rights. He effectively ruled out any of the options with sanctions by quoting the opinion of André Mandelstam in *Les Droits Internationaux de l'Homme:*

> The signature, by all states, of a general convention of the rights of man would be at the present unattainable, if such a convention should include any sanctions. . . . In fact, it would be falling victim to strange illusions to imagine that at the present time, when the Powers have not yet reached an understanding on the subject of the establishment of collective sanctions against the state which breaks its solemn obligations to maintain the *external peace*, that the same Powers would consent to the institution of a juridical system permitting the international community to render judgements followed by sanctions in the demand of interior peace.[57]

As a result of this argument, Sandifer recommended that an international bill of human rights be promulgated without establishing any procedures for enforcement. "This would represent the simplest and least complicated method of putting an international bill of rights into effect," he wrote in a document classified as secret. "It is a device used many times in the past. States agree on the adoption of new rules of law or a formulation of existing rules and proclaim them to the world in a formal international agreement. Reliance is placed primarily upon the good faith of the contracting parties. . . . Such a procedure has the advantage of provoking the minimum of opposition, which is important in a step as radical in character as giving universal legal recognition to individual human rights."[58] This recommendation was to become the guiding principle for U.S. foreign policy—and that of many other nations—in the politics and diplomacy of human rights for the next several decades.

Once it became apparent that an international organization would be created upon the conclusion of the war, the questions of human rights and racial discrimination increasingly came to be considered within the context of drafting appropriate charter provisions. A special project group of the Department of State, in fact, produced draft articles for the United Nations as early as 1943. One of the most important of these prohibited discrimination on the basis of race, nationality, language, political opinion, or religious belief. The purpose of this particular provision, according to the official internal evaluation, could be found in the assumption that a "ban on discrimination [is] fundamental because without it no person's rights are assured and those of all may be undermined. . . . The prohibition of discrimination on the grounds of race is intended to prevent the enactment of laws like the notorious Nuremberg laws, and similar laws in other countries, discriminating against 'non-Aryans.'" Lest this provision be used for other purposes, the report quickly made clear, it would "not interfere with the laws of some of our states for the segregation of races." The reason for this could be found in "the most notable omission": "the absence of guarantees or measures of enforcement" in the article itself. Any such provisions were considered certain to raise "constitutional or political difficulties in various states," to interfere with the doctrine of sovereignty, to be "politically unacceptable" and "out of the question at the present time." The assessment concluded, "There is, therefore, no danger that any state will be forced to accept a standard unacceptable to it."[59]

What various states would or would not accept remained mere speculation until negotiations for a postwar organization actually began at the Dumbarton Oaks Conference in the late summer and early fall of 1944. There, representatives of Britain, the Soviet Union, China, and the United States gathered together in an effort to turn dreams into reality by drafting proposals to maintain peace and security in the world. Yet even before the delegates assembled, they were confronted with the issues of human rights and racial discrimination. The Department of State, for example, already had requested a special study to analyze the circumstances surrounding the denial of the principle of racial equality at the end of the previous war in order to anticipate a strategy now.[60] Moreover, China, well aware of the fate of the Japanese proposal at the Paris Peace Conference, immediately raised the issue of race. In responding to Roosevelt's initial invitation, the Chinese leader, Chiang K'ai-shek, wrote with intensity: "I am particularly grateful to you and Secretary Hull for the insistence on the necessity of China's being represented at the conference. Without the participation of Asiatic peoples, the conference will have no meaning for half of humanity."[61] This was followed by the official Chinese proposal for the new organization's fundamental principles:

1. The International Organization shall be universal in character, to include eventually all states.
2. The principle of equality of all states and all races shall be upheld.[62]

This last provision for racial equality, warned one observer, would produce "a stiff fight."[63]

When the text of this proposal reached the Foreign Office in London, the words about racial equality were singled out for special attention.[64] The British as well as the Americans and Soviets shared a concern over "the equality of race question."[65] During the first phase of the Dumbarton Oaks conversations, representatives of these three powers discussed how they should handle the Chinese proposal specifically and the larger issue of human rights in general.[66] The U.S. delegation, headed by then–Under Secretary of State Edward Stettinius, wanted to include in the draft charter a statement of principle about respecting "human rights and fundamental freedoms" but wanted to shift away from previous State Department draft proposals about nondiscrimination and away from such a stark and explicit article about race as that proposed by China.[67] The Soviet representative, Andrei Gromyko, initially opposed even this proposal, arguing that reference to human rights and basic freedoms was "not germane to the main tasks of an international security organization."[68] Sir Alexander Cadogan, leading the British delegation, also opposed even a general statement of principle in the belief that it would create the possibility that the organization would engage in criticism of the internal policies of member states and thus violate the principle of sovereignty.[69] With reference to the article about race submitted by China, Cadogan telegraphed the following message to the Foreign Office:

Discussion had taken place here of the attitude which should be adopted if the Chinese Delegation press for inclusion in the agreed proposals of a provision on racial equality. Argument strongly advanced is that it would be against our interest and tradition as a liberal power to oppose the expression of a principle denial of which figures so predominantly in Nazi philosophy and is repugnant to the mass of British and foreign opinion. Such action would moreover prejudice British and American relations in a sphere of greatest delicacy by supplying ammunition to critics who accuse us of reactionary policy in the Far East.

He then went on to explain the difference between words and deeds:

Recognition of the principle commits us to nothing more than we have always stood for. But there might be a revival of the quite unfounded fears of 1919 that immigration problems are involved. These are, of course, . . . matters of domestic jurisdiction and would be covered if a satisfactory solution of this question is reached. We may be sure that it if were thought that such questions were involved by the recognition of the principle, the United States Delegation would oppose it.[70]

The delegations of the United States, Great Britain, and the Soviet Union did oppose the language and the form of the original Chinese proposal. Consequently, by the time China received an invitation to participate directly in the second phase of Dumbarton Oaks, the article stating the principle of racial equality already had been eliminated. Similarly, those early drafts from special task groups within the State Department advocating an international declaration on human rights and racial discrimination[71] were never introduced at the negotiations. The leader of the Chinese delegation, Wellington Koo, realized that he could not change the fait accompli by himself but would have to wait until more non-Western states could assemble. As a result, he attempted to maintain at least the appearance of harmony in the deliberations and did not explicitly use that sensitive word, *race*. His initial speech, however, clearly implicated the subject. He spoke of justice rather than politics and diplomacy and of the need to adopt basic international principles of conduct, matters to which China "attached a great deal of importance. It would be highly desirable to do everything possible to remove any suspicion on the part of the peace-loving peoples of the world that this new organization, though originally set up for the maintenance of peace and security, might eventually degenerate into an organization of power politics," he stated. "If we could do something to give a moral tone to the character of the new organization, we would go a long way toward fostering confidence and removing misgivings, possibly based upon cynicism, doubts, or suspicions."[72]

These words of the Chinese delegate, as well as those about racial equality, largely fell on deaf ears at Dumbarton Oaks. Despite Roosevelt's reported feeling that some provision about human rights was "extremely vital,"[73] most of the discussion revolved around the importance of national law, domestic jurisdiction, and the need for the international organization to refrain from intervention in the internal affairs of its members. The resulting draft charter, therefore, said nothing about race and stated only that the organization should "be based on the principle of the sovereign equality of all peace-loving states."[74] Buried deep within the draft, in a section dealing with economic and social cooperation, appeared the phrase that the organization should "promote respect for human rights and fundamental freedoms."[75] When one member of the Chinese delegation asked for an explanation of the meaning of this statement, Leo Pasvolsky of the State Department replied that both the principles and the mechanics would be left to the assembly of the organization, which might propose international agreements with regard to the observance of basic rights if it so desired. He indicated, however, that any such agreements would become effective only when accepted by the respective states, and that this "would not be likely to happen for some time."[76]

These rather meager results did not escape notice. "In the preliminary peace talks at Dumbarton Oaks," said one commentator, "only one colored group participated, the Chinese, and the equality and basic problems of Negroes and colonial colored people were not on the agenda. Will this policy be followed in the coming peace conference?"[77] The answer to this question became apparent when the proposals from Dumbarton Oaks were sent out for the consideration of delegates to the larger and more representative conference that was to meet at San Francisco in spring 1945 to create the United Nations. At the San Francisco Conference, the emphasis on human rights and racial equality would be much different.

Human Rights, Racial Equality, and the Charter

The opening speeches of the delegates at San Francisco conveyed a spirit of unparalleled euphoria. Flushed with success against their military enemies and with the excitement of participating in one of the century's most historic events, hundreds of representatives of fifty participating countries eagerly anticipated creating a new world order that would guarantee peace and security. The gathering was described as a "landmark" and a "milestone in the long march of man to a better future." "For there can be no doubt anymore," declared Prime Minister Jan Smuts of South Africa, "that for us, for the human race, the hour has struck. Mankind has arrived at the crisis of its fate, the fate of its future as a civilized world."[78] The participants were urged to rise above their own national interests and to promote the common international good, to put past practices behind them, and to create an organization founded upon principle.

"If we should pay merely lip service to the inspiring ideals and then later do violence to simple justice," said President Harry Truman, "we would draw down upon us the bitter wrath of generations yet unborn. . . . We must build a new world—a far better world—one in which the eternal dignity of man is respected."[79] Others spoke of the need to be guided by "the vision of the ideal," the faith in justice and the resolve to vindicate the fundamental rights of man, and on that basis to found a better, freer world for the future."[80] Such words sounded marvelous, but lest they become merely "oratorical flourishes which only serve to conceal the real difficulties,"[81] the delegate from India rose to be more specific. "We are all asked to be realists, we are asked to recognize various factors in the world set up as it is today," he stated.

> There is one great reality, one fundamental factor, one eternal verity which all religions teach, which must be remembered by all of us, the dignity of the common man, the fundamental human rights of all beings all over the world. Those rights are incapable of segregation or of isolation. There is neither border nor breed nor color nor creed on which those rights can be separated as between beings and beings. And, speaking as an Asiatic, may I say that this is an aspect of the question which can never be forgotten, and if we are laying the foundations for peace we can only lay them truly and justly. . . . Those fundamental human rights of all beings all over the world should be recognized and men and women treated as equals in every sphere, so far as opportunities are concerned.[82]

This concern with human rights and racial equality was not unexpected. Indeed, various delegations had anticipated it for months. Upon receiving the Dumbarton Oaks proposals for consideration, each government had an opportunity to evaluate the contents, suggest possible amendments, and anticipate likely developments. The Inter-American Conference on Problems of War and Peace, held in Mexico City during March 1945, already had passed a resolution condemning racial discrimination and requesting a draft declaration of international human rights and duties.[83] Others, however, reacted differently. During briefings in advance of the San Francisco Conference, for example, Pasvolsky informed members of the U.S. delegation that reference in the proposal to the promotion of human rights and fundamental freedoms "had caused a great deal of difficulty" during drafting and that this difficulty would likely continue.[84] One of the delegates, Senator Arthur Vandenberg, stated for the record his pleasure in seeing the word "sovereign" in the statement of principles, for it was a matter "dear to our hearts" and would prevent international interference in domestic affairs.[85]

Other countries expressed concern as well. The New Zealand Department of External Affairs worried "that the Chinese will press for formal recognition of the principle of racial equality at the Peace Conference, or before, in the same way as did the Japanese at Versailles."[86] Australia shared this concern; as one official in London wrote, "if 'racial equality' is once written into a basic treaty, it will be easier for China or India in future to challenge the 'White Australia' policy, and an Australian may well see in such an apparently harmless statement of principle the thin edge of a dangerous wedge."[87] The British Foreign Office therefore predicted, correctly, that "the racial equality question will come up again in some form in the postwar settlement."[88]

As feared by some, and as hoped by others, the question of race came up immediately at the San Francisco Conference. The mood and interests of the delegates differed sharply from those of the Americans, British, and Soviets at Dumbarton Oaks. As voiced by Du Bois: "Today as we try in anticipation to rebuild the world, the propositions of Dumbarton Oaks center their efforts upon stopping war by force and at the same time leaving untouched, save by vague implication, the causes of war, especially those causes which lurk in rivalry for power and prestige [and] race dominance." As long as these exist, he declared, "there can be neither peace on earth nor goodwill toward men." Now was the time, argued Du Bois, to shift from the old "for white people only" policies and to recognize that "the day has dawned when above a wounded tired earth unselfish sacrifice, without sin and hell, may join thorough technique, shorn of ruthless greed, and make a new religion, one with new knowledge, to shout from the old hills of heaven: 'Go down, Moses!'"[89] Du Bois and other active observers and participants conveyed an intensity that far surpassed Secretary of State Stettinius's first general expression of the need to work toward "greater freedom and greater opportunity for all peoples of every race and creed and color."[90] They wanted definite changes in international behavior, and said so. In opening speeches to the conference, representatives of India, Haiti, and Uruguay asserted the necessity of realizing the ideals for which so many had suffered and died during the war, particularly the "repudiation of doctrines of racial division and discrimination."[91]

As a first step toward this objective, delegates at the conference began to propose changes regarding human rights in the draft United Nations Charter, starting with the very first chapter. They were by no means satisfied with the vague statements of purpose and stark omissions of the Dumbarton Oaks proposals. The stated purposes of the new organization, they maintained, should go beyond the general ideas of peace and security. Consequently, the representatives of Egypt, India, Panama, Uruguay, Brazil, Mexico, the Dominican Republic, Cuba, and Venezuela, among others, forcefully argued that clear and explicit provisions supporting human rights should be placed in the very beginning of the Charter and perhaps throughout, to replace the relatively meaningless statement buried deep within the text.[92]

Added to these official declarations were those of numerous nongovernmental organizations encouraging their national representatives to take more determined action on human rights. The Council of Christians and Jews in London (composed, in the words of one Foreign Office staff member, of "some heavy backers"[93]) urged that "this essential matter be given prominence" by the British delegation.[94] The group of consultants to the U.S. delegation similarly argued that provisions on human rights represented "a matter of tremendous importance" and therefore should be given "much greater emphasis" in the Charter.[95]

Others joined them in this endeavor, including a relatively large number of U.S. black observers to the conference, like Du Bois and White from the National Association for the Advancement of Colored People, M. W. Johnson from Howard University, and Mary McLeod Bethune from the National Council of Negro Women, and reporters from black newspapers with national circulations, all of whom pressed, in the words of Edgar Brown of the National Negro Council, for "an unequivocal declaration for racial equality" in the Charter.[96] They saw themselves, in their own words, as "aligned with all the colored peoples of the world"[97] and thus maintained enormous interest in the delegations from India, Liberia, Ethiopia, and Haiti, while reserving their greatest scorn for those from the European imperial powers and South Africa.[98] They also gave their support to the Non-European United Committee from South Africa, which declared on behalf of several million blacks, Indians, and groups of mixed color that with extreme racial prejudice all individuals other than white in South Africa "live and suffer under a tyranny very little different from Nazism."[99] They maintained that only the most insensitive could fail to see how ludicrous it would be to speak of a new international order if the world continued to allow apartheid to exist and therefore called upon the delegates at San Francisco to make the Charter specifically opposed to racial discrimination.

These voices—and in many cases, votes—wanted not only articles on human rights but provisions about racial equality and nondiscrimination as well. Fundamental liberties should be guaranteed, in the words of the formal amendment submitted by India, "for all men and women, irrespective of race, color, or creed, in all nations and in all international relations and associations of nations one with another."[100]

The Philippines proposed an amendment declaring the need to establish "racial equality among nations."[101] Others, including Brazil, the Dominican Republic, Mexico, Panama, and (unique among the Europeans) France, actively supported these and similar propositions calling for the prohibition of discrimination on the basis of race.[102] Then, in a move that surprised many delegates when it became public, the Soviet Union joined in support.[103] Given the previous Soviet opposition to human rights at Dumbarton Oaks, the U.S. representatives interpreted this action as being motivated by the politics and diplomacy of the emerging Cold War and as "playing up to the small nations."[104]

Yet it was precisely these non-white, "small nations" that had suffered so much from racial discrimination and been excluded from participation in international deliberations. In the past they had been the victims, the subjects, and the pawns in the chess game of diplomacy, and now they wanted change. This determination surfaced with particular emotion on the issue of colonial territories. Few in the West wanted to discuss the controversial issue of territorial possessions overseas, with its obvious racial dimensions, but at San Francisco it could no longer be ignored. There, China reentered the debate and returned to the point that it had formally raised months before. Arguing against proposals for new trusteeships, the Chinese declared, "Nothing in the Charter should contravene the principle of the equality of all races, and their right to self determination" in the postwar world.[105]

Others from former colonial possessions joined together in asserting that it "was essential that the Conference get away from all ideas of racial superiority and racial inferiority if peace were to be achieved."[106] Iraq argued that racial discrimination constituted a "Nazi philosophy" that had to be "discarded forever" in international relations.[107] General Carlos Romulo of the Philippines reiterated this theme by reminding all the delegates that many different races had fought in World War II together. "This is a victory for the whole world," he declared, "not for one race, one nation, or one leader, but for all men. Before this war broke out, I toured the Asiatic territories and I learned from the leaders and from the people of the flame of hope that swept the Far East when the Atlantic Charter was made known to the world. Everywhere these people asked the questions: Is the Atlantic Charter also for the Pacific? Is it for one side of the world, and not for the other? For one race and not for them too?"[108]

The negotiating power of those states determined to insert provisions on human rights and racial nondiscrimination was, in the words of one astute observer, "considerable," and accounted for the numerous modifications of the Dumbarton Oaks proposals made at San Francisco.[109] As a result of this influence and that of nongovernmental organizations, a number of explicit references and new provisions found inclusion in the Charter. Article 1 listed among the organization's major purposes that of achieving human rights and fundamental freedoms "for all without distinction as to race, sex, language, or religion." Article 13 repeated the same basic provision when discussing the activities of the General Assembly. Similarly, Article 55 spoke of respect "for the principle of equal rights and self-determination of peoples" and the promotion of human rights without discrimination. Articles 62 and 68 reiterated these objectives in terms of the programs of the Economic and Social Council. Finally, Articles 73 and 76, referring to the United Nations trusteeship system, stated that administration of these territories should be regarded as "a sacred trust" where there would be "just treatment" for individuals, "protection against abuses," and respect "for human rights and fundamental freedoms for all without distinction as to race, sex, language, or religion."[110]

Many delegates enthusiastically greeted these provisions and the fact that, for the first time in history, they would appear in a negotiated international document. The delegates prided themselves in obtaining so many references to human rights and nondiscrimination throughout the Charter. They had strongly resisted the attempts made by critics to "eliminate as much repetition as possible" in the "controversial" articles about race, and successfully defended phrases that opponents found "offending."[111] Small nations, minority groups, and colonial subjects also took great pleasure in the fact that instead of speaking of the "high contracting parties" like other international documents, the Charter began with the words, "We the peoples of the United Nations."[112] These proud and pleased advocates soon faced bitter disappointment, however, for the politics and diplomacy of racial discrimination had not yet run its full course.

Although countries might have been willing to consent to the inclusion of words and statements of principle, few were prepared to commit themselves to practical or effective means of implementation. Once again the problem of enforcement provided the greatest obstacle to realizing ideals of human rights in practice. All the proposals that the United Nations be required actively to "safeguard," "protect," "guarantee," "implement," "ensure," "assure," or "enforce" those provisions died a sudden death.[113] Instead, the only verbs that could gain majority acceptance were relatively innocuous ones such as "should facilitate," "assist," "encourage," and "promote."[114] Even then, delegates carefully explained that they did not want these words to assume any greater meaning than they already possessed. As the Costa Rican representative stated with reference to those provisions: "The propagation of ideas and principles whose objectives are these is of immense value to mankind;

but surely if the word 'promote' is understood as implying the ability to coerce states . . . not one of the states concerned will recognize this principle."[115] Human rights and racial nondiscrimination thus foundered, once again, on the rock of national sovereignty.

The difficulty and paradox, of course, stemmed from the fact that governments were being asked to provide active and determined protection against themselves. In matters of human rights, the chief violators are generally governments. Thus, on this matter, the majority of states remained unwilling to sacrifice elements of their sovereignty for the sake of human rights by authorizing the international community to intervene in their own domestic jurisdiction and internal affairs. Many individuals and groups urged leaders of the world to use this unique occasion to advance respect for human beings by changing practices and policies of the past. "We have taught the layman to worship the arch-fiction of the sovereign state," warned international legal scholar Philip C. Jessup before the conference even began, "and thereby have built a Maginot line against the invasion of new ideas in the international world, and behind that rampart the demagogue and the reactionary are enthroned."[116] James T. Shotwell of the Commission to Study the Organization of Peace joined in arguing for a minimum international standard to uphold human rights. "Each state, jealous of its sovereignty, has regarded any expression of foreign interest in the welfare of its citizens at home, as an interference in its own affairs," he stated. "Now as a result of the Second World War, it has become clear that a regime of violence and oppression within any nation of the civilized world is a matter of concern to all the rest."[117] The spokesman of Uruguay similarly asserted that guaranteeing human rights was "the basic problem which this Conference will have to solve."[118]

This problem was not solved, for the delegates at San Francisco remained either unwilling or unable to be convinced. When John Foster Dulles wondered aloud among his U.S. colleagues in the delegation whether the human rights and nondiscrimination provisions might not create difficulties for "the Negro problem in the South,"[119] he was told that the inclusion of a domestic jurisdiction provision would preclude this possibility. When Herbert Evatt, minister for external affairs of Australia, wanted to voice his concern about immigration policy, he received the advice that it would be "embarrassing to India and would provoke an awkward debate in the Conference on the color question," and would be unnecessary as long as the Charter included domestic jurisdiction safeguards.[120] Similarly, when the British worried about the implications of the provisions about human rights and race, their Foreign Office prepared a special memorandum, entitled "World Organization: Racial Equality and Domestic Jurisdiction," which stated that internal policy would be protected by the inclusion of an article regarding domestic jurisdiction.[121] Consequently, the delegates insisted that the United Nations Charter include Article 2, paragraph 7, reading, "Nothing contained in the present Charter shall authorize the United Nations to intervene in matters which are essentially within the domestic jurisdiction of any state or shall require the Members to submit such matters to settlement."[122] In the words of Senator Tom Connally on the U.S. delegation, this article "was sufficient to overpower all other considerations."[123]

The resulting provisions dealing with human rights and racial discrimination in the United Nations Charter evoked a variety of reactions. To many, they marked an unprecedented accomplishment and a culmination of efforts to realize individual dignity in the world. Never before in the annals of diplomacy had those issues been discussed so openly or made such an integral part of a negotiated international agreement. For these reasons, the concluding speeches of many delegates at San Francisco spoke profusely of "one of the great moments in history," of the "welfare of all men," of international justice and equality, and of the cooperation among diverse "races and creeds."[124] To others, those same articles produced either anxiety at having said too much or frustration at having said too little. A number of British officials worried about what all this would mean for restrictive immigration quotas in the Dominions and their own policies in colonial areas.[125] During hearings in Washington, Senator Eugene Millikin asked, "Would the investigation of racial discrimination be within the jurisdiction of this body?" In quick response to this question Senator Vandenberg assured him that the domestic jurisdiction clause would prohibit such an action, would prevent any compulsion or enforcement whatever, and would retain for the various states the right either to accept or reject even recommendations for a change in behavior.[126]

Statements such as these confirmed the worst fears and frustrations of those who, like Du Bois, viewed the results of the United Nations conference as nothing but a compromise between "the national interests, the economic rivalries, and the selfish demands" of the powers. Du Bois argued that the new organization should serve "not only white peoples of English descent, but Latins and Slavs, and the yellow, brown, and black peoples of America, Asia, and Africa." "The proposed Charter," he declared, "should, therefore, make clear and unequivocal the straightforward stand of the civilized world for race equality, and the universal application of the democratic way of life, not simply as philanthropy and justice, but to save human civilization from suicide. What was true of the United States in the past is true of world civilization today—we cannot exist half slave and half free."[127]

Other participants and observers viewed the Charter, including its human rights provisions, neither as a magnificent achievement nor as a horrendous tragedy but rather as a first step toward the future. They considered the practice of politics and diplomacy as the art of the possible and believed that they had accomplished about as much as could be expected, given the circumstances, traditions, and prejudices of the time. "We cannot indeed claim that our work is perfect or that we have created an unbreakable guarantee of peace," said Lord Halifax in a moment of rare candor. "For ours is no enchanted palace to 'spring into sight at once' by magic touch or hidden power."[128] He told the delegates that they had forged an instrument that would work for peace only if nations were ready to make sacrifices for it, and that only time would tell if their efforts rested on shifting sand or solid rock. Smuts, who referred to himself quite accurately as an old veteran of the wars and peace conferences extending over almost a half-century, also emphasized this theme in his comments. "Our Charter is not a perfect document by any means," he admitted. "It is full of compromises over very difficult and tangled problems. But at least it is a good practical, workmanlike plan for peace—a very real and substantial advance on all previous plans for security against war."[129] In his concluding statement before the entire conference, President Harry Truman spoke similarly of the accomplishments as "only a first step." "This Charter, like our Constitution," he said,

> will be expanded and improved as time goes on. No one claims that it is now a final or a perfect instrument. It has not been poured into a fixed mold. Changing world conditions will require readjustments—but they will be readjustments of peace and not of war. . . . The Charter is dedicated to the achievement and observance of human rights and fundamental freedoms. Unless we can attain those objectives for all men and women everywhere—without regard to race, language, or religion—we cannot have permanent peace and security in the world.[130]

What had been achieved, in the words of one delegate, marked "the beginnings of a long and challenging endeavor."[131]

The Beginnings with New Questions

The creation of the Charter of the United Nations did indeed represent the beginnings. It set into motion a whole range of revolutionary changes and practical accomplishments, dashed hopes and callous cynicism, domestic frustrations and international conflicts, jurisdictional disputes and legal controversies, political posturing and diplomatic achievements.

In all of the efforts that followed, the specific issues raised and relative bargaining positions taken at the end of the war would be repeated, refined, reinforced, and in some cases readjusted to fit particular and changing circumstances. In fact, as we shall see, the subject of racial prejudice and human rights quickly became inextricably intertwined with many of the postwar world's most critical and controversial problems. This could be seen immediately with the emergence of a number of serious new questions asked about the politics and diplomacy of racial discrimination in the remaining years of the twentieth century.

One of the most vital questions in this regard centered upon the relative weight that should be given between the letter and the spirit of the Charter and between national and international law. Despite the determined efforts to insert the "domestic jurisdiction" clause in the text of the Charter and the subsequent confident assertions that it would prohibit internal interference, many individuals and groups quickly asserted that the "spirit and purpose" of the Charter imposed important obligations.[132] Even the governments most insistent upon protecting the prerogatives of national sovereignty agreed when pressed that in signing the Charter states assumed certain minimum responsibilities to honor its provisions. The Netherlands explicitly raised this issue by asking the following question: "Does an obligation—at least a moral obligation—result from this Chapter and the Charter as a whole for the states members concerned to eliminate, in the territories under consideration, all discrimination resulting from feelings of racial superiority and to combat such feelings by education and by other adequate means?" The United States representative briefly and tersely responded, "Yes, there is a moral obligation to endeavor to overcome the evils to which you refer."[133]

Others asserted that these provisions constituted solemn, legally binding obligations and not simply statements of public morality. They argued that the Charter, as a legal document, recognized fundamental rights of the individual and thereby for the first time in history transformed individuals from mere objects of international compassion into subjects of international law.[134] India immediately tested this proposition in its long-standing dispute with South Africa, claiming before the United Nations that as a result of discriminatory laws directed against Indians and other Asiatics, the South African government violated the provisions of the Charter regarding human rights. South Africa responded, of course, that its laws were its own business and that the entire matter remained within its own jurisdiction. This defense provoked a sharp reaction by the General Assembly and in particular by the representative of Panama, who asked: "Are human rights essentially within the domestic jurisdiction of the State? My answer is no, and a hundred times no. I submit that by the San Francisco Charter human rights have been taken out of the province of domestic jurisdiction and have been placed within the realm of international law."[135]

These tensions between national and international law occurred not only between states but within them as well. In such cases, aggrieved parties sought to challenge and redress domestic racial discrimination by raising questions about the applicability of the provisions in the Charter. As early as 1945 in Canada, the High Court of Ontario in the *Re Drummond Wren* case dismissed racially restrictive real estate convenants and cited the human rights and fundamental freedoms articles in the United Nations Charter as the reason for doing so.[136] Shortly thereafter, U.S. courts began to hear similar arguments that the nondiscrimination provisions in the Charter required the elimination of segregation and racially discriminatory laws. Within a short time these same cases would face the United States Supreme Court itself.[137]

The Charter also raised fundamental questions about a subject that would directly influence the lives of virtually millions of people around the world: the future nature of colonial empires. How could the members of the United Nations proclaim their support for the principle of racial nondiscrimination, many asked, and at the same time continue to tolerate white domination over much of the globe through imperialism? How could they fight the war for freedom and democracy and then deny self-government to subject peoples? How could they oppose the attitudes of racial superiority proclaimed by the Nazis and yet hold the same opinions toward Asians, Africans, and others within their own empires? How could the Charter speak of equality and at the same time endorse the practice of trusteeships?

These questions, and others like them, helped to provoke tense negotiations whenever any discussions of colonial territories arose at the San Francisco Conference. The issue, as one observer described it in advance, was "loaded with explosive material."[138] The powerful victors had no desire to preside over the demise of their empires or possessions. Britain, France, the Netherlands, Belgium, and South Africa resisted any efforts to interfere in their administration or control over other lands and wished to continue with a League of Nations type of mandate system as they had after World War I. In sharp contrast, China, the Soviet Union, Egypt, and a number of other states pressed to achieve independence for the subject peoples. Somewhere in the middle sat the United States, not wanting to alienate either its European allies or other peoples, while at the same time insisting upon securing important strategic islands that it had just won in the Pacific.[139]

The vast differences of these positions, in the end, brought about an uneasy compromise within the Charter. Article 73 provided the Declaration Regarding Non-Self-Governing Territories, stressing the need for "just treatment" of the inhabitants of these lands and the desire for eventual self-government. The language set no standards, however, and imposed no specific duty of accounting to the General Assembly. Within this context the Charter reiterated in Article 76 the provision "to encourage respect for human rights and fundamental freedoms without distinctions as to race, sex, language, or religion," "to encourage recognition of the interdependence of the peoples of the world," and to ensure "equal treatment" "without prejudice"; but it confined these responsibilities only to members of the United Nations and their nationals and did not specify how even this should be done. Moreover, rather than granting independence to peoples under colonial domination, the Charter established the International Trusteeship System to help oversee whatever changes might take place and declared in Article 77 that it would remain "a matter for subsequent agreement as to which territories . . . will be brought under the trusteeship system and upon what terms."[140] This general and indefinite language raised more questions than it answered, but these questions in turn held the key to the future and would help to launch the beginnings of one of the greatest forces for change in the entire twentieth century: decolonization.

The massive upheaval of World War II unleashed the powerful forces that within a few years would bring about a virtual end to empire.[141] Victory signified that new principles should govern international and interracial relations. The war diminished not only the power but also the self-confidence of Europeans to rule their colonial possessions. In so doing, moreover, it revolutionized the myth of white invincibility and superiority among native peoples. As the African nationalist leader Rev. Ndabaningi Sithole wrote:

> During the war the African came in contact with practically all the peoples of the earth. He met them on a life-and-death basis. He saw the so-called civilized and peaceful and orderly white people mercilessly butchering one another just as his so-called savage ancestors had done in tribal wars. He saw no difference between the primitive and the civilized man. In short, he saw through the European pretensions that only Africans were savages. This had a revolutionary psychological impact upon the African.

But in addition, he continued, World War II taught the African powerful ideas:

> During the war the Allied Powers taught the subject peoples (and millions of them!) that it was not right for Germany to dominate other nations. They taught the subjugated peoples to fight and die for freedom rather

than live and be subjugated by Hitler. Here then is the paradox of history, that the Allied Powers, by effectively liquidating the threat of Nazi domination, set in motion those powerful forces which are now liquidating, with equal effectiveness, European domination in Africa.[142]

With these thoughts in mind and sensing that they stood on the verge of a major turning point in the history of the world, a number of activists eagerly sought to seize the opportunity and bring political pressure upon Western leaders. In June 1945 the Pan-African Federation, Federation of Indian Associations in Britain, West African Students' Union, Ceylon Students' Association, and Burma Association combined their resources and energies to organize the All-Colonial Peoples' Conference to demand independence and an end to racial discrimination.[143] This was soon followed in October by the larger and more influential Fifth Pan-African Congress, meeting in Manchester. As his effective successor, George Padmore, expressed the mood of the delegates to Du Bois: "Living under alien rule, their first manifestation of political consciousness naturally assumes the form of national liberation, self-determination, self-government—call it what you may. They want to be able to rule their own country, free from the fetters of alien domination." Toward this end, he declared, "we would like to break up the French Empire as much as we would like to liquidate the British Empire."[144]

Representatives came from Sierra Leone, Nigeria, Gold Coast, Gambia, Liberia, Uganda, Tanganyika, Nyasaland, Kenya, Union of South Africa, Antigua, Barbados, Bermuda, British Guiana, Jamaica, St. Kitts, St. Lucia, Trinidad, and Tobago, among others. They also came representing a new attitude that revealed the politicizing effect of World War II and the expectations raised by the United Nations Charter. Compared with the bourgeois notables, ministers, and academicians who, with their liberal white friends from Europe in abolitionist or mission societies, had attended the earlier Pan-African congresses, these individuals leaned more toward the left, more toward political activism and trade unions, and more toward taking their destiny into their own hands. From their ranks emerged many like Nkrumah and Kenyatta who became some of the most important leaders of the decolonization movement. They no longer were inclined to ask modestly for some form of recognition or for some slight favor from on high but now were ready to demand independence, respect for human rights, and an end to racial discrimination.[145]

This stronger self-awareness and determination could be seen in the proceedings and resolutions of the congress itself. Individual sessions focused upon racial discrimination and the color bar, imperialism in Africa and the West Indies, oppression under apartheid in South Africa, and the necessity for independence in both Africa and Asia. As one spokesman shouted, "We must be free! We will be free!"[146] The delegates viewed their past and their future as linked to other people similarly victimized by discrimination and sent messages of greetings to Afro-Americans, India, Indonesia, and Indochina. They demanded that the principles of the Atlantic Charter be put into practice around the world and insisted upon "the immediate abolition of all racial and other discriminatory laws at once."[147] Moreover, they agreed to adopt a strategy for organizing their peoples through political parties and trade unions and to engage in a struggle to obtain power. In one of the final resolutions, entitled "The Challenge to the Colonial Powers," they asserted: "The delegates to the Fifth Pan-African Congress believe in peace. . . . Yet if the Western world is still determined to rule mankind by force, then Africans, as a last resort, may have to appeal to force in the effort to achieve Freedom, even if force destroys them and the world." In another, "The Declaration to the Colonial Peoples of the World," the text ended with a slogan reminiscent of the concluding words of the Communist Manifesto: "Colonial and Subject Peoples of the World—Unite!"[148]

Not all people under colonial domination, of course, possessed the patience to wait for the slow deliberations of diplomats at the United Nations or the resolutions of delegates to international congresses. They wanted instead to take matters into their own hands, to exploit the weakness of the European powers after the war, and to seize power by force. Achmed Sukarno led his troops in campaigns against the Dutch in Indonesia to secure independence. Ho Chi Minh battled against the French with his guerrilla forces in Indochina, as did other nationalists in Algeria, Syria, and Lebanon. The British faced armed resistance, terrorism, and rioting against their colonial rule in India, Burma, Malaya, Iraq, Egypt, and Palestine. In each of these struggles, the same question arose: Would decolonization proceed along the gradual and peaceful approach of trusteeship as envisioned by the United Nations Charter, or would it occur with bloodshed and violence between those wanting to retain their empires and those insisting upon ending imperialism and racial discrimination?

The immediate postwar world witnessed these struggles of race not only in the empires but at home as well. Some occurred with particular vehemence in the United States. At the very moment when U.S. delegates in San Francisco proclaimed their support for freedom and opposition to discrimination, Southern Democrats allied with Republicans in Congress to kill by means of a filibuster the Fair Employment Practices Commission. To black ex-servicemen who had returned from a war to defend democracy, such a blow seemed especially vicious. Many were in no mood to live again in a racially segregated society. Within a single year, major race riots broke out at Columbia, Tennessee; Philadelphia; and Chicago. The Ku Klux Klan announced its revival at a meeting in Atlanta; several lynchings occurred in Georgia. In Mississippi Senator Theodore Bilbo declared that the "white primary" election would stay in force forever and that whites should use "any means at their command" to keep blacks away from the polls.[149] Watching all this caused a number of thoughtful Americans to ask whether the era of racial repression that followed World War I would be repeated once more. How could their country fight so fiercely against Nazi doctrines of racial superiority abroad, they questioned, while at the same time blindly tolerating such blatant racial prejudice and discrimination in their own land?[150]

Overseas observers, especially those in Asia, Africa, and the West Indies, also asked these questions about the United States. During the war they had looked to the "arsenal of democracy" and the proclamations of Roosevelt with perhaps exaggerated expectations for a new era of racial toleration. Thus, the apparent return to segregation, public displays of prejudice, and outbreaks of race riots within the United States aroused deep disappointment and bitterness, causing them to ask stinging questions about U.S. hypocrisy. Among the first and most outspoken of these foreign critics was India, whose press steadily began to hammer away with headlines like "Treatment of Negroes a Blot on U.S." and descriptions of discrimination as "shameful manifestations of racial intolerance."[151] Diplomats in the field watched these attacks with alarm and described the attention given to U.S. racial prejudice as an "obsession."[152] When spokespersons from other continents added their voices to this mounting criticism, officials with the Department of State began to ask the important question of whether racial discrimination at home might cause serious postwar problems for U.S. foreign policy abroad.[153]

Even more questions emerged in the wake of two final events in the aftermath of military victory in Europe: the inauguration of the atomic age and the Nuremberg trials, both of which raised the issue of race from still different perspectives. Following their successes against Germany, the United States and the Allies concentrated their efforts on ending the war in the Pacific as soon as possible and thus did not hesitate to drop the first atomic bombs against Hiroshima and Nagasaki. But in so doing, they released the new weapons of mass destruction upon those of a different race. This prompted immediate speculation, with or without facts and even within official circles, about whether Truman and his advisors would have wreaked such terrible devastation upon Caucasians.[154] Subsequent comments by Prime Minister Mackenzie King of Canada that "it is fortunate that the use of the bomb should have been upon the Japanese rather than upon the white races of Europe" only encouraged such speculation even more.[155]

Military victory also provided the opportunity to prosecute publicly the major Nazi war criminals before a tribunal at Nuremberg, which served as the first international attempt to punish premeditated race-related murder. There, the staggering piles of documentary evidence, shocking photographs of the extermination camps, and gruesome films of bulldozers shoving heaps of naked and limp bodies into hastily dug ditches revealed to the world beyond doubt the enormity of the crimes. Up to this point, Nazi atrocities always could be conveniently dismissed or discounted as wartime propaganda too exaggerated to be real. Now, for the first time, they could not, and the words echoed again and again: "Believe the unbelievable!"[156] The testimony and evidence made public by the International Military Tribunal at Nuremberg both allowed and forced the world to peer deep into the abyss of unimagined horror that had claimed the lives of several million human beings in the name of racial superiority. If this happened so recently in the past, people questioned, could it happen again in the future?

*   *   *

These many questions about the politics and diplomacy of racial discrimination burst upon the world in the immediate aftermath of World War II. That conflict and the atrocities that it generated as revealed most dramatically at Nuremberg forced people to examine themselves, their moral values, their attitudes about race, and the consequences of extreme racial prejudice in ways that nothing else had ever been able to do before in history. The signing of the United Nations Charter accelerated this process further, producing what has been called "the start of a revolution in the development of new approaches to human rights issues."[157] That document and the negotiations surrounding it raised serious questions about power and prejudice in the past and, more importantly, deep and troubling questions about directions for the future. In so doing, the questions anticipated and foreshadowed even greater changes to come as the world set out to make its way toward a new beginning.

6
Making a New Beginning

> AND IF WE ACCEPT THE PREMISE—AS WE HOPE the Nations of
> the World do—that peace is indivisible, if we accept that there can
> be no peace as long as the scourge of Nazism exists in any
> corner of the globe, then it follows that the defeat of German
> Nazism is not the final chapter in the struggle against [racial]
> tyranny. There must be many more chapters before the peoples of
> the world will be able to make a new beginning.
> —The Non-European United Committee

The United Nations as the Forum and Focal Point

Those who founded the United Nations understood that the new international organization would play an important role in the politics and diplomacy of the postwar world. The experience of the war, foreign and domestic pressures, and universal hopes for the future persuaded them of the truth of their aspirations. But the precise nature of that role, of course, remained unknown and undefined. The Charter of the United Nations mentioned general principles yet provided few specific guidelines for implementation. Some interpreted this lack of detail as a grand opportunity for activism, avoiding the caution and mistakes of the League of Nations by forging ahead with innovative institutions and instruments to enhance human rights. Others considered the vagueness of language as indicative of nations' desire to discuss general problems but to avoid highly controversial issues and at all costs any interference into the domestic affairs of member states. Both sides agreed that resolution of these very different positions would take time and would depend upon the changing historical circumstances. But few anticipated just how soon that battle would be joined or how quickly the United Nations would become the major forum for debate and the focal point for pressure to eliminate racial discrimination.

The first of many efforts to make this new beginning occurred during the very first session of the United Nations. Encouraged by the principles enunciated in the Charter, acutely aware of the fact that the victors sitting in judgment at Nuremburg were focusing upon racism within Europe rather than toward the non-white world, and firmly determined to raise the question of race before the international community, the Egyptian delegation, with the strong support of all the existing Afro-Asian and most Latin American countries, swiftly introduced a resolution. It condemned racial and religious persecution and called on governments to take prompt and energetic action to end discrimination. Delegates quickly rose to lend their wholehearted support, describing the matter of racial discrimination as a "burning question," a "vital" issue of "immense importance," and as "one of the most important questions which the conscience of this august Assembly must face."[1] Emile Saint-Lot of Haiti passionately spoke of the heavy burden of the recent past and declared:

> It was partly in order to remedy the harmful effects of racial discrimination that the whole world, the civilized world, the world that still attaches a certain value to the human being, to the dignity of the human person, launched a concerted attack on fascism and Nazism. To have got rid of Hitler is not enough. We must also get rid of . . . the exponents of the theory of racialism. . . . We shall, of course, come up against certain tendencies, but we must face them without fear if we genuinely wish to construct peace and a new world based on fresh ideals.[2]

The Indian delegate echoed the same theme by asserting that peace and security must be based "on freedom for all people, on the recognition of human dignity, on the fact that the human soul has the same value whether it is encased in a white, brown, or black body."[3] The force of this principle could hardly be denied, and the assembled delegates, by unanimous vote, passed the resolution condemning racial discrimination.

In politics and diplomacy such unanimity is rare; it can be obtained only in unique circumstances. In the case of this resolution against discrimination, the unanimity was secured because of the horrifying experience of World War II and the fact that the language of the resolution spoke only of a general principle to which all should aspire. The delegates neither singled out a specific country for criticism nor provided any terms for enforcement. Thus, all states believed they could support the resolution. Sharp division immediately replaced this placid unanimous agreement, however, as soon as conditions changed.

Enormously encouraged by this strong support to recognize the international problem of race, for example, India wasted no time before firing the first serious salvo. Since the Indian people had been long humiliated by their experience of racial discrimination from Western imperialism, immigration quotas, and restrictions against their nationals while traveling or living abroad, and since Gandhi had spoken so forcefully and so long about racial equality, they decided to force the issue immediately. Resolutely determined to make the United Nations confront the fact of continuing prejudice and convinced that it possessed a special mission to speak for the oppressed of the world, the Indian government sent a lengthy letter to Secretary General Trygve Lie as early as June 1946. In the letter, they described the history of discrimination to which Indians and others of darker skin color had been subjected on the basis of race, the suffering experienced in the specific case of South Africa, and the need to bring practices into conformity with principles stated in the Charter. In an effort to make a new beginning by recognizing and then correcting the problem, they formally filed a complaint against South Africa and its treatment of people of Indian origin. This move, as they knew it would, once again placed the issue of race directly on the agenda of the United Nations during its very first session.[4]

To launch this debate, the Indian government sent Vijaya Lakshmi Pandit, the intense and articulate sister of nationalist leader Jawaharlal Nehru. She opened her comments by describing the General Assembly as "unique in the annals of history" and reminding the delegates of their special responsibilities under the Charter. They might consider that the immediate question before them involved only South Africa and its Ghetto Act, which placed those of Indian origin under restrictions in business and prohibitions from living in white areas, but the delegates should remember that the larger and more significant problem was clearly that of racial prejudice. "The issue we have brought before you is by no means a narrow or local one," she declared, insisting that discrimination on the basis of race represented not only a widespread phenomenon but also one "totally inconsistent with the objectives and purposes of the United Nations and its Charter."[5] After throwing down the gauntlet with this speech, she stepped away from the podium and waited for the assembled delegates to respond.

This subject possessed explosive ramifications for politics and diplomacy at many levels, and Western members of the General Assembly in particular wanted to move very carefully indeed. They decided that no single existing committee could handle this difficult problem and therefore assigned it to a special joint body composed of the First (Political and Security) and Sixth (Legal) committees. They also decided that they needed time to consider their positions; hence, debate did not begin for nearly one month. But when it started, it began with force and passion.

Pandit rose again and accused South Africa of grossly violating the Charter's fundamental principles regarding human rights by the country's practices of racial discrimination. This case, she stressed, was not a question that concerned only two countries, but one with potential consequences for the entire world. To solve this problem, she declared, the members of the United Nations would have to exercise their collective wisdom and "employ their moral sanction in the interests of justice."[6] The grand old man himself, Jan Smuts of South Africa, immediately rose to respond to these charges. He claimed that the exploitation of domestic issues by other states as a political weapon presented a dangerous development, arguing that "such foreign propaganda in alleged minority interests" would greatly threaten global peace and security. He reminded his fellow delegates that Article 2, paragraph 7, of the Charter explicitly and deliberately stated that within the domain of its own domestic affairs, a state was not subject to interference or control by any others. His government, like that of India, did agree that this issue held enormous consequences for the future, but he argued from an entirely different point of view. The determination of whether or not this question and others like it fell within the domestic jurisdiction of any state, Smuts concluded, was "of the gravest importance."[7]

All sides of the debate recognized that a critical precedent would be set in this case arising out of racial discrimination. Within the joint committee a number of other states rallied behind India's position, including China, Czechoslovakia, Egypt, Ethiopia, Guatemala, Haiti, Honduras, Iran, Mexico, the Philippines, Poland, the various Soviet-controlled states, Uruguay, Venezuela, and Yugoslavia. Their representatives described the issue before them as one with political, international, domestic, and ethical dimensions of the first magnitude and referred to the fact that they had just fought against the racial extremism of Hitlerism and fascism. As Wellington Koo of China stated, they all recognized that this issue arose because of abhorrent practices based "entirely on the principle of discrimination according to race and color."[8] Those who supported the South African position (the major white states: Britain, Australia, Canada, and the United States, as well as the Netherlands), in contrast, moved reluctantly into the discussion and confined their statements largely to legal considerations. None even attempted to deny the existence of racial discrimination in South Africa, but their delegates restricted their arguments instead to the question of whether the United Nations legally had jurisdictional authority to act on this case. Sir Hartley Shawcross of Britain suggested aloud that if the organization could interfere in the domestic affairs of South Africa, it also might do the same regarding the internal laws of any country, thus creating a most dangerous precedent.[9]

This debate burst out with even greater fury when it reached the General Assembly as a whole. With fire in her voice, Pandit dismissed the legal argument about domestic jurisdiction as "late in the day and far-fetched" and as one that made a mockery of the Charter's professions about a world free from the inequalities of race. "Millions of voiceless people," she argued, "who, because of their creed or color, have been relegated to positions of inferiority, are looking to us for justice, and it is only on the foundation of justice that we can create a new world order. . . . We must remember that, in the present case, the minds of millions of people in India and in other parts of Asia and Africa have been moved to intense indignation at all forms of racial discrimination which stand focused on the problem of South Africa. This is a test case."[10]

Others saw it in exactly the same light and eagerly threw themselves into the fray. Koo of China argued that all Asiatics held great interest in this case, believing that racial discrimination no longer could be allowed to exist in the world. The Mexican delegate strongly supported this argument and described it as raising "one of the most important questions of our time," whereas Carlos Romulo of the Philippines called it "a moral question of the first magnitude" that could be ignored only at great risk.[11] Poland's representative similarly attacked racial discrimination as being solely "based on a factor over which no human being has any control: the color of the skin" and as the source of critical international controversy. "Can this Assembly," he asked, "remain indifferent when so fundamental a problem is involved?"[12] Ricardo Alfaro of Panama practically shouted that he would never consider human rights as the exclusive prerogative of individual states, claiming that the Charter gave birth to the new principle that individuals as well as states were subjects of international law. To fail to enforce the Charter, he argued with equal passion, would turn the provisions on nondiscrimination into "eloquent words," "a convenient lie," and "beautiful literary bauble" that "might as well be scratched out, erased, and suppressed."[13]

The opponents did not take this criticism passively and struck back with anger. Smuts, who long before had personally and directly clashed with Gandhi over the issue of racial prejudice, objected to the whole debate as being outrageous and vehemently protested this interference into South Africa's domestic affairs. He lashed out at the South African Indians who had come to New York to advise the Indian delegation and bitterly described the General Assembly as a "mere political forum" of speech makers rather than a body of rational statesmen.[14] Shawcross attacked the previous speeches as being no more than "brilliant appeals to our emotions by practiced political orators." He charged India with hypocrisy, for although India pointed out South African racial discrimination for all the world to see, it conveniently ignored its own caste system. Shawcross then accused those who supported the Indian position of only claiming to want justice but in reality seeking "an emotional political verdict swayed by eloquence and oratory."[15] The debate became so heated, in fact, that the president of the session actually had to stop and remind the delegates of the need "to restore a little serenity to the discussion. I would ask you to be very prudent," he said, " . . . for the question is really delicate and has many subtleties."[16]

After momentarily exhausting itself in debate, the Assembly finally decided to move toward a vote. The resolution recognized that racial discrimination had impaired the relations between two member states, expressed the opinion that the treatment of Indians in South Africa be in conformity with international obligations, and called upon the Indian and South African governments to discuss their problems and report back to the General Assembly. It contained no binding provisions for enforcement.[17] The supporters of the resolution therefore claimed that the terms were so meek and mild that no one possibly could object, but the opponents described it as blatant interference into domestic affairs. When the delegates could say no more, they cast their votes and eagerly awaited the results.

The resolution just barely passed with the necessary two-thirds majority. Thirty-two members supported India, while fifteen sided with South African and seven abstained. Voting with the majority were all the states from Africa, Asia, and the Middle East that had experienced the effects of racial discrimination from the West (Afghanistan, China, Egypt, Ethiopia, India, Iran, Iraq, Lebanon, Liberia, the Philippines, Saudi Arabia, and Syria), all the Communist countries (Belorussia, Czechoslovakia, Poland, the Ukraine, the Soviet Union, and Yugoslavia), many Latin American states (Chile, Colombia, Cuba, Dominican Republic, Guatemala, Haiti, Honduras, Mexico, Panama, Uruguay, and Venezuela), and an extremely small scattering of nations from Europe (France, Iceland, and Norway). Voting with the minority were Britain and the white Commonwealth (Canada, New Zealand, and the Union of South Africa), the traditional friends of South Africa in Europe (the Netherlands, Belgium, Luxembourg, and Greece), the United States, and several Latin American countries (Argentina, Costa Rica, El Salvador, Nicaragua, Paraguay, and Peru). Rebuffed by this loss, Smuts returned home and bitterly complained that the United Nations was becoming dominated by the colored peoples of the world.[18]

This resolution, in addition to the one immediately preceding it that condemned racial discrimination in principle, did indeed appear to mark the way toward a new beginning. Never before in the history of diplomacy had any international body or gathering of official representatives so openly and directly confronted the issue of race. As the editor of the *Crisis* observed, these discussions were "far ahead of Versailles when President Wilson and the British would not even permit race to be discussed formally even in a committee meeting."[19] In acting as the forum and focal point for these two precedent-setting cases, the United Nations revealed that it was willing to wrestle with the global problem of racial discrimination. Yet, in doing so, it also demonstrated during the very first year of its existence a distinct pattern that would be followed time after time in the subsequent politics and diplomacy of discrimination. For non-white, non-Western nations that had suffered from attitudes and policies of racial prejudice, race represented a burning issue of critical importance that they would raise on every possible occasion. These states demonstrated that they were prepared to make antiracism rather than racism the prevailing ideology of the postwar world. In this endeavor, they would receive Communist support and would increasingly focus attention upon South Africa. Representatives from the white West, who found it difficult to comprehend the intensity of feeling about this subject and who would tolerate and even support antiracism resolutions as long as delegates confined themselves to general principles, refrained from attacking the discriminatory practices of specific states and restricted their behavior to words rather than acts of enforcement that might interfere with domestic jurisdiction. To many observers, it seemed as though the United Nations represented a microcosm of the world as a whole, with international relations to a very large degree determined by interracial relations.

It is not surprising, therefore, that those who wanted to eliminate racial discrimination in their own countries would turn to the United Nations for assistance. The principles enunciated in the Charter, which all member states had signed, and especially the determination of the majority in the General Assembly to discuss the issue of race generated enormous hope among those seeking change. This body seemed much more courageous and willing to confront violations of human rights than had the League of Nations before it. Moreover, many U.S. blacks asked in pointed and eager anticipation: If the United Nations could focus attention on discrimination in South Africa, might it not also look at racial segregation in the United States?

With precisely this question in mind, the indefatigable Du Bois, now almost eighty years old, set about to petition the United Nations on behalf of U.S. blacks. Working through the offices of the National Association for the Advancement of Colored People, he supervised the writing of a remarkable 155-page report describing the long history of racial discrimination within the United States, the denial of basic legal rights to blacks solely on the basis of their skin color, and the obligations regarding human rights incumbent upon all members of the United Nations under the Charter. News of this explosive document began to leak out, causing NAACP Executive Secretary Walter White to write privately that newspapermen "from all over the world" were requesting advance copies of the petition and maintaining that "the matter cannot be kept secret, so great is the interest."[20] Du Bois, of course, did not want secrecy or quiet diplomacy. Indeed, when he formally presented the petition to the United Nations in October 1947, he did so in the full light of publicity and media coverage. He entitled the petition "An Appeal to the World: A Statement on the Denial of Human Rights to Minorities in the Case of Citizens of Negro Descent in the United States of America and An Appeal to the United Nations for Redress."[21] In his public statement accompanying this document Du Bois declared that he spoke on behalf of fourteen million black U.S. citizens and asserted:

> This protest, which is open and articulate, and not designed for confidential concealment in your archives, is a frank and earnest appeal to the world for elemental Justice against the treatment which the United States has visited upon us for three centuries. . . . It is to induce the nations of the world to persuade this nation to be just to its own people that we have prepared and now present to you this document. . . . We hand you this documented statement of grievances, and we firmly believe that the situation pictured here is as much your concern as ours.[22]

This petition threw fuel on the fire. Journalists from around the world, sensing that they were witnessing an extremely important event, provided widespread publicity.[23] The delegates anxious to press the issue of race in an international forum, especially from the Afro-Asian group, immediately took it up as their own, offering to provide whatever official assistance might be necessary to pursue the case further.[24] Moreover, and of particular significance for the politics and diplomacy of discrimination in the emerging Cold War, as we shall see, the Communist countries eagerly seized upon it as a source of great embarrassment to the United States that could be exploited to enormous advantage.[25]

In its own assessment of the petition, the National Association for the Advancement of Colored People thus correctly could claim that "this question then, which is without doubt primarily an internal and national question, becomes inevitably an international question, and will in the future become more and more international." The authors described their work as giving hope "to oppressed Africans and colored people throughout the world" and thereby were sure of the work's having "ramifications of universal breadth. Without doubt," they continued with conviction, "the publicity it has commanded, the significant questions the petition raises, and the dynamic problem of racial discrimination with which it deals are sure to motivate some sort of alleviating action on the part of the United Nations and its member governments. The eyes and ears of the chancelleries of the world will be focused and attuned to this petition." "For depending upon what stand the United Nations takes in this appeal," concluded the assessment with considerable insight, "will be determined, in part, the policy to be followed and the measures to be adopted by the colonial powers in their future relations with their wards, and the procedures to be put into practice by countries who practice some form of discrimination. While on the part of the submerged and underprivileged groups, it is likely to inspire and stimulate them to carry their cases directly to the world body in the hope of redress."[26]

In so many different ways, this petition provided a dramatic focal point for demonstrating that the problem of race had become inextricably intertwined with some of the most complicated international issues of the remaining twentieth century. These included the ability of private individuals or groups to challenge their own governments before the world, the limits of domestic jurisdiction, the political and diplomatic consequences of continued racial discrimination, the policies of white colonial powers toward dependent colored peoples, the process of decolonization and emergence of new power blocs in Africa and Asia, the Cold War rivalry between the United States and the Soviet Union, the value placed upon basic human rights by governments and the international community, and the role and authority of the United Nations itself. As both proponents and opponents of the petition alike thus recognized, interracial relations had become an integral part of international relations. Well aware of exactly this fact and its enormous and sensitive complications, officials of the United Nations were not at all eager to receive the petition. On the one hand they could not ignore it, and on the other they could not touch it without the approval of member governments, especially the powerful United States against which it was directed. As one participant observed, United Nations officials simply were "afraid of the document."[27] In order to avoid any direct confrontations, they decided to accept the petition graciously in public and then quickly divert it to the new Commission on Human Rights.

Setting Standards for Human Rights

The Charter of the United Nations largely reflected the powerful Western nations' ideas and priorities regarding peace and security. Provisions dealing with human rights, as we have seen, had not been a part of the original plans for the postwar organization but had been added due to the pressure of other governments and private nongovernmental organizations wanting to eliminate racial discrimination. Once the United Nations began to meet, it became apparent that this concern would not fade away but, to the contrary, grow in intensity. Early indications of complaints by one government against another for its policies toward race, exposure of domestic discrimination before the forum of world opinion, passionate debates on the prejudice relating to skin color, a growing awareness of how many international issues were being affected by racial considerations, and a heightened concern about human rights in general all confirmed this development even further. Consequently, the United Nations had to decide quickly how it proposed to handle these problems of swelling proportions. In 1946, therefore, the secretary general established a Division of Human Rights within the Secretariat, and the Economic and Social Council during its first meeting appointed nine individuals to study this matter and make recommendations concerning the composition and mandate for a special permanent body to be called the Commission on Human Rights.[28]

This "nuclear," or preparatory commission, charged with making recommendations, immediately and by acclamation elected as its chairperson Eleanor Roosevelt, former First Lady of the United States and already described as "the most important person in the United Nations human rights program."[29] With intelligence, compassion, graciousness, and a long-standing interest in the needs of the racially oppressed, she set about to accomplish the assignment with the manner of a schoolmarm. Her enormous popularity and prestige attracted even greater attention to the work of the Commission as it planned for the future. Private citizens wrote her letters pleading for assistance[30] and publicists rushed into the debates by writing articles designed to express their own opinions regarding what should be done.[31] Governments represented on the preparatory commission actively campaigned for their own positions,[32] and those not serving worried about the consequences of having no voice. With Britain being among the latter, the Foreign Office confidentially expressed the opinion that "the work of this commission may be of considerable importance, and that many subjects of particular concern to this country, in particular subjects such as the rights of colonial peoples, may be raised." The absence of a British representative, while at the same time the inclusion of one from India, the Foreign Office worried, "might prove a serious disadvantage."[33] It also wanted to make sure that "controversial subjects such as racial discrimination . . . figure low on the list."[34]

Inspired by its charge to be "at the starting point of a very great enterprise" by making recommendations for the promotion of global human rights, the preparatory commission decided to pursue ambitious goals.[35] Eleanor Roosevelt publicly stated in advance that she knew some people and governments would not like the results. "Sometimes issues arise," she said with courage, "where one has to advocate something that it may be difficult for one's own government to carry through, and yet, if one believes it is right, I think one should advocate it, hoping that if it would be good for the world, it would, therefore, in the end, be good for one's own government and one's own people too."[36] Toward this end, she and the committee recommended, among other suggestions, that the permanent Commission on Human Rights be composed of individual experts rather than representatives of governments so that it might acquire greater independence and integrity, and that the commission actively aid the Security Council by pointing to cases where violations of human rights constituted a threat to the peace.[37]

These ambitious proposals met quick resistance when submitted to the Economic and Social Council as a whole. Many governments considered them too extensive and too threatening to their foreign policies and domestic jurisdiction and set about to use politics and diplomacy to modify them. Within just a few days, one diplomat could observe, "these proposals are at this moment being considerably watered down by the Council."[38] The British delegate received instructions in cypher from the Foreign Office to be very careful about this "extremely delicate" subject with enormous political implications, but "not to give the impression that we are being obstructive. We suggest our right course is to play for time, leaving it as far as possible to other delegations to bring out the difficulties."[39] In this regard, the Soviet delegate certainly obliged by leading the fight against members serving as individuals in favor of instructed representatives from governments.[40] When the dust finally settled, members of the Economic and Social Council decided that they desperately needed to establish a permanent Commission on Human Rights, and did so. Fearing excessive independence, however, the Council determined that the Commission should be composed of eighteen members serving as state-appointed representatives of their own respective governments. The work of this Commission, the Council resolved, should be directed toward submitting proposals, recommendations, and reports to the Council regarding "the protection of minorities, the prevention of discrimination on grounds of race, sex, language, or religion," declarations or conventions on related matters, and an international bill of human rights.[41]

Heartened by this wide-ranging mandate to break new ground in the international arena, despite its several limitations on independence and action, the Commission on Human Rights held its first meeting in January 1947. It unanimously elected Eleanor Roosevelt as chair and did so again for six sessions, a United Nations record. Other members of considerable stature joined her, including René Cassin, who had served as vice president of the French Conseil d'Etat and later as the president of the European Court of Human Rights, Charles Malik from Lebanon, Carlos Romulo of the Philippines, C. P. Chang from China, Hansa Mehta from India, and Charles Dukes from Britain. All were acutely aware of the political and diplomatic realities confronting them, however, and therefore deliberately determined to invest their time where they could and where they believed it would do the most immediate good. For this reason, they agreed during their first session not to touch the sensitive areas of investigations of alleged violations of human rights or to take action on individual complaints and petitions against member states. Instead, they decided, among other things, to create a special Sub-Commission on Prevention of Discrimination and Protection of Minorities and to prepare a preliminary draft for an international bill of human rights that would serve as a basis for further steps on the road toward a new beginning.[42]

The idea of some kind of an international bill of human rights, of course, had been discussed in diplomatic circles since the middle of World War II.[43] In his closing address to the San Francisco Conference, President Harry Truman himself had suggested that once the Commission became established, it should give first priority to drafting such a document. "That bill of rights," he declared, would "be as much a part of international life as our own bill of rights is a part of our Constitution."[44] Other governments, organizations, and private individuals took up the call as well, suggesting specific language, proposing certain concepts, and even submitting complete draft texts. Some came from Cuba and Panama, others from Britain, and still others from the American Law Institute, American Association for the United Nations, American Jewish Congress, American Bar Association, Inter-American Juridical Committee, Pan American Union, and the Institut de Droit International.[45] These many proposals and the force with which they were promoted generated a momentum and a pressure that could not be ignored. Thus, when the Commission sat down to draft an international bill of human rights, it did so knowing that its work would be carefully watched.

In the drafting committee of the Commission it quickly became apparent that politics and diplomacy would continue to determine the course of events. Eleanor Roosevelt desperately, and somewhat naively, wanted to produce a document without delay. But she found herself constantly confronted with the posturings of governments, including her own, and what one participant called "the deep incompatibilities" of ideological orientation.[46] Asian and Latin American members, for example, advocated a bill of rights that provided for maximum goals that all states would strive to attain. Western members like the United States and Britain, however, favored a bill that imposed minimum enforceable standards. The West stressed the importance of individual political and civil liberties such as freedom of expression, association, religion, and due process of law. The Eastern bloc, in contrast, gave priority to economic and social rights such as opportunities for employment, education, health care, and social security. Proponents of individual property rights clashed with those affirming the needs of the larger community. The powers administering trust territories objected to attempts by others to add the right of collective self-determination to guarantees of individual rights. Non-white nations, with the support of Communist countries, advocated group rights for racial minorities beyond the general principles of nondiscrimination.[47]

While trying to cut a path through this thicket of conflicting opinion, Eleanor Roosevelt suddenly received unwelcome instructions from her government. Deeply conscious of determined southern resistance to anything that might interfere with racial policies, the Department of State decided that it wanted a general declaration of principle on human rights rather than any kind of binding international convention with legal force. The United States, she reluctantly had to report to her colleagues on the Commission, "does not feel that anything resembling a generally acceptable convention can be produced at this session. For the U.S. this is necessary among other reasons because it is governed partly by federal law and partly by the laws of its constituent states. . . . My government feels on far safer ground working on the declaration than on the convention."[48] This statement, complained one delegate, was made "without any previous warning" and created a "deplorable impression."[49]

Strangely enough, and for very different reasons, the Americans found themselves supported by the Soviets, who also saw in the idea of a declaration a way to support a principle while at the same time protecting domestic jurisdiction and their own activities in Eastern Europe from outside interference. "The Committee," warned Vladimir Koretsky, "might be embarking on a voyage which would lead it in a direction where it might cross the border which divides international from internal law— the border which divides the inter-relationships of governments from the field where the sovereign rights of nations must prevail."[50] With both the Americans and the Soviets uniquely on the same side of a human rights issue, little else could be done. The drafting committee therefore sent to the Commission on Human Rights a proposed text for a universal declaration.

This draft declaration directly presented a test of conviction. It challenged the Commission on Human Rights, Sub-Commission on Prevention of Discrimination, the Economic and Social Council, Third Committee (Social, Cultural, and Humanitarian Questions), General Assembly, the Secretariat of the United Nations, interested individuals and private organizations, and literally all governments to determine what they were both willing and able to do for human rights. Each had to wrestle with how to respond to a proposal that John Humphrey, the first director of the United Nations Division of Human Rights, described as "revolutionary in character." As he saw it, "There has never been a more revolutionary development in the theory and practice of international law and organization than the recognition that human rights are matters of international concern."[51] When Du Bois submitted his petition on behalf of U.S. blacks suffering from racial discrimination into this setting,[52] members of the international community realized that they were poised on the verge of extremely important decisions. Although they might be able to divert a single petition by burying it in committee, they could not do so with the draft declaration, which had captured the headlines of the world, produced staggering expectations, and now demanded a response.

Many governments therefore found themselves having to devote enormous time and energy to studying carefully the draft language and considering both its domestic and its foreign implications. They exchanged views with each other, asked for different opinions, often received unsolicited proposals from private citizens and organizations, lobbied for drafts of their own, and as always, carefully calculated what could be accomplished in what was called the realm of "practical politics" at home and "the international political situation" abroad.[53] They found themselves constantly caught between the activists who wanted to initiate immediately a revolutionary program for the international protection of human rights and those who insisted upon maintaining all the traditional prerogatives of national sovereignty, and they wondered whether a declaration would have great moral and legal force or whether it would be merely "a basis for propaganda and controversy" or "eyewash."[54] This split became particularly acute in the cases of the British and Americans, both of whom created elaborate interdepartmental committees in an attempt to resolve at least internal differences.[55]

Once negotiated at the national level, proposals were directed to the General Assembly's Third Committee, which alone considered 168 separate amendments in more than eighty different meetings.[56] As one diplomat reported back to his government, all countries wanted to do something for human rights but at the same time to protect domestic jurisdiction and "their own particular sacred cows."[57] In the end, the

General Assembly, meeting in Paris during December 1948, agreed by a vote of forty-eight to zero, with eight abstentions (including South Africa), to work toward a covenant of binding obligations in the future but at the moment to state principles and set standards for all peoples in the Universal Declaration of Human Rights.

A considerable number of the articles in the Declaration focused upon race. Racial discrimination not only had served as the initial and primary source of international concern over human rights but also continued to do so while the memory of the Nazi Holocaust remained vivid.[58] Just a day earlier, as we shall see, members of the General Assembly had approved the Convention on the Prevention and Punishment of the Crime of Genocide, voicing their deep concern about the implications of racial intolerance and persecution.[59] They wanted to emphasize the same point again in the Declaration by placing it within a larger context and stressing their belief that an intimate connection existed between the protection of human rights and peace. The Declaration therefore began with a preamble recognizing before everything else "the equal and inalienable rights of all members of the human family." This equality, Article 2 asserted, must be maintained "without distinction of any kind, such as race, color, sex, language, religion, political or other opinion, national or social origin, property, birth, or other status." Due to pressure from former colonial peoples, the declaration went on to maintain that these rights must be extended to those in non-self-governing territories; that slavery and the slave trade in all their forms be prohibited; and that the political, civil, economic, social, and cultural rights clearly delineated in the text be given "equal protection against any discrimination." Such provisions, declared the General Assembly, established "a common standard of achievement for all peoples and all nations."[60]

This Universal Declaration of Human Rights, as might be expected, produced a wide variety of reactions. To the hopeful, it represented, in the words of René Cassin of France, "the first international document of ethical value" and one certain to "open a new era for humanity."[61] Hernan Santa Cruz of Chile hailed the Declaration as "of exceptional importance" as a "safeguard for all human beings," while Charles Malik of Lebanon praised it as "destined to mark an important stage in the history of mankind."[62] Other delegates also joined their voices to this chorus, like Belarmino de Athayde of Brazil, who described it as "a remarkable achievement" and Mohammed Khan of Pakistan, who declared it to mark "an epoch-making event."[63] Eleanor Roosevelt, who had done so much to guide the Declaration through so many committees, admitted that it was not a perfect document but one that nevertheless "may well become the international Magna Charta of all men everywhere. We stand today," she declared, at the threshold of a great event both in the life of the United Nations and in the life of mankind. . . . At a time when there are so many issues on which we find it difficult to reach a common basis of agreement, it is a significant fact that . . . [so many] states have found such a large measure of agreement in the complex field of human rights. This must be taken as testimony of our common aspirations first voiced in the Charter. . . . The realization that the flagrant violation of human rights by Nazi and Fascist countries sowed the seeds of the last world war has supplied the impetus for the work which brings us to the moment of achievement here today.[64]

Critics viewed the Declaration from sharply different perspectives. All the Communist countries that had worked so hard in committee to prevent its provisions from restricting the power of states over their citizens now found it useful for propaganda in public to criticize the Declaration for not doing enough. Zdenek Augenthaler of Czechoslovakia, for example, complained that it was "vague," while the delegate from Belorussia lamented over its "many gaps" and "deficiencies."[65] Juliusz Katz-Suchy of Poland went as far as to accuse it of being "a step backward" in the movement for human rights.[66] At times, Andrei Vyshinsky of the Soviet Union criticized the declaration for possessing "serious defects" in the absence of implementation provisions, although at other times he complained that it went too far by threatening national sovereignty.[67] In the Soviet Union, *Izvestiia* described the document as "extremely abstract" and "adorned with the flowers of luxuriant phraseology."[68] South Africa, in contrast, vehemently condemned the Declaration as going "far beyond" the rights contemplated by the Charter and thereby interfering with the domestic jurisdiction of member states.[69] Private citizens similarly criticized it for either doing too much or too little.[70]

The Universal Declaration of Human Rights, to the great surprise of many cynics and the critics who complained that little had been accomplished,[71] quickly assumed an unprecedented status and influence. Despite all the efforts made during the negotiations to emphasize the difference between a declaration on the one hand and a binding treaty on the other, the standard-setting nature of the Declaration rapidly took on a life of its own. Governments, by publicly supporting the Declaration's enumerated standards of conduct through their official speeches and votes in an international forum, found themselves making a major contribution to the customary law of nations, whether they intended to do so or not. Their endorsement of the Declaration provided an authoritative interpretation of the Charter, establishing the criteria for judging the conduct of states in their relations with individuals. Many observers correctly described this development as "revolutionary,"[72] and one declared directly, "You are now witnessing, whether you know it or not, the birth of a new concept in the field of law and government."[73]

Sensing this dramatic change, governments and private citizens alike began to invoke the Declaration in challenging existing practices and in creating new laws, thereby endowing it with growing moral, political, and even legal force. It came to inspire a whole series of additional resolutions, binding covenants, international treaties, and even national legislation and judicial decisions designed to combat racial discrimination and other violations of human rights. Within just the first three years of its existence, for example, the Declaration provided not only the inspiration but in many cases the specific language for the terms of the European Convention for the Protection of Human Rights; the Inter-American Declaration on Human Rights; the peace treaty with Japan; the constitutions of Indonesia, Libya, Jordan, and Puerto Rico; and court opinions in the United States, Austria, Belgium, the Philippines, and the International Court of Justice.[74] Through time, innumerable other examples were added to the list. For all these reasons, the Universal Declaration of Human Rights is still described by many observers as "the greatest achievement of the United Nations."[75]

Preventing and Punishing Genocide

The success of all these early efforts to use the United Nations as an international forum and focal point greatly pleased those who desired to combat racial discrimination. The ground-breaking resolution condemning practices that discriminated on the basis of race, the attack against South Africa and its racial policies, the public attention given to the petition from the National Association for the Advancement of Colored People, the Commission on Human Rights and its Sub-Commission on Prevention of Discrimination, and the Universal Declaration of Human Rights all produced a justifiable sense of accomplishment among the majority of states. Far from being satisfied with these many gains that stood in such sharp contrast with past diplomatic practice, however, these states wanted to make their opposition to racial discrimination unequivocally clear and use the momentum to push even further. They therefore sent requests to the Secretariat to prepare a detailed study on the main types and causes of discrimination, and to the United Nations Educational, Scientific, and Cultural Organization (UNESCO) to undertake a program to disseminate scientific facts about race to the world.[76] Even more importantly, they wanted to focus both attention and action on the agonizing subject up to that time considered beyond reach: genocide.

Horrifying brutality and the systematic extermination of millions of innocent human beings during World War II revealed to a heretofore silent and complacent world the extremes that could be reached in the name of unbridled racial superiority. The torture and slaughter of masses of people due to their presumed racial characteristics produced emotional shock, agony, and moral outrage of unimagined proportions among the survivors, who vowed that they would do whatever they could to assure that these things would never be allowed to happen again. Their resolve was strengthened with the release of extraordinarily gruesome evidence from the International Military Tribunal at Nuremburg, which conclusively demonstrated the extent of a deliberate policy to apply the "Final Solution" and exterminate entire populations in a genocidal war. In an effort to prevent and punish any possible recurrence, they approached the international community.

As soon as the United Nations began its sessions, Cuba, India, and Panama called upon the governments of the world to place genocide, "race murder," on the international agenda.[77] Once again, non-white nations initiated the discussion and led the attack. They and their allies observed that genocide had existed for many centuries but that its extreme nature during the recent war demonstrated a great danger to global peace and security that simply could not be ignored. "The monstrous wickedness of the crimes committed by the Nazi and other regimes against the races they considered inferior," said one diplomat, "testifies to the gravity of the situation."[78] Citing the judgments of the Nuremburg trials, the majority of members of the Sixth Committee (Legal Questions) of the General Assembly sought to declare genocide a crime and make it subject to punishment under international law. Toward this end, they submitted a proposed resolution to the General Assembly as a whole.

The international revulsion against genocide was so strong that the General Assembly wasted little time in debate. Moreover, no government wanted to give even the slightest appearance of condoning or being sympathetic to mass extermination based upon prejudice. Consequently, member states quickly approved an important resolution affirming "that genocide is a crime under international law which the civilized world condemns, and for the commission of which principals and accomplices— whether private individuals, public officials, or statesmen, and whether the crime is committed on religious, racial, political, or any other grounds—are punishable."[79] They then went on to invite all countries to enact the necessary national legislation for the prevention and punishment of this crime. In addition, they requested that the Economic and Social Council take the next step by carefully drafting an actual convention against genocide that, after submission to individual states for ratification, would be legally binding upon all signatories.

During the course of the next two years, the Economic and Social Council, its special Ad Hoc Committee on Genocide, the Sixth Committee, and the Committee on the Codification of International Law invested great energy in producing a draft convention. Their efforts once again revealed the relative ease with which a declaration or resolution of principle could be passed and the contrasting difficulty of trying to obtain agreement upon a legally binding convention. Some states actively worked to secure a meaningful text, whereas others reluctantly participated in debate, choosing instead to submit numerous amendments to delay the proceedings.[80] Still others either overtly or covertly attempted to halt the process altogether, believing that the process was either a waste of valuable time that could produce only pious statements or a threat to domestic jurisdiction. From the very beginning, for example, the British considered the effort as "useless" at best and dangerous at worst.[81] "Our course of conduct," concluded the Foreign Office in private, "should be governed by the desirability of getting the whole idea of having a convention on genocide dropped. If we cannot succeed in this . . . then all we can do is to aim at spinning out matters in such a way that nothing ever happens."[82]

The governments that supported the draft convention on genocide would not be put off or allow themselves to be distracted by such tactics. With near obsession, they wanted to mobilize the conscience of the world and to outlaw the intentional destruction of any racial or other kind of minority group. They persistently worked to persuade others about the necessity of eliminating what they described as a "scourge" upon humanity, "inhuman and diabolical" extermination, the "crime of crimes," and "the most odious crime that could be committed against the human race."[83] After great effort, a majority of states succeeded in bringing a draft convention out of committee and before the General Assembly in the glaring light of global publicity. In this setting, governments demonstrated a marked reluctance to engage in tactics designed to delay or obstruct. The British Foreign Office, for example, realized that the subject of genocide now had become of "considerable political importance" and reluctantly concluded that even in abstaining from voting "we shall find ourselves in a minority consisting of the Slav States and South Africa and shall lay ourselves open to severe and . . . justified criticism in the Assembly and at home."[84] For reasons such as these, therefore, members of the United Nations by December 1948 were able to adopt the Convention on the Prevention and Punishment of the Crime of Genocide.

The convention confirmed in its very first article "that genocide, whether committed in time of peace or in time of war, is a crime under international law which [all signatories] undertake to prevent and punish."[85] It held that not only persons committing genocide, but even those inciting others to commit genocidal extermination, would be held responsible for their actions whether they were public officials or private citizens. Those charged with the crime were to be tried either by a national tribunal of a state or by an international court having jurisdiction in particular cases. The signatories also pledged to enact the necessary domestic legislation and to provide effective punishment to implement these provisions. They also promised that genocide would not be considered a political crime, thereby making it possible to extradite those so charged. The convention thus placed genocide, even if perpetrated by a government against its own citizens in its own territory, outside the exclusive confines of domestic jurisdiction and, for the first time, in the realm of international concern and responsibility.

As with all other negotiated international agreements, this genocide convention quickly produced both ardent defenders and strident critics. Some diplomats hailed it as "a milestone in the progress of international law" and "a great step forward."[86] The president of the General Assembly praised it as another "epoch-making event" that established "international and collective safeguards for the protection of human groups" and one that marked "an important advance in the development of international criminal law."[87] Other observers criticized it as flawed and deficient, using adjectives such as "pointless," "purposeless," "problematic," "useless," and "worthless."[88] Some complained that the convention contained too many enforcement provisions while others wanted even fewer. Some, like the Soviet Union, criticized the text for possessing too little reference to doctrines of racial superiority, whereas others, like the United States, believed that it already contained too many.[89]

More reasonable and moderate opinion recognized that the sensitive nature of the subject of genocide, the convention's serious implications for both foreign and domestic policies, and the necessity for compromise precluded any universal satisfaction among more than fifty states with different social and political systems. The majority in the General Assembly sought to achieve not what was perfect, but what in politics and diplomacy was possible. They took pride in reaching a settlement upon the first international treaty dealing with race prepared by the United Nations to be proposed for signature and ratification by governments around the world.[90]

At the same time, however, this majority in the United Nations began to worry about two emerging problems. One of these concerned the relationship between pronouncements and practical accomplishments:

Speaking out publicly and passing resolutions about race, actually setting standards for human rights, and signing conventions to prevent and punish genocide represented significant achievements in the struggle to address the global issue of racial discrimination, especially when compared to the silence and inaction of previous centuries. But what would be the effect of these efforts in practice, and how long would it take them to be implemented?[91] The second problem appeared just as troublesome: It concerned how these efforts to combat discrimination based upon race might be affected, for better or worse, by the emerging Cold War.

The Impact of the Cold War

The years immediately following the upheaval of World War II provided enormous opportunities for new beginnings in many different areas. Allied military successes in Europe, North Africa, the Far East, and the Pacific, and the resulting changes in power relationships, assured the victors that they could remake at least some things in the world as they wanted, and they immediately set about to do so in a variety of ways. Nevertheless, the coalition that won the war was composed of several dozen separate states, all possessing and promoting their own particular agendas. When faced with this situation, these states understood that collective security for the future now depended upon their ability to suppress individual differences and to cooperate in peace as they had in war. At times they all shared a common vision and thus could agree unanimously to endorse the Charter creating the United Nations. On some occasions, as we have seen, the overwhelming majority could reach a remarkable consensus about breaking new ground in setting standards for human rights and explicitly dealing with racial discrimination. During other times, however, any semblance of agreement broke down, especially when the superpowers, the United States and the Soviet Union, locked themselves into their bitter struggle known as the Cold War.

Joyous celebrations and pledges of mutual friendship among U.S. and Soviet troops at the end of the war quickly gave way to confusion, suspicion, and then open hostility. Once the cohesive element of having a common enemy had been removed and cooperation no longer appeared to be a vital necessity, each side began to fall victim to its own national interests, perspectives, and ideologies. Disputes over Soviet behavior in Eastern Europe and U.S. possession of atomic weapons only exacerbated continuing disagreements over the nature of the regime in Poland, occupation policies toward Germany, and the role of the United States in Japan. The confrontation intensified when Winston Churchill's famous "Iron Curtain" speech of March 1946 publicly warned that the Soviets might well observe no limits at all "to their expansive and proselytizing tendencies" and accused them of desiring "the indefinite expansion of their power and doctrines."[92] Joseph Stalin angrily shot back that these comments amounted to nothing less than "a call for war against the Soviet Union."[93] Crises in Iran, Yugoslavia, Greece, and Turkey increased the level of tension even more.

Then, in 1947 the U.S. president enunciated the Truman Doctrine, arguing that in the global ideological struggle the United States should provide assistance to all countries struggling for freedom. "At the present moment in world history," Truman declared, "nearly every nation must choose between alternative ways of life"—either democracy characterized by free institutions and guarantees of individual liberties or totalitarianism based upon terror and political oppression.[94] The Soviets responded by describing this speech as "venomous slander," "aggressive," "hostile and bellicose," and one specifically designed "to interfere in the affairs of other countries on the side of reaction and counter-revolution."[95]

As this confrontation intensified into the Cold War, both the Americans and the Soviets assumed more rigid positions. They, and then their respective allies, increasingly began to view their contest as the paramount and most critical dimension of postwar international politics. Given the power and influence of the protagonists, this global struggle tended to relegate other states and other issues to positions of secondary importance or less. The latter found themselves not simply influenced by but at times caught up in and virtually dominated by the bitter rivalries of the Cold War. This phenomenon could be seen not only in the global issues of peace and collective security, economic recovery and development, international trade, and the rule of law but also in the many different aspects of the politics and diplomacy of racial discrimination.

With the exception of South Africa, perhaps no country in the world at the end of the war possessed such widespread notoriety for its domestic racial policies as the United States. The long history of slavery, Jim Crow laws, Supreme Court decisions, and general discrimination on the basis of race was well known. In an era of U.S. isolation, Western global dominance, and the absence of any serious challenge, many believed that these practices would continue forever. But the experience of World War II and the onset of the Cold War dramatically set into motion forces that would shatter this illusion. Public pronouncements by Roosevelt against the evils of Nazi doctrines of racial superiority, statements by Truman strongly supporting the principles of nondiscrimination in the United Nations Charter, participation in the United Nations and its Commission on Human Rights, the determination of non-white states to raise the issue of race explicitly in international relations, and the eagerness of the Soviet Union to exploit any flaws of its major adversary all combined to form powerful and unexpected external pressures for change. In this context, as the United States assumed leadership for protecting the security and the values of the West in the Cold War, it drew great attention to itself, thereby exposing its domestic racial policies to the world as never before in its history.

It did not take long for the country to realize that when others looked at U.S. society they would see not only the achievements of democracy but also the sores of racial discrimination. Indeed, the country quickly found itself accused of being "a hypocrite in international affairs" for demanding free democratic elections in Eastern Europe while at the same time tolerating laws and practices that denied thousands of black citizens the right to vote at home.[96] The return of victorious black troops from the war only to face continuing segregation and even lynching in the South made a particularly striking impression upon observers throughout the world. In Rome, *Unita* told its readers that "in the land of the Four Freedoms thirteen million Negroes struggle against American racial discrimination."[97] *El Universal, La Prensa,* and *El Nacional* in Mexico City, *Epoca* in Buenos Aires, and *Al Yaqdha* in Baghdad all carried similar accounts, as did the *Manchester Guardian* in England, with its coverage of the Ku Klux Klan.[98]

In India, the *Bombay Chronicle* drew attention to the irony of Americans fighting against Nazi racial doctrines during the war and yet holding the same beliefs themselves at home, while the *Bombay Sentinel* viewed it all as part of a seamless web and declared, "The epic milestone in the march toward full freedom will never be reached as long as whites in Africa, America, and all over the world in fact do not cast off their color prejudices and treat all human beings, irrespective of their color, as members of the same human family." India, the paper said, should see the cause of the blacks in the United States as intimately related to that of the Bantus of Africa and of all other colored people in the world, concluding that "a few million whites should not be allowed to dominate and rule the teeming colored millions who form the bulk of the world's population."[99]

The criticisms that stung the most, however, were those issued by the great emerging rival of the United States, the Soviet Union. *Trud* opened an attack in 1946 by providing details of recent lynchings of blacks in Georgia and describing their inequality within the United States.[100] *Pravda* continued the assault by drawing a connection between imperialism and the exploitation of other races, and between capitalism and racial discrimination. "The ideas of racial and national inequality," it declared, "find concrete expression in the policy which capitalistic governments adopt in connection with colonial and dependent peoples and with minorities within the parent countries." *Pravda* noted that "the Constitution of the U.S. guarantees to all citizens equal rights before the law; however, the Negro population, consisting of 13,000,000 people, actually does not have these rights. Racial discrimination continues to exist in all its forms and in all branches of the economy and culture of the country." To support this contention, the newspaper correctly cited the number of states where blacks were deprived of freedom of speech, obliged to attend segregated schools, prevented from using public facilities equally with whites, prohibited from entering into mixed marriages, and in some cases subjected to murder through lynching. In sharp contrast to this, *Pravda* claimed that the ruling White Russians did not discriminate against racial minorities within the Soviet Union and unabashedly asserted: "Only the Soviet Socialist Government has constantly fought for the real freedom, independence, and equality of all peoples—large and small. Only in the U.S.S.R. has real equality of free peoples, real friendship of peoples, free from all forms of exploitation, of national subjugation, and racial discrimination, been established."[101] Statements such as this, concluded the U.S. ambassador in Moscow, struck at the most vulnerable point and "may portend a stronger emphasis on this theme as a Soviet propaganda weapon."[102]

This external pressure from the Cold War now began to play a monumental role in creating a new beginning for human equality within U.S. politics.[103] Just as the Nazi experience had turned a mirror toward U.S. racial discrimination, so now the Soviet campaign effectively held up a magnifying glass and invited the rest of the world to look through it and see the United States at its worst. Policymakers in Washington found this to be not only a supreme embarrassment but also "extremely dangerous" in global competition.[104] They began to understand more and more that racial policies could no longer be considered as a purely domestic matter as in the past. This assessment weighed heavily upon Truman's decision to create the special President's Committee on Civil Rights, composed of distinguished citizens, which quickly turned to the Department of State and asked for specific information concerning how racial discrimination at home affected U.S. foreign policy abroad.

The Department of State provided a clear answer to the President's Committee on Civil Rights. Charles Fahy, the legal advisor, noted the new postwar international attention focused upon human rights and discussed the various obligations incurred under the Charter of the United Nations concerning nondiscrimination. In addition, he went significantly beyond mere legal aspects and placed the issue within its larger political and diplomatic context, writing, "Irrespective of what the U.S. obligation may eventually prove to be with regard to human rights, it must be realized that *as a leading member of the international community, the eyes of the world will be upon the United States.*"[105]

Both the influential Policy Planning Staff and the United Nations Liaison Committee, perfectly capable of hedging their bets and obfuscating issues through language, also provided straightforward advice on this matter. They each concluded their reports by acknowledging the dangerous liability of prejudice and declaring that "the conduct of our foreign policy is handicapped by our record in the field of civil rights and racial discrimination."[106] Secretary of State George C. Marshall similarly observed the problems created by foreign press coverage of racial prejudice, the wide gap between words and deeds in human rights, and the subsequent vulnerability of the United States to Communist propaganda. These facts led him to conclude solemnly: "The foreign policy of a nation depends for most of its effectiveness, particularly a nation which does not rely upon possible military aggression as a dominant influence, on the moral influence which that nation exerts throughout the world. The moral influence of the United States is weakened to the extent that the civil rights proclaimed by our Constitution are not fully confirmed in actual practice."[107]

Since these assessments of foreign affairs fitted so closely with concurrent pressures from domestic politics to ensure racial equality for all citizens, members of the President's Committee on Civil Rights determined to make bold recommendations. Their famous and uncompromising report, *To Secure These Rights*, issued in 1947, is described by one authority as "one of the most outspoken and impressive documents of all time bearing upon human rights."[108] They began by describing the tragic record of racial discrimination within the United States, the constitutional guarantees for equal protection under the law, and the new obligations for nondiscrimination under the Charter. "The time is now," they declared, for taking action to secure human rights, specifically arguing that in addition to moral and economic factors, the "international reason" must be given very careful attention. "Throughout the Pacific, Latin America, Africa, the Near, Middle, and Far East," they warned, "the treatment which our Negroes receive is taken as a reflection of our attitude toward all dark-skinned peoples," and plays "into the hands of Communist propagandists." To correct these serious problems, the committee members forcefully called for the prohibition of state restrictions on the franchise for blacks, a federal law against lynching, an end to segregation in housing and education, a fair employment act prohibiting discrimination, and a denial of federal aid to those states that refused to comply. All these measures, they declared, should be directed toward one ultimate goal: "The elimination of segregation based upon race, color, creed, or national orgin from American life."[109]

As those who wanted to eliminate racial discrimination observed how international rivalry thus contributed so heavily and unexpectedly to the cause of human rights, they consciously determined to work with, rather than against, the forces of the Cold War. George Padmore of the Pan-African movement, for example, deliberately attempted to use the conflict and the contrast between the Americans and the Soviets as a means to advance freedom and equality for non-white peoples around the world. With considerable determination, he drew a sharp distinction between the ideologies of the emerging superpowers, identifying the United States with the reactionary capitalism and white racism of Western imperialist countries and then holding up the Soviet Union as a model for and supporter of national liberation movements for the oppressed.[110]

A. Philip Randolph also exploited U.S. fears about national security in the face of the Communists to gain attention for action against segregation in the armed forces.[111] In delivering his petition of protest to the United Nations on behalf of the National Association for the Advancement of Colored People, Du Bois warmly welcomed the support given by the Soviet Union and its Communist allies.[112] With almost reckless candor given the tenor of the time, Du Bois openly declared, "It is not Russia that threatens the United States so much as Mississippi; not Stalin and Molotov but Bilbo and Rankin."[113] Some observers viewed speeches like this as entirely appropriate, arguing that if the United States openly criticized the lack of respect for human rights within Russia and its satellites in Eastern Europe, then it should expect others to see the absence of genuine democracy within the United States as well.[114] Others considered such behavior as nothing short of treason, saw supporters of civil rights as being Communist sympathizers, and believed that publicity only served the interests of enemy propaganda by "furnishing Soviet Russia with new ammunition to use against us."[115]

Notions such as these about using ammunition against others in ideological warfare appeared frequently and encouraged the combatants sometimes to fight fire with fire. The Department of State, for example, began to recognize that the Iron Curtain of political repression actually might present fewer difficulties for many in the world than the Mason-Dixon Line of racial segregation.[116] Sensing the country's extraordinary vulnerability on this matter of racial inequality, the State Department sent out an unusual, confidential circular telegram to overseas missions asking diplomatic personnel to report back on "any outstanding incidents of discrimination" that might be used as ammunition against their particular host country if its criticisms of the United States became too strong. The Department of State needed something to throw back in the face of its foreign critics but wanted to hide its intentions. "Make no (repeat no) formal inquiries," it directed.[117]

Responses came back from around the world in just a few days. The embassy in Moscow reported that "it is one of the Soviet regime's most emphasized propaganda claims that it has eliminated racial discrimination" but observed that "despite claims to the contrary, racial discrimination by individual and groups does still exist in the U.S.S.R.," particularly against non-Slav minority races and Jews.[118] Reports from other posts indicated discrimination in China against non-Chinese, in Mexico and Brazil against native Indians, and in Latin America against Asiatic immigration. Responses from white Canada, Australia, New Zealand, and South Africa confirmed a well-known and long tradition of discrimination against those of non-white skin color. Those responding from Cuba, Luxembourg, the Philippines, Iraq, Sweden, and most of the countries of the Middle East indicated that their hosts prided themselves in a near absence of overt racially discriminatory practices. Still others noted that among some nations, including Haiti and India, governments and peoples alike felt extremely sensitive about the issue of racial discrimination and could be expected to raise it at every possible opportunity.[119]

Never were the opportunities to discuss the global problem of race so great as those that occurred at the United Nations. States that had long suffered from the effects of racial discrimination, as we have seen, steadfastly determined to use the new organization as a forum and focal point to change practices from the past. In the United Nations these states were seen by the Americans and the Soviets as the home of the uncommitted non-white peoples of the world—and as the great prize to be won in the Cold War. In this setting, the United States frequently found itself caught off guard and under attack, not only in the highly visible formal debates, but even in logistical matters arising from its role as host to the United Nations. Non-white staff members employed by the Secretariat, for instance, many of whom were carefully selected by their own countries due to impressive personal accomplishments, suddenly found themselves upon arrival in the United States unable to rent or purchase housing solely because of the color of their skin. Official delegates from Africa, Asia, and Latin America similarly were shocked to discover that they might not be served in restaurants or given hotel accommodations simply due to their race. The foreign victims of these U.S. racial practices did not sit back passively but lodged serious and formal complaints against the United States. In thus being forced to confront the problem, the Department of State reached several unavoidable conclusions: Racial discrimination against these overseas visitors caused "ill-will, misunderstanding, and even hostility," created a terrible and frequently lasting impression harmful to U.S. foreign policy, and produced embarrassing incidents useful to Communist governments "in skillful propaganda to the detriment of the United States."[120]

Global press coverage made this bad situation even worse for the United States. One U.S. diplomat in Ceylon, for example, reported that racial segregation attracted more attention than any other subject and that newspapers "lost no opportunity to seize upon any incident, statement, judicial decision, or other item of news emanating from the U.S. to play up the idea of American discrimination on the basis of color."[121] Reports from Moscow, Shanghai, Mexico City, Athens, Bombay, Manila, and many other cities around the world confirmed this story.[122] As the mission in Accra noted in sending the Department of State a copy of the *African Morning Post*, local papers possessed little interest in international news, with one exception: racial discrimination and prejudice against those with black skin within the United States.[123] This unmistakable pattern led one foreign observer to conclude that discrimination on the basis of race in the United States provided "the greatest propaganda gift any country could give the Kremlin in its persistent bid for the affections of the colored races of the world."[124]

All these events seriously embarrassed the United States in its position at the United Nations, particularly when the events were deliberately magnified by the Soviet Union, whose delegates began to appreciate the potent political and diplomatic uses of the rhetoric of antiracism. This caused few problems, of course, for Americans on the political extremes. Those on the far right who opposed both racial equality and communism and who cared little or nothing for the rest of the world or the United Nations felt comfortable with this contest of the Cold War, as did those on the far left who wanted to end racial discrimination by glorifying the Soviets and embarrassing the United States.[125] It did cause agonizing difficulties, however, for those caught in the middle: Americans who genuinely wanted to eliminate discrimination based upon race but at the same time and just as surely wanted to be loyal to their country in its struggle against the Soviet Union.

No one experienced this dilemma more acutely than Eleanor Roosevelt. For years she had fought for racial equality and respect for human rights. She also firmly believed in the necessity of portraying the United States in a favorable light to the rest of the world, particularly when the country was challenged by communism. Heretofore, she had always assumed that these goals could be accomplished together and, hence, saw no serious conflict of interest or ethical values in simultaneously serving as a member of the Board of Directors of the National Association for the Advancement of Colored People and accepting a position as the U.S. representative to the United Nations Commission on Human Rights. The intensification of the Cold War drastically altered this arrangement, for she quickly found herself caught in a vortex of opposing forces. Her old and loyal friends in the civil rights movement pushed her to remain true to her conscience and take a strong, public stand against racial discrimination in the international forum, even if it might on occasion embarrass the United States.[126] Her government, however, strictly instructed her to remain loyal to her country and to represent the interests of the United States correctly and favorably before the world in its pressing rivalry with the Soviet Union, even if doing so might occasionally delay action against racial equality.[127] At times, as in the case of the Du Bois petition publicly protesting U.S. discrimination before the United Nations, she found her position in the middle so personally difficult that she seriously considered the possibility of resignation.[128]

Eleanor Roosevelt courageously attempted to strike a balance between these competing pressures, constantly struggling against being forced to make an exclusive choice between either racial equality at home or the reputation of her country abroad. For this reason, she criticized both the Soviet Union and the United States for their violations of human rights and often remarked on the embarrassment brought to the United States because of its own racial discrimination. "Anyone who has worked in the international field," she wrote publicly, "knows well that our failure in race relations in this country, and our open discrimination against various groups, injures our leadership in the world. It is the one point which can be attacked and to which the representatives of the United States have no answer."[129]

These outspoken statements were not appreciated by the Department of State at all; nor were her private warnings that racial discrimination made blacks particularly susceptible to Communist propaganda.[130] Indeed, her own government pressed Eleanor Roosevelt to make more anti-Soviet speeches and, in the opinion of John Humphrey, who worked closely with her on human rights for many years, "exploited" her for short-term Cold War objectives.[131] This, in turn, aggravated existing Soviet abrasiveness in United Nations deliberations and brought renewed assaults not only against the United States but personal attacks also against her as a "meddling old woman" and "hypocritical servant of capitalism."[132] These intensified Cold War pressures actually seem to have encouraged Eleanor Roosevelt to become even more determined in her beliefs. Consequently, she responded by vehemently criticizing the Soviet Union when it violated liberties at home and in Eastern Europe, forcefully renewing her commitment to work for equality within the United Nations, openly and honestly admitting the problems of racial prejudice within the United States, and proudly announcing new U.S. efforts to correct faults of past discrimination like the hard-hitting report of the President's Committee on Civil Rights.[133]

In this regard, and like others committed to racial equality, Eleanor Roosevelt found her hopes greatly bolstered by several dramatic changes occurring within the United States. The foreign and domestic pressures had mounted to such a degree that the Truman administration began to take several definite actions to combat racial discrimination. In 1948 the U.S. Supreme Court, influenced by the provisions in the United Nations Charter, reversed many decades of its own decisions in the two remarkable landmark cases of *Oyama* v. *California* and *Shelley* v. *Kraemer,* striking down land ownership restrictions and real estate covenants based upon race.[134] During the same year President Truman issued momentous executive orders desegregating the armed forces and requiring that all federal officials when involved in personnel decisions refrain from any discrimination based upon race, color, religion, or national origin. His party platform similarly and publicly declared that racial minorities be given equal protection under the law as guaranteed by the Constitution. The president also consistently fought for just immigration legislation that did not exclude foreigners simply because of their race.[135] In 1951 Truman vetoed a bill seeking to expand segregation, significantly observing the connection between foreign and domestic politics and declaring: "We have assumed a role of world leadership in seeking to unite people of great cultural and racial diversity for the purpose of resisting aggression, protecting their mutual security, and advancing their own economic and political development. We should not impair our moral position by enacting a law that requires a discrimination based on race. Step by step we are discarding old discriminations; we must not adopt new ones."[136]

*   *   *

In their efforts to secure a new beginning for racial equality, members of the international community thus found themselves influenced by a wide variety of different pressures suddenly joined in unique combination. Added to the terrible memories of the Nazi experience and the determination of non-Western nations to raise the global issue of racial prejudice were two forces from the Cold War, specifically the Soviet eagerness to attack the United States on its Achilles' heel of racial inequality and the U.S. desire to avoid embarrassment before the world. When combined with domestic pressures to change past practices, these several powerful challenges of politics and diplomacy pushed both the United States and its Western allies much further than they initially intended to go.[137] Consequently, this resulted in a series of unprecedented achievements in only three short years: an international resolution against racial discrimination, condemnation of South Africa's policies toward race, establishment of the Commission on Human Rights and its Sub-Commission on Prevention of Discrimination, setting of standards in the Universal Declaration of Human Rights, creation of the Convention of the Prevention and Punishment of the Crime of Genocide, and implementation of the first measures toward desegregation in the United States. Each of these important accomplishments marked a milestone on the road toward racial equality and respect for basic human rights. Together they began a process of taking the treatment of citizens out of the exclusive confines of domestic jurisdiction and of transforming individuals from mere objects of international sympathy into subjects of international law.

Much, of course, remained to be done and only time could tell how these decisions and declarations would be implemented in practice. Peoples of different races around the world carefully watched to see whether or not these promises would be kept. But nowhere would this scrutiny be more intense than among those non-white states in Africa and Asia about to emerge from the collapse of white colonial empires and to confront both power and prejudice.

7
The End of Empire

WE OF ASIA AND AFRICA ARE EMERGING into this world as new
nation states . . . [and] besides the issues of colonialism and
political freedom, all of us here are concerned with the matter of
racial equality. . . . In the United Nations [we] have again and
again forced this on the unwilling attention of the other members.
There we could see palpably the extent to which Western men
have had to become defensive about their past racist attitudes. . . .
They have yet to learn, it seems, how deeply this issue cuts and
how profoundly it unites non-Western people who may disagree on
all sorts of questions. [We need to provide] a sober and yet jolting
reminder to them that the day of Western racism is passing along
with the day of Western power over non-Western peoples.
—Carlos Romulo

Decolonization and Collapsing Empires in Asia

In 1945, when the United Nations emerged as an international organization to promote peace and human rights, 51 states were admitted
to membership. Among these, only 3 came from Africa (Ethiopia, Liberia,
and South Africa), and among the mere 3 from Asia only China was
independent of colonial rule. Seven belonged to the Middle East. The
great majority of member states therefore represented the countries of
Europe (including the Soviet Union), the Americas, and the white
Commonwealth countries.[1] Many assumed that this political dominance
by the Western, white world would continue in the future as it had for
several centuries in the past.

They were wrong, for in the simple words of one observer, "time
had run out."[2] Within a single decade, 25 new states had joined the
United Nations. By the end of 1965, 41 more had been added, swelling
the membership to 117 and dramatically changing its composition.[3] This
development marked one of the greatest political changes in human
history, transferring power from whites to non-whites and liberating
perhaps one billion people from colonial rule in Asia and Africa. Once

197

they secured their independence, these states emerged fully determined to use this most powerful shift of power to end the last vestiges of Western imperialism and racial discrimination.

In this regard, as in so many others, the experience of World War II provided the initial, critical impetus. The Atlantic Charter as early as 1941 pledged to "respect the right of all peoples to choose the form of government under which they will live."[4] The signatories of the Declaration of the United Nations also promised that should they be victorious in battle, they would support not only human rights but liberty and independence for peoples as well.[5] This public assertion by precisely those Western powers with the greatest colonial possessions stimulated enormous hope among subject peoples throughout the world who believed that they bore witness to a complete reversal of policy. Confident that the Allies would honor their pledge, many nationalist leaders, particularly in Africa and Asia, spoke of victory in the war as the unique opportunity to bring about political independence and nationhood. How could the Allied governments, they reasoned, fight a war for freedom and democracy and then deny self-government to their own colonial peoples?[6] The Charter of the United Nations, signed in 1945, bolstered their spirits further, for it specifically included nondiscrimination provisions and supported "the principle of equal rights and self-determination of peoples."[7] Its Declaration Regarding Non-Self-Governing Territories did even more by proclaiming a commitment to develop self-government in accordance with the political aspirations of native peoples themselves.[8] Indeed, one diplomat at the time described this as "the most important and far-reaching joint declaration of colonial policy in history."[9]

Yet, as we have seen on other occasions, declarations of principle in politics and diplomacy are not always followed in practice. Despite these solemn pledges and the appearance of recognizing the changing nature of international relations, the white, Western world demonstrated a profound unreadiness to quickly abandon its colonial empires. The British, French, Dutch, Belgians, Spanish, Portuguese, Italians, and South Africans all resolved to remain imperial powers, to retain their possessions, and to conduct postwar colonial policy in their own way and at their own pace free from any dictation by an international organization.[10] Even though exhausted by World War II and confronted by both domestic and foreign arguments in favor of emancipating imperial territories (including outspoken statements from the United States against a resumption of old-fashioned imperialism and the unjustified power of a mere "handful of whites" over millions of colored natives),[11] the colonial powers rushed troops and administrators back into their respective possessions in India, Burma, Indochina, Malaya, Indonesia, the Middle East, Angola, the Congo, Algeria, Madagascar, Kenya, and nearly all the rest of the African continent. There the powers also reasserted their racial attitudes. As one U.S. academic observer at the time wrote with deep concern in an essay entitled "The Colonial Crisis and the Future":

> The first of the universal traits of colonialism [even after the war] is the color line. In every dependent territory . . . the resident white population [is] separated from the native masses by a social barrier that is virtually impassable. The color line, indeed, is the foundation of the entire colonial system, for on it is built the whole social, economic and political structure. All the relationships between the racial groups are those of superordination and subordination, of superiority and inferiority. There is no mistaking this pattern for one of mere segregation, or separation with equality. The color line . . . cuts across every colonial society in such a way as to leave the natives in the lower stratum and the whites in the upper.[12]

This reassertion of physical color and prejudice toward race was reinforced by more subtle means as well. When drafting the Declaration Regarding Non-Self-Governing Territories in the United Nations Charter, for example, the Western powers managed to prevent the inclusion of any provisions for sharing political administration, granting independence by a specific time, or general enforcement that might restrict their authority. In addition, when adhering to a number of subsequent international accords such as the General Agreement on Tariffs and Trade, the genocide convention, and the European Convention on Human Rights, they consistently insisted upon inserting a "colonial application clause" declaring that binding obligations need not be applied to dependent territories.[13] Even when signing the famous Universal Declaration of Human Rights, the Western powers actively sought to delay any publicity about, or application of, its principles regarding racial equality in colonial areas lest it stir up unrest. In a secret despatch to governors of the British colonies, for example, the Colonial Office took great pains to explain that even though the declaration contained no legal commitments and represented "nothing more than a statement of ultimate ideals," it was nevertheless "a source of embarrassment" that might produce "difficulties" and "undesirable implications" in the colonies.[14] Western officials complained of the "obvious effort to undermine the influence and authority of the administering powers" and the "widespread anti-colonial bias in the United Nations."[15] To prevent still further "interference" into the affairs of their empires, the British, French, and Belgian colonial administrators resolved to work closely with each other in developing a common strategy that would protect their interests against the "backward races."[16]

These tenacious efforts to perpetuate colonial empires and white domination over the colored peoples of the world were doomed to failure. The promises for self-determination and political independence, the shattering of the myth of white invincibility during World War II, the weakened position of Europeans and their loss of confidence in the aftermath of the war, the competition between the Americans and Soviets for the affections of emerging nations, and the activism of the new United Nations all played vital roles in helping to shatter colonial empires. But added to all of these forces was the intense determination of nationalist leaders among subject peoples to be free of Western imperialism. If independence could not be obtained through negotiations, they now were prepared to fight and take it by force. As the author of a book entitled *Racism: A World Issue* wrote immediately following the war, "No power in the world can prevent the colored races, the peoples of Asia and Africa, from uniting because of common grievances against the centuries of domination by the white man and ending this domination by the use of means we have taught them so well to use."[17] Together these factors combined in such a startling way that within only fifteen years almost all of the colonial empires created during the previous several centuries crumbled, the power was transferred from whites to non-whites, and in place of the empires there emerged new and independent nation-states.

It is not surprising that this process began in Asia. There, stunning Japanese victories against French, British, Dutch, and U.S. possessions during the first years of World War II dramatically stripped away the facade of Western superiority and brought to the surface slogans from the earlier Pan-Asiatic conferences: Asia for the Asiatics![18] Through a series of defeats and humiliations of the colonial powers, Japan greatly heightened "color consciousness" throughout the region and often found enthusiastic reception for its portrayal of the struggle as a victory of East over West and colored over white.[19] Activists for self-determination described these Asian military successes as "vindicating the prestige of all Asiatic nations" in the face of "Anglo-Saxon imperialism" and saw in the successes the hope that Asia would someday be free.[20] This, of course, raised the whole question about the future role of the white man in Asia. As S. Sjahrir of Indonesia observed the change in *Out of Exile*, virtually everything "was shaken loose from its moorings. . . . All layers of society came to see the past in another light. If these [Japanese] barbarians had been able to replace the old colonial authority why had that authority been necessary at all? Why, instead, hadn't they handled the affairs of government themselves? . . . [Now] national self-consciousness . . . developed a new and powerful drive beyond anything known before."[21]

The Japanese enhanced these feelings even more by inviting nationalist leaders like Subhas Chandra Bose of India, Ba Maw of Burma, José Laurel of the Philippines, and Achmed Sukarno of Indonesia to participate in war conferences at Tokyo. Moreover, the raising of national military units in these territories provided still further guarantees that once the war ended, armed force would stand behind the desire for political independence.[22]

Interestingly enough, Japanese victories in Asia produced very similar thoughts among a number of Western commentators as well. After the fall of Singapore, for example, Margery Perham of Oxford University wrote two perceptive articles in the *Times* reviewing the colonial situation and calling for a drastic reorientation in policy. "Japan's attack in the Pacific," she argued, "has produced a very practical revolution in race relations" by successfully challenging the "great white imperial Powers."[23] She believed that the disasters of empire in Asia easily could be repeated in Africa due to deep-seated racial attitudes and economic exploitation and that these could be avoided only by a major shift in policy that stressed instead partnership and promoted egalitarianism among the races. In the wake of additional humiliation, Queen Wilhelmina of the Netherlands similarly spoke of the need to abolish racial discrimination and consider reconstructing the Dutch Empire "on the solid foundation of complete partnership" and toward the goal of "national evolution."[24] Declared influential U.S. journalist Walter Lippmann with even greater force: "The Western nations must now do what hitherto they lacked the will and imagination to do: they must identify their cause with the freedom and the security of the peoples of the East, putting away the 'white man's burden' and purging themselves of the taint of an obsolete and obviously unworkable white man's imperialism."[25]

The beginnings of this purge of imperialism came when the sudden collapse of Japan threw all of Asia into confusion and opened the door for many dreams of national self-determination to come true. Within less than one year, the United States, as Lippmann had proposed, made the first move to reorient colonial policy. Strongly conscious of setting an example to others in the West and anxious to win the loyalty of those in the East, the United States decided to release a possession that it had held since the end of the nineteenth century. With great fanfare and colorful ceremony and in a remarkable absence of violence, Congress granted long-promised independence to the Philippines in July 1946. The United States was not prepared to abandon all influence, however. As a condition of formal independence, it required that the Philippines adopt a constitution based upon the U.S. model, grant to the United States control over several military and naval facilities, and establish a close economic relationship between the two countries. Yet, despite these initial limitations upon complete sovereignty, Filipino independence marked the first deliberate, major reversal of colonial policy. As such, it served both as a prudent example to other Western powers trying to maintain their overseas possessions and as an inspiration to nationalist leaders elsewhere in the region who also dreamed of securing self-determination.[26]

Perhaps nowhere did these dreams of independence occur with greater frequency and passion than in India, where Gandhi's inspiration had mobilized several million to demand freedom from the mighty British Empire. Deeply frustrated and angered by their treatment after World War I, Indian politicians resolved that they would not let self-determination escape them again. They hoped that U.S. pressure on London would provide some assistance but knew that they needed much more. For this reason, they enthusiastically welcomed the news of the coming to power of the British Labour party. The first postwar election in Britain replaced Churchill (who had been a brilliant war leader but vowed that he would never preside over the dismemberment of the empire) with a government committed to implementing "a revolution in Imperial attitude" by dealing with peoples in Asia, the Middle East, and eventually Africa on a more equal footing.[27] With this change, the British dramatically marked one of the most significant landmarks in the entire global transition from empire to independence: In August 1947 they handed over authority to their heirs in the two new dominions of India and Pakistan. Although the subsequent violence between Indian Hindus and Pakistani Muslims revealed once again that prejudice could take many dangerous and insidious forms, the granting of independence clearly marked the beginning of the end of empire. As historian Wm. Roger Louis wrote, "Everything dwindled in importance in comparison with the transfer of power in India on the 15th of August. New limbs of the Commonwealth might flourish, but the backbone of the old British Empire had been severed."[28]

Several years before, Indian leaders in the Congress party had hoped that if they ever obtained independence, it would serve as an example to others and become "a prelude to the freedom of all Asiatic nations now under domination."[29] It did exactly this. For more than one hundred years India had been regarded as the keystone and crown jewel of the British Empire and, in some cases, the raison d'être for much of the rest of the empire. Thus, once power changed hands there, other areas could be seen in a much different light. Within only a few months, therefore, Britain relinquished control of further imperial possessions as well. In January 1948 it granted independence to Burma and in February gave national freedom to Ceylon (now Sri Lanka).[30] Before the year was out, Britain also withdrew in the Middle East from Palestine, setting into motion events that would make it possible for survivors who had suffered so much from the Holocaust to create the modern state of Israel. With this action of 1948, the British ended the first phase of their new and revolutionary postwar decolonization. The speed of these policies had been so great and the contrast with the past so sharp that they needed time to adjust, time to see whether their strategy of supporting moderate nationalists would prevent the rise of anti-British extremists, time to decide whether their attitudes toward race could change, and time to determine what they would do with the rest of their empire.

This conscious decision by the British at least to begin the process of decolonization from part of their far-flung empire did not always inspire other European imperial powers to do the same. The Dutch, for example, tenaciously refused to give freedom to the Indonesians. Instead, the Dutch sent troops to the islands for "police operations" designed to consolidate their control. For four years they fought against guerrilla forces to retain their East Indian empire. In this action, they attracted the full blast of Communist verbal assaults against Western imperialism, anticolonial speeches within the United Nations, and then counteraction by others. Asian states, together with some from the Middle East, supported the nationalist movement of Sukarno, refused to allow planes from the Netherlands on the way with military supplies to Indonesia to use airfields, and joined in a boycott of Dutch ships. Then, believing strongly that the tide of history worked against any reimposition of empire, both India and Australia took the matter to the Security Council. The Dutch, finding themselves politically and diplomatically isolated from all but the European imperial powers, financially drained, and militarily weakened, finally gave up. In 1949 they granted independence to Indonesia, thus ending a colonial regime begun by the East India Company of Amsterdam three and a half centuries before.[31]

France, like the Netherlands, demonstrated little or no voluntary desire to loosen its reins of empire. Despite vague promises of independence it had made during the war and vocal support for human rights within the United Nations, France clearly wanted to retain all possessions in North and West Africa, the Caribbean, and Southeast Asia and was fully prepared to use armed force if necessary to reestablish its grip. This appeared particularly difficult to accomplish in Indochina, where large numbers of French troops seemed unable to suppress the guerrilla forces loyal to the nationalist and Communist leader, Ho Chi Minh. By 1949 the government in Paris reached accommodation with Laos and Cambodia, making them "associate states" within the French Union, but insisted that it retain control of the wealthy region of Cochin China and its large city of Saigon. For this reason, France could not obtain agreement with Ho and his Vietminh forces. In this case, diplomatic discussions yielded few results, for both sides believed that they could gain more by fighting than negotiating. France therefore committed more soldiers and money to this overseas war, attacked Hanoi, and bombarded Haiphong, but could not break the deadlock. The guerrilla forces, for their part, would not compromise on anything that denied the reality of independence. Violence thus raged for years, first with the French until the decisive 1954 battle of Dienbienphu, and then with other outside powers, including the United States. Before the Vietnamese gained independence, their countryside would be torn to shreds and countless numbers of their people killed.[32]

The guerrilla violence evident in French Indochina also erupted in British Malaya. Although Britain had been prepared to relinquish its power relatively quickly and without a protracted fight in India, Pakistan, Burma, Ceylon, and Palestine, this approach did not necessarily carry over to its other colonies. When it became clear that independence would not be granted in the same way to Malaya, Communist-supported insurgents launched a guerrilla campaign in 1948. The resulting war pitted the "security forces" of British, Commonwealth, Gurkha, and loyal Malayan troops against the Malayan Racial Liberation Army or MRLA, composed of Chinese and Indian immigrants as well as Malays. After several years of bloody and costly fighting, the British commander, General Sir Gerard Templer, concluded, "The answer lies not in pouring more troops into the jungle, but in the hearts and minds of the people."[33] Toward this goal of winning the loyalty of the more moderate nationalist elements, authorities in London began negotiations designed to transfer power to a native government. In the end they succeeded, and by 1957 Malaya (now Malaysia) finally received independence from colonial rule.

Together these particular guerrilla campaigns demonstrated two highly significant features about the decolonization that followed 1948–1949. The first is that the empires of the white Europeans would not collapse overnight or somehow automatically fall of their own weight into independence. An important backbone may have been broken and a revolutionary process started, but the death knell would not sound for a number of years. Stiff resistance still would be mounted when the colonial powers desired to protect their interests, set their own pace and conditions, and in the words of one author, "cling on to their imperial ermine."[34] Moreover, the insurgent wars in both Vietnam and Malaya raised the spector of communism in decolonization. Open Communist involvement in these two struggles and their support for other "wars of national liberation" suddenly cast disengagement from empire in an entirely new light for many in the West, especially the Americans. Mao Tse-tung's Communist Chinese victory, the resulting "loss" of China, and the outbreak of the Korean War only one year later in 1950 compounded this problem even further. The Cold War thus ominously appeared to burst beyond its European confines and now flood Asia and potentially engulf the entire globe. In this crisis-filled and emotion-charged setting, Americans rapidly found themselves shifting away from their immediate postwar support of decolonization and moving instead toward the view that these insurrections were more important as Cold War battlefields rather than as struggles against European colonization, and that the insurrection leaders were "agents of international Communism" and "outright Commies" rather than indigenous nationalists fighting for independence.[35]

Both the Soviets and the Americans saw the stakes in this emerging globalization of the Cold War as extremely high. There was much to win—and much to lose. Here, among colonial or former colonial peoples, the superpowers could demonstrate the appeal of their particular ideological convictions and the strength of their system. Here they could obtain access, resources, markets, strategic air and naval bases, and political loyalty for themselves and their allies—or deny them to the adversaries. Here they could help or hinder international peace, security, and respect for human rights. With these kinds of considerations in mind, Soviet spokesman Andrei Zhdanov attempted to make the contrast as sharp as he possibly could by announcing at the founding meeting of the Communist Information Bureau that there now existed "Two Camps": the "Imperialist and Anti-Democratic Camp" led by the United States and its allies on the one hand, and the "Anti-Imperialist and Democratic Camp" led by the Soviet Union. In the battle between these two, he declared, the Soviets would support all "fighters for national liberation in the colonies and dependencies" in their heroic struggle against capitalist exploitation and imperialist domination.[36] Subsequent efforts consciously sought to portray the West as composed of avaricious imperialists and racists who "prepare for wars and slaughter," "exploit and exterminate the enslaved peoples in the colonies," and "practice and preach racial discrimination."[37] To emphasize a contrast, they presented Communists as champions of peace, self-determination for dependent peoples, and racial equality.[38]

For frustrated, angry, and hungry people who long had suffered from racial discrimination and colonial exploitation and who dreamed of independence, this portrayal of the Soviets as strong and dedicated friends possessed enormous appeal. It promised salvation to the damned and offered hope for the future outside of liberal democracy and capitalism. The West thus had reason to be deeply worried, to recognize that its own policies provided "ready-made ammunition" for Communist accusations, and to determine an effective course of action.[39] "Some 200 million people of the world live in non-self-governing territories," acknowledged one revealing Department of State study, "often under conditions of poverty, disease, and illiteracy. Among these people there are today increasingly powerful movements for self-government and great material well-being." Recent independence achieved by non-whites in the Philippines, India, Pakistan, and Burma, the study stated, created a momentum that probably could not be stopped. Then the report went on to discuss what it regarded as the real problem:

> At the same time international Communism has taken advantage of the situation and is spreading propaganda among these dependent peoples and filling their minds with alluring, if fantastic, promises of independence and economic betterment. If this important phase of the struggle between Communism and democracy is not to be lost by the democracies, they must pursue policies that are evidently consonant with the interests of the peoples in the dependent areas, and must also find means of making this clear to the peoples concerned.[40]

The U.S. government, despite its many efforts, never seemed to be able to find such means or to make them effective. At times it spent its energy trying to focus colonial peoples' attention on the repressiveness of the Soviet regime, the violations of human rights under Stalin, and the beguiling but deceitful nature of Communist promises. During other times, the government attempted to use its vast economic resources in the form of foreign aid to assist newly independent peoples. But each time it seemed either unwilling or unable to recognize what Walter White described to an approving Eleanor Roosevelt as the real problem: "the attitude towards the United States of the non-white peoples of the earth and the skepticism of these two-thirds of the world's population with respect to America's assertions of democracy in the light of continued race prejudice."[41]

On some occasions the United States did demonstrate a willingness to recognize its own past faults in imperialism and racial discrimination and then proudly proclaimed its ability to change. Within only hours after the momentous 1954 Supreme Court decision, in *Brown* v. *Board of Education*, outlawing racially segregated schools, for example, the Voice of America broadcast the news to foreign countries in thirty-five different languages.[42] Sometimes U.S. leaders even professed a revolutionary tradition that supported the nationalist aspirations of others. "We ourselves are the first colony in modern times to have won independence," declared Secretary of State John Foster Dulles in 1954. "We have a natural sympathy with those everywhere who would follow our example."[43] Yet, policy never seemed to match this rhetoric. There may have been times when the United States genuinely wanted to see empires collapse and colonial peoples gain independence—but it wanted to defeat communism more.

The advocates of decolonization watched in dismay as their own struggles for independence became caught up, complicated, confused, and at times overwhelmed by this rivalry of the global Cold War. They found themselves not only fighting to emancipate themselves from their imperial masters but also trapped in the meshes of the battle between East and West over which they had little or no control. Despite his vocal expressions of support for self-determination, Dulles admitted that it and other issues would be pushed into the background if necessary in order to meet the highest U.S. priority: the defeat of communism, which he described as "not only the gravest threat that ever faced the United States but the gravest threat that ever faced what we call Western civilization."[44] To achieve this objective, the United States became a willing contributor of considerable military assistance to Britain and France, the powers with the largest colonial empires, when they needed money and weapons to fight against Communist insurgents in their overseas possessions.[45] Ironically, the same Cold War that actually assisted the movement for racial equality within the United States[46] thus helped to retard decolonization in the world at large. For their part, the Soviets discovered that even though the anticolonialism of Communist doctrine enjoyed wide appeal, they had great difficulty in winning the trust of those subject peoples who saw a vast contradiction between the Soviet Union's rhetoric about self-determination on the one hand and its suppression of human rights at home and of independence in the Baltic States and Eastern Europe on the other.[47]

Many colonial peoples thus found themselves trapped, used, and abused by the Cold War. Although Soviet-American rivalries held out the prospect of perhaps playing one bloc off against the other or even trying to extract aid simultaneously from both sides, this proved to be an extremely dangerous game to play.[48] The superpowers set their own rules and established their own objectives. Both the Soviet Union and the United States resisted any genuinely independent nationalism. Both spoke of the bitter and irreconcilable struggle between "two camps" and desperately tried to push the rest of the world into one or the other. Moreover, and of particular importance to those concerned about the racial factor in international relations, both the Soviets and the Americans were white. For these several reasons, a number of nationalist leaders attempted to break out of this entanglement and advance the cause of decolonization for its own sake by joining forces, setting their own agenda, and creating a nonaligned "Third World."

An Emerging "Third World"
and Independence in Africa

One feature stands above all others in the process of bringing empires to an end: the desire among colonial and former colonial peoples to control their own destinies. Despite their many differences, they held this desire in common. Years of domination and discrimination by Western powers, in some cases going back several centuries to the days of the slave trade,[49] instilled within them a passionate desire for freedom from outside control, some form of self-determination, and racial equality. "The peoples of the colonies know precisely what they want," declared Nkrumah passionately. "They wish to be free and independent, to be able to feel themselves on an equal footing with all other peoples, and to work out their own destinies."[50] In this setting, it is hardly surprising that opinions about imperialism and race would be closely tied to expressions about "Asia for the Asians" and "Africa for the Africans." Yet, as long as the white, European colonial powers maintained their strength and thereby their empires, these slogans could remain only words. World War II and the Cold War revolutionized that situation. By greatly diminishing the once unrivaled strength of Europe, the war gave colonial peoples new opportunities for emancipation. Then, by appearing to impose still another global structure of power, the contest between the Soviets and the Americans provided them with even more reason to seek independence.

A shared sense of common fate and purpose convinced a number of nationalist leaders in the very beginning of the postwar world that they might never achieve independence unless they banded together. Well aware of their individual weaknesses, they sought to gain strength and support through solidarity. Toward this end, in 1945 several countries in the Middle East formed the Arab League, the first regional organization committed to liberating colonial areas from Western control. Egypt, Iraq, Syria, Lebanon, Jordan, Saudi Arabia, Yemen, and a representative of the Palestinian Arabs all joined together to proclaim their belief that a people under colonial rule should be considered equal to recognized states if they formed a nation or an ethnic or racial family. Libya, Morocco, the Sudan, and Tunisia subsequently joined the Arab League at a later date. In 1948 one of its members, Iraq, seemed to speak for many of the others when it declared nazism, communism, and Zionism all to be crimes of imperialism against humanity and international peace.[51]

Other groups also organized to present united resistance against colonial rule and secure independence. Out of the Pan-African movement came the West African National Secretariat, led by Nkrumah and taking as its motto: For Unity and Absolute Independence, for all the peoples in Africa. Its major publication, the *New African*, began by announcing that "imperialism and colonial liberation are two irreconcilable opposites" and that since compromise between them was impossible, "the death of one is the life of the other." It stated the purpose of the organization directly: "fearlessly to inspire the youths of Africa for definite political action, and arouse in them a burning desire for freedom."[52] Similar expressions against colonial domination and racial discrimination were voiced at the Asian Relations Conference convened in New Delhi in 1947 and the Asian Socialist Conference, held at Rangoon during 1953, which established a permanent Anti-Colonial Bureau.[53] During the first of these two occasions, Jawaharlal Nehru uttered those words subsequently so frequently cited in the Afro-Asian world: "Far too long have we . . . been petitioners in Western courts and chancelleries. That story must now belong to the past. We propose to stand on our own legs and to cooperate with all others who are prepared to cooperate with us. We do not intend to be the playthings of others."[54]

As the tension of the Cold War intensified, many nationalist leaders began to believe that their own independence had to be wrestled not only from old colonial masters of the past but also from new attempts by the Soviets and Americans to push them into one camp or the other. For example, when in 1954 the United States, in order to combat communism, wanted to form the Southeast Asian Treaty Organization (SEATO) and include all the states in that region, India, Burma, Ceylon, and Indonesia resisted pressure to join and declared their intention to remain "neutral" in the Cold War.[55] During the same period, sixteen Latin American nations that frequently criticized the "Yankee imperialism" of the North took the unusual step of outlawing the Communist party in their states, prompting one observer to remark, "Latin Americans can be depended upon to adopt a solidarity opposition to Soviet and every other imperialism . . . in defense of their independence and their institutions."[56] With a growing frequency, nations around the globe announced that they would not be subjugated either by the West or the East. Although these countries had very different political regimes and philosophies and suffered from inexperience in international politics and diplomacy, deep religious and ethnic divisions, and many internal rivalries between themselves, they all shared a determination to be independent. Instead of being under the control of the "Free World" led by the United States or the "Communist World" led by the Soviet Union, they wanted to be "neutral," "nonaligned" states forming their own "Third World."[57]

The most dramatic and influential of these several attempts to gain and then maintain independence was the famous Asian-African Conference convened at Bandung in Indonesia. Recently freed from colonial rule themselves, the governments of Burma, Ceylon, India, Indonesia, and Pakistan first conceived of a conference as a means of bringing together the anticolonial movements in Asia with those in Africa and together developing an effective strategy for advancing their mutual interests. Toward this end they sent invitations to twenty-nine nations as diverse as Japan and Jordan, China and Ethiopia, North and South Vietnam and the Gold Coast, Laos and Liberia. Together they represented one and one-half billion people, and together they shared the experience of domination and discrimination at the hands of Western whites. Consequently, the organizers deliberately and specifically refused to invite any white power, including the United States and the Soviet Union, both of which they regarded as part of their problem. Protests from the West about being excluded from an important diplomatic conference brought little sympathy and prompted one black writer to comment that it could not be forgotten that "for centuries Asian and African nations had watched in helpless silence while white powers had gathered, discussed, and disposed of the destinies of Asian and African peoples—gatherings in which no Asian or African had ever had any say."[58] As one Western newspaper tersely concluded: "The West is excluded. Emphasis is on the colored nations of the world. And for Asia it means at last the destiny of Asia is being determined in Asia, and not in Geneva, or Paris, or London, or Washington. Colonialism is out. Hands off is the byword. . . . This is perhaps the great historic event of our century."[59]

When the delegates themselves assembled at the Bandung Conference in April 1955, they too spoke of its historic importance. In his opening comments, President Sukarno described the gathering as a "new departure in the history of the world." Deeply conscious of the symbolism of the occasion, he announced, "This is the first international conference of colored peoples in the history of mankind." Sukarno saw the struggle as one between the old established forces of the white imperial powers led both by the United States and the Soviet Union on the one hand and the new emerging forces of the non-white Afro-Asian world on the other. What brought this second group together for the first time, he believed, was a shared experience among them all of colonial domination and racial discrimination. "We are united," declared Sukarno, "by a common detestation of colonialism in whatever form it appears. We are united by a common detestation of racialism."[60]

Speaker after speaker rose to reiterate this theme. Ali Asatroamidjojo of Indonesia, Prince Sihanouk of Cambodia, Ato Akliliou of Ethiopia, Jawaharlal Nehru of India, Gamal Nasser of Egypt, Tatsunosuke Takasaki of Japan, and Kojo Botsio of the Gold Coast, among others, all spoke movingly about their shared experiences due to the black, brown, and yellow color of their skins. In this regard they placed particular significance on the presence and participation at the conference of the capable Chou En-lai from the People's Republic of China, who certainly could not qualify as "nonaligned," but who more importantly could represent the largest and most powerful non-white country in the world. Together they denounced imperialism in both its traditional and Soviet-American Cold War varieties and the persistent continuation of racial prejudice by the West. Again and again they stressed that colonial domination and discrimination against race must be seen as the intimately interrelated policy manifestations of an overwhelming attitude of racial superiority.

One of the most articulate, interesting, and thought-provoking speeches of the entire Bandung Conference came from President Carlos Romulo of the Philippines. He began by noting that only a few years before no one would have been bold enough to predict such remarkable changes in politics and diplomacy as the creation of the United Nations, the international efforts to promote human rights and nondiscrimination, and the beginning of the end of empire, with several new states gaining independence. These efforts could be continued and the achievements further increased, he maintained, if Asians and Africans worked together to make themselves "conscious instruments" of historic decision and if the world recognized that the very "touchstone" of their motivation was racial equality. "There has not been and there is not a Western colonial regime which has not imposed, to a greater or lesser degree, on the people it ruled the doctrine of their own racial inferiority," asserted Romulo. "We have known, and some of us still know," said this normally very conservative, Catholic man with emotion,

the searing experience of being demeaned in our own lands, of being systematically relegated to subject status not only politically and economically, and militarily—but racially as well. . . . To bolster his rule, to justify his own power to himself, Western white man assumed that his superiority lay in his very bones, in the color of his skin. This made the lowliest drunk superior, in colonial society, to the highest product of culture and scholarship and industry among the subject people.

"I do not think in this company," he continued before an audience now spellbound by his words, "I have to labor the full import of this pernicious doctrine and practice. . . . I do not think I have to try to measure the role played by this racism as a driving force in the development of the nationalist movements in our many lands. For many it has made the goal of regaining a status of simple manhood the be-all and end-all of a lifetime of devoted struggle and sacrifice."[61]

Interestingly enough, Romulo did not stop at that point as he certainly could have done with the loud applause of the other delegates ringing in his ears. Instead, he warned the Asians and Africans assembled at Bandung that they had a particular responsibility not to repeat this repulsive behavior by falling into the "racist trap" themselves. One of the worst possible developments, he said, would be the emergence of a "counter-racism" in which the black, brown, and yellow of the world responded "to the white man's prejudice against us as non-whites with prejudice against whites simply because they are white." Romulo then leveled his heaviest blast: "What a triumph it would be for racism if it should come about. How completely we would defeat ourselves and all who have struggled in our countries to be free! . . . Our quarrel with racism is that it substitutes the accident of skin color for judgment of men as men. Counter-racism would have us do the same: to lump white men by their supposed racial grouping and govern our acts and reactions accordingly." He challenged the delegates to rise above this human weakness and courageously called upon them to remember the important fact "that this kind of racist attitude has been the practice not of all white men, but only of some, and that it flies in the face of their own profoundest religious beliefs and political goals and aspirations." Romulo concluded this remarkable challenge with these words: "Let us not preserve stupid racial superstitions which belong to the past. Let us work to remove this ugly disease wherever it is rooted, whether it be among Western men or among ourselves."[62]

In the same way that Hitler's atrocities had turned a mirror toward the West and forced them to see their racial attitudes of the past, so Romulo's speech turned that mirror back toward Afro-Asians and challenged them to be honest with themselves and with others by examining their own attitudes toward race and by avoiding the strong tendency to pretend that racism somehow applied only to whites. In neither case was the task easy. Some of the delegates at Bandung wanted to ignore their own prejudices and seek revenge against whites for slavery, imperialism, immigration quotas, and countless other forms of racial discrimination inflicted against them. They wanted to humiliate those who for so long had humiliated them or at least secure some form of compensation for centuries of injustices.[63] The majority understood this instinctive reaction to the heavy burden of the past and knew perfectly well that the colored peoples of the earth vastly outnumbered the whites of the West. But they also knew that such a response would make them fall victim to what Romulo called the "racist trap" and merely perpetuate the very prejudice of race they wished to destroy.

On the touchstone issue of race, therefore, the final communiqué from the Bandung Conference reflected the more moderate position of the majority. It called not for revenge or antiwhite solidarity but rather declared its full support for racial equality as set forth in the United Nations Charter and the Universal Declaration of Human Rights. The conference participants extended their sympathy to all victims of racial discrimination, pledging to eliminate "every trace of racialism" and to "guard against the danger of falling victims to the same evil in their struggle to eradicate it." To emphasize the importance of neutrality and nonalignment, the delegates condemned the superpowers for possessing nuclear weapons of mass destruction and promised to abstain from collective security arrangements that served "the particular interests of any of the big powers." Moreover, they declared that "colonialism in all its manifestations [read traditional European, U.S., and Soviet] is an evil which should speedily be brought to an end," and called upon all major powers to grant freedom and independence to dependent, colonial peoples.[64]

This conference provided unparalleled inspiration and self-confidence for Asians and Africans. A newfound sense of "belonging" and a spirit of "solidarity" against racial domination and discrimination greatly impressed the participants. Indeed, there was hardly a delegate from any of the twenty-nine countries represented at Bandung who on his or her return home did not call the conference a resounding success.[65] Despite their differences and contrasts, they demonstrated to themselves and to others that they could work together, manage their own affairs without outside interference, and discuss their common future. Here they expressed pent-up frustrations developed over generations and found release from the psychological chains of presumed inferiority and unity among those of color; here they expressed support for the underdog trying to shake off the vestiges of empire and a craving for independence and racial equality. Léopold Senghor even went as far as to describe the Bandung Conference as the most important event since the Renaissance and the one that spelled "death to the inferiority complex of colonial peoples."[66] For many of the leaders at Bandung who had spent years of their lives under arrest and in prison for opposing Western colonialism, it was the fulfillment of a dream. "We have made history," declared Nehru, and we have acted as "agents of historic destiny."[67]

Like a heavy rock thrown into a still but deep pond, the Bandung Conference immediately sent waves rushing across the world. It did not take long for governments to decide how they would respond. Sensing a unique opportunity to support their ideology of anticolonialism, emphasize their unity with other non-white peoples, and at the same time extend their own influence in Asia and Africa, the Chinese quickly stressed Chou En-lai's personal contributions to the "spirit of Bandung" and their strong support for national liberation movements. Although it had not been invited to the conference, the Soviet Union also quickly praised the meeting, hailing it as a beacon of light in the struggle of the Afro-Asian peoples against European and U.S. imperialism.[68] The *Times of India* viewed this response as particularly interesting and commented at the time: "Russia with one foot in Europe and another in Asia has been more quick to appreciate the significance and implications of Bandung than the West. While Washington and London fumble feebly, obsessed by visions of colored hordes clouding a lily-white horizon like locusts swooping on pastures new, Moscow, Moses-like, beckons the dispossessed hosts onwards to the Promised Land."[69]

In sharp contrast to the Chinese and Soviets, who presented themselves as friends and thus built up a reservoir of goodwill, which would last well into the postindependence period, the West reacted to the Bandung Conference with silence, vacillation, or opposition. Dulles, in fact, even went as far as to condemn Third World neutrality as "an obsolete, . . . immoral, and short-sighted conception."[70] The military attack by Britain, France, and Israel in 1956 against Egypt (one of the active participants at Bandung) made this situation even worse and strengthened the resolve of the Afro-Asian group to push further. Undeterred by either these statements or actions by the West and encouraged by the support given from Communist countries, the Afro-Asian group determined to reinforce the principles of Bandung by holding additional international conferences, by creating the more militant Afro-Asian Peoples' Solidarity Organization,[71] and of particular importance for global politics and diplomacy, by actively supporting the nationalist movements for independence emerging throughout Africa.

For many Asian countries the Bandung Conference marked the end of the transition from colonial rule to independence, but for Africans it marked the beginning. As late as 1955, still only three countries in the entire continent other than South Africa could claim to be independent: Ethiopia, Liberia, and Egypt. All the rest remained under some form of control from Europe or from what one African termed simply "the white hand of authority."[72] Efforts of the Arab League and Pan-African movement, publications like the *New African*, and the growing popularity of self-assertion through concepts such as Negritude and "Africanity" provided inspiration for emancipation,[73] but they could not bring it about by themselves. In this regard, Africans received enormous assistance from Asians. The collapse of empires in Asia demonstrated to those nationalists in Africa that independence could be won, that some Europeans could change their minds voluntarily while others could be defeated in guerrilla warfare if necessary, and that Third World unity against domination and discrimination, against power and prejudice, could help them all.

One of the first and most obvious examples of this connection between these events and Asia and the gaining of independence in Africa occurred in possessions controlled by France. The stunning defeat delivered to French power, prestige, and self-confidence at Dienbienphu in Indochina brought the Pierre Mendes-France government to power in Paris and with it the conscious decision to accept the loss of empire in Asia. This, in turn, greatly inspired nationalist movements in Tunisia and Morocco, where the Neo-Destour party under the leadership of Habib Bourguiba and the Istiqlal organization with the support of the popular Sultan Muhammad V both sought their respective freedom from heavy-handed colonial rule. Confronted by the strength of these movements, violent disturbances, pressure from the United Nations and the Bandung Conference, and the prospects of even greater losses, the French decided to relinquish control. In 1956 they therefore granted independence to Tunisia and Morocco, thus setting into motion a process of ending the French empire in Africa.[74]

The beginning of this retreat of the European powers from their extensive African holdings continued with the British. Like the French, they determined that they simply could not continue to fight against these tremendous pressures for change and indefinitely cling to all their possessions gained in the past. Attacks from Sudanese nationalists frequently supported by the Egyptians, for example, led the British to recognize the futility of their efforts. They decided to abandon their claims, withdraw from their positions, and concede independence to the Sudan in 1956. Such a startling reversal of British policy in Africa offered dramatic new hope for determined nationalists, particularly Kwame Nkrumah, who for years had been active in the Pan-African movement and dreamed of ways to gain freedom for his homeland of the Gold Coast. Working closely with the moderate British governor, Sir Charles Arden-Clarke, this radical nationalist surprised a watching world by reaching an agreement for a peaceful transfer of power. After lengthy negotiations Nkrumah finally announced with tears in his eyes that the colony formerly exploited for its gold and black slaves would gain independence in 1957 under the new name of Ghana. Well aware that his was the first black African state to be liberated from colonial rule, Nkrumah pledged to make it an example to others and proclaimed: "The independence of Ghana is meaningless unless it is linked to the liberation of Africa."[75]

In order to realize this dream, Nkrumah immediately set about to use the new sovereign state of Ghana as a base from which to assist other African peoples struggling for independence. He invited the well-known Pan-African activist George Padmore to help him organize a conference that would bring together representatives of nationalist movements from twenty-eight African territories still under colonial rule. Their purpose, stated one spokesman, would be to formulate concrete plans regarding several common problems, the most important of which appeared under the headings of "colonialism and imperialism" and "racialism and discrimination."[76] The result was the highly successful All-African People's Conference, held in Accra during 1958. Delegations from anglophone West and East Africa, francophone black Africa, the Belgian Congo, and the Arab lands to the north made this the first genuinely all-African assembly in history. It also marked the first time that a meeting of Pan-Africanism had ever met on African soil itself. Not about to miss a unique opportunity like this, the remarkable ninety-year-old Du Bois demonstrated that he had lost none of his passionate fire and exhorted the assembled delegates to unite in a common effort: "You have nothing to lose but your chains! You have a continent to regain! You have freedom and human dignity to attain!"[77]

Inspired by speeches such as these, the delegates agreed to set up a body that would direct and assist anticolonial struggles throughout the entire continent of Africa. They applauded the acquisition of independence by Guinea earlier that year, reaffirmed their determination to remain nonaligned, and then declared their support for the Algerian revolution against the French, for Tom Mboya of Kenya and Julius Nyerere of Tanganyika and their Pan-African Freedom Movement of East and Central Africa, and Patrice Lumumba and his efforts in the Belgian Congo. These actions at Accra instilled in a number of African leaders, many of them previously unknown to one another, a new sense of solidarity, purpose, and hope for the future.[78]

Within just a few short years, a virtual revolution occurred. Encouraged by their mutual efforts, Africans, with the support of many Asians, pushed for more. Europeans, frightened by events and forces they could no longer control and recognizing the need to respond to drastically changing circumstances if they wanted to retain any influence at all with former colonial peoples, reluctantly realized that they would have to do with less. In one dramatic shift of policy, for example, Charles de Gaulle of France suddenly declared that "the colonial era is over" and with a flourish announced his intention to become a champion of the decolonization movement.[79] The dam burst in 1960—frequently described as "The Year of Africa."[80] In a sudden flood approximately half of the continent became politically independent: Within this single year, seventeen separate states gained nationhood. These included Cameroon, Senegal, Mauritania, Mali, Niger, Ivory Coast, Upper Volta (now Burkina Faso), Togo, Dahomey (now Benin), Central African Republic, Chad, Congo (Brazzaville), Malagasy Republic, Zaire, Somalia (former Italian and British Somaliland), Gabon, and Nigeria.[81] As he personally witnessed this collapse of empire before his eyes, British Prime Minister Harold Macmillan felt compelled to deliver his now-famous "Wind of Change" speech before a surprised and angry audience of whites in Cape Town. "We have seen," he said,

> the awakening of national consciousness in peoples who have for centuries lived in dependence upon some other power. Fifteen years ago this movement spread through Asia. Many countries there of different races and civilizations pressed their claim to an independent life. Today the same thing is happening in Africa. The most striking of all the impressions I have formed since I left London a month ago is the strength of this national consciousness. The wind of change is blowing through this continent. Whether we like it or not this growth of national consciousness is a political fact. We must all accept it as a fact. Our national policies must take account of it.[82]

That same wind continued to blow even where the existence of whites as permanent settlers rather than simply temporary administrators greatly complicated any transfer of power. In East Africa, for example, British experiments with "multiracial constitutions" that, in order to retain some control, prescribed a certain number of legislative representatives for each racial group rather than open elections for majorities quickly failed to gain black support. Protracted guerrilla insurrections made the situation all the more volatile. When Sierra Leone and Tanganyika gained independence in 1961, still more cracks in the edifice of empire opened. Uganda, Rwanda, and Burundi joined them the next year, as did Algeria after a terribly bloody war against the French. Then, in 1963, both Kenya and the former slaving center of Zanzibar became free.[83] To emphasize their break with the past, almost all of these new governments immediately passed laws prohibiting racial discrimination.[84] Never in the history of the world have so many peoples gained independence and emancipation in such an incredibly short period of time, and throughout it all rang the cry of Chief A. J. Luthuli of the African National Congress: "Let My People Go!"[85]

This sudden shift of power in Africa did not come without difficulties and hardships. Independence brought many benefits of freedom but also the very real practical problems of self-government. The thrust from colonial status to nationhood brought with it the responsibilities of politics and diplomacy heretofore assumed by others and for which few African leaders had been trained. Many understandably argued with rhetorical flourish and defiance that they would rather govern themselves poorly than continue being governed well by others, but this provided no substitute for a realistic approach to the tasks before them. They quickly discovered, for example, that in all too many cases there existed little relationship between political independence on the one hand and economic viability, social cohesion, or modernization on the other. At home they faced the problems of governing, educating, financing, and feeding themselves, problems made all the more difficult when many whites took their skills and their capital and left for Europe or their last holdout on the continent, South Africa. Moreover, the African leaders found themselves confronting a bewildering array of complicated international problems, not the least of which was trying to chart a neutral course of nonalignment through the morass of the Cold War.

Acutely aware of these difficult problems that they all shared, a number of African leaders anxiously sought some means to overcome their individual limitations and differences. The split between the radicals in the "Casablanca group," who wanted immediate Pan-African unity (Ghana, Guinea, and Algeria), and the gradualist or functionalist states in the "Brazzaville-Monrovia group," for example, convinced many that they desperately needed to combine their efforts and develop a common strategy. For this reason, they enthusiastically welcomed the call from Haile Selassie for the Summit Conference of Independent African States. Thirty-two African heads of state or government accepted his invitation and assembled in Addis Ababa in 1963. Within only a few days they unanimously agreed to create the Organization of African Unity, complete with its own charter, assembly, council of foreign ministers, secretariat, and specialized commissions, to advance their common interests. The charter emphasized their belief in the inalienable right of all people to control their own destiny, the principles enunciated in the Universal Declaration of Human Rights, the importance of achieving freedom and equality, the need to maintain a position of nonalignment between the Cold War blocs, and the necessity to promote unity and solidarity among African states.[86]

The first three resolutions passed by the Organization of African Unity delineated its objectives clearly and unequivocally. In the very beginning, the delegates unanimously passed a resolution entitled "Decolonization" on that burning issue. In it they denounced colonialism; announced their determination "to support dependent peoples in Africa in their struggle for freedom and independence" from foreign control; and called for the severance of all diplomatic and consular relations with Portugal and South Africa as long as they continued to practice imperialism, genocide, and apartheid. They then turned their attention to the second resolution, "Apartheid and Racial Discrimination," which expressed deep concern over "measures of racial discrimination taken against communities of African origin living outside the continent" and in this context singling out the plight of blacks in the United States for special attention. As could be expected, they used the strongest language to condemn racial discrimination "in all its forms in Africa and all over the world." Finally, the Organization of African Unity passed its third resolution, called "Africa and the United Nations," which provided even further indications of things to come by insisting that Africa as a geographical region have greater representation in the principal organs of the United Nations and pledging that there they would coordinate their growing number of votes in order to assert themselves more effectively on matters of common concern—especially when pursuing decolonization and when challenging racial discrimination.[87]

Pursuing Decolonization and Self-Determination

This revolutionary emergence of independent states in Africa and Asia virtually transformed the composition, character, tone, language, and much of the agenda of the United Nations. As we have seen, when the world organization began, its membership included only three countries from all of Africa, three from Asia, and seven from the Middle East. The overwhelming bulk of the members, by contrast, came from the white, Western countries. The tide began to turn after the significant Bandung Conference, for in 1955, after five years in which not a single new member had entered the United Nations, sixteen countries were allowed to join. Four more states joined the next year, all from Africa and Asia. Ghana and Malaya became members in 1957, and Guinea did so one year later. The great flood came in 1960 and 1961. During these two years alone, nineteen African and two Asian countries swelled the ranks of the United Nations as never before. Together they dramatically shifted the organization's voting strength. By the end of 1961, in fact, there existed fifty-three members from the Afro-Asian world and fifty-one from all other continents combined. With this achievement, the Afro-Asian countries secured a majority. Seven more Afro-Asian countries joined the next year, thus demonstrating that this majority only would continue to increase through time.[88]

It did not take long for this trend to become evident. Indeed, even at an early stage, one high official from South Africa complained bitterly that "the complexion of the United Nations has changed from white to black."[89] India viewed the situation in the same way but, instead of opposing the change, openly welcomed it and sought to use it to full advantage. As early as 1950, twelve countries from Africa and Asia met under Indian leadership to discuss means of coordinating common approaches within the United Nations. By 1956 this group had increased in size to twenty-eight, making it the largest single regional bloc and able to prevent any proposal from obtaining a two-thirds majority in the General Assembly without the support of at least some of its members. After 1961 the Afro-Asians secured an absolute majority and thus a position from which they could express themselves on any subject, determine agenda items, assert themselves, and reaffirm their political independence to the world. This served as a powerful stimulant to Afro-Asianism, for voting power tended to elevate Afro-Asian countries to a new international status that, by the sheer weight of its numbers, was far higher than the rank that any of its single members could ever hope to attain on their own.[90]

The emergence of this new Afro-Asian group within the United Nations, of course, did not entail automatic uniformity. Indeed, its members unquestionably represented the most heterogeneous bloc in the entire organization. Geographically, they spread all the way from Japan to Morocco and Iraq to the Malagasy Republic. In religion, they differed from Hindu to Muslim and from Christian to Buddhist. Politically, they ranged from vociferously nonaligned Egypt and Indonesia, to pro-Western Thailand and Lebanon, to pro-Communist Mongolia. Even those leaning toward communism found themselves sharply divided in the Sino-Soviet split. Their acute differences surfaced time and time again in disputes within the United Nations as each state voted in its own national self-interest.[91] Only two issues could bring them together to close ranks for a common purpose, but about these they were consistent: first, the fate of those peoples still under colonial domination; and second, the plight of those still suffering from racial discrimination.

Efforts within the United Nations to bring an end to empires began with the Trusteeship Council. The Charter initially had established an International Trusteeship System to oversee the administration of at least some colonial possessions. It also proclaimed a desire for just treatment without prejudice and eventual independence for the inhabitants through the Declaration Regarding Non-Self-Governing Territories.[92] The General Assembly assigned supervision of this system to the Trusteeship Council, composed of representatives from those states in the United Nations administering trust territories, nonadministering permanent members of the Security Council, and others elected at large by the General Assembly itself.

At first, the colonial powers believed that this rather weak arrangement would be sufficient for their continued control of overseas possessions, little suspecting what revolutionary changes were in store. Indeed, they even had enough votes to block the application of Du Bois and the Pan-African Congress for consultative status, as one United Nations administrator wrote, on the grounds that "your organization adopted a resolution in opposition to the Trusteeship System and that, therefore, you are opposing the aims of the Charter."[93] Very quickly, however, the

Soviet and Chinese representatives from the Security Council indicated their strong opposition to Western colonialism on the Trusteeship Council and the General Assembly deliberately elected its open members from the Afro-Asian or Latin American states. Together they began using their influence and their votes to do what they could to dismember empires, allowing petitioners representing nationalist organizations to testify before the council and thus make their claims widely known and sending visiting missions into trust territories to provide increased pressure for independence.[94]

In this endeavor, the Trusteeship Council received great assistance from the General Assembly as it changed composition. As early as its first session in 1946, for example, the General Assembly drew the attention of United Nations' members to the fact that the obligations of the Charter for eventual self-government for all dependent peoples, and not just those in designated trust territories, were in force. It did not have the power, however, to do anything more than simply receive whatever material about the economic, social, and educational conditions in the dependencies the administering countries chose to give it "for informational purposes" only, as stated in the Charter.[95]

Through time, this situation began to change, as a growing number of members argued that the dependent territories' goal of full self-government necessitated the receipt of information about constitutional and political developments as well. The Afro-Asian states thus passed resolutions establishing special committees to receive and study information from trust and other non-self-governing territories. By 1955 they even secured a sufficient number of votes to assert that the General Assembly itself was competent to examine this information and to determine whether these territories were progressing toward independence or not.[96] Furious debates within the Assembly followed over the violence in Kenya, Algeria, Cameroon, and then the Congo, increasing the level of intensity. As one senior Belgian official who served on a number of delegations to the United Nations to defend the colonial performance of his country declared: "Anti-colonial nationalism has become one of the main revolutionary forces of our times. Its virulence has grown in the course of recent years to subjecting the colonial powers, both within and without their non-self-governing territories, to a pressure which—failing recourse to totalitarian methods—tends to become irresistible."[97]

With the admission to the United Nations in 1960 of seventeen new members—all of which were formerly dependent territories—this movement for the immediate liberation of colored, colonial peoples indeed did appear irresistible. Now the states forming the majority in the General Assembly knew that they possessed the necessary votes and momentum to take a more determined position. In addition, they knew that the eyes of the world would be focused upon the 1960 assembly session, for it was scheduled to bring together a remarkable array of international leaders, including Dwight Eisenhower of the United States, Nikita Khrushchev of the Soviet Union, Marshall Tito of Yugoslavia, Fidel Castro of Cuba, Nehru, Nkrumah, Nasser, and Sukarno, among many other heads of state.

The time had come, said the representative of Libya, for the world to acknowledge universally "that the practices of colonialism, which consist purely and simply of the domination of certain countries by others and the subjugation of certain peoples by others, are flagrant violations of the principle of 'equal rights and self-determination of peoples' laid down in the Charter."[98] Krishna Menon of India reiterated this theme but specifically emphasized one particular issue when he asserted, "We must not forget that the real objective is to abolish from this world any kind of rule by one nation or people of another nation or people, particularly if it is based upon racial discrimination."[99] Others from Africa and Asia added their voices to this discussion as well, continually stressing the need to build upon and then go beyond the historic decisions reached during the Asian-African Conference in Bandung and the All-African Peoples' Conference in Accra. The "complete, unconditional, and immediate liquidation of colonialism in all its manifestations," declared one spokesman, "must be our irreducible decision."[100]

Toward this end, forty-three African and Asian states joined together and submitted to the United Nations General Assembly a resolution called the Declaration on the Granting of Independence to Colonial Countries and Peoples. This resolution proclaimed the necessity of bringing colonialism in all its forms and manifestations to a speedy and unconditional end. It declared that the subjugation of peoples to alien domination, discrimination, and exploitation constituted a flagrant violation of fundamental principles in the Universal Declaration of Human Rights, an infraction against the Charter of the United Nations, and an impediment to the promotion of world peace and cooperation. For this reason, the declaration called for immediate steps that would bring an end to empire by transferring power to all peoples of trust and non-self-governing territories, without any conditions or reservations, to enable them to enjoy complete independence and freedom—"without any distinction as to race, creed, or color."[101]

As one might imagine, this striking Declaration on the Granting of Independence to Colonial Countries and Peoples opened up an emotionally charged and heated debate of the first magnitude. The states recently released from the grips of colonialism spoke passionately about their sufferings in the past and the insidious nature of racial prejudice by which whites subjected black, brown, and yellow men and women around the world. Representatives of these states also declared their determination to assist their brothers and sisters still under foreign domination and discrimination to gain freedom and independence. Some emphasized the importance of nonalignment in this struggle, while others spoke in favor of either one side or the other in the Cold War, some criticizing the Soviet Union for its own brand of imperialism and some castigating the United States for its overseas interventions and its toleration of the Ku Klux Klan. The Soviets, with their satellites in tow, eagerly entered the fray, giving full verbal support to the declaration and claiming that Communists always supported the national liberation of subjected peoples.[102]

Debate on the declaration raged on for days, but finally the time approached to vote. A silence fell across the General Assembly. Each state recorded its decision and anxiously awaited for the tally to be announced. When the president finally read the result, most delegates rose to their feet with loud cheers. Eighty-nine states supported the declaration, including all those from Africa, Asia, Latin America, and from the Communist countries. No one directly opposed it. But to the continued anger and frustration of the rest, eight white powers all allied on one side in the Cold War and all with either troops or extensive interests in territories beyond their own borders cast abstentions: Portugal, Spain, South Africa, Britain, Australia, France, Belgium, and the United States.[103]

Fearful that these abstaining states might deliberately fail to live up to either the letter or the spirit of the Declaration on the Granting of Independence to Colonial Countries and Peoples, the General Assembly sought to monitor carefully progress toward implementation. As early as the Assembly's next session, therefore, thirty-eight African and Asian states sponsored a resolution noting with deep regret that most of the provisions of the declaration had not been carried out. They deplored the fact that armed force and repression continued to be used in certain areas "with increasing ruthlessness" against dependent peoples, depriving them of their right to independence. The majority in the assembly thus called upon all states concerned to "take action without further delay with a view to the faithful application and implementation of the Declaration."[104] At the same time they voted to establish a special committee to explore ways in which the United Nations could use its authority and the declaration to accelerate the process of bringing an irrevocable end to empire.[105]

This special committee tackled its task with determination and vigor, quickly going far beyond the rather limited terms of reference initially imposed upon the Trusteeship Council. Over the objections of the

Australian, British, and U.S. committee members, it invited petitioners from dependent territories to come and express their grievances before an international body. It held meetings outside of the United Nations headquarters in places such as Tangier, Addis Ababa, Dar-es-Salaam, and Lusaka when necessary to make direct observations and obtain on-site information. The special committee consciously sought to utilize the resources of other United Nations agencies that might contribute to eliminating domination and discrimination, including the International Labor Organization, the Food and Agriculture Organization, UNESCO, and the World Health Organization. It also boldly requested specific information from administering powers about the political conditions in their dependencies, made explicit recommendations on how the declaration should be implemented, and established deadlines for the granting of independence to non-self-governing peoples.[106]

Through their efforts in spearheading these many concerted actions in the special committee, General Assembly, and Trusteeship Council, the Afro-Asian countries thus placed decolonization high on the agenda of international politics and diplomacy. They took it upon themselves to use the various organs of the United Nations in whatever way they could to assist other peoples seeking emancipation. For this reason, they took enormous pride in seeing other states follow them through the recently opened door of independence. Only one year after the Declaration on the Granting of Independence to Colonial Countries and Peoples, Sierra Leone, Mauritania, Mongolia, and Tanganyika became free. Burundi, Jamaica, Rwanda, Trinidad, Tobago, Algeria, and Uganda followed in 1962. Kuwait, Kenya, Zanzibar (which united with Tanganyika to form Tanzania), Malawi, Malta, and Northern Rhodesia (Zambia) all joined the United Nations as sovereign members during the next two years. Then in 1965 and 1966, Gambia, the Maldive Islands, Singapore, British Guiana (Guyana), Basutoland (Lesotho), Bechuanaland (Botswana), and Barbados all gained their independence as well.

These revolutionary developments brought a dramatic end to empire in most places of the world—but not all. Despite the remarkable and unprecedented successes in decolonization initiated by the Afro-Asian countries and supported by most others, a number of non-self-governing territories still remained. These included certain islands in the Atlantic, Pacific, and Indian oceans, and the Caribbean, in addition to particular enclaves that those in power refused to relinquish. The most important of these by far were the "hard-core" territories in southern Africa, all controlled by white minority regimes: Angola, Mozambique, and Guinea-Bissau under Portuguese authority; Southern Rhodesia; and South-West Africa, or Namibia, ruled by South Africa with the same policies that it used against blacks at home.[107] The occupation of these lands not only continued to resist firmly the tide of decolonization, as we shall see,[108] but also to confront blatantly the second vital concern of all Afro-Asian countries: racial discrimination.

Challenging Racial Discrimination

From the very inception of the United Nations, it was clear that all noncolonial powers would use the organization as a forum and a focal point to express their undying antagonism toward any system of white domination and to promote racial equality. Due to their pressure and that from nongovernmental groups, the Charter itself specifically included several important provisions supporting the principle of equal treatment.[109] The first session of the General Assembly not only passed a resolution condemning discrimination on the basis of race, but also directly called upon South Africa to change its policies toward Africans and Asians. It then went on to create the Commission on Human Rights, establish the Sub-Commission on Prevention of Discrimination and Protection of Minorities, set standards in the Universal Declaration of Human Rights, and write the Convention on the Prevention and Punishment of the Crime of Genocide.[110]

Each of these important accomplishments marked a milestone on the road toward international concern for racial equality and basic human rights that had never existed before. For this reason and in this context, they were hailed as remarkable achievements. Nevertheless, each suffered from a serious flaw. Neither the Charter of the United Nations nor the Universal Declaration of Human Rights contained any binding commitments or the threat of enforcement with sanctions for noncompliance in this area. The genocide convention imposed obligations not upon all states, but only those that voluntarily agreed to sign, thus leaving countries like the United States and South Africa not bound by its provisions. Moreover, during these first years, the new Commission on Human Rights and its Sub-Commission on Prevention of Discrimination, like the United Nations itself, remained under the control of white, Western powers, which already had been pushed much further than they initially intended to go in discussing the issue of racial discrimination. At this stage many wanted to slow down or perhaps even stop the process entirely.

During the early years of the Commission on Human Rights, for example, the majority of member governments demonstrated a distinct reluctance to move very fast or to take meaningful action. From the very beginning, both the British Foreign Office and the British Colonial Office wanted the commission to avoid any extensive study of the global problem of racial discrimination and colonialism in "backward" colored territories.[111] The British delegate consistently received instructions to render the Commission's decisions "as innocuous as possible."[112] Similarly, the United States wanted to use the considerable reputation of Eleanor Roosevelt in the area of human rights but would not allow her to participate in any discussion at all about explosive complaints from the National Association for the Advancement of Colored People or other groups regarding domestic racial discrimination.[113] When Dulles became secretary of state he not only removed her from the chair of the Commission, but with the full support of southern senators concerned about race, he announced that he would never bring a binding human rights covenant before the U.S. Senate for ratification.[114]

Other governments also constantly refused to let their representatives on this commission take any action upon individual petitions submitted to it that complained of human rights violations, thus creating what even the former director of the Division of Human Rights described as "probably the most elaborate wastepaper basket ever invented."[115] Some actually attempted to eliminate completely the Sub-Commission on Prevention of Discrimination due to what they regarded as its excessive independence.[116] After drafting the Universal Declaration of Human Rights, the Commission then spent its next decade and a half debating language on covenants designed to implement the Declaration, arguing whether self-determination should be tied to other human rights, and confining itself merely to written or verbal informational activities. "The hopes have been so far sadly frustrated," complained one observer bitterly as he likened the inaction of the Commission to that of the League of Nations and sarcastically gibed, "It touched nothing which it did not adjourn."[117]

This distinct pattern of deliberate inaction was dramatically and primarily changed by one phenomenon: the rise of the Afro-Asians. Passionately committed not only to pursuing decolonization but also to challenging racial discrimination, they immediately began to make their influence felt when they gained independence and entered the United Nations. Collectively, these new states from Africa and Asia exerted enough pressure to begin a radical and turbulent transformation in their favor in the composition and character of the Commission on Human Rights, its Sub-Commission on Prevention of Discrimination, the Third Committee, General Assembly, and other organs of the United Nations.[118] As this process continued, the Afro-Asian states increasingly could use their newly acquired positions to focus attention on the global problem of discrimination based on race. "An age-old sore had come to light," wrote Eleanor Roosevelt about this development, "and I felt the weight of history for which the nations of the Western world are now to be called to account." Tensions and emotions would occupy the United

Nations, she accurately predicted from firsthand experience, due to the intense feeling among those from Africa and Asia "that we, because our skins are white, necessarily look down upon all peoples whose skins are yellow or black or brown. This thought is never out of their minds."[119]

Throughout all the many discussions about decolonization and self-determination for dependent peoples, for example, the delegates from Africa and Asia never lost sight of the issue of race. At the Asian-African Conference in Bandung, the All-African Peoples' Conference in Accra, the formation of the Organization of African Unity in Addis Ababa, the meetings of the Afro-Asian Peoples' Solidarity Organization in Cairo, and the debates within the United Nations in New York and Geneva, the delegates always coupled colonialism and racial discrimination.[120] Their attitude was captured with particular perceptiveness by Frantz Fanon in his powerful and angry book, *The Wretched of the Earth* (1961), which gave expression to the deep and painful connection between the politically subjugated and the racially oppressed.[121] As the delegate from Morocco tried to explain during a General Assembly debate about self-determination and human rights, both colonialism and racial discrimination violated the principle of equality and ignored the most elementary right of all people. Through their own perverse logic, he continued, they signified the "domination, enslavement, and exploitation of the individual" and created extreme forms of inequality and racial segregation wherever they appeared.[122] For this reason, once Africans and Asians gained political independence, they set about to determine the terms of discourse in international bodies and to challenge as directly as they possibly could the integrally interrelated issue of racial discrimination.

Not content with the early, ground-breaking decisions and resolutions of the United Nations in the area of racial discrimination, the states vitally concerned about human rights pushed for additional action. They initiated negotiations that led to the Economic and Social Council's Supplementary Convention on the Abolition of Slavery and the Slave Trade in 1956. Due to their efforts, the International Labor Organization adopted the Convention Concerning Discrimination in Respect to Employment and Occupation two years later. They also encouraged UNESCO to approve in 1962 the Convention Against Discrimination in Education.[123] Each of these new international agreements, as well as continuing resolutions against South Africa's policy of apartheid,[124] contained specific provisions prohibiting racial discrimination, but none went so far as the African and Asian countries wanted to go. As long as they remained in a minority, there was little they could do. Once they captured the majority, however, they set about to take much more determined action.

In this regard, they received assistance from a most unexpected source: the outbreak of renewed neo-Nazi racial hatred in Europe which again reminded the world of the dangerous persistence of prejudice.[125]

There can be little question about the fact that this new majority within the United Nations found itself motivated by several different factors to place the racial discrimination issue so prominently upon the international agenda. The matter of racial equality touched them deeply and sincerely and raised one of the most fundamental of all questions about the application of justice irrespective of the color of one's skin. But this, it must be admitted, was not all. The emotionally charged subject of race, they quickly learned, could provide a ready means of unifying a wide variety of different states, cultures, and ideologies for a common purpose. The rhetoric of antiracism against whites in the West could divert attention away from troublesome problems at home such as political turmoil, economic instability, tribal strife, the denial of other kinds of human rights by repression, or even their own forms of discriminating practices. In addition, and not at all insignificant for the politics and diplomacy of discrimination, the racial issue could allow new states of Africa and Asia to join forces in a bloc and exert influence upon the international community. In the United Nations, where members counted votes before wealth or military might, they could exercise power—especially against those from the white West at whose hands they long had experienced domination and discrimination.[126]

For a wide variety of different but related reasons, therefore, the Afro-Asian states raised the issue of race repeatedly and with fixed determination. This frequently caused them to turn a blind eye toward other violations of human rights, especially those in their own countries and in the Soviet Union. They pressured countries like the United States over segregation and immigration quotas so much, in fact, that President Dwight Eisenhower publicly regretted the harm done "to the prestige and influence and indeed to the safety of our nation and the world" due to racial discrimination.[127] The Afro-Asian nations also circulated the story that when then–Vice President Richard Nixon attended the independence celebrations in Ghana, he turned to his black neighbor at the dinner table to ask, "How does it feel to be free?" The reply came: "I wouldn't know. I am from Alabama."[128] Accounts of insensitivity and prejudice such as these created a most difficult image for the United States, eventually forcing Dean Rusk, secretary of state under the Kennedy administration, to admit, "The biggest single burden that we carry on our backs in our foreign relations in the 1960s is the problem of racial discrimination."[129] To increase the pressure on the United States and to expose its policies toward race even more, African nations openly feted

Malcolm X of the militant Black Muslims and endorsed his call for active self-defense by the racially oppressed against white supremacists.[130]

Then, working first within the Commission on Human Rights, its activist Sub-Commission on Prevention of Discrimination, and the Third Committee, the Afro-Asian majority sponsored a series of educational seminars on the global problem of race and successfully brought before the General Assembly in 1963 a proposed resolution called the Declaration on the Elimination of All Forms of Racial Discrimination.[131] With this document the Afro-Asian countries wanted to express their deep alarm over continuing manifestations of racial discrimination, their conviction that prejudice on the basis of color seriously threatened interracial and international relations, and their sincere belief "that any doctrine of racial differentiation or superiority is scientifically false, morally condemnable, socially unjust and dangerous, and that there is no justification for racial discrimination in theory or in practice." To eliminate such prejudice and assure equality, the sponsoring states pledged that they would do whatever was necessary to end racial discrimination "without delay."[132] Debate and discussion raged furiously, primarily among the Afro-Asians and Communists on one side and Western powers on the other. The latter argued that they certainly supported the ethical principle of racial equality but did not want to violate the principle of freedom of speech in a democratic society by being forced to prosecute those who happen to express ideas of racial superiority.[133] In the end, the declaration passed by eighty-nine votes in favor, none against, and the now-familiar seventeen abstentions.

Most delegates quickly hailed the Declaration on the Elimination of All Forms of Racial Discrimination as a truly historic statement by the international community.[134] For the first time, the declaration placed states on record not only as condemning ideologies that promoted prejudice and policies that applied racial discrimination (including segregation and apartheid) but also for taking some action against them. "It is an undoubted fact," stated one representative, "that . . . the peoples of Africa and Asia, who throughout history and in all continents have suffered the most from racial discrimination, attach the greatest importance to this question."[135] As Moreno Salcedo of the Philippines declared:

This is a momentous occasion, for in this hall and for the first time the equality of man, regardless of race or color, has been unanimously proclaimed. In our long and troubled journey towards a better life, one of the greatest tragedies of all times has been the iniquitous degradation of the human being by reason of the color of his skin. The Declaration . . . now definitely shatters the myth that one race is superior to another or that one person is better than another simply because his complexion is lighter or darker. . . . We entertain the hope that the noble sentiments in this Declaration will now be translated into deeds.[136]

Diallo Telli of Guinea echoed the same theme by maintaining that the declaration represented a great affirmation "to all representatives of the so-called 'colored' peoples who, on every continent, have suffered most through the centuries, and who still suffer most from racial discrimination. . . . However," he warned, "we are not forgetting for a single instant that even the best resolutions are of value only in so far as they are effectively *applied*. . . . The hour for decisive action has struck. Let us not allow it to pass by."[137]

In order to assure that this opportunity not be missed and that definite actions accompany these words of resolutions, the majority in the General Assembly immediately called for a two-pronged approach: a legally binding International Convention on the Elimination of All Forms of Racial Discrimination and similar covenants with obligations to finally put teeth into the Universal Declaration of Human Rights.[138] The latter, of course, had been discussed since the days of Eleanor Roosevelt; but it had always been put off and delayed by Western states that opposed any threats to their sovereignty and by Communist countries that resisted international attention to civil and political rights within their borders.[139] This prolonged and fruitless deadlock lasting for eighteen years finally was broken by the Afro-Asians, who now demanded that action be taken.

The remarkable International Convention on the Elimination of All Forms of Racial Discrimination, adopted in 1965, provided the first concrete result of this new determination. For the first time in history, states negotiated among themselves a binding treaty designed "to adopt all necessary measures for speedily eliminating racial discrimination in all its forms and manifestations, and to prevent and combat racist doctrines and practices in order to promote understanding between races and to build an international community free from all forms of racial segregation and racial discrimination." In this regard, they referred to the principles of both the Universal Declaration of Human Rights and the Declaration on the Granting of Independence to Colonial Countries and Peoples, and then finally provided a working definition of what they meant by racial discrimination. "In this Convention," stated Article 1, "the term 'racial discrimination' shall mean any distinction, exclusion, restriction, or preference based on race, color, descent, or national or ethnic origin which has the purpose or effect of nullifying or impairing the recognition, enjoyment or exercise, on an equal footing, of human rights and fundamental freedoms in the political, economic, social, cultural, or any other field of public life."[140]

The signatories then went on to bind themselves legally and morally to prevent, prohibit, and eradicate racial segregation and apartheid, to guarantee equality before the law, and to adopt immediate and effective measures to combat prejudices that lead to racial discrimination. Toward this end, they pledged to nullify any national or local laws that had the effect of creating or perpetuating racial discrimination in their countries, to punish by law those who disseminated ideas based upon racial superiority or hatred, and to provide annual reports to the United Nations on their compliance with the treaty's provisions. The signatories even agreed that they could be subjected to criticism by other states party to the convention and by individual petitions charging them with violations of nondiscrimination. Moreover, to monitor and implement these terms, they established the special Committee on the Elimination of Racial Discrimination, the first—and for several years, the only—international machinery created within the framework of measures for implementation in a United Nations–sponsored treaty in the field of human rights. The convention entered into force in 1969 and within a short period of time obtained more ratifications than any other single United Nations human rights instrument,[141] beginning, in the words of one scholar, "the most comprehensive and unambiguous codification in treaty form of the idea of the equality of races."[142]

Greatly encouraged by this achievement, but not yet satisfied and still uncertain how the convention would be implemented in practice,[143] the new majority within the United Nations also pushed for additional legal instruments designed specifically to implement the Universal Declaration of Human Rights. Due to the Afro-Asian efforts and pressure, the General Assembly successfully adopted in 1966 the important International Covenant on Economic, Social, and Cultural Rights as well as the International Covenant on Civil and Political Rights.[144] Both obligated the signatories to recognize and enforce the right of self-determination for subject peoples and the right to be treated equally without discrimination. Then, in order to provide even more teeth to these commitments, the covenants provided the opportunity for states to sign the Optional Protocol, permitting individuals to petition the Human Rights Committee created by the covenants for a redress of grievances before an international tribunal. These treaties justifiably generated enormous enthusiasm for constituting a major breakthrough in the implementation of human rights and the principles of equality. Collectively, they went far beyond anything achieved before. As one delegate declared, they represented "the culmination of twenty years of work."[145] Another spoke in similar praise but wisely cautioned that the task ahead required avoiding "pompous statements" and "tempting promises" while seeing to it "that these new covenants are strictly observed everywhere."[146]

*   *   *

The end of empire primarily in Africa and Asia brought in its wake not only the demise of white, Western dominance in the world but also the rise of new states fully determined to exercise their independence and nonalignment by promoting self-determination among peoples and challenging racial discrimination. Once they obtained a majority within the United Nations, they secured a mechanism for doing precisely this. First with a number of declaratory resolutions and then with a series of binding treaties, they sought to bring about a world free from the domination and discrimination of the past. Only the most intransigent refused to join in this effort and refused to ratify the International Convention on the Elimination of All Forms of Racial Discrimination. These included the "hard-core" territories in southern Africa under the control of white minority regimes, Israel, and despite its most impressive record at home during the "Black Revolution" in the mid-1960s in advancing civil rights and racial equality, the United States.[147] The continued refusal of a small number of states to make concessions in the face of such an overwhelming movement greatly angered and frustrated the rest, prompting them to intensify their determination by designating 1973 as the beginning of a still further international effort known as the Decade for Action to Combat Racism and Racial Discrimination.

8

A Decade for Action

COME THEN, COMRADES; IT WOULD BE AS WELL to decide at
once to change our ways. We must shake off the heavy darkness
in which we were plunged, and leave it behind. The new day
which is already at hand must find us firm, prudent, and resolute.
. . . It is a question of the Third World starting a history which will
have regard to the sometimes prodigious theses which Europe has
put forward, but of which the most horrible was committed in the
heart of man, and consisted of the pathological tearing apart of his
functions and the crumbling away of his unity . . . by racial
hatreds, slavery, exploitation, and above all the bloodless genocide
which consisted in the setting aside [because of race] of fifteen
thousand millions of men.

—Frantz Fanon

Launching the Decade
for Action to Combat Racism

The striking successes of the Third World in raising and then pressing
the issue of race before the international community stood in sharp
contrast to the record of several prior centuries of politics and diplomacy.
Conscious of their growing numbers and influence, Third World states
used declarations, resolutions, treaties, and various institutional mech-
anisms within the United Nations to do whatever they could to remove
the racial domination of empire from colonial peoples and to end racial
discrimination wherever it might exist. In this endeavor, they greatly
welcomed the news, for which they took some credit, of the 1964 and
1965 Civil Rights Acts in the United States and the 1965 and 1968 Race
Relations Acts in Britain.[1] Despite all their many gains, however, pockets
of resistance remained firm, as a few states steadfastly refused to change
their policies toward race. For this reason and because they deeply
believed that international relations were yet another manifestation of
interracial relations, the vast majority of countries determined that they
would devote themselves to even greater efforts to eliminate this scourge

from the earth. Indeed, their concern about obtaining racial equality has often been described as the most dominating theme of the entire postwar world, the central issue permeating the United Nations, and the question capable of eliciting the "absolute commitment" and "passionate intensity" of the entire Third World.[2]

When the International Convention on the Elimination of All Forms of Racial Discrimination entered into force as a binding treaty, it was a demonstration of what could be accomplished among nations with the will and the ability to effect change. Consequently, it provided an enormous stimulus to take further action. In 1969, therefore, the General Assembly approved an important resolution entitled "Measures to Be Taken Against Nazism and Racial Intolerance" and declared 1971 to be the International Year for Action to Combat Racism and Racial Discrimination "in the name of the ever-growing struggle against racial discrimination in all its forms and manifestations and in the name of international solidarity with those struggling against racism."[3] Other statements continued to draw attention to the fact that the issue of race affected international peace and security, economic development, decolonization, education and the welfare of youth, social conditions, and all basic aspects of human rights.[4] Throughout this entire process, however, many expressed the opinion that the words of resolutions, declarations, and studies alone might be ineffective or insufficient and would not bring about the kinds of practical solutions necessary to end racial discrimination.[5] To confront precisely this problem, the Sub-Commission on Prevention of Discrimination challenged the members of the United Nations to give "highest priority" to a program of concrete action rather than abstract words and to designate an entire ten-year period as the Decade for Action to Combat Racism and Racial Discrimination.[6]

Rising to this challenge, the General Assembly declared that 1973 was the beginning of such a Decade for Action, expressed its determination to speak out for the dignity and equality of all human beings, and reaffirmed its resolve to achieve a total and unconditional elimination of racial discrimination, including the policy of apartheid. "The ultimate goals of the Decade," stated its members, "are to promote human rights and fundamental freedom for all, without distinction of any kind on grounds of race, color, descent, or national or ethnic origin, especially by eradicating racial prejudice, racism, and racial discrimination"; and then using harsh and unequivocal language:

> to arrest any expansion of racist policies, to eliminate the persistence of racist policies, and to counteract the emergence of alliances based on mutual espousal of racism and racial discrimination; to resist any policy

and practices which lead to the strengthening of the racist regimes and contribute to the sustainment of racism and racial discrimination; to identify, isolate, and dispel the fallacies and mythical beliefs, policies, and practices that contribute to racism and racial discrimination; and to put an end to racist regimes.[7]

To accomplish these goals and objectives, the member states of the United Nations agreed upon a specific and well-defined Program for the Decade for Action to Combat Racism and Racial Discrimination. At the national level, the vast majority agreed to provide assistance to victims of racial discrimination, to abrogate any policies or regulations of their own that had the effect of creating or perpetuating racial hatred, to nullify any immigration laws based upon race, to provide legal protection for basic human rights, and to deny any political or diplomatic support to governments that practice racial discrimination. At the regional and international levels, the majority consented to isolate regimes that advocated racial superiority, to convene seminars for educational purposes, to assist liberation movements struggling against racial domination in colonialism, to create new and binding instruments against apartheid, and to sponsor a world conference on combating racial discrimination. Finally, within the United Nations system itself, the states pledged to conduct studies on race, to require periodic reports on human rights, and to address ways and means of definite action to ensure the practical implementation of resolutions, declarations, and treaties relating to apartheid and racial discrimination.[8] Never before in history had an international body adopted such a comprehensive and ambitious plan to combat the global problem of race.

The overwhelming majority of governments represented in the United Nations immediately set the tone and the standard for this program of action by adopting at the end of 1973 the International Convention on the Suppression and Punishment of the Crime of Apartheid. Drawing upon a series of previous resolutions and declarations,[9] they declared that the policy of apartheid as practiced in southern Africa to separate blacks from whites and similar policies of racial segregation and dis-crimination henceforth would be regarded as crimes against humanity, violations of international law, and serious threats to peace and security. They identified acts of apartheid as those that established domination of one racial group over another, denied life or liberty to persons because of their race, divided and segregated people along racial lines, created separate reserves or ghettos for members of particular racial groups, prohibited mixed marriages, exploited others because of their race, or prohibited any racial group from participation in the political, social, economic, or cultural life of the country. The treaty stipulated that criminal responsibility applied to individuals, members of organizations and institutions, and representatives of states, irrespective of motive. Signatories pledged themselves to adopt legislative, judicial, and administrative measures to prosecute, bring to trial, and punish persons accused of acts of apartheid; to submit periodic reports about racial conditions in their own states; to accept and carry out decisions of the Security Council aimed at the prevention, suppression, and punishment of apartheid; and to cooperate with the Commission on Human Rights and other organs of the United Nations to achieve racial equality.[10] Through such action, said one delegate on behalf of many, the international community could protect the victims, punish the guilty, and attack racial prejudices that "paralyze and destroy" the world and thereby establish "a sure guide" for future generations to promote equality.[11]

Within this context of the Decade for Action, a growing number of states devoted much more attention to the work of the Commission on Human Rights. There, in the words of one analyst, members from Africa, Asia, and Latin America joined forces "in a systematic assault on white racism," a subject that, to the dismay of the West, "often dominated Commission debates and programing."[12] They then focused upon the two bodies previously created under Third World pressure: the Special Committee on Apartheid and a unit of the Department of Political and Security Council Affairs of the Secretariat named the Centre Against Apartheid.[13] Through these organizations they vigorously concentrated their efforts upon arousing global public opinion against the practices of racial domination and discrimination, particularly in southern Africa, by holding educational seminars and international conferences on race, sponsoring training programs, cooperating closely with the Commission on Human Rights, establishing trust funds for victims of apartheid, and issuing numerous publications about the politics and diplomacy of racial discrimination.[14] The majority of states also sought to coordinate their activities with those of the Organization of African Unity, several antiapartheid movements, and numerous nongovernmental organizations accredited to the United Nations. In addition, they unrelentingly pushed to achieve acceptance by the international community of the Declaration Against Apartheid in Sports and, more importantly, the comprehensive Program of Action Against Apartheid.[15]

Not content with these measures, the states party to the International Convention on the Elimination of All Forms of Racial Discrimination actively worked to secure other signatures and to strengthen essential means of compliance. They did not want the convention to become a mere declaration of verbiage or abstract principle and therefore centered their attention upon the autonomous Committee on the Elimination of Racial Discrimination (CERD), designed as the machinery to implement the treaty itself by creating a system of international accountability. Toward this end, they strongly encouraged the committee to establish procedures for receiving and reviewing obligatory reports from each country on its legislative, judicial, and administrative measures adopted to provide practical effect to the antidiscrimination provisions of the convention.

Despite many problems of non- or partial compliance and a lack of power for enforcement, members of this committee took their assignments very seriously, especially after the launching of the Decade for Action, and began to pressure the states that did not fully comply with the reporting procedure. They did not hesitate at all, for example, to declare publicly that incomplete or insufficient reports were "unsatisfactory" or to announce that they would not accept a government's flippant explanation that racial discrimination "does not exist" within a particular country. Committee members noted with great pride and a sense of achievement when states responded to their recommendations and adopted concrete measures for eliminating racial discrimination or when they could assist the Special Committee on the Situation with Regard to the Implementation of the Declaration on the Granting of Independence to Colonial Countries and Peoples.[16] But, with similar zeal, they did not back away from openly criticizing those countries that refused to sign the treaty, identifying a variety of sources of continued racial discrimination rather than those solely of white and black relations, and expressing their frustration with "an international system in which national sovereignty is vigilantly guarded by the component states."[17]

Throughout all of these activities of the Decade for Action to Combat Racism and Racial Discrimination, most governments within the international community proceeded with a high degree of consensus about what constituted racial discrimination and what should be done to eliminate it. That agreement collapsed, however, whenever debate erupted over one of the most sensitive and controversial issues ever raised in the context of racial prejudice: Zionism. Many countries in the Third World long had believed that not in its religious faith, but rather in its effort to expand power and influence, the modern state of Israel, in the name of a "chosen race," exhibited dangerous manifestations of discrimination directed against Palestinians in occupied territories, non-Jews and non-Westerners in immigration policies, and Arabs throughout the Middle East.[18] Some delegations raised this issue as early as the famous Bandung Conference, yet were outvoted due to others' belief that Zionism was not the same thing as racism and continued sympathy about Jewish persecution during the Holocaust—which had helped to raise the issue of basic human rights before the world's conscience in the first place.[19]

But the sympathetic attitude of a majority of states dissipated through time, as they watched a series of wars in the Middle East and began to perceive an increasing intolerance and inflexibility in Israeli policies and a growing bond between Israel and South Africa. They knew that South Africa had been one of the earliest states to recognize Israel and that its prime minister, D. F. Malan, was the first foreign chief of government to visit Israel. They perceived that both South Africa and Israel had been settled by pioneers originating from the West, that both regarded themselves as religious outposts under siege and as anticommunist, that both were small states surrounded by hostile peoples of a different race, and that both found themselves as the major outcasts of the United Nations. This perception of similar backgrounds and common interests, whether correct in fact or not, was strengthened even more by Prime Minister John Vorster of South Africa when he declared in a notable interview with the *New York Times* that South Africans also viewed Israel's "apartheid problem" with sympathy and understanding.[20]

Angry and frustrated over this perceived connection between South Africa and Israel and fearful of the growing economic and military ties between the two countries, the majority of members within the United Nations determined to reaffirm their commitment to eliminate apartheid and therefore in 1973 formally condemned what they described as the "unholy alliance" between "South African racism and Zionism."[21] In heated debate the Israeli representative lashed out against these charges, accusing the others of profaning "the memory of our six million martyrs" and shouting, "Sinister analogy, calumny, falsification of facts, tendentious insinuations, even lies tied with white threads—nothing, virtually nothing, was spared in order to cast mud upon a people who throughout its history has suffered more than any other from discrimination and racism of the most abject nature."[22] Yet neither these rebuttals, nor the imprecise and politically motivated use of the word "racist," nor the supreme irony of a nation once created because of racial persecution now being accused of racial discrimination itself deterred the majority of states from pressing further.

In fact in the politics and diplomacy of discrimination these countries' attitudes received additional reinforcement from many Arab states whose economic and political power grew remarkably due to increased global dependence upon oil. Thus in 1975 a series of international declarations emerged from a variety of settings and organizations. The World Conference of the International Women's Year, held at Mexico City, for example, announced that peace required the "elimination of colonialism and neo-colonialism, foreign occupation, Zionism, apartheid, and racial discrimination in all its forms."[23] The Assembly of Heads of State and Government of the Organization of African Unity meeting in Kampala declared that "the racist regime in occupied Palestine and the racist regime in Zimbabwe and South Africa have a common imperialist origin."[24] Moreover, during the same year, the Conference of Ministers for Foreign Affairs of Non-Aligned Countries, meeting in Lima, asserted that Zionism represented a most dangerous "racist and imperialist ideology."[25]

The intense political and diplomatic pressures from these several international meetings continued to mount and converged upon the United Nations in fall 1975 in the shape of an explosive resolution designed to condemn Zionism itself as a form of racism. Several states from the Middle East, Africa, and Asia rushed headlong into the fray, arguing that they had no quarrel with Judaism, but rather with Zionism, which propagated a political ideology with racial discrimination, made all the less excusable because Zionists themselves had been so severely persecuted in the name of racial purity. "Jews should not be confused with Zionism any more than Italians should be confused with Fascism or Americans with the Ku Klux Klan," declared the representative of Jordan. "Within every people," he continued, "it is possible to find movements and ideologies harmful and subversive. They must be identified and condemned in the interest of humanity. Such is the case with apartheid; such is also the case with Zionism."[26]

The Israeli delegate shot back that this kind of argument smacked of "unbelievable nonsense," "flagrant anti-Semitism," and an indication, once again, that his state "because it is Jewish, is being made a scapegoat."[27] Such an assault amounted to an official endorsement of anti-Semitism, declared one observer, who described the proceedings as "an obscene act."[28] Nevertheless, when states in the General Assembly cast their ballots upon the matter, they determined by seventy-two votes to thirty-five, with thirty-two nervous abstentions, in their shortest and perhaps most fateful resolution, that "Zionism is a form of racism and racial discrimination."[29] Voting in the minority with Israel were the nine members of the European Common Market, Canada, Australia, New Zealand, and the United States. The U.S. ambassador, Daniel Patrick Moynihan, angrily described the resolution as an "infamous act," declared that it "drained the word 'racism' of its meaning" by confusing the whole concept of race as it was understood, and announced that it might make the United States radically change its attitude toward the entire Decade for Action to Combat Racism and Racial Discrimination.[30]

Among most members of the international community, of course, the U.S. attitude toward the Decade for Action always caused confusion and encouraged considerable skepticism. Although the United States had taken impressive strides toward achieving racial equality at home during the civil rights movement of the mid-1960s (often, as we have seen, under considerable pressure from African and Asian states abroad and from its competition with the Soviet Union in the Cold War) and although the Congress began taking significant steps of its own in 1973–1974 to make the promotion of human rights an integral part of the nation's foreign policies,[31] the United States assiduously rejected any suggestion of working within the internationally established legal framework. Indeed, throughout the decade it remained one of the only countries in the entire world consistently to refuse to ratify even one of the major international instruments on human rights and racial equality, including the genocide convention; International Convention on the Elimination of All Forms of Racial Discrimination; Covenant on Civil and Political Rights; Covenant on Economic, Social, and Cultural Rights; Convention Concerning Discrimination in Employment; Convention Against Discrimination in Education; and the International Convention on the Suppression and Punishment of the Crime of Apartheid, among others.[32] To make this situation even worse, in the minds of the majority of states, the United States appeared to support not only Israel, but of particular importance and through much of the decade, also South Africa, Portugal, and Southern Rhodesia with their racial policies in the "hard core" of southern Africa.

Attacking the "Hard Core" in Southern Africa

Time and time again throughout the politics and diplomacy of discrimination, as we have seen, the overwhelming majority of the international community firmly believed that domination in colonialism abroad and segregation in policy at home were but two sides of the same coin of racial prejudice. All of the major postwar conferences, declarations, resolutions, and treaties on this subject emphasized the intimate relationship between the two.[33] Thus, it came as no surprise when the official program of the Decade for Action to Combat Racism and Racial Discrimination announced that major efforts would focus upon "the struggle of all oppressed peoples, in particular in the territories under colonial, racial, or alien domination" and their desire "to obtain racial equality and freedom."[34] Lest there be any question about the precise targets of such action, the General Assembly identified them as South Africa, Portugal, and other "illegal" and "racist" minority regimes in Africa that continued to suppress the rights of people for self-determination and racial equality.[35]

Despite overwhelming odds against them, these several governments, known collectively as the "hard core,"[36] had been able tenaciously to resist the pressures for change. Even though most of the world gained independence through the collapse of empire and the revolutionary development of decolonization around them, these few white minority regimes refused to relinquish power in Africa. They included: (1) the Portuguese colonial possessions in Angola, Mozambique, and Guinea-Bissau; (2) the government of Southern Rhodesia; and (3) the South African regime, which dominated not only the majority of blacks in its own country but also those in neighboring Namibia. One prescient observer traced a line around the borders of these territories on a map and declared, "That twisting line is the moving edge of history" that will be a "symbolic battleline" drawn around land under white control "but under siege by all the revolutionary ideas and influences in the contemporary world."[37] The Decade for Action sought to move precisely that line and to contribute to that siege against the hard core.

The Portuguese bore the strange distinction of being not only the first white power to enter southern Africa—but also the last to leave. From the fifteenth century to nearly the end of the twentieth, they left a legacy of contact stretching from the age of discovery through the slave trade and on to colonialism. By means of Angola and Mozambique, the Portuguese empire controlled the main shipping lines of access to both the Atlantic and the Indian oceans. It is remarkable that despite the upheavals of World War II that changed so many other attitudes and power relationships across the globe, for almost thirty postwar years Portugal appeared practically immune to the onslaught of African nationalism and the pressures for decolonization. In fact, with the advent of the Cold War, the authoritarian and strongly anticommunist government of Antonio Salazar, who ruled from 1932 to 1968, found that it could use the desire of the North Atlantic Treaty Organization (NATO) allies for air bases in the Azores Islands for political and diplomatic leverage to make its possessions in Africa even more secure.[38] At a time when Harold Macmillan delivered his courageous "Wind of Change" speech regarding British colonial policies in Africa and recognizing the need for self-determination among the continent's black majority,[39] a Portuguese spokesman declared in sharp contrast that there were still many profits to be made in the colonies and that "it is necessary for us to be what we have always been, and we will not change."[40]

This kind of fierce determination by Portugal to resist any alteration of its colonial and racial policies, as might be expected, sparked violent revolts. In February 1961 serious rioting occurred in Luanda, the capital of Angola, after armed members of the Movimento Popular de Libertação de Angola (MPLA) tried to free political prisoners from the city's prison. This action sparked another insurrection the next month in the northern part of the country led by the União das Populações de Angola (UPA). Over six thousand blacks loyal to the Portuguese were killed by the nationalistic guerrilla forces, and some two thousand whites—the largest number of European civilians killed in any African territory during the anticolonial struggles.[41] Violence spread during 1962 to Guinea-Bissau and then in 1964, under the leadership of the Frente de Libertação do Mocambique (FRELIMO), to Mozambique. In each of these insurrections, Portugal, to crush the African guerrillas, responded swiftly by sending military forces trained and equipped by NATO.

In successfully resisting decolonization, the Portuguese government found itself condemned by the vast majority of the world, including African, Asian, Latin American, and Communist countries.[42] It argued that the international community possessed absolutely no jurisdiction over the issue of colonies, claimed that no race problem at all existed in these territories, and charged its critics with perpetrating "the most shameless accusations," a "brazen recourse to lies," and a "gross distortion of statements and policies."[43]

Only a handful of states generally could be counted upon to support Portugal: South Africa, Australia, New Zealand, neighboring Spain, and Portugal's NATO allies Britain, France, and the United States. Although the administration of John Kennedy in Washington imposed a partial arms embargo on weapons that the Portuguese might use against colonial peoples, that did not last long, especially after the Gulf Corporation discovered large amounts of oil reserves in Angola. President Richard Nixon even increased assistance when his advisor on national security affairs, Henry Kissinger, recommended that U.S. policy toward the hard core of southern Africa "maintain public opposition to racial oppression, but relax political isolation and economic restrictions on the white states." Kissinger dismissed the possibility of "a black victory at any stage" and concluded in a calculating assessment leaked to the press:

> The whites are here to stay and the only way that constructive change can come about is through them. There is no hope for the blacks to gain the political rights they seek through violence, which will only lead to chaos and increased opportunities for the Communists. We can, by selective relaxation of our stance toward the white regimes, encourage some modification of their current racial and colonial policies. . . . Our tangible interests form a basis for our contacts in the region, and these can be maintained at acceptable political cost.[44]

When Nixon offered generous financial help to Lisbon in exchange for an extension of the lease of the strategically important Azores base, even the *New York Times*, which was not usually known to champion liberation movements, commented that this "will help Portugal meet the costs of its colonial wars to preserve the white minority in Angola, Mozambique, and Guinea-Bissau."[45]

There were numerous efforts to change this situation, to force a reassessment of "acceptable political costs," and to bring about black majority rule in African territories under Portuguese control. The Conference of Heads of State or Government of Non-Aligned Countries, for example, strongly condemned not only the "racist colonial regime" of Portugal but also those NATO allies who assisted it. Governments participating in the conference joined together to initiate a series of political, diplomatic, and economic measures against the Portuguese and all others that sought "to perpetuate the supremacy of a white minority in southern Africa."[46] The Soviets, Chinese, and Czechs provided arms for black rebels fighting against Portugal. The Organization of African Unity similarly worked to increase pressure on Lisbon by means of political and diplomatic isolation and economic boycotts. Within the United Nations, Third World members described Portugal as "the last bastion of colonialism," accused it of conducting gross "atrocities against the black man," and promised to continue their efforts "until it renounces its policy of racial discrimination and colonial oppression."[47] With the launching of the Decade for Action to Combat Racism and Racial Discrimination, they vowed to do even more to mobilize the Security Council, General Assembly, Special Committee, the International Labor Organization, UNESCO, and many nongovernmental organizations to take meaningful actions against persistent Portuguese colonialism. These several determined measures lacked sufficient power to achieve their ultimate purpose, however, so long as Portugal's NATO allies remained willing to supply military and economic assistance and so long as the authoritarian government in Lisbon remained secure.

Amid a flurry of activity and a military coup d'état, that government suddenly collapsed in April 1974. The fateful decision by Salazar's successor, Marcello Caetano, to airlift ten thousand more troops to join the one hundred and sixty thousand already involved in the bloody and costly wars in Africa ignited the long-smoldering resentment within the army against his regime. Officers of the Movimento das Forças Armadas moved in to overthrow Caetano and to install as president their own General Antonio de Spinola, an outspoken critic of Portugal's debilitating colonial wars. The leaders of the revolt quickly declared their intention to establish a democratic government and thereby dismantle not only the domestic dictatorship of the past but also many of its overseas policies. With this announcement, one journalist who covered the story wrote, "In time, the shock waves sent out by the coup may be felt more strongly in Africa than in Lisbon itself, and the end of the Lisbon dictatorship [may signal] profound changes for Portugal's vast colonial holdings, the first—and the last—great European empire."[48] Predicted another observer with reference to Portugal's African territories, "Full independence is now regarded as inevitable."[49]

Indeed, in an emotional address beamed from the porticoed halls of Lisbon's presidential palace to the balmy streets of the Mozambique capital on the Indian Ocean, the jungles of Guinea-Bissau on the Atlantic, and oil fields of Angola, Spinola delivered his message: "The moment has come," he declared before an electrified audience, "for our overseas territories to take their destinies in their own hands. This is the historic moment for which Portugal, the African territories, and the world have been waiting: peace in Portuguese Africa, finally achieved in justice and freedom."[50] He pledged that he would work to achieve some form of self-determination and a peaceful transition of power for those under Portuguese control.

In less than six months during 1974, therefore, Portugal set into motion a process that abandoned an empire it had acquired and held for more than five hundred years. The new government successfully negotiated with the nationalist African Party for the Independence of Guinea and Cape Verde (PAIGC) to grant self-determination to Guinea-Bissau; with the leftist liberation organization FRELIMO to achieve freedom for Mozambique; and with several organizations to attain independence for Angola.[51] Independence there proved to be particularly difficult due to the intense competition among rival guerrilla movements, the military intervention of South Africa and Cuba, and the active involvement of the Americans and Soviets, who viewed the country as yet one more Cold War battleground for influence. Yet in the end, independence and black majority rule finally came to all three former Portuguese possessions. One white businessman observed, as he watched many of his friends leave Africa with their personal possessions for safer locations, "It is the end of one world and the beginning of another."[52]

This shattering collapse of the Portuguese empire created profound implications for politics and diplomacy in Africa. It encouraged the governments involved with the Decade for Action to Combat Racism to intensify their efforts. It forced outside powers to recognize the unrelenting pressures for decolonization. And, of particular importance, it confronted the remaining hard core, Southern Rhodesia and South Africa, with a most serious challenge. Both countries might be able to ignore verbal condemnations and resolutions within the United Nations, but the coming to power of three states governed by new black majorities presented acute difficulties. Southern Rhodesia and South Africa now suddenly faced the harsh reality of being dangerously exposed to several thousand miles of hostile borders and being surrounded by opponents. In fact, to emphasize precisely this point, Angola, Zambia, Mozambique, Botswana, and Tanzania openly began to refer to themselves as the "Front

Line States" in the final battle to overthrow white minority regimes.[53] They made preparations to use their combined political, economic, and unique geographical resources to deny landlocked Rhodesia its lifeline to the sea, to support neighboring black liberation movements, and to provide bases and sanctuary for guerrilla forces.

The effects of this radical new development could be seen first in Southern Rhodesia. Ever since 1965, when the white-dominated government of Prime Minister Ian Smith in Salisbury rejected demands for majority rule, unilaterally seceded from the British Commonwealth, and began to impose systematically a series of laws designed to enforce racial segregation, the country had attracted international attention.[54] The attempts of its intransigent two hundred and fifty thousand whites to dominate more than five million blacks by denying them basic rights solely because of their race quickly made Southern Rhodesia a target for action. Secretary-General U Thant of the United Nations angrily denounced Smith's regime as "the product of the kind of racism which is abhorrent to the vast majority of mankind."[55] The General Assembly urged nations around the world to refuse diplomatic recognition to the government of Smith and condemned it as an "illegal racist minority regime," and the Security Council imposed economic sanctions against Southern Rhodesia to force a change in its policies.[56] Members of the Organization of African Unity, the Soviet Union, and China even supplied arms to the insurgents. These collective efforts produced only partial success, however, for South Africa, Portugal, Britain, and the United States, among others, which were willing to cooperate with the international community at times, did not always enforce the rules of the sanctions against their own citizens who profited financially from importing tobacco, beef, and chrome and exporting the vital commodity of oil to Southern Rhodesia. South Africa went as far as to provide military forces to fight the black guerrillas.

But the stalemate that these competing internal and external pressures created was shattered by the 1974 coup d'état in Lisbon and the decision by Portugal to abandon its African empire. When faced with the new reality of being nearly surrounded by a ring of openly hostile black states, three hundred more miles of exposed hostile border, growing guerrilla forces, and the suggestion from his South African benefactors that they might not be able to provide sufficient assistance, Ian Smith told his startled countrymen that he could see no way out but to release political prisoners, open discussions with neighboring Zambian President Kenneth Kaunda, and begin negotiations for majority rule in Southern Rhodesia. Careful observers described this revolutionary shift as something that "would have seemed unthinkable as recently as nine or ten months ago" and as "one of the most amazing turnabouts in history."[57]

Yet, change did not necessarily mean immediate resolution. Skeptical of Ian Smith's rapid conversion and believing that more could be gained by fighting than talking, Southern Rhodesia's black nationalist guerrillas escalated their attacks into a virtual civil war along racial lines. The armies of the Zimbabwe African People's Union (ZAPU) and Zimbabwe African National Union (ZANU) launched devastating raids from their bases in the strongly supportive Front Line States of Zambia, Botswana, and Mozambique, frequently attacking innocent civilians in the process. This, in turn, forced the highly unpopular conscription of most adult white males into at least part-time military service to defend the regime. Negotiations initiated by Smith to reach an "internal settlement" with rebel leaders Joshua Nkomo and Robert Mugabe proved fruitless, and various attempts by the British, Soviets, and Chinese to effect the outcome most favorable to their own interests prolonged the crisis even longer. Then, badly shaken by its inability to anticipate and influence the Angolan civil war, the United States sought to intervene as well. In 1976 Henry Kissinger, then secretary of state, visited southern Africa and met with all the major actors in the Rhodesian drama. But his manipulative style and secret sessions with the white minority regimes of Southern Rhodesia and South Africa raised such deep suspicions that ZAPU and ZANU actually decided to combine their respective forces to form a united Patriotic Front and to step up the scale of fighting. With this, the credibility of U.S. policy among blacks in Africa plummeted even further.[58]

It was thus with considerable surprise and anticipation that most of Africa and much of the world watched when Jimmy Carter became president of the United States in 1977. Earlier he had openly declared that "the time for racial discrimination is over" for politics,[59] and now observers wondered if the same principle might influence his diplomacy as well. Carter addressed this question immediately in his inaugural speech when he spoke of the need for a "new beginning" that would emphasize compassion, justice, equality, and an "absolute" commitment to human rights.[60] His secretary of state, Cyrus Vance, repeated the same point shortly thereafter when he stated that basic human rights and respect for the individual were sacred to the best traditions of the United States and pledged that they now would be explicitly interwoven into the fabric of the nation's foreign policy.[61] Anthony Lake, director of the Department of State's Policy Planning Staff, made this new approach even more direct when he focused upon the problems in southern Africa and declared: "Here our interests in calming warlike tensions and honoring the values of our own society are too obvious to be belabored. Our nation was founded on the principle of majority rule: we cannot support or condone the systematic denial of that principle to other peoples anywhere in the world . . . the United States cannot enforce a peace in southern Africa. But we can and must encourage it in every way possible. And there will be no peace until there is racial justice."[62]

These public declarations of general principle received significant endorsement and enhanced credibility when Carter appointed Andrew Young as the U.S. ambassador to the United Nations. By selecting a civil rights activist, former aide to Martin Luther King, Jr., ordained minister, and member of the congressional Black Caucus, Carter appeared to be not only acknowledging but also confirming the importance of dealing with the racial factor in international relations. As the *New York Times* editorialized: "The symbolism of a black American speaking for his country to all the nations of the world will not be lost either inside our boundaries or across the globe. Both the symbolism and the reality will be particularly important to the increasingly expectant Third World."[63] The outspoken Young, of course, wasted no time in making precisely the same point himself, for with more impulsiveness than political acumen, he described former President Nixon and Secretary of State Kissinger as "racists" who lacked any understanding of the global problems of those of color and who failed to recognize that opposition to racial discrimination and colonial domination represented "one of the most powerful dynamics in the world today."[64]

Such statements by an official representative of the U.S. government marked something quite new in the annals of international politics and diplomacy. Although some people in the United States called for Young's resignation after this outburst, his colleagues within the United Nations welcomed his blunt remarks and what appeared to be a dramatic change in U.S. foreign policy toward race. They hoped that the United States now would support the Decade for Action to Combat Racism and Racial Discrimination, sign the international conventions on human rights and racial equality, join the Committee for the Elimination of Racial Discrimination, and finally lend its constructive assistance to attacking the remaining hard core in southern Africa.

Members of the international community thus enthusiastically responded to the Carter administration's announcement of a new "African-centered" policy that would support human rights and black majority rule in that troubled continent. Carter began the process himself by successfully pushing Congress to repeal the Byrd amendment, which had authorized the country under U.S. law to purchase strategically important chrome from Southern Rhodesia in direct violation of Security Council sanctions. He then instructed Andrew Young to participate actively in a United Nations–sponsored conference designed to support liberation movements in Africa. Young joined the representatives of ninety-one other countries, in addition to numerous nongovernmental organizations and observers, meeting during 1977 in Maputo, Mozambique, and told them that the United States wanted to assist those who sought freedom and independence from the "last vestiges of colonialism" in southern Africa. "We firmly believe there must be an end," he declared, "to the deprivation of human dignity and fundamental rights for the majority of people . . . solely because of the color of their skin."[65] Young pledged that the United States would support the Program of Action from the Maputo Conference and would join other nations in working to eliminate racial domination and discrimination in Southern Rhodesia, Namibia, and South Africa.[66]

With reference to Southern Rhodesia, the United States honored this particular pledge and agreed to cooperate closely with Britain in trying to reach some kind of settlement for this strife-torn country. The dynamic British foreign secretary, David Owen, worked well with Andrew Young, for they both believed in promoting racial equality and wanted to bring about a peaceful transfer of power in Salisbury. In this endeavor, however, they and their immediate successors began to realize that speeches and the decisions of majorities did not always bring about immediate results and that their objectives could be realized only through great patience and persistence. The diverse and often difficult positions held by Smith's minority government, white settlers and property owners, the Patriotic Front (with its continuing internal ZANU-ZAPU rivalries), the neighboring Front Line States, the various members of the Organization of African Unity and United Nations, the United States, Britain, and the Commonwealth, among others, proved to be particularly frustrating and at times extremely dangerous. But, in the end, and through the skillful diplomacy of Lord Carrington at Lancaster House (the scene of previous decolonizing conferences), a negotiated settlement was finally reached in 1979. All sides agreed upon holding free and secret elections, and more than two years after the Maputo Conference, a black majority government under Robert Mugabe came to power. With this, the former British colony named after Cecil Rhodes achieved independence under the native name of Zimbabwe.[67] As a result, one more pillar of the hard core collapsed. The ring around the white minority regime in Pretoria that controlled South Africa and Namibia thus became even tighter, and the international concern about racial discrimination even greater.

Convening the World Conference to Combat Racism

Even before Zimbabwe became independent, the majority of governments within the international community that supported the Decade for Action to Combat Racism and Racial Discrimination had determined to hold a world conference. They agreed that they should gather together to review the progress made toward eliminating racial discrimination, to evaluate the effectiveness of their methods in achieving the goals of the decade at its midpoint, and then to devise specific proposals for further action. Such a conference, they stated, "should have as its main theme the adoption of effective ways and means and *concrete measures* for securing the full and universal implementation of United Nations' decisions and resolutions on racism, racial discrimination, apartheid, decolonization and self-determination, as well as the accession to and ratification and enforcement of the international instruments relating to human rights and the elimination of racism and racial discrimination."[68] With these goals in mind, they agreed that August 1978 would be set aside as the time to convene what they would call the World Conference to Combat Racism and Racial Discrimination.

To prepare for this conference, the United Nations began to assemble a number of important studies and position papers dealing with the global problem of race. Secretary-General Kurt Waldheim submitted a detailed report describing the international resolutions and declarations issued on the subject of racial discrimination, discussing the legal instruments designed to protect basic human rights and racial equality, and delineating the various efforts made under the Decade for Action to combat the manifestations of racial prejudice.[69] The Committee on the Elimination of Racial Discrimination established by international convention prepared a thorough paper concerning its own work and deliberations.[70] A revised and updated version of the influential study entitled *Racial Discrimination* was included especially for the occasion as well.[71] Additional reports from the Sub-Commission on Prevention of Discrimination and Protection of Minorities, "The Adverse Consequences for the Enjoyment of Human Rights of Political, Military, Economic, and Other Forms of Assistance Given to Colonial and Racist Regimes in Southern Africa," from the Commission on Human Rights' Ad Hoc Working Group of Experts on Southern Africa, and from the Special Committee Against Apartheid were submitted.[72] Together, they acknowledged not only all the many accomplishments of the decade with respect to race but also the many tasks and obstacles still ahead.

Hundreds of participants from around the world assembled in Geneva for this important conference and what they eagerly anticipated would be the highlight of the Decade for Action. Gathering first at the registration desk in the spacious lobby of the new building at the Palais des Nations, they intently observed the crowd congregating near Door 41 to see who else had come to participate. There were representatives from Africa to Latin America and from Asia to Europe, from reactionary to revolutionary regimes, from industrialized to developing countries, and from aligned to nonaligned states. Some represented governments; others served as observers for national liberation movements, nongovernmental organizations, and regional bodies such as the Organization of African Unity and the Organization of American States. Still others came in their capacity as members of the Special Committee on Apartheid, Council for Namibia, Special Committee on the Situation with Regard to the Implementation of the Declaration on the Granting of Independence to Colonial Countries and Peoples, Commission on Human Rights, and the Committee on the Elimination of Racial Discrimination. The delegates watched with pleasure as the number expanded to include official representatives of 125 separate states. But when they examined the list of participants carefully and looked throughout the lobby more closely, they were shocked to discover that one notable country was missing: the United States.

Despite the obvious problems that this absence would create for foreign relations throughout the Third World and for the credibility of his policy toward human rights and racial equality, Jimmy Carter decided that the United States would not participate in the World Conference to Combat Racism. In fact, he announced that the country would deliberately boycott the conference. When pressed by other governments and the media to provide at least some explanation for this behavior, he said that the answer could be found in the General Assembly's irresponsible 1975 resolution on Zionism.[73] As he stated during a press conference: "The United States is unable to participate in this potentially important conference . . . because the definition of 'racism' has been perverted for political ends by including Zionism as one of its forms. The United States cannot associate itself with the Decade so long as it endorses the patently false definition of Zionism as a form of racism."[74] Critics immediately responded that if any perversion of a definition of "racism" for political purposes existed, then it surely came from the United States whose unquestioned support for Israel prevented it from being honest about discrimination when practiced by Zionists.[75]

When confronted once again with the controversy over Zionism, the other delegations quickly determined that they most certainly were not prepared to let this issue hold the entire world conference hostage. Although intensely angered by the U.S. and Israeli position and undeterred by their own lack of clear definition for racism, they decided to proceed. Consequently, Kurt Waldheim called upon all nations to put politics aside, draw together, and commit themselves to fulfilling the promises they already had made in the Charter of the United Nations and the Universal Declaration of Human Rights. "It is my hope," he said during the opening ceremonies, "that the Conference will mark a decisive turning point in the international struggle against all forms of racial prejudice, inequality, and injustice." Conveniently ignoring his own questionable past, he described discrimination on the basis of race as totally contrary to even the most rudimentary of ethical norms and legal standards, an evil within individuals and societies, and as a source of danger to international peace and stability. Waldheim reminded the participants that much already had been accomplished during the Decade for Action and that they all had good reason to be encouraged. "But this Conference also knows only too well," he continued soberly, "that, notable as this progress has been, much more remains to be done before we will have achieved our goal. . . . As we begin, our aim must be an effective program that will enable us to hold out real hope that these evil practices [of racial discrimination] are coming to an end."[76]

To develop precisely such a program of effective action, the delegates divided themselves into two separate working committees and assigned each group very specific tasks. They charged the First Committee with evaluating the progress achieved toward realizing the goals of the Decade for Action at the national, regional, and international levels and with identifying the obstacles encountered in combating racial prejudice and discrimination. The Second Committee received the difficult assignment of formulating effective ways, means, and concrete measures "for securing the full eradication of racism, racial discrimination, and apartheid."[77] Toward this end, its members were instructed to explore methods of implementing existing international instruments guaranteeing racial equality, supporting peoples and movements still struggling against colonialism, and assisting those suffering under apartheid.

Each committee worked diligently over the course of more than one week, frequently conducting meetings well into the evening. The members listened to official government delegates, representatives from regional and international organizations, consultants, observers, and others who they believed could contribute to their deliberations. These sessions proceeded with few surprises, and it did not take long to reach a general concurrence on the need to focus upon the racial aspects of apartheid and continuing forms of colonialism. Ready agreement upon the ends, however, could not be matched with agreement on the means. Western nations, for example, generally favored a cautious and conservative approach, proceeding slowly, using verbal persuasion, and providing economic incentives to eliminate manifestations of racial discrimination. Most African, Asian, and Communist countries, in contrast, called for some form of comprehensive sanctions against white minority regimes in southern Africa and active support for national liberation movements. Libya even went as far as to demand an armed revolt against offending governments and instructed its chief delegate to declare that "the best way to combat them is to start armed revolution against these regimes and to confront racist violence with revolutionary violence."[78] It did not take long for most delegates to reject these extreme positions, but they found themselves agonizing over how to find means that would be effective in combating racial discrimination but at the same time would not jeopardize international peace.

Yet, just when it appeared that the efforts to overcome these differences and to reach a consensus had been successful, the conference received a shocking blow. For days, the Arab countries remained largely silent on the sensitive issue of Zionism. One correspondent even described their behavior on this matter as "stepping softly" so as not to offend others.[79] But on the next to the last day of deliberations, they insisted upon inserting a clause condemning the relations between "the Zionist state of Israel and the racist regime of South Africa," deploring the Israeli refusal to comply with United Nations resolutions, and calling for the cessation of all practices of racial discrimination against the Palestinians.[80] This move suddenly forced everyone else's hand, compelling them either to support the provision about Zionism or to reject it. Uncomfortable with the general tenor of the conference and what appeared to be an unfair and one-sided emphasis upon white racism alone, several Western nations used their defeat when the vote was taken on this question to announce that they "could no longer participate" in any remaining discussions.[81] With this announcement, the representatives of the nine members of the European Common Market (Britain, Ireland, France, the Federal Republic of Germany, Italy, the Netherlands, Belgium, Luxembourg, and Denmark), Norway, Iceland, Canada, Australia, and New Zealand all packed their bags and walked out of the conference completely.

To the overwhelming majority of nations that remained, the dramatic departure of precisely this group of countries rather than a simple and customary abstention appeared to confirm, correctly or not, the majority's long-standing suspicion that white, Western nations never had, never could, and never would be serious about combating racial discrimination. This judgment seemed all the more accurate in their minds when they witnessed the strong political and economic ties between North America, Western Europe, Australia and New Zealand, Israel, and South Africa. Conversely, to the minority that walked out in protest and was unsure about whether Zionism actually did represent a form of racial discrimination, the vote appeared to confirm, correctly or not, that through their superior voting numbers the majority states were seeing only what they wanted to see and using the vague label *racist* to attack any regime, practice, or policy that they viewed with hostility.[82]

The more than one hundred governments that remained at the conference refused to be stopped by these negative charges and criticisms.

Therefore they worked during the remaining hours to complete the comprehensive Declaration and Program of Action already carefully negotiated over the course of many days with all the participants. When finally finished, they reconfirmed the goals of the Decade for Action to Combat Racism and Racial Discrimination and recommitted themselves to the principle of achieving equality for all, irrespective of race, color, descent, national or ethnic origin. They urged all nations to abide by their solemn past promises to promote human rights through the implementation of international conventions, declaring that "racism, racial discrimination, and apartheid, which continue to afflict the world, are crimes against the conscience and dignity of mankind, and constitute serious dangers which will inevitably lead to greater conflict with enormous repercussions for international peace and security."[83]

To realize these objectives, the World Conference to Combat Racism and Racial Discrimination then adopted a major Program of Action. The participants agreed to engage both individually and collectively in national, regional, and international efforts to combat racial discrimination. Some of these efforts consisted of taking necessary legislative, judicial, and administrative action within their own domestic setting to prohibit any form of discrimination on the basis of race (including measures regulating immigration) and to punish all dissemination of ideas based upon racial superiority or hatred. Others entailed providing assistance to indigenous peoples, immigrants, and migrant workers denied basic human rights because of their race and giving support to national liberation movements and victims of racial discrimination. Still others involved seeking ratification of, or accession to, the international instruments to protect racial equality such as the genocide convention, International Convention on the Elimination of All Forms of Racial Discrimination, and the International Covenant on Civil and Political Rights, among many others. The Program of Action also asked the United Nations as a whole to consider proclaiming that racism and racial discrimination constituted a matter of "the highest priority" for international politics and diplomacy.[84]

Among all of the specific endeavors identified by the Program of Action, however, none received greater attention than those directed against South Africa. Believing that the government of Pretoria constituted the most blatantly racist regime in the world, the conference participants called upon all nations to bring increased pressure to bear upon South Africa's white minority leaders. The participants agreed to work for an arrangement that would deny all military, economic, political, diplomatic, and any other form of assistance that might help South Africa perpetuate its policies. This included calling for comprehensive and mandatory sanctions, with the complete prohibition on sending any technical assistance, nuclear collaboration, weapons, loans and investments, and oil and other strategic commodities to the South African government. In addition, they pledged to provide substantial material support to the Front Line States in their struggles, to groups seeking independence for Namibia, to refugees and other victims of racial discrimination from the remaining hard core, and to those persecuted because of their opposition to apartheid in South Africa. Such a program, said M. V. Molapo of Lesotho, "should give a clear signal to all the racists in the world and in particular the Pretoria government that the world community is prepared to take drastic action" in combating South Africa's white minority regime and its domination over Namibia and "grotesque" policy of apartheid.[85]

Combating South Africa over Namibia and Apartheid

No country in the entire world has been more consistently and soundly condemned for its racial policies than South Africa. Indeed, beginning with the very first session itself of the United Nations, as we have seen,[86] the international community focused global attention upon that country's racially discriminatory practices against Indians and other Asiatics. Once it became apparent that the white minority government treated the majority of blacks even worse, the dimensions of the problem became particularly clear, especially when former colonial territories in Africa gained their independence from white masters and thereby a voice in international diplomacy. In fact, the question of South Africa's racial policies, in one form or another, has been on the General Assembly's agenda at every single session except one. As John Humphrey observed, "Violations of human rights in South Africa have posed one of the most difficult questions with which the United Nations has ever had to deal, and more time and energy has been devoted to it than to any other human rights issue."[87]

Long before the time of the creation of their state, white South Africans recognized that they constituted less than 20 percent of the population. In no province did they even come close to forming a majority. Hence, they believed that the retention and extension of their power required systematic segregation and racial discrimination against the non-whites, who constituted more than 80 percent of the total inhabitants. The whites' resulting policies thus were severely discriminatory and created an inflexible system of racial stratification, but through the end of World War II their policies at least recognized the multiracial character of South African society and did not seem to contemplate the total elimination of all non-whites from any kind of participation in the life of the community. In the immediate postwar years, however, the resistance of many whites to racial concessions hardened, encouraging them to support the radical National party, which called for severing ties with Great Britain, tightening control over South-West Africa (Namibia), propagating doctrines of white racial superiority, and intensifying rigid segregation between the races. This party won a majority of white votes in the critical year of 1948 and thereafter began to implement its new racial program under the slogan of "separate development," or apartheid.

The leaders of the Nationalist government saw in their program of apartheid a means to ensure white superiority over all others. As Prime Minister Johannes Strijdom stated at the time: "Call it paramountcy, *baaskap* [racial control], or what you will, it is still domination. I am being as blunt as I can. I am making no excuses. Either the white man dominates or the black man takes over. The only way the Europeans can maintain supremacy is by domination . . . and the only way they can maintain domination is by withholding the vote from the non-Europeans. If it were not for that we would not be here in Parliament today."[88] To make sure that this "take over" by a majority of blacks never occurred, he and his followers repudiated any concept of equality and even the idea of coexistence among various racial groups. Their goal was not only to maintain non-whites in an inferior status, as before, but also to eliminate them from any meaningful participation in the political, social, economic, or cultural life of the country and to achieve territorial separation between the races.

With these particular objectives in mind and in blatant contrast to the new directions of the rest of the world, the white minority regime in South Africa began to impose a series of rigid laws making race the sole criterion for authorized behavior. The Prohibition of Mixed Marriages Act of 1949 and the Immorality Act of 1950 prohibited members of different races from having intimate relations. The notorious Population Registration Act of 1950 made race a legal as well as a biological concept and classified all people in South Africa into rigid categories based solely on the racial characteristic of color. These included "Whites," or Europeans; "Asians" of Indian or Pakistani origin; "Coloreds" for those of mixed descent; and at the very bottom, "Bantus," or black Africans. The Natives Act of 1952 made it compulsory for all African men (and later women) to carry a "reference book," or "pass," and established a countrywide system to control the movements of blacks and to restrict their entry into white urban areas. The Group Areas Act of 1950 and its amendments and the Separate Amenities Act of 1953 attempted an even more rigid social and physical separation of the races by forcing Africans, Asians, and other coloreds to move to the outskirts of cities and towns; use separate and inferior facilities in education, recreation, and transportation; and observe the rash of new "Whites Only" signs appearing across the land. The Suppression of Communism Act of 1950, the Criminal Law Amendment Act of 1953, and the 1960 Unlawful Organizations Act aimed further at suppressing or restricting of all but the most tame opposition, including those who called for majority rule.[89] Together, these various acts created a system, to use the words of one authority, in which a small minority of whites dominated the majority of all others and in which race became "the sole determinant of power in South Africa."[90]

It is hardly surprising that this kind of repression would provoke serious reaction. In 1952 an organization known as the African National Congress (ANC) swung into a concerted Defiance Campaign of peaceful, passive resistance to what its members called these "unjust laws" or apartheid based solely on race.[91] One year later, a number of sympathetic whites joined forces with Africans, Asians, and other coloreds to form the multiracial Congress Alliance and adopt a Freedom Charter calling for majority rule. The South African government's reaction to this was to charge 156 leaders of the alliance with high treason. The formation of the more militant Pan-Africanist Congress (PAC) created even greater tension, especially when its leaders were arrested after calling for a massive bus boycott. Then, during the course of further resistance to the hated pass laws, an event occurred that some careful observers describe as "the most tragic confrontation between the white regime and the African people opposed to it."[92] On 21 March 1960, police opened fire on an unarmed crowd gathered at Sharpeville in the southern Transvaal. They killed 72 people and wounded nearly 200 others, including women and children, shooting many in the back as they tried to flee.

The news of the massacre at Sharpeville and the massive protests among blacks that followed in its wake throughout South Africa reverberated around the world, as shocked nations moved to express their horror over this killing of innocent civilians. Building upon a series of earlier resolutions,[93] members of the General Assembly voted to condemn South Africa universally, call for an independent Namibia, and request all states to take both separate and collective action to force South Africa to abandon its racial policies.[94] A special session of the Security Council, at the formal request of more than thirty African and Asian countries, met to consider for the first time in its history the dangers of the policy of apartheid. Without a single dissenting vote, and with the support of even the United States, the Security Council recognized the international turmoil caused by racial prejudice, condemned the white minority regime that caused the Sharpeville massacre, and called upon South Africa to "abandon its policies of apartheid and racial discrimination."[95] Within the Commonwealth, the non-white nations vowed to force South Africa out of their organization, and Nkrumah of Ghana publicly and passionately exclaimed, "I will not be silent on the issue" of such blatant racial discrimination.[96] Declared London's *Daily Herald* in support, "Who wants a Commonwealth that Hitler could have belonged to?"[97]

Although shaken by this strong international reaction to the Sharpeville killings, the government of South Africa defiantly refused to modify its policies. Husky, silver-haired Prime Minister Hendrik Verwoerd, the former editor of the pro-Nazi *Die Transvaler* during World War II, adamantly asserted that he would not allow outside powers to dictate his domestic policies. He declared a state of emergency, imposed censorship on the press, arrested blacks without warrant, and declared the opposition African National Congress and Pan-Africanist Congress to be unlawful organizations. Verwoerd also announced his determination to strengthen South Africa's control over Namibia. In addition, his white minority regime withdrew from the Commonwealth and then took steps to implement its plan for "separate development" or segregation by moving blacks into Bantustans, or "homelands," which constituted only 13 percent of the country's total area. When the victims of this policy turned from passive to more active resistance, the government imposed even more draconian measures. It arrested black leaders Nelson Mandela and Robert Sobukwe, among many others, on charges of treason. The charismatic and articulate Mandela used the occasion of his trial to judge the conditions in South Africa by the new international standards of human rights and to condemn the inflexible policy of apartheid by declaring for all the world to hear:

> The Universal Declaration of Human Rights provides that all men are equal before the law, and are entitled without any discrimination to equal protection of the law. . . . But [here in South Africa] the real truth is that there is in fact no equality before the law as far as our people are concerned. . . . In relationships with us, South African Whites regard as fair and just to pursue policies which have outraged the conscience of mankind, and of honest and upright men throughout the civilized world. They suppress our aspirations, bar our way to freedom, and deny us opportunities in our moral and material progress, to secure ourselves from fear and want.

"All the good things in life," he continued, expressing his passionate abhorrence of racial discrimination, "are reserved for White folks, and we Blacks are expected to be content to nourish our bodies with such pieces of food as drop from the table of men with a White skin." Mandela accused whites of having one set of ethics for themselves and yet another and very different set for blacks, whom they maltreated as inferior solely because of the color of their skins. "I make no threats," he concluded before beginning his prison sentence, "when I say that unless these wrongs to which I have pointed are remedied without delay, we might well find that even plain talk before the country's courts is too timid a method to draw attention to our grievance."[98]

All this attracted international attention even more, and the overwhelming majority of nations in the world significantly hardened their positions against South Africa. A number of states, on their own, severed all economic ties with South Africa.[99] Acting collectively through the General Assembly, others established the Special Committee on the Policies of Apartheid to monitor South African behavior carefully. They requested that member countries break off diplomatic relations with South Africa, boycott all South African products, refrain from exporting goods (including all arms) to the white minority regime, and enact legislation prohibiting South African ships or aircraft from using their port facilities.[100] In addition, through both the General Assembly and the Security Council, they called upon South Africa to abandon its arbitrary arrests and trials of opponents of apartheid.[101]

When the Pretoria government persisted in its refusal to comply with these resolutions, members of the General Assembly recommended still stronger measures to one particular group of states: the major trading partners of South Africa. Knowing full well that the white minority regime could not survive without foreign trade, they urgently appealed throughout the 1960s to Britain, France, the United States, Italy, the Federal Republic of Germany, and Japan to stop providing economic assistance that allowed this government to persist in its racial policies.[102] Moreover, working through the General Assembly, Security Council, and International Court of Justice, they established the Council for Namibia to administer that territory until independence was achieved and declared South Africa's control over Namibia and its imposition of apartheid there to be immoral and illegal and in gross violation of fundamental human rights.[103]

At the launching of the Decade for Action to Combat Racism and Racial Discrimination, the vast majority of these states became even more insistent upon taking determined action, particularly when they saw South Africa arrogantly flouting their solemn resolutions and the legal opinions of the International Court of Justice. The white minority regime in Pretoria remained confident that its wealth, strategic resources, geopolitical position, and anticommunist stance would keep its important Western political and economic partners from imposing mandatory sanctions or punitive arms embargoes, and thus continued to hold out on both apartheid and Namibia. For this reason, members of the General Assembly pushed even further and in 1973 adopted the International Convention on the Suppression and Punishment of the Crime of Apartheid. During the same year, with strong support from the Organization of African Unity, they demanded the immediate withdrawal of South African forces from Namibian territory and then took the significant step of recognizing the national liberation movement of Namibia, the South-West African People's Organization (SWAPO), as the authentic representative of the Namibian people in their struggle for independence.[104]

When these measures appeared to have little effect upon the intransigent white minority regime, members of the General Assembly voted to ask the Security Council to expel South Africa from the United Nations completely due to its policies of apartheid, occupation of Namibia, and "the constant violation by South Africa of the principles of the Charter and the Universal Declaration of Human Rights."[105] Never before in the history of the organization had expulsion of a member nation been formally considered. After stormy debate during 1974, ten members of the Security Council (including the Soviet Union and China) voted to expel South Africa, but for the first time three permanent members cast vetoes together on a resolution. Britain, France, and the United States gave their support to South Africa and thus spared it from expulsion. Furious about this vote by the major white Western powers, the members of the General Assembly decided to take their own unprecedented action and successfully moved to suspend South Africa from any participation in their deliberations. They refused to allow the South African delegation to speak, make proposals, vote, or even take its seat in the assembly's proceedings.[106]

In the midst of all this international—and interracial—tension, the military coup in Portugal shocked the world, bringing in its wake, as we have seen, the collapse of the oldest colonial empire in Africa.[107] The resulting achievement of independence and majority rule in Guinea-Bissau and Mozambique, the failure of the South African military adventure in Angola, and the tightening of the ring of Front Line black states around the hard core of whites in southern Africa not only revolutionized much in the international balance of power but also gave many victims of apartheid new political consciousness, pride, support, determination, and a belief that in the long run they would emerge triumphant.[108] This larger setting is essential to understanding why increasing numbers of blacks suddenly became much more willing to endure the risks of possible bloodshed by striking out against the regime in South Africa.

The effects of these dramatic international changes upon domestic opposition became vividly evident in 1976 when numerous schoolchildren and their parents in Soweto, the country's largest black urban area, determined to launch a massive strike in protest against segregated and unequal education. Their local action in Soweto, however, quickly ignited explosions and other violent disturbances in most other African townships as well. These grew in intensity and continued well into 1977, resulting in several hundred deaths and the massive arrests of leading blacks, other non-whites, and several sympathetic whites, all under various security laws. One of those arrested and held in custody was Steven Biko, a powerful spokesman for black consciousness and a man who at the age of thirty had become one of the most influential and respected of a new generation of African leaders. Biko openly stated what he and his followers had hoped to achieve. "We are looking forward to a non-racial, just, and egalitarian society," he said,

> in which color, creed, and race shall form no point of reference. We have deliberately chosen to operate openly because we have believed . . . that we can penetrate even the deafest of white ears and get the message to register that no lie can live forever. In doing this we rely not only on our strength but also on the belief that the rest of the world views the oppression and blatant exploitation of the black majority by a minority as an unforgiveable sin that cannot be pardoned by civilized societies.[109]

These words did not please the white authorities and after several weeks of silence, the South African police announced that Biko had gone on a hunger strike while in prison and that, as a result, he unfortunately had died of malnutrition.

Despite the efforts of police to keep them away, fifteen thousand mourners gathered for Steven Biko's funeral. When they opened his coffin, however, they saw not the skin and bones of a corpse emaciated by hunger, but rather a well-built body that they recognized. Everything appeared to be normal—all except for the head. The mourners immediately noticed a huge lump on the left side of the temple. When they removed the unusually large amount of velvet padding on which his head rested, they saw to their horror that the entire back of his skull had been crushed. This shocking spectacle in the midst of grief and emotion proved to be too much to bear, and the mourners suddenly raised their fists high in the air with black power salutes and began to lash out in fury and violence against the white minority regime. South Africa's Prime Minister John Vorster reacted by ordering his security forces to impose even harsher measures of repression, censorship, and arrest for those who protested against the racial policies of his government.[110] His foreign minister, R. L. "Pik" Botha, publicly announced that whites would never agree to changes in their apartheid policy. "Forget it," he said. "No way. We shall not accept that; not now, not tomorrow, never, ever."[111]

Biko's brutal murder in 1977, following as it did the violent Soweto riots, provided yet another shocking reminder of the policy of apartheid and provoked unparalleled revulsion against South Africa throughout the world. Well aware of their commitment to the new Program of Action Against Apartheid[112] and the larger Decade for Action to Combat Racism and Racial Discrimination, most nations now agreed that they simply must take more determined and concrete measures. Deliberately avoiding the prospect of rhetoric alone in the General Assembly, they focused their attention upon the more powerful Security Council. Here, and to the surprise of many, the United States agreed to cooperate with the others in taking meaningful action. Andrew Young announced to his nearly incredulous fellow representatives that in view of Biko's death, President Carter had authorized him to join in an arms embargo against South Africa. The purpose of U.S. support, said Young, was to embark "on a course aimed at ending racial discrimination."[113]

After unanimously condemning the policy of apartheid and declaring that "the violence and repression by the South African racist regime have greatly aggravated the situation in South Africa and will certainly lead to violent conflict and racial conflagration with serious international repercussions," members of the Security Council then took the unprecedented step of imposing a mandatory arms embargo against South Africa. This applied to the sale or transfer of weapons and ammunition, military vehicles and equipment, paramilitary police supplies, and even spare parts.[114] Such action marked the first time in the history of politics and diplomacy at the United Nations that punitive, mandatory sanctions had been imposed against a member state. For this reason, Kurt Waldheim correctly called it a "historic occasion" and a "momentous step" indicating a new determination by the international community to take clear action in combating apartheid and racial discrimination.[115]

This increased attention to and outrage over South Africa's racial policies encouraged most nations to mobilize and coordinate their actions in other ways as well. During the same year of 1977, for example, the Commonwealth countries meeting in London joined together in signing the Gleneagles Agreement, condemning the "detestable" policy of apartheid and adamantly declaring, "The member countries of the Commonwealth, embracing peoples of diverse races, colors, languages, and faiths, have long recognized racial prejudice and discrimination as a dangerous sickness and an unmitigated evil and are pledged to use all their efforts to foster human dignity everywhere."[116]

Shortly thereafter, 92 states participated in the Maputo Conference in Mozambique, declaring that "the South Africa apartheid regime has been the bastion of racism and colonialism" and giving their full support to SWAPO in its struggle to free Namibia from control by South Africa.[117]

Within months, 111 governments sent official representatives to the World Conference for Action Against Apartheid meeting in Lagos, Nigeria. There, they agreed that "South Africa belongs to all its people irrespective of race, color, and creed and that all have the right to live and work there in conditions of full equality," and reiterated their "universal abhorrence of apartheid and racism in all its forms and manifestations and the determination of the international community to secure its speedy elimination."[118] This kind of sentiment was voiced again with even greater force in 1978 when the Security Council explicitly stated its determination to secure independence for Namibia and when, as we have seen, most of the representatives from 125 states gathered for the World Conference to Combat Racism and Racial Discrimination and served notice that they were prepared to take "drastic action" against the white minority regime in South Africa.[119]

Despite these many determined endeavors and a series of multilateral negotiations and resolutions,[120] members of the international community found themselves increasingly frustrated and angered to the breaking point by South Africa's adamant refusal to modify its racial policies. Contemptuous of all this attention, pressure, and opinion mobilized against it, the white minority regime in Pretoria resolutely continued tightening its grip on Namibia and enforcing its repressive system of apartheid. When several countries presented a carefully drafted plan for independence and majority rule for the Namibian people, R. L. Botha immediately rejected the proposal, declaring it to be "completely unacceptable."[121] When the United Nations offered still another possible peaceful solution to the problem of racial discrimination, he refused to accept it, saying that South Africa would rather risk international disfavor and sanctions than change its policies and capitulate to external pressure.[122] Much of Botha's abrasive self-assuredness, of course, came from his belief that he could make such statements with impunity. He and other members of the South African government believed that for reasons of politics, strategy, ideology, and economics, the Western governments of Britain, France, and the United States would never allow full-scale sanctions to be imposed against them. Indeed, they became all the more persuaded in this conviction with the election of Ronald Reagan.

The South African government greeted the news of Reagan's election as president of the United States in November 1980 with enthusiasm. Within hours, Prime Minister P. W. Botha expressed the belief that the victory of Reagan would initiate a new era of "reasonable" deliberation between Washington and Pretoria that would reverse Carter's open emphasis on human rights and opposition to apartheid.[123] When Jeane Kirkpatrick was named as the new U.S. representative to the United Nations, the white South African press widely quoted her as saying that "racial dictatorship is not as onerous as Marxist dictatorship."[124] Newspapers also noted with satisfaction that the designated secretary of state, Alexander Haig, viewed South Africa favorably as a supplier of strategic minerals to the West, as a protector of the sea-lanes sailed by oil tankers, and as a loyal ally against Communist expansion into Africa rather than as an international outlaw that should be condemned for its racial policies.[125] For all of these reasons, the South African state radio hailed the Reagan victory as the defeat of "pseudo liberalism, permissiveness, state intervention, appeasement, and antipatriotism," concluding that now "Western Christian culture" still had a chance to triumph over communism.[126]

An indication of the effects of the U.S. election upon South Africa's boldness came with the opening of the United Nations Conference on Namibia in January 1981. Delegates from around the world gathered in Geneva to negotiate a settlement that would create a cease-fire between SWAPO and South African forces, then provide international supervision for elections leading to independence and majority rule. South Africa not only rejected all such proposals, but walked out of the conference as well, launched a commando raid into Mozambique, and then stepped up its military activities in Angola. When asked about U.S. reaction to this behavior, President Reagan stated that the United States should "keep the door open and continue to negotiate with a friendly nation like South Africa."[127] Then, Kirkpatrick's defense of South Africa in her maiden speech before the United Nations and subsequent meeting with a South African military delegation that had covertly entered the United States seemed to confirm the earlier rumors of a dramatic shift in policy. Beamed one banner headline in the white Afrikaans newspaper *Die Vaderland*: "U.S. Will Not Leave South Africa in the Lurch." "Not only is it virtually the opposite of that [policy] adopted by the Carter Government," exulted the paper, "but it is even more friendly than the policy of Richard Nixon."[128] A close advisor to Prime Minister P. W. Botha described the mood of the South African government resulting from this U.S. support with one word: "euphoria."[129]

The Reagan administration argued that such a new and positive dialogue, called "constructive engagement," with Pretoria would be the most effective means not only to serve U.S. interests but also to coax South Africa to end its occupation of Namibia and ameliorate its policy of apartheid. Proven, traditional, diplomatic practice of maintaining positive discussions rather than negative pressure, it claimed, would yield the best results over time.[130] Few countries, however, found themselves persuaded by this argument or willing to give it a chance. Indeed, many actively organized and mobilized themselves to speak out and to work against it. A diplomatic summit conference of the presidents of the Front Line States, for example, denounced the growing friendship between Washington and Pretoria as "a clear affront and challenge to independent Africa."[131] A meeting of nonaligned foreign ministers similarly condemned this U.S. policy of support for South Africa based upon strategic and economic considerations rather than human rights and adopted a program of action for Namibia's independence, part of which called for the imposition of mandatory sanctions against the white minority regime.[132] To their dismay, when the Security Council considered resolutions to impose such sanctions against South Africa, the United States, Britain, and France all cast vetoes.

Encouraged by this support, the South African government immediately launched a new military campaign from Namibia against SWAPO forces in Angola. In response, Assistant Secretary of State for African Affairs Chester Crocker said simply that "it is not our task to choose between black and white," and the United States again, but all alone, vetoed a Security Council resolution condemning the South African attack.[133] Shocked and angered by this statement about the United States' not wanting to "take sides," Ambassador Olara Otunnu, speaking for the Africa Group within the United Nations, observed: "The choice is between the forces of apartheid which have brutalized and dehumanized the vast majority of South Africans and the forces that seek to set them free. How can a country that professes democracy remain neutral between an oppressive system which has deprived eighty percent of the citizens of their basic rights and a movement of people that seeks to restore these democratic rights? . . . How long," he asked plaintively, "will the friends of South Africa protect the aggressor?"[134]

Subsequent policy decisions made it appear as though the answer to this question might be that this kind of U.S. protection and support would continue for several years. During the negotiations among the Western "Contact Group" of the United States, Britain, France, the Federal Republic of Germany, and Canada, to find some solution to the Namibian problem in 1982, for example, the Americans suddenly insisted that independence for Namibia from South African occupation could not take place until the Cubans withdrew their forces from Angola. When the other members of this group criticized such a position of "linkage," Vice President George Bush obdurately proclaimed that the United States "will not bend" to international pressure. "That's our position," he asserted. "We are going to stay with it."[135] Moreover, in yet another move that reinforced the impression of a similar lack of commitment to racial equality, the Reagan administration announced that the United States would refuse to participate in or even attend the 1983 Second World Conference to Combat Racism and Racial Discrimination.

The many participants in the Decade for Action unanimously agreed that the elimination of all forms of racism and discrimination based upon race represented an issue "of high priority to the international community," and hence recognized the importance of convening the Second World Conference to Combat Racism and Racial Discrimination to review and assess their efforts during the previous ten years and to formulate "ways and means of specific measures aimed at ensuring the full and universal implementation of United Nations resolutions and decisions on racism, racial discrimination, and apartheid."[136] A wide variety of nations from Europe, Latin America, Africa, and Asia, bodies such as the International Labor Organization and UNESCO, regional associations like the Council of Europe and Organization of African Unity, nongovernmental organizations, churches, and individuals invested several years of intense effort in preparing for this conference.[137]

They thus found themselves greatly heartened when the representatives of 128 states sent official representatives (mostly at the ambassadorial level) to join with several hundred other participants in Geneva for the Second World Conference to Combat Racism and Racial Discrimination. The 3 countries that believed that they would be singled out for special attention chose not to attend: South Africa, the United States, and Israel. Secretary-General Javier Perez de Cuellar refused to let the nonparticipation of these three halt the proceedings, however, saying that the conference had "a special responsibility to the world community" and must be held "because it forms an integral part of the battle which must be fought. We must be relentless," he declared with his opening statement, "in our struggles to eradicate racism and racial discrimination universally."[138]

From the very first session of the conference it immediately became apparent that the participants wanted to take even more determined action than they had in the past. They refused to remain content with their many accomplishments of the previous ten years and decided that they could not rest until the "morally condemnable" and "dangerous" practices of racism, racial discrimination, and apartheid were eradicated completely.[139] In this regard they focused in particular upon what the Xinhua News Agency of China called "the most stubborn fortress of racism today": South Africa.[140] The conference participants condemned its "systematic oppression and discrimination against the overwhelming majority of the population," its "continuing illegal occupation of Namibia," and its "acts of military aggression and destabilization" against the neighboring states of Angola, Botswana, Lesotho, Mozambique, Seychelles, Swaziland, Zambia, and Zimbabwe. To confront these problems directly, the delegates voted 104 to 0 to launch the Second Decade for Action to Combat Racism and Racial Discrimination and quickly adopted a new and comprehensive Program of Action calling upon all states to render assistance to oppressed blacks in South Africa, to support the Front Line States, to impose stronger and mandatory sanctions against the Pretoria government, and to cease all collaboration and investment with the South African apartheid regime. Such action, declared the participating nations, representing the overwhelming majority in the world, would confirm their "unalterable determination" to mobilize maximum international pressure in order to finally achieve global recognition of the principle of racial equality.[141]

*   *   *

When the initial Decade for Action reached its conclusion, those many nations that had participated so actively could view their accomplishments with pride. As a result of their efforts, the world was much more keenly aware of the global problems of power and prejudice, of racial discrimination, and of apartheid and much more sensitive as to how international relations could be seen as interracial relations than it had been only ten years before. Because of their work, the International Convention on the Elimination of All Forms of Racial Discrimination had become one of the United Nations instruments receiving the greatest number of ratifications. During the Decade for Action, and with their active support and encouragement, several countries gained independence from white colonial rule in the hard core of Africa, including Guinea-Bissau, Mozambique, Angola, and Zimbabwe. Moreover, due to their activities, the international community for the first time in the history of politics and diplomacy had convened two major world conferences on racial discrimination and brought newfound pressures, especially from the Third World, to bear upon South Africa for its occupation of Namibia and its policy of apartheid.

These many accomplishments gained during a time of action marked considerable achievement in the struggle for racial equality but obviously did not eliminate all problems associated with race. Pious statements, rhetorical flourishes, and well-meaning resolutions do not automatically provide results in practice. "While recognizing the progress which has been made," observed Perez de Cuellar with remarkable candor during the 1983 conference, "we must nevertheless face the fact that as the Decade nears its end racism and racial discrimination are still far from eradicated." The occupation of territory belonging to others, the policy of apartheid, and the often subtler forms of racial discrimination in different and non-white societies around the world continued, in his words, to cast "an obscene shadow on humanity as a whole."[142] For this reason, he challenged members of the international community to involve themselves energetically in the Second Decade for Action to Combat Racism and Racial Discrimination and to renew their commitment to achieving racial equality as they moved toward the future.

Epilogue: Toward the Future

ALTHOUGH THERE HAS BEEN PROGRESS, racism and racial discrimination are very far from being eliminated. . . . We should not be content merely with denouncing unacceptable situations; we should endeavor to correct them. We should not confine ourselves to the normative approach, but get down to the hard facts.
—Hector Charry-Samper

Continuing and Persistent Problems

Among the most difficult and frustrating of the "hard facts" in politics, diplomacy, and discrimination is the continuing and persistent nature of many racial problems. Despite all of the extraordinary accomplishments of the international community and individual nations since the end of World War II, racism and racial discrimination remain in existence. Although greatly diminished in a wide variety of countries around the world, prejudice on the basis of race tenaciously persists. Several hundred participants in one recent international conference, for example, felt compelled to address precisely this issue and concluded that the significant and profound advances made during the past several years should not blind people to the fact that in some cases racism and racial discrimination "are continuing scourges which must be eradicated throughout the world."[1] "The truth," declared Colombian diplomat Hector Charry-Samper with deep conviction, "is that there [continue to be] various degrees of racism, both direct and more or less covert forms of discrimination, anachronistic vestiges of theories based upon the notion of supremacy of certain human groups, which science has shown to be false. In a number of regions, new forms of racism quickly emerge, and the catalogue of discrimination is lengthening before our very eyes, adding detestable types of persecution, intolerance, segregation, and exploitation."[2]

Some forms of racial prejudice, of course, remain subtle and covert, often running just below the surface as individuals and nations continue to allow physical characteristics to influence their attitudes toward those of different races. Others are more clearly evident, manifesting themselves in ways that demonstrate blatant practices of discrimination on the basis of race. These include restrictions upon educational and employment opportunities, exploitation in the marketplace, expropriation of land, forced relocation or emigration, privation of civil or political rights, discriminatory laws on immigration and citizenship, and restrictions upon migrant workers, among other policies. They also include persecution of indigenous or aboriginal peoples and genocide. Even want, it is said, has a color; as the relative abundance of the predominantly white North of the globe towers above the poverty of the largely non-white South.[3] Indeed, from Asia to Africa and Europe to the Americas, no area of the world is completely immune from at least some of these problems.[4]

Among this wide range of racial discrimination, however, nothing has attracted more global attention in the late 1980s than the case of South Africa. The indictment against the white minority regime in Pretoria is not that it is guilty of doing things that no other country has ever done but that it *continues* to enforce government-sanctioned policies of gross racial discrimination to degrees unmatched anywhere on the globe,[5] and at a time when so many, as author David Lamb wrote in *The Africans*, consider that "the world's ultimate crime is the racism of whites toward blacks."[6] The South African government continues to occupy Namibia and deny self-determination to its people, thereby presenting the last unfinished business on the agenda of African emancipation. It persists in armed military attacks against its black neighbors, Angola, Lesotho, and Botswana, among others. And of particular significance, it refuses to change the policy of apartheid even when the country is faced with intense opposition; thus, it prohibits its huge black population majority from voting, traveling or working without permits, residing in areas of choice, expressing their opinion without penalty, or living with even minimum human rights.

As the leaders of east and central Africa charged in a manifesto several years ago with words that have remained true: "There is one thing about South African oppression which distinguishes it from other oppressive regimes. The apartheid policy adopted by its government . . . is based upon a rejection of man's humanity. A position of privilege or the experience of oppression in the South African society depends upon the one thing which it is beyond the power of any man to change. It depends upon man's color." They then felt compelled to explain what this meant in human terms by saying:

> If you are black, you cannot escape this characterization nor can you escape it if you are white. If you are a black millionaire and a brilliant

political scientist, you are still subject to the pass laws and still excluded from political activity. If you are white, even protests against the system and an attempt to reject segregation, will lead you only to the segregation and the comparative comfort of the white gaol. Beliefs, abilities, and behavior are all irrelevant to a man's status; everything depends upon race.[7]

For all these reasons, the white minority regime in South Africa is seen as a dangerously explosive and continuing source of extreme racism, tension, and aggression that menaces not only its own people but the international community as well. Millions of non-whites see it as a living symbol of white domination from the past and vow that they will not rest until they have achieved black majority rule here. In fact, no issue in global politics and diplomacy can unite more countries so quickly than this one of South Africa.[8] Its abhorrent racial policies are verbally condemned by virtually every nation in the world. When confronting the hard facts of the Pretoria regime, for example, even Ronald Reagan maintained that he and other Americans "view racism with repugnance" and deplore "the human and spiritual cost of apartheid in South Africa."[9] Others, of course, have spoken with more force and determination, describing South Africa as "the bastion of institutionalized racism," and its policies as "the most unjust of all the current situations of segregation," "the most extreme and shameful form of racism," and "the most serious and threatening" manifestations of racial discrimination in the entire world.[10]

In the face of this kind of international condemnation, South Africa has remained largely unmoved. Countless resolutions opposing apartheid, legal judgments against continued occupation of Namibia, treaties promoting human rights and prohibiting racial discrimination, reports documenting cases of brutal racial persecution, protests against invasions of the Front Line States, and partial sanctions have been unable to change the basic nature of the white minority regime in Pretoria. In fact, no form of political or diplomatic pressure has been able to significantly influence South Africa since Gandhi first brought the situation to international attention before World War I. "There is no doubt," wrote one scholar, "South Africa presents a threat to international peace and security. . . . [But] relatively undisturbed by the commotion she has created, South Africa continues on her path towards a racist empire."[11]

This well-worn path has remained as a deep and unhealed scar slashed across the body politic, and thus far South Africa has provided little evidence that it intended to change course. After its universal condemnation during the Second World Conference to Combat Racism and Racial Discrimination, for example, South Africa defiantly launched yet another punishing raid into Angola to attack the SWAPO black nationalist guerrillas fighting for Namibian independence. Even though it signed a "non-aggression and good neighborliness" pact with Mozambique in exchange for Mozambique's promise not to aid black guerrillas of the African National Congress, South Africa was not prepared to extend this offer to others. In addition, the Pretoria government persisted in its apartheid policies of residential and educational segregation and of forced relocation of several million of the country's twenty-three million blacks, most of them to remote and impoverished "homelands." Although it attempted minor reform in 1984 by creating a new tricameral parliament, which gave a limited voice to those of mixed race and Indians, the less than five million whites retained their control over all important matters and refused to give blacks any representation at all. Those black leaders who protested this arrangement immediately found themselves arrested, like Nelson Mandela, for subversion or treason, and detained without trial, and many have been killed while undergoing police interrogation.

Only a powerful and visible black opponent like Anglican Archbishop Desmond Tutu, who heads the thirteen-million member South African Council of Churches, has been able to escape this fate and publicly express his outrage. Although subjected to government criticism and harassment, Tutu has still managed to plead with black audiences for interracial concord and peaceful change, to warn of a coming "bloodbath" if whites do not share power with the black majority, and to declare that "apartheid is as evil and as vicious as Nazism and Communism."[12] When physically out of South Africa and standing before an international audience on the occasion of receiving the prestigious 1984 Nobel Peace Prize, he said: "Blacks are systematically stripped of their South African citizenship and are being turned into aliens in the land of their birth. . . . This is apartheid's final solution, like the solution the Nazis had for the Jews in Hitler's Aryan madness."[13]

Within only a few months, Tutu's compelling words tragically and ironically came to life with death. In February 1985, black residents of the wretched squatters' camp called Crossroads, just outside Cape Town, feared that they would be resettled by force. For this reason, they quickly began blocking the roads around their shacks with makeshift barricades of oil drums, stones, and old tires. When government police and riot squads approached the scene, they found themselves confronting nearly three thousand protestors, some of them lifting their arms in a black-power salute and shouting *"Amandhla!"* (Power!). The government forces answered hurled stones with rubber bullets and bird shot, and then the riot turned into a battle. Once the smoke finally cleared, 26 policemen had sustained injuries, whereas among the blacks 250 suffered wounds and 18 were dead.[14]

This rioting and upheaval only fanned the flames of unrest. As the twenty-fifth anniversary of the bloody and highly symbolic Sharpeville massacre[15] approached, the situation became even more volatile. The explosion came quickly. In March 1985, a highway procession of four thousand blacks commemorating all those who lost their lives at Sharpeville marched toward the town of Uitenhage, not far from Port Elizabeth on the Eastern Cape. Suddenly, the police opened fire upon the crowd. They killed on the spot nineteen demonstrators. According to a number of eyewitnesses, the police then not only placed sticks and stones in the hands of the dead to make them appear as the aggressors but also shot others who sprawled wounded on the ground and summoned a fire engine to hose away the blood. "This," said Rev. Allan Boesak of the World Alliance of Reformed Churches, "was summary execution and cold-blooded murder."[16] In the days that followed, the white minority government banned twenty-nine black organizations from holding any meetings, including the broadly based antiapartheid alliance of blacks and whites known as the United Democratic Front, sixteen of whose leaders already faced charges of treason. This ban provoked even greater violence, attacks against authority, arson, massive civil disobedience, and more loss of life, resulting in South Africa's bloodiest confrontations in twenty-five years. "Enough!" cried Johannesburg's *Rand Daily Mail* in anguish. "This country is tearing itself apart. We are writing our history in blood."[17]

These tragic deaths and the spiraling violence caused the Pretoria regime not to modify or abandon apartheid, but rather to dig in its heels even deeper. Government spokesmen continued to fall back upon *kragdadigheid,* or a mailed-fisted attitude of determined resistance. Declared President P. W. Botha defiantly, "I am going to keep order in South Africa, and nobody in the world is going to stop me."[18] His reaction and its subsequent repression sparked yet further violence and counterviolence, convincing many South Africans, black and white, that the vicious circle would continue—and perhaps grow worse. Such fear appeared recently in a haunting cartoon in the Johannesburg *Star,* which showed three gravestones side by side. The first recorded, "Sharpeville. 1960." The second read, "Uitenhage. 1985." The third tombstone said: "Watch This Space."[19]

Standards—and Double Standards

It is not difficult, when one views this tragic record of bloodshed and discrimination, to understand why South Africa is so universally condemned and despised. Despite years of struggle and promises of reform, violence still holds sway in this troubled land and in those countries that it touches. In attacking its black neighbors, in occupying Namibia and denying its people self-determination, and in enforcing apartheid, the white minority regime of South Africa has violated every international legal and moral standard of human rights and racial equality now in existence. To make matters worse, the Pretoria government has seemed to do so with impunity, defiant arrogance, and complete disregard for these very standards themselves. This compels not simply South Africa's opponents (of whom there are many) in the world but also its few friends to condemn its abhorrent actions in the strongest possible terms. "The system of apartheid is totally repugnant," declared Secretary of State George Shultz in exasperation when responding to questions about the Uitenhage tragedy, for example. "The pattern of violence has underlined how evil and unacceptable that system is."[20]

This particular condemnation, among many others, however, points to another of the "hard facts" of global racial discrimination. That is, although virtually all states may criticize the gross violations of human rights standards by South Africa verbally, some remain unwilling to enforce these standards in practice. The friends of Pretoria have either refused to acknowledge that their political and financial support helped to perpetuate these racial policies or argued that the immediate strategic, economic, and ideological interests were more important than defending human rights. For these reasons, they continued not only to circumvent boycotts and embargoes imposed against South Africa but, for a considerable time, actually increased trade and financial investment with the white minority regime. The *Washington Post* summarized the hypocrisy of this approach with a biting political cartoon showing a straight-faced government spokesman announcing, "I'm in charge of our 'constructive engagement' policy toward South Africa." With a flourish he said, "I claim successes, object to sanctions, emphasize the positive." Then, while piously folding his hands, he concluded solemnly, "and deplore massacres as often as necessary."[21]

Such double standards have not gone unnoticed by the international community. Those few diplomats who wished to remain discreet on this matter simply and positively emphasized the need for *"all governments"* to join together in enforcing established standards of racial equality.[22] Others became more direct and negatively criticized "all those who contribute to the maintenance of the system of apartheid [and thus] are accomplices in the perpetuation of this totally abhorrent system of institutionalized racism."[23] Some sought to point their fingers slightly more directly and identified such accomplices as "certain Western powers" who benefited from racial exploitation[24] or, like the Chinese delegation, charged that "one superpower has all along been abetting and generously supporting the South African authorities, thus becoming the chief patronage of that racist regime."[25] Still others lashed out with vehement specificity against the countries that actively collaborated in an "unholy alliance" with South Africa, using their strongest language against the United States and Israel. The participants in one recent and widely representative gathering, for example, deplored "in particular the policies of the U.S. administration which, under the guise of 'constructive engagement,' has provided comfort and encouragement to the apartheid regime."[26] Tutu himself has described U.S. policy toward Pretoria as "immoral, evil, and totally unChristian."[27] Even harsher words were used by diplomatic officials at yet another important international meeting when they issued the following statement against such collaboration:

> The Conference condemns any form of cooperation with South Africa, notably the existing and increasing relations between Israel and the racist regime of South Africa . . . ; it particularly deplores the expansion and intensification of those relations at the time when the international community is exerting all its efforts toward the objective of completely isolating the regime of South Africa; the Conference views this cooperation as an act of deliberate choice and a hostile act against the oppressed people of South Africa, as well as a defiance of the resolutions of the United Nations and the efforts of the society of nations to ensure freedom and peace in South Africa.[28]

Open castigation of this kind of practice by several nations that condemn racism verbally, while at the same time collaborating with South Africa, helps to draw attention to the difficult problem of double standards and to explain why so many nations and individuals have increasingly regarded international relations as interracial relations. It also indicates why the Soviets (despite their own discrimination against racial minorities and anti-Semitism at home) found it so easy to use the issue of race against the Americans in their Cold War rivalry. In sharp contrast to the United States, the Soviet Union and its allies have consistently supported decolonization, signed all treaties seeking to prevent racial discrimination, actively supported sanctions against South Africa, and participated in programs to combat apartheid and racism. Their task was made all the easier when the United States deliberately chose not even to attend the World Conferences to Combat Racism and Racial Discrimination, thus leaving the field completely open to critics. In this setting, it did not take much effort to portray the Americans as grossly insensitive to the global issue of race at best or as openly racist at worst. As the chief representative of the African National Congress to the United Nations described the results, people throughout Africa and Asia tended to believe that, unlike many in the West, Communists "at least are concerned about our problem" and "support us by pouring water rather than gasoline on the fire of racism."[29] A black Namibian recently put the matter even more bluntly by saying, "The Soviets are probably just as racist as the other white Europeans, but at least they support the right cause against South Africa."[30]

Here it is of critical importance to acknowledge honestly that in the politics and diplomacy of discrimination the dimensions of double standards cannot be confined to the relatively easy target of the white minority regime in Pretoria and its few friends. The majority of states in the international community have been quick to jump upon the abhorrent racial policies of whites in South Africa or the West but extremely reluctant to condemn racial injustices and violations of human rights perpetrated by others and by themselves. In this light, the Decade for Action to Combat Racism and Racial Discrimination appropriately might be named the "Decade for Action Against Apartheid" or the "Decade to Combat White Racism."[31]

Members of the United Nations, for example, even when dealing just with Africa, have been quick to condemn whites for their financial dealings with Pretoria, but remained almost silent when Nigeria, using fraudulent destination papers, shipped oil to the South African Government through Rotterdam and when even the Front Line States themselves continued their active trading with South Africa. Although ready to criticize apartheid, they said little when Idi Amin of Uganda expelled whites and Asians from his country and then proceeded to kill a quarter of a million of his own citizens. Few speeches in the General Assembly deplored tribal warfare in Nigeria or expressed deep concern about "Emperor" Jean Bokassa's brutality in the Central African Republic. In addition, many of those who vocally welcomed Archbishop Tutu's Nobel Peace Prize acceptance speech condemning South Africa remained conspicuously quiet when two other human rights activists, Andrei Sakharov of the Soviet Union and Lech Walesa of Poland, were denied exit visas by their Communist governments to accept exactly the same award.

It is precisely this use of double standards in the world that prompted Jeane Kirkpatrick to deliver one of her most contentious, but courageous, speeches as U.S. ambassador before the United Nations. Although others had discussed the problem before,[32] she decided to launch an attack in the full light of publicity by saying that it was neither fair nor reasonable to judge the human rights violations of some nations harshly, while completely ignoring the gross abuses of others. She accused some nations of attempting to "use human rights less as a standard and a goal than as a political weapon; less to expand the domains of freedom and law than to expand the scope of their hegemony." The application of standards, she charged, "has grown more distorted and more cynical," while human rights have "become a bludgeon to be wielded by the strong against the weak, by the majority against the isolated, by the blocs against the unorganized." Kirkpatrick then went as far as to accuse the United Nations of "moral hypocrisy," relating her criticism to the specific problem of racism with the following words:

> My government believes that apartheid is a morally repugnant system which violates the rights of black peoples and colored who live under it. . . . As such, it is reprehensible. It cannot be condoned. . . .
>
> But let us be clear, apartheid is not the only system for denying people the enjoyment of freedom, the right to choose and criticize their rulers, the rule of the law, the opportunity for a good job, a good education, a good life. There are other grounds on which other regimes in the last decade have denied their citizens dignity, freedom, equal protection of the law, material well being, and even life; other regimes that have more cruelly and more brutally repressed and slaughtered their citizens.

Kirkpatrick ended her blunt speech by calling upon members of the United Nations to affirm and to adhere to a common human rights standard. "If we do not have a single standard," she accurately concluded, "then our resolutions and recommendations are merely tendentious political statements without moral content."[33]

Once this charge of double standards became public, others began to level criticism as well. The focus of their attention centered not simply upon Communist governments, which effectively *used* the issue and the rhetoric of racism, in alliance with Asian and African countries, to attack the West but upon other international organizations and media coverage of world events as well. The Geneva-based World Council of Churches, which had done so much effective work in raising people's consciousness of the global problems of racial discrimination, for instance, found itself suddenly accused of being only too ready to condemn violations of human rights by right-wing regimes while keeping more or less silent about such abuses by left-wing governments. Said one recent, sharp critique, the council "will need to show, more than hitherto, that its compassion for those who suffer under Communism is as real as for those who are racially and economically oppressed elsewhere."[34] As one critic wrote to the *Times* of London after a story about brutality by Pretoria authorities: "Had it happened in Matabeleland or Uganda it is very doubtful whether you would have wasted a paragraph on it. It is white South Africa which has to be got at, and for the one and only reason that it is white in a black continent."[35] Accusations of this nature make it easier for Foreign Minister Roelof Botha to respond by saying, "South Africa is sick and tired of the hypocrisy" of other nations,[36] and for the Durban-based *Sunday Tribune* unashamedly to tell its foreign critics: "Go to hell!"[37]

Such charges and countercharges demonstrate not only the difficult nature but also the pervasive role played by politics and diplomacy in the problem of double standards. The charges and countercharges indicate that while much global attention is appropriately focused upon some of the most egregious cases of racial abuse, it is often and deliberately selectively blind to the many other examples or other degrees of discrimination in the world. Attacks upon South Africa's flagrant violations against blacks with apartheid and the occupation of Namibia, for example, rarely are accompanied by criticism of the caste system and the treatment of untouchables in India or discrimination against the ethnic Chinese in Malaysia and Indonesia. Condemnations of practices in the United States and Canada toward blacks, Native Americans, Hispanics, and other racial minorities seldom are coupled with accusations against Brazil's extermination of its Indians, of the fate of tribal peoples in the Philippines, or of Japan's attempt to keep its own people "racially homogeneous." Few in the General Assembly rose in protest when Pol Pot murdered approximately three million Kampucheans through genocide. Denunciations of British immigration practices and domestic racial riots, Australian or New Zealand aboriginal policies, or Israeli treatment of the Palestinians are scarcely found alongside protests deploring "reverse discrimination" against whites in black Africa or the ruling White Russians' maltreatment in practice of racial minorities within the Soviet Union and Afghanistan while occupied by the Soviet army.

Charges of racial discrimination against the former colonial powers rarely are accompanied by acknowledgments that Western European governments now have ratified almost all of the major human rights instruments and, through their Commission of Human Rights and Court, often have displayed far more willingness than the Afro-Asian countries to submit to enforcement procedures. By contrast, the Asian states have created no regional body to protect human rights, and the signatories of the African Charter on Human and Peoples' Rights now in force still have not instituted an effective mechanism to provide genuine means of enforcing equal treatment.[38] In this particular political and diplomatic setting, accusations of "racist" and "racism," although frequently accurate, thus often offer contemporary evidence of the classic problem among nations and individuals of seeing the mote in the eyes of others while at the same time ignoring—or deliberately diverting attention from— the beam in their own.

"Speeches and Majority Votes"— or "Iron and Blood"?

The difficulties presented by these kinds of problems are compounded by yet another of the several "hard facts" of the politics and diplomacy of discrimination: that is, the question of determining the best means of confronting and then overcoming abuses. Although members of the international community might well be able both to attain and then to sustain some general consensus about the *end* of securing racial equality, they are not likely to reach an agreement upon the *means* to do so. Some, for example, are inclined to discuss gradual and peaceful solutions politely over a long period of time, claiming that only in this way will long-lasting results and mutual understanding be achieved. Others find this argument not at all convincing, are prepared to use violence if necessary to secure immediate gains, and find themselves agreeing with the famous statement by the nineteenth-century German chancellor, Otto von Bismarck, that "the great questions of the day will be decided not by speeches and majority votes . . . —but by iron and blood."[39]

Bismarck's outspoken and rather crass words remain as thought provoking today as when they were first voiced. The reason for this is that they verbalize the classic debate as to whether the great questions of politics and diplomacy are resolved by speeches and resolutions or by might and war. This debate rages with particular poignancy over racial discrimination, for in this case both extremes have been employed in the past and continue to be advocated for the future. Many things, as we have seen, have been achieved and mark major advances on the road toward global racial equality. But the fact remains that the effectiveness of the United Nations and other international bodies ultimately rests upon the willingness of their sovereign nation-state members to enforce decisions. International concern over questions of human rights has frequently been in open conflict with the basic principles of sovereignty and nonintervention, which govern the politics and diplomacy of states in their internal and external relations. Hence, solemn agreements and commitments can be ignored or broken. Such conditions easily can lead to what one author described as "the shoals of disappointment and disillusion"[40] and to bitter conclusions like that of the observer who wrote: "No major power—white, black, or brown; Communist, capitalist, or non-aligned—has committed its resources . . . purely out of moral conviction. Nations undertake the use of force, military or economic, only when their national interests are threatened or can be greatly enhanced."[41]

In this setting, speeches often produce only more speeches, and violence often breeds only more violence. It takes little effort or imagination, of course, to criticize the use of "mere words" and dismiss the many pious statements and verbal declarations issued by those members of the international community lacking power to implement their decisions. Words alone, if unaccompanied by action, are hardly likely to lead to many practical results. But, while recognizing this fact, it is also of great importance to acknowledge what values words do possess. As scholar Thomas Franck perceptively concluded after many years of personal experience in observing diplomats make speeches and pass resolutions, "it is quite as wrong to take words in U.N. resolutions *too* seriously as not to take them seriously enough."[42] Although words can be used by the poor and the powerless to inflict pain on those who always seem to win without having to raise their voices, they also communicate heartfelt aspirations as well as authentic rage, and they particularly express pleas for attention to extremely serious problems that simply cannot be ignored.

The agony of trying to find an appropriate path between this Scylla of mere words and the Charybdis of war was made acutely visible during the recent Second World Conference to Combat Racism and Racial Discrimination. Well aware of the sharp criticism leveled against a constant flow of declarations and resolutions without teeth, of promises without performance, and even descriptions of the United Nations as the "House of Hypocrisy,"[43] Perez de Cuellar challenged the delegates to develop "*realistic* programs of action which can address problems concretely."[44] Hector Charry-Samper developed this theme even more fully by candidly and honestly acknowledging, "It is no secret to anyone that we face certain difficulties which we must surmount—to start with, the pessimism which some have publicly expressed about our chances of success." To effectively combat racial discrimination in the world, he warned, diplomats and others must consciously and assiduously avoid simply producing "documents and rhetorical statements or conventions" that verbally strike out against racism and then are "pigeon-holed" and forgotten. "How can we fail to recognize," he asked, "that there is a crisis of confidence about what we who are gathered here represent in one way or another? There is a sort of shifting, recurrent scepticism about the effectiveness of the United Nations and its methods and instruments which encourages conflict and endorses the call to hatred, violence, and the intolerance and self-centered sense of superiority which finds its ultimate and unacceptable expression in war."[45]

Such tensions over means have been evident in all discussions of standards and double standards of human rights, but nowhere were they more striking than in the continuing and persistent arguments about South Africa. Despite the years of serious speeches and the mountains of solemn resolutions by majority votes, the white minority government in Pretoria has refused to end its attacks against neighboring black states, its occupation of Namibia, or its basic policy of apartheid. Indeed, daily news reports in the late 1980s gave every indication that racial tensions in southern Africa were growing even worse.

South African commandos attacked Angola in late May 1985, for example, and in June struck against strongholds of the African National Congress in Botswana. Then, in marked defiance of United Nations resolutions calling for majority rule and independence, P. W. Botha installed a new administration in Namibia. Throughout this period and in townships across South Africa, unprecedented rioting against police and those suspected of collaborating with white rule became so intense that the authorities could hardly contain it. After the loss of nearly five hundred black lives and well over one thousand arrests, the protests intensified even further. By July, the explosive situation became so tense that Botha determined that he and his regime could rule only by declaring a state of emergency for the entire country. This in turn provoked more violence, protests against South African embassies around the world, calls in the U.S. Congress for action, and a recall by all the members of the Common Market of their ambassadors in Pretoria.[46] There appeared to be no end in sight at all. By October, several hundred more deaths had occurred, and violent clashes broke out beyond the confines of the black townships and, for the first time, escalated into the white-controlled territory of Johannesburg itself. There, enraged blacks not only fought against police and security forces, but also attacked white civilians caught in the middle. All these events simply seemed to confirm Mandela's judgment that in South Africa there would be "no easy walk to freedom."[47]

This cycle of racial violence and confrontation continued unabated throughout South Africa during 1986. In January and February both blacks and whites died in racial attacks in the towns and cities of Moutse, Bekkersdal, and Alexandra. During the first part of May, an estimated one and one-half million black workers went out on strike, and shortly thereafter the white South African government launched raids into neighboring Botswana, Zambia, and Zimbabwe against bases of the black African National Congress. Then, in preparation for anticipated violence that might accompany the tenth anniversary of the start of the June 1976 uprising in Soweto,[48] one of the most emotion-charged dates in the calendar of black resistance to white rule, the government declared a nationwide state of emergency, which gave sweeping powers of arrest and detention to police, imposed stringent controls on expression of political dissent, and prohibited press and television coverage of racial unrest. Simultaneously with this declaration, the government arrested several hundred dissidents in predawn raids against trade unionists, church workers, moderate members of the United Democratic Front coalition against apartheid, and radical opposition groups. In taking this action, President Botha announced that the white government of South Africa was quite prepared to "go it alone" and would not "crawl before anyone" to avert international pressure.[49]

Ironically, and poignantly, on the very day that Botha declared his state of emergency, the Commonwealth Secretariat released its special report entitled *Mission to South Africa*. During the preceding months, a distinguished array of Commonwealth leaders (known as the Eminent Persons Group) from Australia, Nigeria, and India, among other Commonwealth countries, made successive visits to South Africa in order to assess its racial problems and prospects. They were given the opportunity to conduct lengthy discussions with a diverse spectrum of opinion including white government ministers, businessmen, women's groups, and black opposition leaders; to travel to both white and black areas of the country; and to interview individuals ranging from Botha to Mandela. After conducting a lengthy study, the group concluded that the white minority government, despite claims to the contrary, was in no way prepared to dismantle or even modify its apartheid policy of racial segregation. Their report observed that racial violence within as well as between the races had escalated, that the color barrier in South Africa had been fortified rather than diminished, that political freedom and respect for human rights had been curtailed, and that there appeared to be little respect for the peaceful establishment of representative government. "From these and other recent developments," they wrote, "we draw the conclusion that while the Government claims to be ready to negotiate, it is in truth not yet prepared to negotiate fundamental change, nor to countenance the creation of genuine democratic structures, nor to face the prospect of the end of white domination and white power in the foreseeable future. Its program of reform does not end apartheid, but seeks to give it a less inhuman face. Its quest is powersharing, but without surrendering overall white control." The eminent Commonwealth group concluded that there was "little doubt that the alternative to a negotiated solution would be appalling chaos, bloodshed, and destruction."[50]

In response to the explosive combination of the frightening conclusions of this report, the white-imposed state of emergency, the anniversary of the Soweto uprising, and the continued refusal of South Africa to voluntarily change its policy of apartheid, a number of peoples and governments heretofore on the sidelines began to reconsider whether peaceful gradualism had been used in the past simply as an excuse for doing nothing to combat institutionalized and legalized racial discrimination. For this reason, they began to register their protest, take more determined action, and in the words of former British Foreign Secretary

David Owen, "to get tough with South Africa."[51] In Paris, more than one thousand demonstrators marched to the South African embassy, and in The Hague, five thousand antiapartheid protestors staged a march. The government of Canada immediately denounced P. W. Botha for "intransigence" and announced a series of economic measures against Pretoria, including terminating Canadian procurement of South African products. In Brussels, the multilateral European Economic Commission reported that economic sanctions were now a necessary last resort to pressure South Africa to end apartheid and publicly asserted, "Not only is Pretoria doing nothing to avert civil war and carnage, all its actions are calculated to provide it."[52] By August, the forty-nine-nation Commonwealth (over the objections of Prime Minister Margaret Thatcher) also voted to support sanctions against the white minority regime, and shortly thereafter, British Foreign Secretary Sir Geoffrey Howe and U.S. Assistant Secretary of State Chester Crocker actually met with the outlawed African National Congress president, Oliver Tambo. In October, Pretoria's growing isolation was further underscored by an unprecedented rebuke of the 136-nation International Red Cross in Geneva, an organization that long has prided itself in adhering to principles of universality and impartiality, when it refused to seat the delegation from South Africa.

Perhaps the most surprising reaction and indication of change came from the United States. Here the Congress initiated and passed a measure to impose a comprehensive trade embargo against the white minority regime of Pretoria and to require U.S. companies and individuals to divest themselves of existing investments in South Africa. When the bill was sent to President Reagan (who strongly supported tough trade measures against such Communist countries as Cuba, Vietnam, Kampuchea, North Korea, and Nicaragua), he immediately vetoed it, claiming that over the long haul only gradual change with the support of the white government would be effective, even though this approach might be criticized during the short term. Said one senator in anger, "the President persists in locking himself into a failed and lonely policy that has put America on the side of racism in South Africa."[53]

In response, and with the support of many churches, trade unions, universities, human rights groups, state and local governments, the congressional Black Caucus, and major figures in both the Republican and Democratic parties, Congress voted by overwhelming margins in both houses to override the presidential veto. Thus, in October 1986 the Comprehensive Anti-Apartheid Act became the law of the land, imposing a package of economic sanctions stronger than those adopted by any other of South Africa's former major trading partners, providing for expanded assistance and support of education and training for black

South Africans, and mandating a further escalation of sanctions if substantial progress was not made toward ending discrimination and establishing a nonracial democracy. Then, in a remarkable assessment and confession, the secretary of state's own Advisory Committee on South Africa concluded in 1987 that "the Administration's strategy of 'constructive engagement' has failed to achieve its objectives" and that a more activist policy was now needed to end racial apartheid.[54]

Yet, using economic sanctions and divestiture as a means of achieving racial equality, it must be acknowledged, was certainly not universally accepted. Some considered that external pressure from foreign powers could exert only limited influence, for in the end, the solution in its glories or in its tragedies would have to come from the South African people themselves. Even some of the most vehement opponents of apartheid among South African blacks strongly opposed restrictions upon foreign trade and investment. Among these was the prominent leader, Chief Gatsha Buthelezi, head of the large Zulu tribe and president of the Inkatha political organization, who continued to argue that the growing disinvestment campaign could not succeed in ending white minority rule but would only compound the economic distress suffered by blacks. For this reason, he encouraged sympathetic foreigners to pursue their financial investments and to create employment opportunities in South Africa but, at the same time, to follow the so-called Sullivan Principles, which obliged corporations to treat black and white workers equally. Other antiapartheid leaders, of course, branded such a position as a form of shameful collaboration and a betrayal of the cause of racial equality.[55]

The one certainty in this heated and emotionally charged controversy over sanctions and disinvestment, however, has been the strong opposition of the white minority regime in Pretoria. Roelof Botha characteristically and combatively lashed out against any foreign critics and anyone who would dare withdraw funds or restrict trade with South Africa. "We reject demands and prescriptions," he thundered in Parliament, denouncing disinvestment as "misplaced and perverse. Indeed," he said, "we can and will not allow it," and shouted defiantly at the world: "We have faced sanctions before. We have faced this threat for more than two decades. We beat the arms embargo. We beat the oil embargo. With the country's help we will once again beat this threat."[56] By February 1988 this firm stance against threats and refusal to change reached such proportions that the government banned the activities of seventeen leading antiapartheid organizations in South Africa, including those of the large United Democratic Front. Opposition leaders vowed to defy the crackdown and warned that this ban would lead only to further bloodshed. Speaking at a news conference in Cape Town, Desmond

Tutu ominously warned: "Peaceful paths to change are being closed off one by one, and those wanting real change are being encouraged by the government's actions to turn to violence. White South Africans must realize that they are at the crossroads. If they don't stop this government soon, and there's not much hope that they will, we are heading for war."[57]

Such defiance and refusal by South African whites to share power with blacks have convinced many critics that even the threat of economic sanctions could not possibly be sufficient to change course and end apartheid. They, like Bismarck before them, believed that only "iron and blood" could resolve this great question. They argued that the claims of racial equality transcended prohibitions against violence. Even one committee of the World Council of Churches, although taking pains to emphasize that "force should only be used as a last resort" to achieve justice, reluctantly but rather starkly concluded, "The struggle against racism is a struggle about power."[58] Others demonstrated no hesitation at all in reaching the same conclusion. The guerrilla fighters of liberation movements like SWAPO and the African National Congress, and those governments and organizations that provided assistance to them, for example, argued that the only effective means of changing the minority regime was to bring it to its knees, either through ironclad economic sanctions or through the blood of armed force. "The racists," stated Romesh Chandra of the World Peace Council (despite the name of his organization), "cannot be 'educated.' They must be defeated."[59] The white leaders of South Africa, likewise maintained Nigerian Ambassador Alhaji Maitama-Sule, "do not understand the language of cooperation, the language of constructive engagement." Hence, their racial policy of apartheid "cannot be amended . . . cannot be reformed," but instead "has to be totally abolished, totally eradicated, totally wiped out."[60]

Similar, but even stronger statements about the necessity for uncompromised armed struggle were heard throughout the 1980s in Africa. They increasingly attracted more and more listeners and adherents as that continent and the world at large witnessed the continued refusal of the regime in Pretoria to end racial discrimination voluntarily. "Those racist whites," claimed Namibian activist Alfred Moleah, "are incapable of reform or change" and "are so wedded to their racist beliefs, and so hopelessly victims of their own racist propaganda that they cannot help themselves even if they wanted to." Brutal combat and violent struggle, he argued, is the only fact that these "apartheid racists and their imperial cohorts" understood. With focused anger and determination, he concluded:

> For racial peace to ever come to South Africa and Namibia, those racist whites will have to be forced to accommodate themselves to the reality

of their location and situation. . . . It will have to be forcefully impressed upon them that theirs is a lost cause, and that the African is more than the racist caricature of their image—that he is possessed of a will and desire, and ability to make his history and to determine his destiny. They have to be made to realize that an alien minority, however smart, ruthless, or perverse, cannot indefinitely rule over a majority. Otherwise the consequences are bound to be more regrettable and unfortunate.[61]

Such results are likely to be catastrophic, causing what Desmond Tutu characterized as a "bloodbath" of violence,[62] what black and white South Africans alike defined as nothing short of a "race war,"[63] and what members of the international community described as a "collision course" with "tragic consequences for the country, for Africa, and for the world."[64] Predicted one recent observer of the frightful polarization between black and white: "Sanctions will weaken the economy to some extent, but the effects will not be deep and will be overcome in time. The younger generation of blacks is permanently committed to struggle. The armed conflict will intensify; it will become increasingly brutal; it will polarize into a race war. Millions will die."[65]

Things of the Spirit
in the Past and the Future

When one faces these many hard realities of politics, diplomacy, and racial discrimination, one cannot avoid acknowledging the role that power plays in the world. The struggle against racial prejudice and for racial equality, as we have seen beginning with Chapter 1's description of the effort to abolish the slave trade, always has proceeded in the wake of wars and revolutions. From the emancipation of slaves after the French Revolution and U.S. Civil War to the gaining of independence by colonial peoples after World Wars I and II, the cause of human rights invariably has required some drastic upheaval to shift power away from those unwilling to share it voluntarily. As John Humphrey concluded after years of experience working in this area, "in matters relating to human rights, individuals and governments are usually on opposite sides of the ring. In such matters, governments usually move when and only when they are forced to do so."[66]

In recognizing the significance of power, however, it is essential not to assume thereby that the things of the spirit can be simply ignored or easily dismissed. The fact remains that these wars and revolutions in the past provided not only shifts in power but also special opportunities for reassessments, self-examinations, and reflections on ethical values for both nations and individuals. By bringing a non-white victor to the

Paris Peace Conference, World War I enabled the Japanese to succeed in raising the problem of race for global attention. By struggling against Hitler and his Final Solution and then seeing itself in the mirror of Nazi racial atrocities, the world discovered its conscience pricked as never before in history. By signing the Universal Declaration of Human Rights with the onset of the Cold War, members of the international community saw their own racial policies in new perspectives and changed many of their practices regarding race accordingly. By witnessing the successes of revolutions and wars of national liberation, Western colonial powers found themselves examining the meaning of their own political and religious principles in unprecedented ways. In each of these cases, among the many others that we have explored, the reassessments and reflections brought about by upheaval in turn produced actions heavily influenced by an overwhelming sense of moral conviction and responsibility for the values of freedom, justice, and respect for all regardless of their race.

The upheavals against apartheid in South Africa have been producing similar effects in the late 1980s. By bringing global attention to the extreme and tragic injustices perpetrated solely because of the color of some people's skin, these convulsions again forced peoples around the world to examine their own fundamental values and beliefs. This occurred not long ago with George Shultz who, after watching yet another white South African attack against blacks, conceded that the regime's racial policies are simply "morally indefensible," and "an affront to everything we believe in."[67] The Reagan administration's policy of "constructive engagement" was not the same in the late 1980s as it was when first enunciated, and the State Department's own advisory committee recently concluded, "The racial aspect of South Africa's existing political system repels most Americans; indeed, it repels all people who reject race as a criterion of human value."[68] Time and time again, those participating in demonstrations and actions in support of racial equality for South Africa expressed a powerful and renewed sense of moral commitment to religious and political principles, and a strong desire to do what they believed was right even though other consequences might follow. As one member of the U.S. Congress said when sponsoring legislation for economic measures against Pretoria that he knew might entail significant political, strategic, and economic costs, "It is time for us as a nation to put our beliefs into action."[69]

Astonishingly, very similar words have been heard from the leadership of the white church in South Africa, once one of the principal pillars of the country's system of racial segregation. The synod recently experienced a fundamental crisis of conscience and completely reversed the church's traditional stand by declaring, "The Dutch Reformed Church is convinced that the application of apartheid as a political and social system which injures people and unjustly benefits one group above another cannot be accepted on Christian ethical grounds since it conflicts with the principle of neighborly love and righteousness."[70] Racial discrimination must end, according to the church's new silver-haired moderator, Johan Heyns, for as he explained to his white congregations, "We aren't heading for a revolution in our country, we are already in the midst of one; and by that I mean it's a revolution of ideas, a revolution of our system of values."[71]

Indeed, in the long global struggle for racial equality there always have been those who emphasized these values of ethics and moral conviction rather than sheer or mere power. From Gandhi to Martin Luther King, Jr., from the abolitionists to the anti-imperialists, from Christians to those of other faiths who believed in justice, from the champions opposed to immigration quotas based upon race to the campaigners against apartheid, from the creators of the Declaration on the Elimination of All Forms of Racial Discrimination to those who composed the Declaration of Conscience in support of racial equality,[72] these men and women understood the importance of moral force. Many assigned it the preeminent place. During his controversial career in South African politics, for example, Jan Hofmeyr courageously spoke out for his white compatriots to "measure up to what are coming to be accepted internationally as standards of values." He acknowledged the political and economic dimensions of discrimination but then focused upon what in his mind was the most important factor:

> But our chief loss is a moral loss. As long as we continue to apply a dual standard . . . , to determine our attitudes towards, and our relationships with European and non-European on different ethical bases, to assign Christian doctrine a significance which varies with the color of men's skins, we shall suffer as a nation for what Plato would have called the lie in the soul—and the curse of the Iscariot may yet be our fate for our betrayal of the Christian doctrine we profess.[73]

President John F. Kennedy used similar words to describe the challenge of combating racial discrimination in the United States, calling it as "primarily a moral issue" as "old as the Scriptures."[74]

Others with long, personal experience with politics, diplomacy, and discrimination also have understood that might alone is not sufficient to change hearts and minds when dealing with prejudice of race. "In the final analysis," wisely observed one UN secretary-general several years ago, "racial discrimination cannot be countered by legislation alone, indispensable though it is. Its roots lie not only in organized society by also in the hearts and minds of individual men and women." It was sustained, he said, by ignorance and a tendency to judge people on the basis of the color of their skin rather than by their real qualities, thereby denying the common humanity that bound us all. For this reason, he believed, "Racial discrimination is an evil which we can and must defeat both within society and within ourselves."[75] After serving many years with courage and conviction on the Human Rights Commission, Eleanor Roosevelt spoke in very similar terms about the need to emphasize the essential values of "equal justice, equal opportunity, and equal dignity without discrimination" of race in order to enhance the "ethical conscience of mankind."[76] More recently, the chairman of the Special United Nations Committee Against Apartheid echoed the same theme after much agonizing thought by concluding: "The world can never be governed by force, never by fear, never by power. In the end what governs is the spirit and what conquers is the mind."[77]

This issue of moral conviction and things of the spirit, of course, raises innumerable and tormenting questions about the application of ethical values to the world of power politics and diplomacy. From at least the time of Thucydides to the present, arguments have raged over whether or not in the intense competition of international affairs the strong simply do what they can while the weak do what they must.[78] In this kind of a world of bitter rivalry and violence where restraints are seldom observed at all, do—or can—moral considerations play any role at all? The structure of the international system itself often places severe limits upon opportunities for moral action, for there the chief actors are sovereign nation-states, themselves the most frequent violators of human rights. The consequences of introducing explicitly ethical considerations of one kind into the affairs of state easily can result in heavy political, strategic, or economic costs that might threaten other values in turn. The conflicts among different political, religious, and cultural value systems around the world often cause sharp disagreements over both conceptions and priorities of human rights. Moreover, problems of assessment, evaluation, and double standards, as we have seen, also are manifest and can lead to confrontation, failure, or distorted uses of the issue of race for purposes of political or diplomatic warfare at home and abroad.

Yet, despite these many problems and centuries of wrestling to find solutions, normative questions about the *ought* rather than simply the *is* of global politics and diplomacy remain before us. Indeed, such questions are particularly pressing and acute in the area of racial discrimination. Race was the subject that placed the whole issue of human rights upon the international agenda in the first place, and for a vast majority in the world race remains the most critical and universal test of how people deal with other people on the basis of an ethical standard. The principle of racial equality itself flows from a basic ethical concept, that of human dignity, which implies in its simplest terms that every human being is an end in himself or herself, not a mere means to an end, and should be treated as such.[79] Thus, it is only natural for people to ask whether the conduct of politics and diplomacy supports or opposes racial discrimination, which is the very negation of the principle of equality. This should not be at all surprising, for as scholar Stanley Hoffmann wrote in his penetrating book entitled *Duties Beyond Borders: On the Limits and Possibilities of Ethical International Politics,* "We must remember that states are led by human beings whose actions affect human beings within and outside: considerations of good and evil, right or wrong, are therefore both inevitable and legitimate."[80]

We should not conclude from this that the answer to all questions of politics, diplomacy, and racial discrimination can be found in morality alone, any more than we should look to solutions that rely exclusively upon explanations of power. Here, arguments that we must somehow choose between either the extreme of the "idealists" on the one hand or that of the "realists" on the other provide precious little assistance or insight in judging either our past or our future. If the historical experience treated in this book is any guide, then whatever solutions are available most likely will be found by those who search for ways to skillfully combine and delicately balance the two. The key to these matters of human rights in global politics and diplomacy, confirmed David Owen from personal experience, was "to balance morality with reality." One must remain deeply committed to applying ethical principles to policy while at the same time being "hard-headed and practical," working for "realizable objectives," and avoiding what Winston Churchill described in his own inimitable way as "mush, slush, and gush." "The art," Owen observed, "lies in striking the right balance."[81]

This is exactly the conclusion reached by Hector Charry-Samper as well. To strike that balance in dealing with race across the globe is never easy, but it provides the only practical means of solving one of the most difficult problems the world has ever known. "It would be defeatist to ignore what has been achieved . . . ," he solemnly asserted,

> [but] we would be wanting in common sense if we espoused an unpractical perfectionism which, far from solving all problems might well strengthen the hands of the enemies of racial equality and delay the elimination of all kinds of discrimination.
>
> We need a strong admixture of realism which does not preclude, but is indeed fortified by, a sense of idealistic solidarity. The two combined will make it possible to find a common path, to build a true alliance

against all forms of racism, from the most serious to the most carefully concealed.[82]

In the long and often tortuous global struggle with power and prejudice for racial equality, it has been precisely this kind of combination that has proved to be the most successful. Whether by conscious design of the participants or not, the cause of ending discrimination based upon race has been advanced the most when the realities of power and self-interest were balanced with those values of the human spirit. From the emancipation of slaves to freedom for non-white colonial peoples, from standards of the Universal Declaration of Human Rights to the genocide convention, from the binding terms of international conventions protecting equality to the Program of Action Against Apartheid, and from the independent Committee on the Elimination of Racial Discrimination to the Decade for Action to Combat Racism and Racial Discrimination, success has come when those with some degree of power and interest also possess some degree of compassion, a sense of justice, and a moral conviction that all individuals should be treated with respect regardless of the color of their skin.

*   *   *

These remarkable successes by those with both power and principle mark significant and impressive achievements on the road toward global racial equality. Each new effort faced determined opposition, vested interests, entrenched habits of mind, and a heavy burden from the past; and the continued existence of some forms of discrimination, polemics of self-righteousness, and one-sided condemnation of others should not detract from the many genuine and widespread accomplishments. Their full appreciation calls for a sense of proportion. From a historical perspective, these achievements of only the last forty years must be measured, not against completely utopian or abstract goals, but against the gains of the past four thousand years.[83] For most of that period, an overwhelming proportion of the non-white world lived subjected to the worst kinds of discrimination based upon race, in slavery, imperialism, segregation, and various forms of exploitation and exclusion, all reinforced by explicit and publicly proclaimed ideologies of racial superiority. During that time, the practices, institutions, and laws of the international community remained deathly silent on the subject of human rights and equal treatment, and individuals possessed no recourse against the discriminatory abuses of their state. Indeed, as late as the beginning of the twentieth century, even the words "racial discrimination" and "prejudice of race" were never allowed in diplomatic parlance.

Since then, however, there has been a virtual revolution in the global approach to race and what Du Bois called "the problem of the twentieth century."[84] As a result of the politics and diplomacy that we have seen, although filled with hopes and frustrations, careful calculations of interest and raw emotions, victories and defeats, there has been a remarkable and dramatic shift of unprecedented proportions. The issue of race is now at the forefront of the international agenda, and no government can claim to be unaware of its implications. Most states now make racial equality a goal integral to both their domestic and their foreign policies and participate in efforts to eliminate discrimination. A substantial legal and institutional framework of law, covenants and treaties, judicial rulings, declarations, organizations, and procedures now are devoted to actively promoting human rights, preventing discrimination on the basis of race, and combating racism. The availability of these collective and continuous means and norms afford both states and individuals opportunities to air grievances, express aspirations, and seek practical protection for racial equality.[85] Moreover, there is now a nearly universal recognition that racial issues are not exclusively confined to the internal affairs of any state but in one way or another affect the peace and security of us all.

Knowing of these impressive achievements, those most intimately involved in the global effort to achieve an equality of race speak with confidence about the road ahead. The successes of the immediate past convince them that despite the continuing problems, limits, and difficulties of power and prejudice, there is an "historic trend," "the movement of history," and a "moral inevitability" that is on their side and will not be denied.[86] Said one diplomat recently, this effort is an "irreversible process," for those millions of people around the world who have secured justice and gained protection for their freedom from racial discrimination "will never give it up and now will never go backward."[87] The struggle to secure racial equality thus is a continuous one that will proceed with determination and conviction. It is hoped that in this process the historical experience of politics, diplomacy, and racial discrimination discussed in this book will suggest not only some answers but also raise questions about ourselves, our values, our past, and perhaps even our future.

Notes

Introduction: "The Problem of the Twentieth Century"

1. Harold Isaacs, "Color in World Affairs," *Foreign Affairs* 47 (January 1969): 236.
2. Will and Ariel Durant, *The Lessons of History* (New York: Simon and Schuster, 1968), pp. 25–31.
3. Claude Lévi-Strauss, *Race et histoire* (Paris: UNESCO, 1952).
4. See Robert K.A. Gardiner, "Race and Color in International Relations," in John Hope Franklin (ed.), *Color and Race* (Boston: Houghton Mifflin, 1968), pp. 18–33; Patrice de Comarmond and Claude Duchet (eds.), *Racisme et société* (Paris: Maspero, 1969); and the various working papers of the Sous-Comité sur le racisme, la discrimination raciale, l'apartheid et la décolonisation du Comité special des ONG pour les Droits de l'homme prepared for their meeting in Geneva, 5–8 July 1983.
5. Mr. Driberg, 6 May 1949, in the House of Commons, as cited in Great Britain, Public Record Office, Foreign Office, 371/78946 [hereafter cited as Great Britain, PRO/FO]; and United Nations, Centre Against Apartheid, *International Tribute to William E.B. Du Bois* (New York: United Nations, 1982).
6. Carl Degler, *Neither Black Nor White* (New York: Macmillan, 1971), p. xi.
7. Ronald Segal, *The Race War* (New York: Bantam, 1967), p. 1. Also see Moses Moscowitz, *The Politics and Dynamics of Human Rights* (Dobbs Ferry: Oceana, 1968), p. 175.
8. Hugh Tinker, *Race, Conflict, and the International Order* (London: Macmillan, 1977), pp. 134–35.
9. See Harold Isaacs, "Group Identity and Political Change: The Role of Color and Physical Characteristics," in Franklin (ed.), *Color and Race*, p. 75; and a discussion of the lengthy, but frequently important, debates over definitions in Eugene Lerch, "Der Rassenwahn von Gobineau zur UNESCO Erklärung," *Der Monat* (1950); G.E. Simpson and J. Milton Yinger, *Racial and Cultural Minorities* (New York: Harper & Row, 1965 ed.); M.F. Ashley Montagu, *Statement on Race* (New York: Oxford University Press, 1972 ed.); Phil Tobias, *The Meaning of Race* (Johannesburg: South African Institute of Race Relations, 1961); Pierre L. van den Berghe, *Race and Racism* (New York: Wiley, 1967); John R. Baker, *Race* (New York: Oxford University Press, 1974); and E.W. Vierdag, *The Concept of Discrimination in International Law* (The Hague: Nijhoff, 1973), pp. 87–90; among others.
10. M.F. Ashley Montagu, *Man's Most Dangerous Myth* (New York: Harper Brothers, 1952), p. 1.
11. See Roy Preiswerk, "Race and Color in International Relations," *The Year Book of World Affairs, 1970* (New York: Praeger, 1970), p. 55.
12. Tinker, *Race, Conflict, and the International Order*, p. 2. Also see George W. Shepherd, *The Study of Race in American Foreign Policy and International Relations* (Denver: University of Denver Press, 1969).
13. Preiswerk, "Race and Color in International Relations," pp. 64–65.

14. See United Nations Document A/CONF.119/26, "Report of the Second World Conference to Combat Racism and Racial Discrimination," Geneva, 1–12 August 1983.

Chapter 1: The Heavy Burden of the Past

1. The literature on the nature of prejudice, discrimination, and group conflict is vast. See G.E. Simpson and J.M. Yinger, *Racial and Cultural Minorities* (New York: Harper & Row, 1965 ed.); Arnold Rose, *The Roots of Prejudice* (Paris: UNESCO, 1951); United Nations Document E/CN.4/Sub.2/288, "Special Study of Racial Discrimination in the Political, Economic, Social and Cultural Spheres," 25 July 1968 [hereafter cited as UN Document]; Gordon Allport, *The Nature of Prejudice* (New York: Doubleday, 1958 ed.); and William Wilson, *Power, Racism, and Privilege: Race Relations in Theoretical and Sociohistorical Perspectives* (New York: Free Press, 1976 ed.).

2. Jean Filliosat, "Classement des couleurs et des lumières en Sanskrit," and P. Metais, "Vocabulaire et symbolisme des couleurs en Nouvelle Caledonie," in Ignace Meyerson (ed.), *Problèmes de couleur* (Paris: S.E.V.P.E.N., 1957), pp. 309 ff.; Pierre van den Berghe, *Race and Racism: A Comparative Perspective* (New York: Wiley, 1967), pp. 12–15; John Hope Franklin (ed.), *Color and Race* (Boston: Houghton Mifflin, 1968), passim, and Hannah Arendt, "Race Thinking Before Racism," *Review of Politics* 6 (1944):36–73.

3. William Cohen, *The French Encounter with Africans: White Responses to Blacks* (Bloomington: Indiana University Press, 1980), p. 1. Also see Harold Isaacs, "Group Identity and Political Change: The Role of Color and Physical Characteristics," in Franklin (ed.), *Color and Race*, p. 75, and Philip Mason, *Patterns of Dominance* (New York: Oxford University Press, 1970), pp. 1–20.

4. Madeleine Reberioux, "Préhistoire du racisme," in Patrice de Comarmond and Claude Duchet (eds.), *Racisme et société* (Paris: Maspero, 1969), p. 106.

5. M.I. Finley, *Economy and Society in Ancient Greece* (New York: Pelican Books, 1983 ed.), p. 104.

6. Aristotle, *Politics,* translated by Ernest Barker (London: Oxford University Press, 1961), bk. 1, ch. 1, p. 3; bk. 7, ch. 7, p. 296; and bk. 1, ch. 5, pp. 13–14.

7. Michael Banton, *Race Relations* (London: Tavistock, 1967), p. 12.

8. Frank Snowden, Jr., *Blacks in Antiquity: Ethiopians in the Greco-Roman Experience* (Cambridge, Mass.: Harvard University Press, 1970), pp. 2 and 9. Snowden does not believe, however, that this judgment of color resulted in discriminatory practices.

9. Herodotus, *History,* translated by George Rawlinson, in Francis Godolphin (ed.), *The Greek Historians* (New York: Random House, 1942), bk. 4, pp. 188–291.

10. See Donald Lach, *Asia in the Making of Europe* (Chicago: University of Chicago Press, 1965), vol. 1, bk. 1, pp. 5ff.

11. Tacitus, *The Complete Works of Tacitus,* translated by A.J. Church and W. Brodribb (New York: Modern Library, 1942), pp. 700–18.

12. Jacques Barzun, *Race: A Study in Superstition* (New York: Harper & Row, 1965), p. 18. Also see A.N. Sherwin-White, *Racial Prejudice in Imperial Rome* (London: Cambridge University Press, 1967).

13. Caius Julius Solinus, *The Excellent and Pleasant Worke,* translated by Arthur Golding (Gainesville: Scholar's Facsimiles & Reprints, 1955), ch. 42.

14. Saint Augustine, *The City of God,* translated by Marcus Dods (New York: Modern Library, 1950), pp. 530–32.

15. David Brion Davis, *Slavery and Human Progress* (New York: Oxford University Press, 1984), pp. 43 and 45; and David Brion Davis, *The Problem of Slavery in Western Culture* (Ithaca: Cornell University Press, 1966), p. 50.

16. See Snowden, *Blacks in Antiquity*, pp. 169–95; William Westermann, *The Slave Systems of Greek and Roman Antiquity* (Philadelphia: American Philosophical Society, 1964), pp. 78ff.; and Davis, *The Problem of Slavery*, p. 49.

17. Cited in Ronald Sanders, *Lost Tribes and Promised Lands*, (Boston: Little, Brown, 1978), p. 7.

18. Ibn Khaldun, *The Muqaddimah*, translated by Franz Rosenthal, 3 vols. (New York: Pantheon, 1958), 1:118–19.

19. Cohen, *The French Encounter with Africans*, p. 15.

20. See Meyerson, *Problèmes de couleur*, pp. 329ff.; Roger Bastide, "Color, Racism, and Christianity," in Franklin (ed.), *Color and Race*, pp. 34–49; Davis, *Slavery and Human Progress*, pp. 41ff.; and Bernard Lewis, *Race and Color in Islam* (New York: Harper & Row, 1971).

21. See Garrett Mattingly, *Renaissance Diplomacy* (London: Cape, 1962), passim.

22. Gomes Eannes de Azurara, *Chronicle of the Discovery and Conquest of Guinea*, translated by C.R. Beazly and Edgar Prestage, 2 vols. (London: Hakluyt Society, 1896), 1:54.

23. Pierre d'Ailly, *Imago Mundi* (Louvain: Paderborn, 1483), Chap. 12, p. 15.

24. Christopher Columbus, *Select Letters of Christopher Columbus, with Other Original Documents Relating to the Four Voyages to the New World*, translated and edited by R.H. Major (London: Hakluyt Society, 1870), pp. 25–31.

25. See H. Vander Linden, "Alexander VI. and the Demarcation of the Maritime and Colonial Domains of Spain and Portugal, 1493–1494," *American Historical Review* 22 (October 1916): 1–20.

26. C.R. Boxer, *The Portuguese Seaborne Empire, 1415–1825* (New York: Knopf, 1969), p. 46.

27. J.H. Plumb, in Introduction, ibid., p. xxv. Also see K.M. Panikkar, *Asia and Western Dominance* (New York: Collier, 1969 ed.).

28. Shepard Clough et al., *European History in a World Perspective*, 3 vols. (Lexington: D.C. Heath, 1975 ed.), 2:576.

29. These are the words of Lewis Hanke, *Aristotle and the American Indians: A Study of Race Prejudice in the Modern World* (Bloomington: Indiana University Press, 1970), p. 10.

30. As Philip Wayne Powell observed in his book *Tree of Hate* (New York: Basic Books, 1971), the "Black Legend" often has been exaggerated for political reasons. The cruel practices of Spain should not be viewed as significantly different from those of the other European powers.

31. Bartholomé de las Casas, *In Defense of the Indians*, translated and edited by S. Poole (DeKalb: Northern Illinois University Press, 1974), p. 362.

32. J.H. Parry, *The Spanish Seaborne Empire* (New York: Knopf, 1966), p. 150. For an interpretation more sympathetic to Spain, see Salvador de Madariaga, *The Rise of the Spanish American Empire* (New York: The Free Press, 1965 ed.), pp. 12–26.

33. Gonzalo Beltrán, *La Problación Negra de Mexico*, as cited in van den Berghe, *Race and Racism*, p. 43.

34. See Davis, *The Problem of Slavery in the Western Culture*, pp. 62–128; Davis, *Slavery and Human Progress*; James Watson (ed.), *Asian and African Systems of Slavery* (Berkeley: University of California Press, 1980); and Orlando Patterson, *Slavery and Social Death* (Cambridge, Mass.: Harvard University Press, 1982).

35. J.H. Plumb, in "Introduction," Boxer, *The Portuguese Seaborne Empire*, p. 20.

36. See Davis, *Slavery and Human Progress*, pp. 52 and 64.

37. Duarte Pacheco Pereira, *Esmeraldo de situ orbis*, translated by George Kimble (London: Hakluyt Society, 1937), p. 2.

38. Cited in Boxer, *The Portuguese Seaborne Empire*, p. 101.

39. Pacheco Pereira, *Esmeraldo de situ orbis*, p. 89.

40. André Thevet, *Cosmographie universelle* (Paris: Huilier, 1575), p. 67.

41. Alexandre Valignamo, as cited in Boxer, *The Portuguese Seaborne Empire*, p. 252. Also see Richard Cole, "Sixteenth-Century Travel Books as a Source of European Attitudes Toward Non-White and Non-Western Culture," *Proceedings of the American Philosophical Society* 116 (February 1972):59–67.

42. Lach, *Asia in the Making of Europe*, vol. 1, bk. 2, p. 822.

43. Ibid., p. 827.

44. As cited in J.M. Roberts, *History of the World* (New York: Knopf, 1976), p. 580.

45. This paragraph is based on George Fredrickson, *White Supremacy: A Comparative Study in American and South African History* (New York: Oxford University Press, 1981), p. 7.

46. See Basil Davidson, *The African Slave Trade* (Boston: Little, Brown, 1980 rev. ed.), pp. 53–85; and Parry, *The Spanish Seaborne Empire*, p. 268.

47. Richard Hakluyt, *The Principal Navigations, Voyages, Traffiques, and Discoveries*, 12 vols. (Glasgow: MacLehose & Sons, 1903–1905), 10:7.

48. Hugo Grotius, *De jure belli et pacis*, translated by Louise Loomis (Roslyn, N.Y.: Black, 1949), bk. 2, ch. 5, and bk. 3, ch. 7.

49. Robert Herzstein, *Western Civilization* (Boston: Houghton Mifflin, 1975), p. 428.

50. Davis, *Slavery and Human Progress*, pp. xvii and 51.

51. "Board of Trade to the Governors of the English Colonies," 17 April 1708, in E. Donnan (ed.), *Documents Ilustrative of the History of the Slave Trade to America*, 4 vols. (Washington, D.C.: Carnegie Institution, 1930–35), 2:45.

52. See Eric Williams, *Capitalism and Slavery* (New York: Capricorn Books, 1966 ed.); Eugene Genovese, *In Red and Black: Marxist Explorations in Southern and Afro-American History* (New York: Vintage, 1972 ed.), especially pp. 55–63, 72, 189, and 381; Kenneth Little, *Race and Society* (Paris: UNESCO, 1952), pp. 11ff.; and Davis, *Slavery and Human Progress*, pp. 51–82.

53. Fredrickson, *White Supremacy*, p. 70.

54. These expressions are constantly and consistently used throughout the literature of the seventeenth century, as the many volumes published by the Hakluyt Society dealing with European encounters with Africa make clear.

55. Winthrop Jordan, *White Over Black* (Chapel Hill: University of North Carolina Press, 1968), pp. 4–6. For a more moderate view, see Fredrickson, *White Supremacy*, pp. 73–74.

56. George Best, as cited in Hakluyt, *Principal Navigations* 7:262–63.

57. The "Hamitic myth" is discussed in several sources, as indicated by Sanders, *Lost Tribes and Promised Lands*, pp. 55, 224–25, and 343–44; Davis, *The Problem of Slavery*, pp. 217, 317, and 340; and Hakluyt, *Principal Navigations* 7:263–64.

58. Jordon, *White Over Black*, p. 97.

59. See Davis, *The Problem of Slavery*, p. 453; Jordon, *White Over Black*, p. 80; and Anthony Barker, *The African Link: British Attitudes to the Negro in the Era of the Atlantic Slave Trade, 1550–1807* (London: Cass, 1978). As Edmund Morgan demonstrated in his book *American Slavery, American Freedom* (New York: Norton, 1975), this process occurred over a period of many years.

60. Fredrickson, *White Supremacy*, p. 93.

61. On the differences, see note 109.

62. Boxer, *The Portuguese Seaborne Empire*, pp. 249–72.

63. Harley Ross Hammond, "Race, Social Mobility, and Politics in Brazil," *Race* 4 (1963):4.

64. *Colección de documentos para la formación social de Hispanoamérica, 1493–1810*, as cited in Magnus Morner, *Race Mixture in the History of Latin America* (Boston: Little, Brown, 1967), p. 47.

65. Gabriel Debien, *Les esclaves aux antilles françaises* (Basse-Terre: Société d'histoire de la Guadeloupe, 1974), pp. 121, 177, 181, and 236–38.

66. Cited in George F. Tyson, Jr. (ed.), *Toussaint L'Ouverture* (Englewood Cliffs: Prentice-Hall, 1973), p. 5.

67. "Act to Regulate the Negroes," as cited in John Hope Franklin, *From Slavery to Freedom* (New York: Knopf, 1974 ed.), p. 51. Also see Morgan, *American Slavery, American Freedom*, pp. 316–37.

68. "The Fundamental Constitutions of 1669," in *The Federal and State Constitutions, Constitutions, Colonial Charters, and Other Organic Laws*, 2 vols., compiled by B. Poore (New York: Franklin, 1972 reprint), 2:1408.

69. C.R. Boxer, *The Dutch Seaborne Empire*, (New York: Knopf, 1965), p. 233. Also see the detailed discussions in Fredrickson, *White Supremacy*.

70. See the excellent discussion in Cohen, *The French Encounter with Africans*, pp. 100–10; and Lucien Peytraud, *L'Esclavage aux antilles françaises* (Paris: Hachette, 1897), pp. 143ff.

71. Fenelon, as cited in Gaston Martin, *Histoire de l'esclavage dans les colonies françaises* (Paris: Presses universitaires de France, 1948), p. 122.

72. Cited in Peytraud, *L'Esclavage aux antilles françaises*, p. 381.

73. Cohen, *The French Encounter with Africans*, p. 126.

74. Jordon, *White Over Black*, p. 104. In the northern colonies these laws were less detailed, more haphazard, and less harsh than those to the south. It must also be recognized that the British were certainly capable of cruel discrimination against whites as well, as indicated by their actions against the Irish.

75. "An Act for the Better Ordering and Governing of Negroes and Slaves," in South Carolina, *Statutes at Large of South Carolina*, 10 vols., compiled by Thomas Cooper and David McCord (Columbia: Johnston, 1836–41), 7:352.

76. Jordon, *White Over Black*, pp. 252–53. Also see George L. Mosse, *Toward the Final Solution: A History of European Racism* (New York: Harper & Row, 1978); Louis Snyder, *Race: A History of Modern Ethnic Theories* (New York: Longmans, 1939); and Earl Count (ed.), *This Is Race* (New York: Schuman, 1950).

77. Carl Linne, *Systema naturae* (London: British Museum, 1939, facsimile of the 1758 ed.), 1:22.

78. Johann Friedrich Blumenbach, *On the Natural Varieties of Mankind*, 3d edition 1795 (New York: Bergman, 1969 reprint), pp. 209, 264, and 269. See also John R. Baker, *Race* (New York: Oxford University Press, 1974), pp. 24ff.

79. See Michele Duchet, "Esclavage et préjugé de couleur," in Comarmond and Duchet (eds.), *Racisme et société*, p. 122. For a similar conclusion from the English-speaking world, see Edward Long, *History of Jamaica*, 3 vols. (London: Lowndes, 1774).

80. Petrus Camper, *The Works of the Late Professor Camper*, translated by T. Cogan (London: Hearne, 1812 ed.), pp. 9 and 50.

81. Charles White, *An Account of the Regular Gradation of Man, and in Different Animals and Vegetables* (London: Dilly, 1799), p. 134. For an excellent discussion of

these various attitudes with an emphasis upon the British, see Philip Curtin, *The Image of Africa: British Ideas and Action, 1780–1850* (Madison: University of Wisconsin, 1964), pp. 24–57.

82. *Encyclopaedia Britannica*, 1798 edition, as cited in Richard Popkin, "The Philosophical Basis of Eighteenth-Century Racism," in Harold Pagliaro (ed.), *Racism in the Eighteenth Century* (Cleveland: Case Western Reserve University, 1973), p. 249.

83. David Hume, "Of National Characters," in *The Philosophical Works*, 4 vols., edited by T. Green and T. Grose (London: Longmans, Green, 1882–1886), 3:252n.

84. Baron de Montesquieu, *De l'Esprit des lois*, livre 12, chap. 2, in *Oevres complètes*, 3 vols. (Paris: Hachette, 1908 ed.), 2:15.

85. Voltaire, as cited in Cohen, *The French Encounter with Africans*, pp. 88, 133, and 137. Also see Davis, *Slavery and Human Progress*, pp. 107–08.

86. Thomas Jefferson, *Notes on the State of Virginia* (New York: Harper & Row, 1964 ed.), p. 138.

87. The best discussion on this subject is found in Davis, *Slavery and Human Progress*, pp. 107–53. Also see Barker, *The African Link*, passim.

88. James Beattie, *Elements of Moral Science*, 2 vols. (Edinburgh: Creech, 1793), 2:164.

89. See Fredrickson, *White Supremacy*, pp. 140ff.; and Morgan, *American Slavery, American Freedom*, passim.

90. Cohen, *The French Encounter with Africans*, p. 113. Also see Marcel Garaud, *La Révolution et l'égalité civile* (Paris: Sirey, 1953).

91. Jefferson, *Notes on the State of Virginia*, p. 156.

92. T. Lothrop Stoddard, *The French Revolution in San Domingo* (Boston: Houghton Mifflin, 1914), p. vii, who provided a good discussion of these events, along with C.L.R. James, *The Black Jacobins: Toussaint L'Ouverture and the San Domingo Revolution* (New York: Vintage, 1963 ed.), and Jordon, *White Over Black*, pp. 375–78.

93. Peytraud, *L'Esclavage aux antilles françaises*, pp. 398–99.

94. "Report of the New Jersey Abolition Society," as cited in Arthur Zilversmit, *The First Emancipation: The Abolition of Slavery in the North* (Chicago: University of Chicago Press, 1967), p. 189.

95. As cited in Davis, *Slavery and Human Progress*, p. 116. Also see Roger Anstey, *The Atlantic Slave Trade and British Abolition* (Atlantic Highlands: Humanities Press, 1975).

96. Leslie Bethell, *The Abolition of the Brazilian Slave Trade* (Cambridge: Cambridge University Press, 1970), p. ix.

97. See Betty Fladeland, "Abolitionist Pressures on the Concert of Europe, 1814–1822," *Journal of Modern History* 38 (December 1966): 358–60.

98. Lord Castlereagh, as cited in F.J. Klingberg, *The Anti-Slavery Movement in England* (New Haven: Yale University Press, 1926), p. 144.

99. See Bethell, *The Abolition*, pp. ix–x.

100. Great Britain, Foreign Office, *British and Foreign State Papers, 1815–1816* (London: Ridgway & Sons, and others, 1841–), 3:946–70; Harold Nicolson, *The Congress of Vienna* (New York: Harcourt, Brace, 1946), pp. 211ff.; and Martha Putney, "The Slave Trade in French Diplomacy from 1814–1815," *Journal of Negro History* 60 (July 1975):411–27.

101. "Déclaration des 8 cours, relative à l'abolition universelle de la traite des nègres," 8 February 1815, in Great Britain, Foreign Office, *British and Foreign State Papers, 1815–1816* 3:971–72.

102. Great Britain, Public Record Office, Foreign Office, [hereafter cited as Great Britain, PRO/FO] 92/30, "Traité définitif entre Grande Bretagne et la France," 20 November 1815. With reference to human rights issues at the Congress of Vienna, it also can be noted that the efforts of the Rothschilds resulted in a recognition of citizenship for Jews by those who signed the agreement.

103. Treaty of Peace and Amity, 18 February 1815, in United States, Department of State, *Treaties and Other International Agreements of the United States of America,* compiled by Charles Bevans, 12 vols. (Washington, D.C.: Government Printing Office, 1974), 12:47.

104. These are the words of Sir Charles Webster, *The Foreign Policy of Castlereagh,* 2 vols. (London: Bell, 1963), 1:423.

105. Fladeland, "Abolitionist Pressures," p. 366. Also see Suzanne Miers, *Britain and the Ending of the Slave Trade* (New York: Africana, 1975), p. 11.

106. Nicolson, *The Congress of Vienna,* p. 214.

107. *Seventeenth Annual Report of the Directors of the African Institution,* 16 May 1823, as cited in Fladeland, "Abolitionist Pressures," p. 373. Also see her more detailed book, *Men and Brothers: Anglo-American Anti-Slavery Cooperation* (Urbana: University of Illinois Press, 1972).

108. Great Britain, Public Record Office, *The Records of the Foreign Office, 1782–1939* (London: Her Majesty's Stationery Office, 1969), p. 16. On the matter of how foreign ministries adapt to new conditions and priorities, see Paul Gordon Lauren, *Diplomats and Bureaucrats: The First Institutional Responses to Twentieth-Century Diplomacy* (Stanford: Hoover Institution Press, 1973).

109. W.E.B. Du Bois, *The Suppression of the African Slave Trade* (Baton Rouge: Louisiana State University Press, 1969 reprint), pp. 133–46.

110. Daniel Mannix and Malcolm Cowley, *Black Cargoes: A History of the Atlantic Slave Trade* (New York: Viking Books, 1962), p. 274.

111. John Forsyth, as cited in Great Britain, Foreign Office, *British and Foreign State Papers, 1834–35,* p. 136.

112. The most thorough quantitative analysis is found in Philip Curtin, *The Atlantic Slave Trade* (Madison: University of Wisconsin Press, 1969). On the period from 1811 to 1830, see pp. 234, 266–67, and 269. Quantification of the slave trade, of course, generates much debate, as can be seen in J.E. Inikari, "Measuring the Atlantic Slave Trade," *Journal of African History* 17 (1976):197–223 and the resulting discussion on pp. 595–627. For a discussion of the little-known Zanzibar-Arabia traffic, see Mannix and Cowley, *Black Cargoes,* pp. 241–62.

113. Thomas Buxton, *The African Slave Trade and Its Remedy* (London: Murray, 1840), pp. 32–48. These figures, of course, can only be considered as very rough estimates, and Curtin believes that most are exaggerated. The estimate of Buxton is cited here simply to provide a contemporary example that was widely publicized at the time.

114. Bethell, *The Abolition,* p. x.

115. David Brion Davis, *The Problem of Slavery in the Age of Revolution, 1770–1823* (Ithaca: Cornell University Press, 1975), pp. 59–60.

116. Curtin, *The Atlantic Slave Trade,* p. 234.

117. Great Britain, House of Commons, *Sessional Papers,* 1845 49 (73), "Return of the Numbers of Slave Vessels Arrived in the Transatlantic States Since 1814," pp. 593ff.; and *Sessional Papers, 1847–48* 22 (623) "Fourth Report from the Select Committee on the Slave Trade," pp. 705ff.

118. Carl Degler, *Neither Black nor White* (New York: Macmillan, 1971), p. 61.

119. Franklin, *From Slavery to Freedom,* pp. 138–39.

120. On the differences, see Frank Tannenbaum, *Slave and Citizen: The Negro in the Americas* (New York: Vintage Books, 1963 ed.); Stanley Elkins, *Slavery: A Problem in American Institutional and Intellectual Life* (Chicago: University of Chicago Press, 1968 ed.); and van den Berghe, *Race and Racism*, passim.

121. Degler, *Neither Black nor White*, pp. 67–92.

122. Ibid., p. 25. Also see Arnold A. Sio, "Interpretations of Slavery," *Comparative Studies in Society and History* 7 (April 1965):289–308.

123. See Eric McKitrick (ed.), *Slavery Defended: The Views of the Old South* (Englewood Cliffs: Prentice-Hall, 1963).

124. Alexis de Tocqueville, *Democracy in America*, Phillips Bradley edition, 2 vols. (New York: Vintage Books, 1945), 1:397.

125. "Dred Scott v. Sandford," *U.S. Supreme Court Reports* 60 (1856):408–10.

126. Franklin, *From Slavery to Freedom*, p. 210.

127. Davis, *The Problem of Slavery in the Age of Revolution*, p. 49. Also see his longer discussion of the moral impulses in *Slavery and Human Progress*, pp. 131ff.

128. From this larger perspective one must consider the abolition of hereditary serfdom in Prussia during 1807, the Catholic Emancipation Act of 1829 in Britain, the emancipation of the serfs in Austria and Hungary during 1848 and in Russia during 1861, and the gradual relaxation of many legal restrictions against those of the Jewish faith throughout the century. In this context it is particularly important to note that some writers believe that the emancipation of black slaves was primarily a question of class struggle. One of the most articulate of these is Eugene Genovese, *The World the Slaveholders Made* (New York: Vintage Books, 1971).

129. Salvador de Madariaga, *The Fall of the Spanish American Empire* (New York: Collier Books, 1963 rev. ed.), p. 340.

130. R.R. Palmer and Joel Colton, *A History of the Modern World*, 2 vols. (New York: Knopf, 1978 ed.), 2:454. The most thorough discussion of the British case can be found in Davis, *Slavery and Human Progress*. For the French case, see Martin, *Histoire de l'esclavage dans les colonies françaises*, pp. 280–96.

131. Arthur Corwin, *Spain and the Abolition of Slavery in Cuba, 1817–86* (Austin: University of Texas Press, 1967); Richard Graham, "Causes for the Abolition of Negro Slavery in Brazil," *Hispanic American Historical Review* 46 (May 1966):123–37; and Bethell, *The Abolition*, passim.

132. The best discussion can be found in Miers, *Britain and the Ending of the Slave Trade*, passim. Also see David Murray, *Odious Commerce* (Cambridge: Cambridge University Press, 1980).

133. See Sir E. Hertslet, *The Map of Africa by Treaty*, 3 vols. (London: Harrison and Sons, 1909), 2:488.

134. The best discussions about this dual nature of the Brussels Act can be found in Miers, *Britain and the Ending of the Slave Trade*, pp. 236–319; and, more briefly, in Davis, *Slavery and Human Progress*, pp. 302–07.

135. Tannenbaum, *Slave and Citizen*, p. 21; and Davidson, *The African Slave Trade*, pp. 95–101 and 271, both largely agree on this figure, which includes those who disembarked alive, those who died during the "Middle Passage" across the Atlantic, and those who perished before being placed on the slave ships. It should be emphasized again, however, that such figures can only be considered as rough estimates.

136. Tocqueville, *Democracy in America* 1:372–73.

137. Ibid., p. 390.

138. See Harry W. Fritz, "Racism and Democracy in Tocqueville's America," *The Social Science Journal* 13 (October 1976):65–75; Leon Litwack, *North of Slavery* (Chicago: University of Chicago Press, 1965 ed.); and most recently, Joel Williamson, *The*

Crucible of Race: Black-White Relations in the American South Since Emancipation (New York: Oxford University Press, 1984).

139. Thomas Carlyle, "Occasional Discourse on the Nigger Question," *Fraser's Magazine* 40 (December 1849):670–79.

140. See George Fredrickson, *The Black Image in the White Mind: The Debate on Afro-American Character and Destiny, 1817–1914* (New York: Harper & Row, 1971), especially the chapter entitled "Prejudice and Reform," pp. 1–42; and Philip Staudenraus, *The African Colonization Movement, 1816–65* (New York: Columbia University Press, 1961), passim.

141. Augustin Cochin, *L'Abolition de l'esclavage* (Paris: Guillaumin, 1861), p. xxiv.

142. Alfred Michiels, as cited in Cohen, *The French Encounter with Africans*, p. 209.

143. Van den Berghe, *Race and Racism*, pp. 16–17.

144. This discussion is based on Davis, *The Problem of Slavery in the Age of Revolution*, p. 14.

145. Morgan, in *American Slavery, American Freedom*, argued that this central paradox of U.S. history took place over a long period of time from the seventeenth to the nineteenth centuries.

146. Fredrickson, *White Supremacy*, pp. 154–55, and *The Black Image in the White Mind*, p. 91; Pierre van den Berghe, *South Africa: A Study in Conflict* (Middletown, Conn.: Wesleyan University Press, 1965), in which he first coined the expression, and *Race and Racism*, pp. 17–18; Davis, *The Problem of Slavery in Western Culture*, p. 286; and Fritz, "Racism and Democracy," pp. 70–71.

147. Philip Curtin (ed.), *Imperialism* (New York: Walker, 1971), pp. 1–3; and Cohen, *The French Encounter with Africans*, p. 262.

148. Curtin, *The Image of Africa*, p. 377.

149. Robert Knox, *The Races of Man: A Philosophical Enquiry into the Influence of Race over the Destinies of Nations* (London: Renshaw, 1862 ed.), p. 244. Also see the earlier work by P.P. Broc, *Essai sur les races humaines* (Paris: Librairie des sciences médicales, 1836).

150. See William Stanton, *The Leopard's Spots: Scientific Attitudes Toward Race in America, 1815–1859* (Chicago: University of Chicago Press, 1960), pp. 161–73, discussing Nott's book.

151. See the excellent and highly suggestive discussion on the French scientific community in Cohen, *The French Encounter with Africans*, pp. 210–62.

152. Barzun, *Race*, pp. 97–132.

153. Leon Poliakov, *The Aryan Myth: A History of Racist and Nationalist Ideas in Europe*, translated by Edmund Howard (New York: New American Library, 1977), pp. 2 and 226.

154. For a detailed discussion of his predecessors, successors, and influence, see E.J. Young, *Gobineau und der Rassismus: Eine Kritik der anthropologischen Geschichtstheorie* (Meisenheim am Glan: Hain, 1968); and more briefly, Baker, *Race*, pp. 33–38.

155. Arthur de Gobineau, *Essai sur l'inégalité des races humaines*, 2 vols. (Paris: Firmin-Didot, 1938, 5th ed.), 1:1–7; 2:502–23.

156. Young, *Gobineau und der Rassismus*, pp. 221ff.; and Barzun, *Race*, pp. 50–77.

157. Karl Marx, *Das Kapital: Kritik der politischen Okonomie*, 3 vols. (Hamburg: Meissner, 1922 ed.), 3:325; and Marx to Engels, 30 July 1862, in Karl Marx and Friedrich Engels, *Werke*, compiled by the Institut fur Marxismus-Leninismus, 37 vols.

(Berlin: Dietz, 1959–1970), 30:257. Also see Léon Poliakov, *Histoire de l'antisémitisme*, 4 vols. (Paris: Calmann-Levy, 1955–1977), 3:432–40.

158. Engels to Marx, 2 October 1866, in Marx and Engels, *Werke* 31:256.

159. Charles Darwin, *The Origin of the Species* (London: Murray, 1859).

160. See Fredrickson, *The Black Image in the White Mind*, p. 230.

161. Charles Darwin, *The Descent of Man* (New York: Appleton, 1888 ed.), pp. 159–60.

162. See, for example, Robert Huttenback, *Racism and Empire: White Settlers and Colored Immigrants in the British Self-Governing Colonies* (Ithaca: Cornell University Press, 1976), pp. 26–79.

163. Rutherford Hayes, as cited in Stuart Miller, *The Unwelcomed Immigrant* (Berkeley: University of California Press, 1974 ed.), p. 190.

164. John Macdonald, 12 May 1882, in Canada, House of Commons, *Official Debates, 1882* (Ottawa: Maclean, Roger, and Co., 1882), 12:1477.

165. Great Britain, PRO/FO, 371/35917, File F 1647/877/61, "The 'White Australia' Policy," 19 March 1943; and Huttenback, *Racism and Empire*, pp. 47, 91–115, and 195.

166. Paul Leroy-Beaulieu, *De la colonisation chez les peuples modernes* (Paris: Guillaumin, 1874), especially pp. i–vii, 465–69, and 605–06.

167. For general discussions see Carlton Hayes, *A Generation of Materialism, 1871–1900* (New York: Harper & Brothers, 1941), pp. 216–29; and Roberts, *History of the World*, p. 703.

168. Robert Cornevin, *Histoire de l'afrique: l'afrique précoloniale* (Paris: Payot, 1976); Gordon A. Craig, *Europe Since 1815* (New York: Holt, Rinehart, & Winston, 1971 ed.), pp. 407–12; Roland Oliver and Anthony Atmore, *Africa Since 1800* (Cambridge: Cambridge University Press, 1981 ed.); and Henri Brunschwig, *L'Avènement de l'Afrique noire* (Paris: Colin, 1963).

169. Earl Grey, as cited in Little, *Race and Society*, p. 16. Also see V.G. Kiernan, *The Lords of Human Kind: Black Man, Yellow Man, and White Man in an Age of Empire* (Boston: Little, Brown, 1969).

170. Benjamin Disraeli, as cited in Poliakov, *The Aryan Myth*, pp. 231–33; and Curtin, *The Image of Africa*, p. 381.

171. See Jules Ferry, 28 July 1885, in France, Assemblée nationale, Chambre des Députés, *Débats parlementaires, 1885,* Session ordinaire (Paris: Imprimerie du Journal Officiel, 1885), 2:1065–66; Madeleine Reberioux, "L'essor du racisme nationaliste," in Comarmond and Duchet, *Racisme et société*, pp. 139–40; and Panikkar, *Asia and Western Dominance.*

172. William Seward, as cited in Fredrickson, *The Black Image in the White Mind*, p. 141, in his chapter on "White Imperialism." Also see Reginald Horsman, *Race and Manifest Destiny* (Cambridge: Harvard University Press, 1981).

173. Ray Allen Billington, *Land of Savagery, Land of Promise* (New York: Norton, 1981), p. 107.

174. Felix Cohen, *Felix Cohen's Handbook of Federal Indian Law*, Rennard Strickland (ed.), (Charlottesville: Michie, Bobbs-Merrill, 1982 ed.); and William Hagan, *American Indians* (Chicago: University of Chicago Press, 1979 ed.), pp. 66–144.

175. *Annual Report of the Commissioner of Indian Affairs*, 1 November 1872, in Francis Prucha (ed.), *Documents of United States Indian Policy* (Lincoln: University of Nebraska Press, 1975), pp. 138–40.

176. See Clough et al., *European History in a World Perspective* 3:1350 and 1425.

177. Great Britain, House of Commons, *Sessional Papers 1884–1885*, 55(4284), "Protocols and General Act of the West African Conference," p. 297.

178. *Lagos Observer,* 19 February 1885, as cited in J.F.A. Ajayi, "Colonialism: An Episode in African History," in L.H. Gann and Peter Duignan (eds.), *Colonialism in Africa,* 5 vols. (Cambridge: Cambridge University Press, 1969), 1:507n.

Chapter 2: The Rising Tide

1. Ludwig Gumplowicz, *Der Rassenkampf* (Innsbruck: Wagner'sche univ.-buchhandlung, 1883); Nicholas Danielevsky, *Rossiya i Evropa,* first published in 1871, translated into German by Karl Notzel as *Russland und Europa* (Stuttgart: Deutsch verlags-anstalt, 1920); and Herbert Spencer, *The Principles of Sociology,* 3 vols. (New York: Appleton, 1876–97).

2. Richard Hofstadter, *Social Darwinism in American Thought* (Boston: Beacon, 1955 ed.), pp. 3–66; and Jacques Barzun, *Darwin, Marx, and Wagner* (Garden City: Doubleday, 1958 ed.), pp. 94–100.

3. Otto Ammon, *Die natürliche Auslese beim Menschen* (Jena: Fischer, 1893); Ludwig Woltmann, *Die Darwinische Theorie und der Sozialismus* (Dusseldorf: Michels, 1899); and Iakov Novikov, *L'avenir de la race blanche* (Paris: Alcan, 1897).

4. See Magnus Morner, *Race Mixture in the History of Latin America* (Boston: Little, Brown, 1967), pp. 140–42.

5. "Biological View of Our Foreign Policy," by "A Biologist," *Saturday Review* (February 1896):118–20.

6. Georges Vacher de Lapouge, *Les sélections sociales* (Paris: Fontemoing, 1896), p. 68. Also see pp. 3–7 and 69–80.

7. Georges Vacher de Lapouge, *L'Aryen* (Paris: Fontemoing, 1899), p. vii.

8. Georges Vacher de Lapouge, "L'anthropologie et la science politique," *Revue d'Anthropologie* 16(1887):151.

9. Houston Stewart Chamberlain, *Die Grundlagen des neunzehnten Jahrhunderts,* 2 vols. (Munchen: Bruckmann, 1907 ed.), 1:320.

10. Introduction, by Lord Redesdale, in Houston Stewart Chamberlain, *The Foundations of the Nineteenth Century,* translated by John Lees, 2 vols. (London: Lane, 1910), 1:v.

11. Roderick Stackelberg, *Idealism Debased* (Kent, Ohio: Kent State University Press, 1981), p. 114.

12. Letter from Wilhelm II to Chamberlain, 31 December 1901, as cited in Leon Poliakov, *The Aryan Myth: A History of Racist and Nationalist Ideas in Europe* (New York: New American Library, 1977), p. 319.

13. Adolf Stoecker, as cited in Carlton Hayes, *A Generation of Materialism* (New York: Harper & Brothers, 1941), p. 261.

14. Louis Snyder, *The Idea of Racialism* (Princeton: Van Nostrand, 1962), p. 81.

15. See Hayes, *A Generation of Materialism,* p. 264, and the vituperative Edouard Drumont, *Le Peuple juif* (Paris: Librairie antisémite, 1900).

16. Josiah Strong, *Our Country: Its Possible Future and Present Crisis,* 1891 rev. ed. (Cambridge: Belknap Press, 1963 reprint), pp. 213–14.

17. John Fiske, *The Discovery of America,* 2 vols. (Boston: Houghton Mifflin, 1893), 1:22; and Brooks Adams, *The Law of Civilization and Decay* (New York: Macmillan, 1896), p. xi.

18. Theodore Roosevelt, *The Winning of the West,* in *The Works of Theodore Roosevelt,* 20 vols. (New York: Scribner's, 1926), 9:56–57. Also see Thomas Dyer, *Theodore Roosevelt and the Idea of Race* (Baton Rouge: Louisiana State University Press, 1982).

19. George Fredrickson, *The Black Image in the White Mind: The Debate on Afro-American Character and Destiny, 1817–1914* (New York: Harper & Row, 1971), p. 246. This paragraph is based upon Fredrickson's excellent discussion.

20. Joseph Le Conte, *The Race Problem in the South,* from the Man and State Evolution Series, no. 29 (New York: Appleton, 1892), pp. 359–60.

21. Eugene Rollin Corson, "The Vital Equation of the Colored Race and Its Future in the United States," in *The Wilder Quarter-Century Book* (Ithaca: Comstock, 1893), pp. 169 and 175.

22. Frederick Ludwig Hoffman, *Race Traits and Tendencies of the American Negro* (New York: Macmillan, 1896).

23. Fredrickson, *The Black Image in the White Mind,* pp. 249–50.

24. C. Vann Woodward, *The Strange Career of Jim Crow* (New York: Oxford University Press, 1957), chapter entitled "Capitulation to Racism," pp. 49–95; and John Hope Franklin (ed.), *From Slavery to Freedom* (New York: Knopf, 1974), pp. 272–76.

25. "Plessy v. Ferguson," *U.S. Supreme Court Reports* 163 (1896):544 and 548.

26. Theodor Herzl, *Der Judenstaat: Versuche einer modernen Lösung der Judenfrage* (Vienna: Breitenstein, 1896).

27. Edwin S. Redkey, *Black Exodus: Black Nationalist and Back-to-Africa Movements, 1890–1910* (New Haven: Yale University Press, 1969).

28. Cited in the autobiography of W.E.B. Du Bois, *Dusk of Dawn* (New York: Harcourt, Brace, 1940), p. 90.

29. See the various contributions in the *Archiv für Rassen- und Gesellschaftsbiologie,* founded in 1904.

30. John Higham, *Strangers in the Land* (New Brunswick: Rutgers University Press, 1955), p. 151.

31. Charles Carroll, *The Negro a Beast* (Miami: Mnemosyne, 1969 reprint), p. 105.

32. William B. Smith, as cited in Fredrickson, *The Black Image in the White Mind,* p. 257.

33. Charles Maurras, in his newspaper *L'Action française,* which began publication in 1899, passim; and Fritz Stern, *The Politics of Cultural Despair* (Berkeley: University of California Press, 1974 ed.), pp. 201–02.

34. Klaus Wagner, as cited in Poliakov, *The Aryan Myth,* p. 302.

35. E.J. Young, *Gobineau und der Rassismus: Eine Kritik der anthropologischen Geschichtstheorie* (Meisenheim am Glan: Hain, 1968), pp. 145ff; and Juan Comas, *Racial Myths* (Paris: UNESCO, 1951), pp. 33–46.

36. John Fiske, *The Discovery of America* 1:22.

37. Jacques Barzun, *Race: A Study in Superstition* (New York: Harper & Row, 1965 ed.), p. 134.

38. Sir Samuel Griffith, "Australia and the Coloured Races," *Review of Reviews* 9 (May 1894):577–78.

39. See Robert Huttenback, *Racism and Empire: White Settlers and Colored Immigrants in the British Self-Governing Colonies, 1830–1910* (Ithaca: Cornell University Press, 1976), pp. 141–43.

40. Britain, Colonial Office, 179/202 of 1897, as cited in ibid., p. 144.

41. As cited in Robert Huttenback, *Gandhi in South Africa* (Ithaca: Cornell University Press, 1971), p. 343.

42. See Britain, Public Record Office, Foreign Office [hereafter, PRO/FO], 371/6684, Memorandum entitled "Racial Discrimination and Immigration," 10 October 1921, "Confidential," F 4212/223/23, p. 11.

43. "Indians and the Empire," *Times* (London), 12 September 1910.

44. Britain, PRO/FO, 371/35917, Memorandum entitled "The 'White Australia' Policy," 19 March 1943, F 1647/877/61, p. 5.

45. *Sydney Daily Telegraph,* 14 October 1896, as cited in Huttenback, *Racism and Empire,* pp. 161–62.

46. Britain, PRO/FO, 371/6684, Memorandum entitled "Racial Discrimination and Immigration," 10 October 1921, "Confidential," F 4212/223/23, p. 10.

47. C.H. Kirmess, *The Australian Crisis* (London: Scott, 1909), p. 335.

48. Immigration Act of 1910, in W.G. Smith, *A Study in Canadian Immigration* (Toronto: Ryerson, 1920), p. 102. The titles of Smith's chapters indicate his concerns: "The Beginning of the Immigration Tide," "The Tide in Flood," and "The Refuse of the Tide."

49. "White Canada Forever," as cited in Huttenback, *Racism and Empire,* p. 277. Also see his full discussion, pp. 168–94; and Kazuo Ito, *Issei: A History of Japanese Immigrants in North America,* translated by S. Nakamura and Jean Gerard (Seattle: Japan Publications, 1973), pp. 101–09.

50. See Magnus Morner, *Race Mixture in the History of Latin America,* pp. 140–42.

51. These various immigration laws are reviewed in Britain, PRO/FO, 371/6684, Memorandum entitled "Racial Discrimination and Immigration," 10 October 1921, "Confidential," F 4212/223/23, pp. 39, 47, and 49.

52. Morner, *Race Mixture in the History of Latin America,* p. 138; and Ito, *Issei,* pp. 64–66.

53. Strong, *Our Country,* p. 51.

54. Josiah Strong, *The New Era* (New York: Baker & Taylor, 1893), p. 77.

55. "Unguarded Gates," *Atlantic Monthly* 70 (July 1892):57.

56. Francis A. Walker, as cited in Thomas Gossett, *Race: The History of an Idea in America* (Dallas: Southern Methodist University Press, 1963), p. 303.

57. Edward A. Ross, "The Causes of Race Superiority," *Annals of the American Academy of Political and Social Science* 18 (1901):85–88; M.S. Iseman, *Race Suicide* (New York: Cosmopolitan Press, 1912); Senator Rawlings, 1 February 1899, in United States, Congress, *Congressional Record* (Washington, D.C.: Government Printing Office, 1899), 32:1348.

58. See William K. Roberts, *The Mongolian Problem in America: A Discussion of the Possibilities of the Yellow Peril* (San Francisco: Organized Labor Print, 1906).

59. Theodore Roosevelt, speech of 10 February 1908, as cited in Britain, PRO/FO, 371/473, Despatch No. 59, "Secret," from J. Bryce (Ottawa) to Grey (London), 20 February 1908. Also see Huttenback, *Racism and Empire,* p. 189.

60. Glenn Altschuler, *Race, Ethnicity, and Class in American Social Thought, 1865–1919* (Arlington Heights: Davidson, 1982), pp. 40–66; Barbara Miller Solomon, *Ancestors and Immigrants* (Cambridge: Harvard University Press, 1956); and Milton Gordon, *Assimilation in American Life: The Role of Race, Religion, and National Origins* (New York: Oxford University Press, 1964), pp. 97–98, 129, and 136.

61. Roger Daniels, *The Politics of Prejudice: The Anti-Japanese Movement in California and the Struggle for Japanese Exclusion* (Berkeley: University of California Press, 1977 ed.).

62. See John Higham, *Strangers in the Land,* pp. 112, 129–30, and 171; and Oscar Hanlin, *Race and Nationality* (Boston: Little, Brown, 1948).

63. United States, Congress, Senate, Immigration Commission (The Dillingham Commission), *Reports of the Immigration Commission,* 42 vols., 61st Congress, 3rd Session (Washington, D.C.: Government Printing Office, 1911).

64. *California Christian Advocate,* 8 May 1913, as cited in Daniels, *The Politics of Prejudice,* p. 64.

65. T. Lothrop Stoddard, *The Rising Tide of Color Against White World Supremacy* (New York: Scribner's, 1921), p. 9.

66. Hugh Tinker, *Race, Conflict, and the International Order* (London: Macmillan, 1977), p. 21.

67. Joseph Chamberlain, as cited in Huttenback, *Racism and Empire*, p. 164.

68. See ibid., p. 172.

69. *Mainichi Shimbun*, 22 October 1906, as cited in Thomas A. Bailey, *Theodore Roosevelt and the Japanese-American Crisis* (Stanford: Stanford University Press, 1934), p. 50.

70. "Resume of the Administrative Means Proposed by the United States . . . and Acceptance Thereof or Counter Proposals by Japanese Government, 1907–1908," in United States, Department of State, *Foreign Relations of the United States, 1924,* 2 vols. (Washington, D.C.: Government Printing Office, 1939), 2:339–69; and Britain, PRO/FO, 371/6684, Memorandum entitled "Racial Discrimination and Immigration," 10 October 1921, "Confidential," F 4212/223/23, pp. 1–10.

71. Daniels, *The Politics of Prejudice*, pp. 31–45 and 65.

72. David Brion Davis, *Slavery and Human Progress* (New York: Oxford University Press, 1984), p. 307.

73. Karl Pearson, *National Life From the Standpoint of Science* (London: Adam & Charles Black, 1905 ed.), pp. 21 and 26–27.

74. Robert Cornevin, *Histoire de l'afrique* (Paris: Payot, 1976), pp. 531ff.

75. Benjamin Kidd, *The Control of the Tropics* (New York: Macmillan, 1898); Léopold de Saussure, *Psychologie de la colonisation française dans ses rapports avec les sociétés indigènes* (Paris: Alcan, 1899); and Karl Peters, *Die Gründung von Deutsch-Ostafrika* (Berlin: Schwetschke, 1906).

76. Robert Cornevin, "The Germans in Africa Before 1918," in L.H. Gann and Peter Duignan (eds.), *Colonialism in Africa*, 5 vols. (Cambridge: Cambridge University Press, 1969), 1:388.

77. Lord Milner, as cited in Leonard Thompson, *The Unification of South Africa, 1902–1910* (Oxford: Oxford University Press, 1960), p. 6.

78. See L.H. Gann and Peter Duignan, "Imperialism and the Scramble for Africa," in Gann and Duignan, *Colonialism in Africa* 1:109.

79. "Deutsche Wacht in Kiautschau," *Simplicissimus*, 19 Jahrgang, Nr. 27 (6 October 1914); Germany, Auswärtiges Amt, *Die Grosse Politik der Europäischen Kabinette, 1871–1914*, 40 vols. (Berlin: Deutsche Verlagsgesellschaft für Politik, 1922–27), 14, nos. 3688–90; Otto Ammon, *Warum siegten die Japaner?* (Berlin: Duemmler, 1895); and Hayes, *A Generation of Materialism*, pp. 310–11.

80. Ernest R. May, *American Imperialism: A Spectulative Essay* (New York: Atheneum, 1968); Hofstadter, *Social Darwinism in American Thought*, pp. 170–200; and the useful summary of opinion in Thomas Paterson (ed.), *American Imperialism and Anti-Imperialism* (New York: Crowell, 1973).

81. Secretary of War E. Root, as cited in M. Storey and M. Lichauco, *The Conquest of the Philippines by the United States* (New York: Putnam, 1926), p. 171.

82. Franklin, *From Slavery to Freedom*, pp. 306 and 312.

83. See Rubin Weston, *Racism in U.S. Imperialism* (Columbia: University of South Carolina Press, 1972); David Healy, *U.S. Expansionism: The Imperialist Urge in the 1890s* (Madison: University of Wisconsin Press, 1970); Philip Kennedy, "Race and American Expansion in Cuba and Puerto Rico, 1895–1905," *Journal of Black Studies* 1 (March 1971):306–16; and James P. Shenton, "Imperialism and Racism," in Donald Sheehan and Harold Syrett (eds.), *Essays in American Historiography* (New York: Columbia University Press, 1960), pp. 230–50. For a different perspective, emphasizing

economics rather than racism, see William Appleman Williams, *The Tragedy of American Diplomacy* (New York: Dell, 1962 ed.).

84. Roosevelt, *The Winning of the West*, pp. 57–58. His exuberant essay on "The Strenuous Life" conveys a similar attitude. Also see Thomas Dixon, *The Leopard's Spots* (New York: Doubleday, 1902), especially pp. 381–84.

85. Benjamin Tillman, as cited in Christopher Lasch, "The Anti-Imperialists, the Philippines, and the Inequality of Man," *Journal of Southern History* 24 (August 1958): 325. Also see Frederickson, *The Black Image in the White Mind*, pp. 305–08: and Woodward, *The Strange Career of Jim Crow*, pp. 55–56.

86. Franklin, *From Slavery to Freedom*, p. 313.

87. Frederickson, *The Black Image in the White Mind*, p. 309.

88. Rudyard Kipling, "The White Man's Burden," in *Rudyard Kipling's Verse* (New York: Doubleday, 1939 ed.), pp. 321–23.

89. See William L. Langer, *The Diplomacy of Imperialism, 1890–1902* (New York: Knopf, 1968), pp. 90–96; and Senator Albert Beveridge, 9 January 1900, in United States, Congress, *Congressional Record* (Washington, D.C.: Government Printing Office, 1900), 33:704–12.

90. Roberts, *History of the World*, p. 739.

91. See, for example, John L. Stevens to John W. Foster, 1 February 1893, in United States, Department of State, *Foreign Relations of the United States, 1894* (Washington, D.C.: Government Printing Office, 1895), Appendix 2, p. 402.

92. William Appleman Williams, *Empire as a Way of Life* (New York: Oxford University Press, 1980), p. 25.

93. The "Relatorio da Comissao" of 1899, as cited in James Duffy, *Portuguese Africa* (Cambridge, Mass.: Harvard University, 1959), p. 155.

94. Immanuel Geiss, *Panafrikanismus: Zür Geschichte der Dekolonisation* (Frankfurt am Main: Europäische Verlagsanstalt, 1968), pp. 139ff.

95. W.E.B. Du Bois, as cited in United Nations, Centre Against Apartheid, *International Tribute to William E.B. Du Bois* (New York: United Nations, 1982 ed.), p. 48.

96. See Roland Oliver and Anthony Atmore, *Africa Since 1800* (Cambridge: Cambridge University Press, 1981 ed.), pp. 114–40 and 144–45.

97. Langer, *The Diplomacy of Imperialism*, pp. 271–82; "La bataille d'Adowa d'après un récit Abyssin," *Revue française de l'étranger et des colonies* 21 (November 1896):656–58; and Gordon A. Craig, *Europe Since 1815* (New York: Holt, Rinehart, and Winston, 1971 ed.), pp. 418–19.

98. "The Italian Disaster," *Times* (London), 4 March 1896.

99. A French history professor, as cited in ibid., 5 March 1896.

100. Germany, Auswärtiges Amt, *Die Grosse Politik* 16, especially nos. 4598ff.

101. Craig, *Europe Since 1815*, pp. 423–24.

102. Among many examples, see V. Veresaev, *In the War*, translated by Leo Wiener (New York: Mitchell Kennerley, 1917), p. 5; and Adam Ulam, *The Bolsheviks* (New York: Collier, 1968), p. 221.

103. Alfred Zimmern, *The Third British Empire* (London: Oxford University Press, 1926), p. 82. Also see Ito, *Issei*, p. 3, for a Japanese perspective reaching the same conclusion.

104. René Pinon, *La Lutte pour le Pacifique* (Paris: Perrin, 1906), p. 165.

105. W.E.B. Du Bois, as discussed in Ronald Segal, *The Race War* (New York: Bantam, 1967), p. 220.

106. B.L. Putnam Weale, *The Conflict of Color: The Threatened Upheaval Throughout the World* (New York: Macmillan, 1910), pp. 97–99 and passim.

107. Stoddard, *The Rising Tide of Color*, p. 12. Also see pp. 21, 23, 97, 149, 153, 203, and 228.

108. For a more complete discussion, see Germany, Auswärtiges Amt, Politisches Archiv, Politisches Archiv und Historisches Referat; France, Ministère des Affaires étrangères, Archives diplomatiques, Comptabilité, Cartons 44ff., and Direction du Personnel, "Projet de Réorganisation"; and Paul Gordon Lauren, *Diplomats and Bureaucrats* (Stanford: Hoover Institution Press, 1976), pp. 34–44.

109. Queen Victoria, as cited in Bernard Porter, *The Lion's Share: A Short History of British Imperialism, 1850–1970* (London: Longmans, 1975), p. 185.

110. Maurice Paleologue, *Un grand tournant de la politique mondiale, 1904–1906* (Paris: Plon, 1934); and Gabriel Hanotaux, "L'Europe qui nait," *La revue hebdomadaire* 48 (30 November 1907):561–70. Also see Otto Hammann, *Deutsche Weltpolitik, 1890–1912* (Berlin: Hobbing, 1925), pp. 35ff.

111. Sir Valentine Chirol, *Fifty Years in a Changing World* (London: Cape, 1927), p. 207.

112. Jean Jaurès, 28 June 1912, in France, Assemblée nationale, Chambre des Députés, *Débats parlementaires* (Paris: Imprimerie des Journaux officiels, 1912), p. 923.

113. T. Lothrop Stoddard, *The French Revolution in San Domingo* (Boston: Houghton Mifflin, 1914), p. vii.

114. Stoddard, *The Rising Tide of Color*, p. 13.

115. Mohamed Duse, "War!" *African Times and Orient Review*, 4 August 1914.

116. Achmed Abdullah, "Seen Through Mohammedan Spectacles," *Forum* (October 1914):484 and 496. Also see Yone Noguchi, "The Downfall of Western Civilization," *Nation* (8 October 1914):432.

117. W.E.B. Du Bois, "The African Roots of War," *Atlantic Monthly* (May 1915):714.

118. For a discussion on the use of black forces by the British, complete with illustrations, see *Times*, "The Campaign in German East Africa," *The Times History of the War*, 22 vols. (London: The Times, 1919), 19:37–72.

119. Cornevin, "The Germans in Africa Before 1918," p. 415.

120. Bernard Porter, *The Lion's Share*, p. 235; and C.E. Carrington, "The Empire at War, 1914–1918," in *The Cambridge History of the British Empire* (Cambridge: Cambridge University Press, 1959), 3:605–44.

121. See Geiss, *Panafrikanismus*, pp. 180–83 and 237; and Du Bois, *Dusk of Dawn*, p. 261.

122. Geiss, *Panafrikanismus*, p. 180.

123. Tinker, *Race, Conflict, and the International Order*, p. 38; and Geiss, *Panafrikanismus*, pp. 237–40.

124. Robert Delavignette, as cited in Rupert Emerson, *From Empire to Nation: The Rise to Self-Assertion of Asian and African Peoples* (Cambridge: Harvard University Press, 1960), p. 24.

125. See Great Britain, PRO/FO, 371/6683, Imperial Conference Secretariat, July 1917, Confidential, "Further Correspondence 1914–1915 Relating to the Treatment of Asiatics in the Dominions."

126. Mohamed Duse, "Today: India and Africa," *African Times and Orient Review*, March 1917, p. 46.

127. Franklin, *From Slavery to Freedom*, pp. 314, 315, and 335; and Du Bois, *Dawn of Dusk*, p. 239.

128. Madison Grant, *The Passing of the Great Race* (New York: Scribner's, 1916). The film, *The Birth of the Nation*, appeared in 1915.

129. This discussion is based upon Franklin, *From Slavery to Freedom*, pp. 336–41; Chester Heywood, *Negro Combat Troops in the World War* (New York: Ams Press, 1969 ed.); and Arthur Little, *From Harlem to the Rhine* (New York: Covici-Friede, 1936).

130. See Gossett, *Race*, p. 368.

131. W.E.B. Du Bois, "Close Ranks," from *Crisis*, July 1918, as cited in Du Bois, *Dawn of Dusk*, p. 254.

132. Cited in Franklin, *From Slavery to Freedom*, pp. 343–44.

133. V.I. Lenin, "The Present War is an Imperialist War," in *Collected Works of V.I. Lenin* (New York: International Publishers, 1930), 18:221ff.; and Porter, *The Lion's Share*, pp. 238–46.

134. V.I. Lenin, "The Right of Nations to Self-Determination," in ibid., pp. 235 and 367ff.; Arno Mayer, *Wilson vs. Lenin: The Political Origins of the New Diplomacy, 1917–1918* (New York: Meridian, 1964), pp. 298–303; and Segal, *The Race War*, pp. 316–17.

135. Stoddard, *The Rising Tide*, p. 220.

136. Georges Bonnet, *Le Quai d'Orsay sous trois républiques* (Paris: Fayard, 1961), p. 40.

137. Kelly Miller, *The World War for Human Rights* (New York: Negro Universities Press, 1969 reprint), p. 474, originally published in 1919. Also see Arthur Barbeau and Florette Henri, *The Unknown Soldiers: Black American Troops in World War I* (Philadelphia: Temple University Press, 1974).

Chapter 3: Racial Equality Requested— and Rejected

1. E.J. Dillon, *The Inside Story of the Peace Conference* (New York: Harper & Brothers, 1920), p. 5.

2. Harold Nicolson, *Peacemaking 1919* (New York: Grosset & Dunlop, 1965), pp. 31–32.

3. For a fuller discussion, see Paul Gordon Lauren, *Diplomats and Bureaucrats* (Stanford: Hoover Institution Press, 1976), especially pp. 34–78 and 222–28.

4. Jean Jaurès, 2 séance of 28 June 1912, in France, Assemblée nationale, Chambre, *Débats parlementaires* (Paris: Imprimerie nationale, 1912), p. 923; and Immanuel Geiss, *Panafrikanismus: Zur Geschichte der Dekolonisation* (Frankfurt am Main: Europäische Verlagsanstalt, 1968), pp. 180ff.

5. W.E.B. Du Bois, "Opinion," *Crisis* 18 (May 1919): 7.

6. Dillon, *The Inside Story*, p. 6.

7. Du Bois, as cited in Clarence Contee, "Du Bois, the NAACP, and the Pan-African Congress of 1919," *Journal of Negro History* 57 (January 1972):16.

8. *Crisis* 17 (January 1919):130–31.

9. Geiss, *Panafrikanismus*, p. 186.

10. Georges Clemenceau, as cited in W.E.B. Du Bois, *The World and Africa* (New York: International Publishers, 1965 ed.), p. 10.

11. They are the words of the *New York Evening Globe*, 22 February 1919. According to Du Bois, *The World and Africa*, p. 7, there had been an earlier, prototype meeting in London during 1900, but this had attracted only about thirty delegates.

12. See United Nations, Centre Against Apartheid, *International Tribute to William E.B. Du Bois* (New York: United Nations, 1982 ed.); and *Freedomways* 5 (Winter 1965):8.

13. Du Bois, *The World and Africa*, p. 12. Also see Du Bois, *Dusk of Dawn* (New York: Harcourt, Brace, 1940), pp. 260–62.

14. See Akira Iriye, *Pacific Estrangement* (Cambridge, Mass.: Harvard University Press, 1972), especially his excellent chapter, "Confrontation: The Japanese View," pp. 126–50.

15. K.K. Kawakami, *Japan and World Peace* (New York: Macmillan, 1919), pp. 53–59.

16. Britain, Foreign Office, Historical Section, *Peace Handbooks*, vol. 73, *Japan* (London: His Majesty's Stationery Office, 1920), pp. 89–94.

17. Among many examples, see "Deutsche Wacht in Kiautschau," *Simplicissimus* 19 Jahrgang, Nr. 27 (6 October 1914); "The Terror," *Sun* (New York), 17 October 1914; and Norman Lindsay's poster, "?," Imperial War Museum, Catalog Number 3242.

18. Robert E. Park, introduction to Jesse F. Steiner, *The Japanese Invasion* (Chicago: McClurg, 1917), p. xiv.

19. Akira Iriye, *Across the Pacific: An Inner History of American-East Asian Relations* (New York: Harcourt, Brace, & World, 1967), p. 131.

20. This speech was reproduced in United States, Congress, *Congressional Record*, 1st Session, 64th Congress, vol. 53, pt. 1 (Washington, D.C.: Government Printing Office, 1916), pp. 754–55.

21. Lest this account of the peace conference appear to assign moral superiority to the Japanese, it should be noted clearly that many Koreans at that time believed that they were treated as definite inferiors by the Japanese, who subjected them to a whole range of indignities bordering on, if not actually amounting to, racial discrimination. Korea petitioned the Paris Peace Conference to recognize the human rights of its people and to support their claim to self-determination. These remonstrances largely were ignored, however, and riots in Korea during March 1919 for independence were forcibly crushed by Japanese troops. See, among others, E.S. Bisbee, "Korea Appeals to Wilson for Freedom," *New York Times Magazine*, 26 January 1919; "Tell of Japanese Cruelty to Koreans," *New York Times*, 18 March 1919.

22. *Hochi*, as cited in "Racial Discrimination," *Japan Times*, 3 December 1918.

23. *Hochi*, as cited in "Mission's Importance Cannot Well Be Surpassed," ibid., 11 December 1918.

24. *Yorozu*, as cited in "What Are Japan's Peace Terms?" ibid., 29 December 1918.

25. *Nichinichi*, as cited in "League May Prove an Organ of Oppression," ibid., 31 January 1919.

26. *Asahi*, as cited in "Parting Word to Peace Delegates," ibid., 11 December 1918.

27. *Asahi*, as cited in "Racial Discrimination Question to End," ibid., 31 January 1919. Also see Russell H. Fifield, *Woodrow Wilson and the Far East* (New York: Crowell, 1952), pp. 158–59.

28. For a summary, see S. Hishida, *Japan Among the Great Powers* (London: Longmans, Green, 1940), pp. 231–32.

29. Masamichi Royama, *Foreign Policy of Japan* (Tokyo: Institute of Pacific Relations, 1941), p. 28. Also see Hugh Borton, *Japan's Modern Century* (New York: Ronald, 1955), p. 287.

30. See the historical study entitled "Japan and the Issue of Racial Equality at Paris," dated 3 February 1943 and sent to the Foreign Office by the U.S. Embassy in London, in Britain, Public Record Office, Foreign Office [hereafter, PRO/FO], 371/35949.

31. Kawakami, *Japan and World Peace*, p. 49. Also see "Mr. Wilson, Democracy Incarnate," *Japan Times*, 7 December 1918.

32. Woodrow Wilson, as cited in Kawakami, *Japan and World Peace*, p. 49.

33. *Asahi*, as cited in "Racial Discrimination Question to End," *Japan Times*, 31 January 1919. The importance of this matter in Japan also was reported by U.S. Ambassador Roland S. Morris in Tokyo to the secretary of state, as indicated by his despatches in United States, Department of State, *Foreign Relations of the United States, Paris Peace Conference, 1919*, 13 vols. (Washington, D.C.: Government Printing Office, 1942), 1:490–93.

34. See the many statements from *Nichinichi, Hochi, Yomiuri*, and *Jigi* in *Japan Times*, 29 and 30 November 1918.

35. *Asahi*, as cited in "Hearty Approbation," ibid., 30 November 1918.

36. Patrick Gallagher, *America's Aims and Asia's Aspirations* (New York: Century, 1920), p. 232. For a different opinion, see Ian Nish, *Alliance in Decline* (London: Athlone, 1972), p. 266.

37. "Saionji Sails Amid Banzais," *Japan Times*, 15 January 1919.

38. *Asahi*, as cited in "What Japan Should Demand at Paris," ibid., 15 January 1919.

39. See David Hunter Miller, *My Diary*, 21 vols. (New York: privately printed, 1924), 3:455, doc. no. 211.

40. Charles Seymour, *The Intimate Papers of Colonel House*, 4 vols. (Boston: Houghton Mifflin, 1928), 4:310. He also noted on p. 314, however, that the Japanese once thanked him for his "considerate sympathy."

41. Ibid.

42. Chinda, as cited in ibid., entry of 6 February 1919, p. 312.

43. Wilson, as cited in Roger Daniels, *The Politics of Prejudice* (Berkeley: University of California Press, 1977 ed.), p. 55.

44. Wilson, as cited in *Crisis*, 9 (January 1919):119–20. Also see Joel Williamson, *The Crucible of Race* (New York: Oxford University Press, 1984), pp. 385ff.; and Henry Blumenthal, "Woodrow Wilson and the Race Question," *Journal of Negro History* 48 (1963):1–21. I am also indebted to Alexander and Juliette George for discussions helping me understand Wilson's personality and his attitude toward race.

45. Kelly Miller to Woodrow Wilson, 4 August 1917, as reproduced in Kelly Miller, *The World War for Human Rights* (New York: Negro Universities Press, 1969 reprint), pp. 492–93.

46. See John Hope Franklin, *From Slavery to Freedom: A History of Negro Americans* (New York: Knopf, 1974 ed.), p. 352.

47. The words are those of Contee, "Du Bois, the NAACP, and the Pan-African Congress of 1919," p. 17.

48. Nicolson, *Peacemaking 1919*, p. 145.

49. Britain, PRO/FO, 371/6684, Memorandum entitled "Racial Discrimination and Immigration," 10 October 1921, "Confidential," F 4212/223/23, p. 10.

50. Hughes, as cited in L.F. Fitzhardinge, *William Morris Hughes: A Political Biography* (Sydney: Angus & Robertson, 1964), pp. 116 and 136.

51. Miller, *Diary*, entry of 8 February 1919, 1:114.

52. Ibid., entry of 9 February 1919, 1:116. See also Britain, PRO/FO, 410/69, Confidential Files, Despatch No. 148, "Confidential," from B. Alston (Tokyo) to Curzon, Annual Report 1919, 19 March 1920, p. 2, which expressed the attitude that for Japan "the war had gone somewhat to the nation's head."

53. As cited in Britain, PRO/FO, 371/3817, Despatch No. 55 from Conyngham Greene (Tokyo) to Curzon (London), 6 February 1919. Also see "Do To Others," *Japan Times*, 9 February 1919.

54. As cited in Britain, PRO/FO, 371/6684, Memorandum entitled "Racial Discrimination and Immigration," 10 October 1921, "Confidential," F 4212/223/23, p. 17.

55. Seymour, *Papers of Colonel House,* 4:309.

56. Conférence de la Paix, 1919–1920, *Recueil des actes de la Conférence,* "Secret," Partie 4, Commission de la Société des Nations (Paris: Imprimerie nationale, 1922), pp. 89–90. Technically, this amendment was an addition to an article favored by Wilson on religious toleration.

57. Ray Stannard Baker, *Woodrow Wilson and the World Settlement,* 3 vols. (New York: Doubleday, Page, 1922), 2:235.

58. Conférence de la Paix, 1919–1920, *Recueil des actes de la Conférence,* "Secret," Partie 4, p. 90.

59. Baker, *Wilson and the World Settlement* 2:235.

60. Britain, PRO/FO, Memorandum entitled "Racial Discrimination and Immigration," 10 October 1921, "Confidential," F 4212/223/23, p. 10.

61. This was done by temporarily withdrawing Wilson's favorite religious toleration clause, to which the Japanese had coupled their amendment.

62. See the interesting account in Gallagher, *America's Aims,* pp. 94 and 322.

63. Conférence de la Paix, 1919–1920, *Recueil des actes de la Conférence,* "Secret," Partie 3, Séances plénières de la Conférence, p. 60.

64. Paul Birdsall, *Versailles Twenty Years After* (New York: Reyal & Hitchcock, 1941), p. 95.

65. "Time to Give Up Race Prejudice, Japanese View," *New York Herald,* 17 February 1919.

66. Gallagher, *America's Aims,* p. 323.

67. See the several works in Japan, Delegation to the Paris Peace Conference, Documents Distributed to the Public, such as "Le Japon et le problème des races," by Saito Man, located at the Hoover Institution, Stanford, California.

68. *Asahi,* as cited in "Japan's Great Mission," *Japan Times,* 13 March 1919.

69. *Nichinichi,* as cited in "Must Stick to Racial Discrimination Question," ibid., 15 March 1919. Also see Stephen Bonsal, *Unfinished Business* (Garden City: Doubleday, Doran, 1944), pp. 169–70; and Roy Watson Curry, *Woodrow Wilson and Far Eastern Policy, 1913–1921* (New York: Bookman, 1957), pp. 255–56.

70. The words are those of Vernon Bartlett, *Behind the Scenes at the Peace Conference* (London: Allen & Unwin, 1919), p. 104. For more discussion of these meetings, see Nish, *Alliance,* p. 270n.; Fifield, *Far East,* pp. 164–65; and Henry Borden (ed.), *Robert Laird Borden: His Memoirs,* 2 vols. (Toronto: Macmillan, 1938), 2:926–28.

71. "The Doctrine of the Legal Equality of States," Document No. 575, in Miller, *Diary* 7:84–85. See also the derogatory statements in Britain, PRO/FO, 410/69, Despatch No. 148, "Confidential," from B. Alston (Tokyo) to Curzon (London), Annual Report 1919, 19 March 1920.

72. Malcolm Lyon, "Last Days," *English Review* (April 1919):351.

73. Gallagher, *America's Aims,* p. 95.

74. Hughes, as cited in "Equality of Races," *Age* (Melbourne), 21 March 1919. Also see Stephen Bonsal, *Suitors and Suppliants: The Little Nations at Versailles* (New York: Prentice-Hall, 1946), p. 229.

75. Seymour, *Papers of Colonel House* 4:415.

76. Britain, PRO/Cabinet, 29/28/1, British Empire Delegation, "Secret," 17th Minutes, 3 April 1919, p. 3.

77. Hughes, as cited in Britain, PRO/FO, 371/6684, Memorandum entitled "Racial Discrimination and Immigration," 10 October 1921, "Confidential," F 4212/223/23, p. 18.

78. Bonsal, *Unfinished Business*, p. 154. Also see Robert Lansing, Diary, entry of 8 April 1919, Lansing Collection, Library of Congress, Manuscript Division, Washington, D.C.

79. Seymour, *Papers of Colonel House* 4:413–15.

80. Breckinridge Long to Wilson, 4 March 1919, 8, No. 22, p. 11626, Woodrow Wilson Papers, Library of Congress, Manuscript Division, Washington, D.C. [hereafter cited as Wilson Papers].

81. Memorandum from the Japanese government, 4 March 1919, as enclosed in ibid.

82. "Ishii Looks to End of Race Prejudice," *New York Times*, 15 March 1919. This official Japanese position on immigration was stated subsequently on numerous occasions. See, for example, Japan, Delegation to the Paris Peace Conference, Documents Distributed to the Public, "Statement Made by Y. Matsuoka in Regard to the Proposed Amendment to the League of Nations about Race Equality," 21 March 1919, located at the Hoover Institution; and "Japan Doesn't Raise Immigration Question," *Japan Times*, 30 March 1919.

83. "Ishii's Plea Stirs Western Senators," *New York Times*, 16 March 1919.

84. Ibid.

85. "Land Law Must Be More Drastic," *Sacramento Union*, 1 April 1919. See also "Wilson Calls Halt to State's Anti-Japanese Bills," *San Francisco Chronicle*, 11 April 1919.

86. J.S. Dunnigan, clerk of the Board of Supervisors, to American Delegates at Paris, 7 April 1919, 8, no. 33, p. 16431, Wilson Papers.

87. Miller, *Diary* 17:254.

88. *Asahi*, as cited in "The Racial Question at Versailles," *Japan Times*, 30 March 1919.

89. United States, American Mission to Negotiate Peace, Supreme Headquarters Records, "Bulletins," Bulletin No. 121 (mimeographed), located at the Hoover Institution.

90. See Morinosuke Kajima, *The Diplomacy of Japan, 1894–1922*, 3 vols. (Tokyo: Kajima Institute of International Peace, 1980), 3:403, based upon Japanese Foreign Ministry Archives.

91. Miller, *Diary* 1:243, 245.

92. Nish, *Alliance*, p. 270.

93. As cited in Gallagher, *America's Aims*, p. 236.

94. See, for example, "Japan's New Proposal Probably Accepted," *Japan Times*, 2 April 1919.

95. Kajima, *Diplomacy of Japan* 3:404.

96. Ibid., p. 405.

97. Japan, Delegation to the Paris Peace Conference, Documents Distributed to the Public, "Interview du Baron Makino, 2 avril 1919" (mimeographed), located at the Hoover Institution. Also see "Japan May Bolt World League," *San Francisco Chronicle*, 3 April 1919.

98. Bonsal, *Unfinished Business*, p. 192.

99. House, as cited in Miller, *Diary* 1:242.

100. Dillon, *Peace Conference*, p. 493.

101. Bonsal, *Unfinished Business*, p. 169.

102. Japan, Delegation to the Paris Peace Conference, Documents Distributed to the Public, "Interview du Baron Makino."

103. "Australia Remains Unalterably Opposed," *Japan Times*, 3 April 1919.

104. See Conférence de la Paix, 1919–1920, *Recueil des actes de la Conférence,* "Secret," Partie 4, p. 174.

105. Ibid., pp. 173–74.

106. Miller, *Diary* 1:245.

107. See Dillon, *Peace Conference,* p. 494; *Le Matin,* "Pas d'égalité des nations," 14 avril 1919; Baker, *Wilson and the World Settlement,* 2:237; "Monroe Doctrine Amendment Adopted," *Japan Times,* 15 April 1919; and Birdsall, *Versailles,* p. 97.

108. Birdsall, *Versailles,* p. 98.

109. Conférence de la Paix, 1919–1920, *Recueil des actes de la Conférence,* "Secret," Partie 4, p. 174.

110. David Hunter Miller, *The Drafting of the Covenant,* 2 vols. (New York: Putnam, 1928), 1:461. Also see Miller, *Diary* 1:245.

111. The words are those of Fifield, *Far East,* p. 166.

112. Conférence de la Paix, 1919–1920, *Recueil des actes de la Conférence,* "Secret," Partie 4, p. 175.

113. Ibid., pp. 175–76.

114. Document No. 767, in Miller, *Diary* 8:268a.

115. Birdsall, *Versailles,* p. 99.

116. Document No. 773, "Notes by Clancy," in Miller, *Diary* 8:277–78. The coverage of Wilson's speech is more thorough in this version than in the official French transcripts.

117. Conférence de la Paix, 1919–1920, *Recueil des actes de la Conférence,* "Secret," Partie 4, p. 176. Those in favor were Japan (2), France (2), Italy (2), China, Brazil, Greece, Yugoslavia, and Czechoslovakia. Also see Bonsal, *Unfinished Business,* p. 197.

118. These two issues were the Monroe Doctrine qualification and the location of the League. For more discussion on the technicalities of this controversial ruling, see Seymour, *Papers of Colonel House* 4:428n; Dillon, *Peace Conference,* p. 494; Gallagher, *America's Aims,* pp. 330–31; and Bartlett, *Behind the Scenes,* pp. 107–08, who wrote, "it would be interesting to hear what explanation can be given for the different treatment accorded to his [Wilson's] and to the Japanese amendments."

119. Conférence de la Paix, 1919–1920, *Recueil des actes de la Conférence,* "Secret," Partie 4, p. 177.

120. Document No. 773, in Miller, *Diary* 8:279.

121. Conférence de la Paix, 1919–1920, *Recueil des actes de la Conférence,* "Secret," Partie 4, p. 177.

122. *Sacramento Union,* 13 April 1919.

123. *San Francisco Chronicle,* 13 April 1919.

124. *Kokumin,* as cited in "Racial Equality Defeated by Anglo-Saxons," *Japan Times,* 20 April 1919.

125. "Japan and Racial Equality," *Japan Times,* 19 April 1919.

126. Du Bois, "Opinion," *Crisis* 18 (May 1919):11.

127. *Nichinichi,* as cited in "Anglo-Saxons Want to Dominate the World," *Japan Times,* 26 April 1919.

128. *Kokumin,* as cited in "Racial Equality Bill Defeated by Anglo-Saxons," ibid., 20 April 1919.

129. "Japan and Racial Equality," ibid., 19 April 1919.

130. Gallagher, *America's Aims,* p. 331.

131. Conférence de la Paix, 1919–1920, *Recueil des actes de la Conférence,* "Secret," Partie 3, pp. 116–18. Also see Japan, Delegation to the Paris Peace Conference, Documents Distributed to the Public, "Speech Delivered by Baron Makino," (mim-

eographed), located at the Hoover Institution; and Hoover Institution Archives, Vance C. McCormick Diaries, entry of 28 April 1919.

132. Gallagher, *America's Aims*, p. 97.

133. *Hochi*, as cited in "An Excellent Stimulant," *Japan Times*, 17 April 1919.

134. *Kokumin*, as cited in "Italy's Attitude at the Peace Conference," ibid., 27 April 1919.

135. *Asahi*, as cited in "The League's Amended Covenant," ibid., 18 April 1919; and *Nichinichi*, as cited in "Anglo-Saxons Want to Dominate the World," ibid., 26 April 1919. Also see Arata Ninagawa, *Les réclamations japonaises et le droit international* (Paris: Pedone, 1919), pp. 30–32; and Dillon, *Peace Conference*, pp. 469 ff.

136. Patrick Gallagher, "Marquis Saionji Moves," *Asia* 19 (September 1919):896; Miller, *Drafting of the Covenant* 1:463–64; and *Hochi*, as cited in "An Excellent Stimulant," *Japan Times*, 17 April 1919.

137. T. Yamada, as cited in "Hughes Would Now Be Gazing," *Japan Times*, 1 May 1919; Seymour, *Papers of Colonel House* 4:314, 413–14; Borden, *Memoirs* 2:926–28; and H.W.V. Temperley (ed.), *A History of the Peace Conference of Paris*, 6 vols. (London: Institute of International Affairs, 1924), 6:352; among others.

138. "Pas d'égalité des nations," *Le Matin*, 14 avril 1919; Gallagher, "Marquis Saionji," p. 896; Dillon, *Peace Conference*, p. 79; and the several editorials in *Yorozu* at this time.

139. *Yorozu*, as cited in "The Yorozu Tries to Be a Prophet," *Japan Times*, 27 April 1919.

140. *Yomiuri*, as cited in "Why Racial Proposal Failed," ibid., 13 April 1919; and *Hochi*, as cited in "An Excellent Stinulant," ibid., 17 April 1919.

141. *Yorozu*, as cited in "The League's Amended Covenant," ibid., 18 April 1919.

142. See "How Japan Set Her Diplomatic Snares to Catch Shantung," *Chicago Tribune*, 4 May 1919; "Paris Is Warned," *New York Herald*, 22 July 1919; and T. Lothrop Stoddard, *The Rising Tide of Color Against White World Supremacy* (New York: Scribner's, 1921), pp. 42–43.

143. Japan, Delegation to the Paris Peace Conference, Documents Distributed to the Public, "For Information Given Out to 'The New York Herald,'" 22 July 1919, by Yosuke Matsuoka (mimeographed), located at the Hoover Institution. Also see Nish, *Alliance*, p. 271, where he maintains that the racial equality issue "was a genuine conviction, honestly held"; and Fifield, *Far East*, p. 158, where he states that "the Japanese were absolutely sincere in their request for racial equality."

144. See Britain, PRO/FO, 410/69, Confidential Files, Despatch No. 148, "Confidential," from B. Alston (Tokyo) to Curzon (London), Annual Report 1919, 19 March 1920, p. 4.

145. Dillon, *Peace Conference*, p. 495. Also see Seth Tillman, *Anglo-American Relations at the Paris Peace Conference of 1919* (Princeton: Princeton University Press, 1961), p. 301. The Japanese would have been seemingly more vulnerable to the charge that they themselves discriminated against foreigners owning land in Japan, yet this matter was not pursued, as indicated in "Ishii's Plea Stirs Western Senators," *New York Times*, 16 March 1919. Also see note 21.

146. Royama, *Foreign Policy*, p. 28; and Kawakami, *Japan and World Peace*, pp. 47–48.

147. Gallagher, *America's Aims*, p. 317.

148. Asahi Shimbun, *The Pacific Rivals: A Japanese View of Japanese-American Relations* (New York: Weatherhill/Asahi, 1972), p. 73; Stoddard, *The Rising Tide of Color*, p. 43; and Du Bois, "Opinion," pp. 8–11.

149. *Asahi*, as cited in "Japan's Great Mission," *Japan Times*, 13 March 1919.

150. Chinda, as cited in "League Has Japan's Full Approval," ibid., 27 March 1919.

151. Japan, Delegation to the Paris Peace Conference, Documents Distributed to the Public, "Statement Made by Y. Matsuoka in Regard to the Proposed Amendment to the League of Nations About Race Equality," located at the Hoover Institution.

152. After the crucial meeting of 11 April, for example, the *Times* (London), "Geneva the League Capital," 12 April 1919, made no mention of the racial issue at all. In the United States, the best coverage was provided by the *Sacramento Union, San Francisco Chronicle, New York Times,* and *New York Herald,* but even these provided sparse information.

153. See, for example, Britain, PRO/CAB, 29/28/1, British Empire Delegation, "Secret," passim; and United States, Department of State, *Foreign Relations of the United States, Paris Peace Conference,* where the issue is hardly mentioned at all in thirteen volumes of detailed material.

154. See, for example, the personal accounts of Lord Robert Cecil, *A Great Experiment* (New York: Oxford University Press, 1941), where the issue is ignored completely; David Lloyd George, *Memoirs of the Peace Conference,* 2 vols. (New Haven: Yale University Press, 1939), 1:425, where it is mentioned only in passing; and Robert Lansing, *The Peace Negotiations: A Personal Narrative* (Boston: Houghton Mifflin, 1921), pp. 243–44, 255, where it is discussed in passing and even then, only in the context of the Shantung question.

155. Wilson, 8 January 1918, Point V of the Fourteen Points, in United States, Congress, *Congressional Record,* 65th Congress, 2nd Session, vol. 56 (Washington, D.C.: Government Printing Office, 1918), p. 680.

156. Leopold Amery, as cited in Bernard Porter, *The Lion's Share* (London: Longmans, 1975), p. 248.

157. This double standard, naturally enough, produced much cynical comment, as evident in Britain, PRO/FO, 371/3817, Patrick Ramsay's notation on Despatch No. 155 from B. Alston (Tokyo) to Curzon (London), 12 April 1919.

158. Cited in Lloyd C. Gardner et al., *Creation of the American Empire,* 2 vols. (Chicago: Rand McNally, 1976 ed.), 2:341.

159. George Louis Beer, *African Questions at the Paris Peace Conference* (New York: Macmillan, 1923), pp. 9 and 23.

160. Charles L. Mee, Jr., *The End of Order: Versailles 1919* (New York: Dutton, 1980), pp. 66–67; and Miller, *The Drafting of the Covenant* 1:116.

161. Hughes, as cited in Mee, *The End of Order,* p. 66.

162. Cited in Roland Oliver and Anthony Atmore, *Africa Since 1800* (Cambridge: Cambridge University Press, 1981 ed.), p. 161.

163. See the preconference paper entitled "Memorandum on the Formula for 'The Self-Determination of Peoples' and the Moslem World," "Secret," written by Arnold Toynbee, November 1918, in Britain, PRO/FO, 371/4353; and the brief discussion in Porter, *Lion's Share,* p. 249.

164. William Roger Louis, "The United States and the African Peace Settlement of 1919: The Pilgrimage of George Louis Beer," *Journal of African History* 4 (1963):413–33.

165. H.A.L. Fisher, *A History of Europe,* 3 vols. (London: Eyre & Spottiswoode, 1938), 3:1174; and Segal, *The Race War,* p. 58.

166. J.M. Roberts, *History of the World* (New York: Knopf, 1976), p. 820.

167. Robert K.A. Gardiner, "Race and Color in International Relations," in Franklin (ed.), *Color and Race,* p. 20.

168. Porter, *Lion's Share,* pp. 251–52.

169. Du Bois, as cited in Franklin, *From Slavery to Freedom*, p. 355.

170. Program of the Ku Klux Klan, as cited in ibid., p. 356.

171. William Tuttle, Jr., "Views of A Negro During 'The Red Summer' of 1919," *Journal of Negro History* 51 (July 1966):209–18.

172. See United States, Congress, House, Committee on Judiciary, *Anti-Lynching Hearings*, 66th Congress, 2nd Session (Washington, D.C.: Government Printing Office, 1920).

173. Franklin, *From Slavery to Freedom*, p. 357. Also see Woodward, *The Strange Career of Jim Crow*, pp. 100 ff.

174. *Mainichi*, as cited in Britain, PRO/FO, 371/3821, Despatch No. 344 from B. Alston (Tokyo) to Curzon (London), 20 August 1919.

175. *Asahi*, as cited in ibid.

176. *Hochi*, as cited in ibid.

177. Shigenobu Okuma, "Illusions of the White Race," in K.K. Kawakami (ed.), *What Japan Thinks* (New York: Macmillan, 1921), p. 170.

178. Kikujiro Ishii, *Diplomatic Commentaries*, translated by W.R. Langdon (Baltimore: Johns Hopkins University Press, 1936), pp. 270–71.

Chapter 4: From One War to Another

1. Conférence de la Paix, 1919–1920, *Recueil des actes de la Conférence*, "Secret," Partie 4, Commission de la Société des Nations (Paris: Imprimerie nationale, 1922), pp. 89–90, located at the Ministère des Affaires étrangères in Paris.

2. Britain, Public Record Office, Foreign Office [hereafter, PRO/FO], 371/6684, Memorandum entitled "Racial Discrimination and Immigration," "Confidential," 10 October 1921, F 4212/223/23.

3. Ibid., [my emphasis].

4. Ibid., [my emphasis].

5. See Asahi Shimbun, *The Pacific Rivals: A Japanese View of Japanese-American Relations* (New York: Weatherhill/Asahi, 1972), p. 73; and T. Lothrop Stoddard, *The Rising Tide of Color Against White World Supremacy* (New York: Scribners, 1921), p. 43; and W.E.B. Du Bois, "Opinion," *Crisis* 18 (May 1919):8–11.

6. Nobuaki Makino, in Conférence de la Paix, 1919–1920, *Recueil des actes de la Conférence*, "Secret," Partie 3, Séances plenières de la Conférence, p. 118.

7. As cited in Britain, PRO/FO, 371/6684, Memorandum entitled "Racial Discrimination and Immigration," "Confidential," 10 October 1921.

8. Ibid.

9. *Ta Ya*, as cited in Britain, PRO/FO, 371/3823, Despatch No. 553 from Sir J. Jordon (Peking) to Curzon (London), 10 December 1919.

10. Immanuel Geiss, *Panafrikanismus: Zür Geschichte der Dekolonisation* (Frankfurt am Main: Europäische Verlagsanstalt, 1968), pp. 220–27 and 238–41.

11. Cited in Britain, PRO/FO, 371/11700, Memorandum A.D. 35/24, "Secret," from J.G. Fearnley to Naval Secretary (Melbourne), 30 December 1925. Also see "Mr. F.A. Graham to Leave for Orient," *Victoria Daily Colonist*, 27 January 1926.

12. Louis Snyder, *The Idea of Racialism* (Princeton: Van Nostrand, 1962), pp. 300–01.

13. Stoddard, *The Rising Tide of Color*, pp. 183 and 228–29. Also see Robert Ketels, *Espoir en la Formation d'un Parti Raciste* (Brussels: Le Racisme Paneuropéen, 1936).

14. Ramsay MacDonald, 23 March 1925, in Great Britain, House of Commons, *Parliamentary Debates: Official Report* (London: His Majesty's Stationery Office, 1925), 182:78–79.

15. "Le nouveau 'Peril jaune', Conférence de M. Sarraut," *Independance Belge,* 16 February 1925. Also see the articles in *Courrier Saigonnais* and *Courrier d'Haiphong* as enclosed in Britain, PRO/FO, 371/10959.

16. Memorandum A.D. 35/24, "Secret," from J.G. Fearnley to Naval Secretary (Melbourne), 30 December 1925, in Britain, PRO/FO, 371/11700.

17. David Lloyd George, as cited in David Hunter Miller, *The Drafting of the Covenant* (New York: Putnam, 1928), 1:116.

18. France, Ministère des Affaires étrangères, "Les Troupes de Couleur dans l'armée française," *Recueil de documents étrangers* (Paris: Ministère des Affaires étrangères, 1921); France, Commissariat General des Troupes Noires, *La Campagne allemande contre les troupes noires* (Paris: Gauthier-Villars, 1922); and Archives de la Société des nations, Political, 11/19766/4150 and 11/4150/4150 [hereafter cited as Archives de la S.D.N.].

19. See the reports from the Deutscher Volksbund "Rettet die Ehre," to the League of Nations, 21 September 1921, in Archives de la S.D.N., Political, 11/9047/4150; and the *Frankischer Kurier,* 18 and 24 February 1921.

20. Letter from the Deutscher Volksbund "Rettet die Ehre" to the League of Nations, 21 September 1921.

21. Hayford, as cited in Geiss, *Panafrikanismus,* p. 189, whose book contains the best treatment of the Pan-African movement.

22. Second Pan-African Congress, as cited in W.E.B. Du Bois, *The World and Africa* (New York: International Publishers, 1965 ed.), p. 238.

23. W.E.B. Du Bois, *Crisis* (December 1923):53–58.

24. See Geiss, *Panafrikanismus,* pp. 205–19.

25. Marcus Garvey, as cited in Edmund David Cronon, *Black Moses: The Story of Marcus Garvey and the Universal Negro Improvement Association* (Madison: University of Wisconsin Press, 1969), p. 66.

26. Ibid., p. 3.

27. Marcus Garvey, as cited in ibid., p. 39.

28. Peter Abrahams, as cited in Amy Jacques Garvey, *Garvey and Garveyism* (New York: Collier, 1970 ed.), p. 315.

29. See Léopold Senghor, *Négritude et civilization de l'universel* (Paris: Seuil, 1977), pp. 8, 217, 277ff., and 398; and Geiss, *Panafrikanismus,* chapter 15.

30. The journal *Race and Class* devotes its quarterly issues to precisely this relationship.

31. George Padmore, *Pan-Africanism or Communism?* (Garden City: Doubleday, 1971 ed.), pp. 83–84, and 282–83; and Cronon, *Black Moses,* pp. 196–97.

32. Geiss, *Panafrikanismus,* p. 193.

33. Frank Burke, as cited in Cronon, *Black Moses,* p. 99.

34. Geiss, *Panafrikanismus,* p. 194.

35. See ibid., pp. 251ff.; and Edward Wilson, *Russia and Black Africa Before World War II* (New York: Holmes & Meier, 1974), pp. 211ff.

36. Stoddard, *The Rising Tide of Color,* p. 220.

37. Britain, PRO/FO, 371/11700, Letter from Edward O'Donoghue (Victoria, B.C.) to Foreign Office, 28 January 1926.

38. Stoddard, *The Rising Tide of Color,* passim; and Britain, PRO/FO, 371/5367, File 2872/2872/23.

39. David Hellwig, "Black Leaders and U.S. Immigration Policy, 1917–1929," *Journal of Negro History* 66 (Summer 1981):119.

40. See Ronald Segal, *The Race War: The World-Wide Clash of White and Non-White* (New York: Bantam, 1967), pp. 58–59; Richard Gray, *The Two Nations* (New

York: Oxford University Press, 1960), chapter 1; and C. Palley, *The Constitutional History and Law of Southern Rhodesia* (New York: Oxford University Press, 1966).

41. See Britain, PRO/FO, 371/5367, Memorandum entitled "Australian and Canadian Legislation Restricting the Immigration of Japanese," 11 December 1920; and PRO/FO, 371/15520, Despatch No. 58, "Confidential," from T.M. Snow (Tokyo) to A. Henderson, 10 February 1931.

42. Senator David Reed, as cited in "Our New 'Nordic' Immigration Policy," *Literary Digest* 81 (10 May 1924):12.

43. Shigenobu Okuma, as cited in Arthur Brown, *Japan in the World of Today* (New York: Revelle, 1928), p. 207.

44. This ideology is discussed in "Fascism and National Socialism," below.

45. See E. Fournier-Fabre, *Le Choc suprême ou la melée des races* (Paric: Ficker, 1921); Maurice Muret, *Le Crépuscule des nations blanches* (Paris: Payot, 1925): Léon Daudet, *Au temps de Judas* (Paris: Nouvelle librairie nationale, 1920); the various anti-Semitic writings of Charles Maurras and Maurice Barrès; and Ada Martinkus-Zemp, *Le Blanc et le noir* (Paris: Nizet, 1975), for a discussion.

46. Sydney Oliver, *White Capital and Colored Labor* (London: Hogarth Press, 1929 ed.), pp. 19–48; M.F. Lindley, *The Acquisition and Government of Backward Territory* (London: Longman's, 1926); and see Jacques Barzun, *Race: A Study in Superstition* (New York: Harper & Row, 1965 ed.), pp. 184–87.

47. John Higham, *Strangers in the Land* (New Brunswick: Rutgers University Press, 1955), p. 270.

48. Thomas Gossett, *Race: The History of an Idea in America* (Dallas: Southern Methodist University Press, 1963), p. 373.

49. Stoddard, *The Rising Tide of Color*, pp. 201–02 and 307–08; and *The Revolt Against Civilization: The Menace of the Under Man* (New York: Scribner's, 1922), passim. Also see the writings of Madison Grant, Henry Fairfield Osborn, S.J. Holmes, Charles Gould, Kenneth Roberts, and Alfred Wiggam during this period.

50. Alfred Zimmern, *The Third British Empire* (London: Oxford University Press, 1926), p. 81. For a similar contemporary assessment, see Ralph Bunch, *A World View of Race* (Port Washington: Kennikat Press, 1936, 1968 reprint), p. 25.

51. Guiseppe Molta, in Société des nations, *Actes le la première assemblée, Séances plenières* (Geneva: Renaud, 1920), pp. 25–27.

52. Paul Hymans, in ibid., p. 31.

53. Guiseppe Molta, in ibid., p. 29.

54. The words are those of Robert K. Gardiner, "Race and Color in International Relations," in John Hope Franklin (ed.), *Color and Race* (Boston: Houghton Mifflin, 1968), p. 21. This conclusion certainly is confirmed by viewing the photographs in the museum of the Société des nations at the Palais des Nations in Geneva and seeing very few non-white faces.

55. See Société des nations, "Garantie de la Société des nations a l'égard des clauses contenues dans certains traités relatifs aux minorités," *Journal officiel* 8 (November–December 1920):8ff.; Myres McDougal, Harold Lasswell, and Lung-chu Chen, *Human Rights and World Public Order* (New Haven: Yale University Press, 1980), p. 582; Warwick McKean, *Equality and Discrimination Under International Law* (Oxford: Clarendon, 1983), pp. 27–51; and Ali Nusret Sun, "La Discrimination raciale et l'Organisation des Nations Unies" (Paris: unpublished dissertation, 1954), pp. 49–51.

56. Britain, PRO/FO, 371/50843, Memorandum entitled "Minority Protection Under the League of Nations," RRI/101/ii, "Restricted," 2 March 1945. Also see

UN Document E/CN.4/Sub.2/6, "The International Protection of Minorities Under the League of Nations," 7 November 1947.

57. Britain, PRO/FO, 371/50843, Memorandum entitled "Policy with Regard to Protection of Minorities After the Present War," 9 April 1945; and PRO/FO, 371/50843, "Minority Protection Under the League of Nations."

58. Britain, PRO/FO, 371/50843, "Minority Protection Under the League of Nations."

59. James Reed, as cited in Ralph Stone, *The Irreconcilables* (Lexington: University of Kentucky Press, 1970), p. 88.

60. Archives de la S.D.N., General, 40/151/78, "Petition for an Amendment to the League of Nations," 3 July 1919.

61. Archives de la S.D.N., General, 40/1827/1827, letter from the "Alliance Universelle pour Favoriser le Développement des Relations Amicales entre les Nations," 30 October 1919.

62. Archives de la S.D.N., Mandates, 1/15865/13940, letter from W.E.B. Du Bois, 15 September 1921.

63. Archives de la S.D.N., Mandates, 1/37672/21159, letter from Marcus Garvey, 23 May 1923.

64. Archives de la S.D.N., Mandates, 6A/3628/3628, letter from S.M. Miles, 21 December 1935 [written as it appears].

65. Archives de la S.D.N., Mandates, 1/37672/21159, note by A.S., 12 August 1922.

66. Ibid., note from E.H.F. Abraham, 15 June 1922.

67. Archives de la S.D.N., Mandates, 1/37672/21159, letter of Sir Eric Drummond to Marcus Garvey, 20 June 1922; and letter of Sir Eric Drummond to G.O. Marke.

68. See Archives de la S.D.N., Mandates, 6A/7158/7158, passim.

69. Société des nations, *Official Journal* 9 (July 1928):942.

70. Nobuaki Makino, in Conférence de la Paix, 1919–1920, *Recueil des actes de la Conférence*, "Secret," Partie 3, pp. 116–18.

71. See Archives de la S.D.N., General, 40/2427/2427; Mandates, 1/3093/2392; Britain, PRO/FO, 371/35917, Memorandum entitled "The 'White Australia' Policy," dated 19 March 1943; and Masatoshi Matsushita, *Japan in the League of Nations* (New York: Columbia University Press, 1929), pp. 64–76 and 162–66.

72. Mineichiro Adatci, in Société des Nations, *Official Journal, Minutes of the First Committee*, Special Supplement No. 24 (September 1924):80–81.

73. See Archives de la S.D.N., Mandates, 1/15865/13940, letter from W.E.B. Du Bois, 15 September 1921.

74. This is made clear by the archival evidence and the many published reports issued by the Commission permanente des mandates, beginning with C.416.M.296. Also see Bernard Porter, *The Lion's Share* (London: Longmans, 1975), pp. 259–302; and Roland Oliver and A. Atmore, *Africa Since 1800* (Cambridge: Cambridge University Press, 1981), pp. 160–99.

75. The only exception was Iraq.

76. J.S. Smit, in Société des nations, *Official Journal, Records of the Assembly*, Special Supplement No. 64 (September 1928):93.

77. Archives de la S.D.N., Mandates, 1/2444/2444, note by Cecil.

78. Joseph Cook, in Société des nations, *Official Journal, Minutes of the Sixth Committee*, Special Supplement No. 19 (September 1923):15.

79. Henry de Jouvenel, in ibid., p. 20.

80. Société des nations, *Official Journal* (November 1926):1517. Also see F.P. Walters, *A History of the League of Nations*, 2 vols. (London: Oxford University Press, 1952), 1:258 and 396–98.

81. Archives de la S.D.N., Mandates, 6A/3628/3628, letter from S.M. Miles, 21 December 1935.

82. Hugh Tinker, *Race, Conflict, and the International Order* (London: Macmillan, 1977), p. 33.

83. See Geiss, *Panafrikanismus*, p. 254.

84. The words are those of Tinker, *Race, Conflict, and the International Order*, p. 38.

85. See Geiss, *Panafrikanismus*, pp. 265 ff.; Kenneth Little, *Negroes in Britain* (London: K. Paul, Trench, Trubner, 1948); and David Vaughan, *Negro Victory: The Life Story of Dr. Harold Moody* (London: Independent Press, 1950).

86. See George Mosse, *Toward the Final Solution* (New York: Harper & Row, 1978 ed.), p. 191.

87. Juan Linz, "Some Notes Toward a Comparative Study of Fascism in Sociological Historical Perspective," in Walter Laqueur (ed.), *Fascism: A Reader's Guide* (Berkeley: University of California Press, 1978), p. 86.

88. Denis Mack Smith, *Mussolini* (New York: Knopf, 1982), p. 182.

89. "Razza e razzismo," *Il Popolo d'Italia*, 8 September 1934; and Ernst Nolte, *Three Faces of Fascism* (New York: Holt, Rinehart, & Winston, 1966), p. 226.

90. Smith, *Mussolini*, p. 174.

91. See, among other examples, "Situation in Ethiopia: Memorandum by the Italian Government," in Société des nations, *Official Journal* (October 1935):1415.

92. Haile Selassie, in Société des nations, *Official Journal, Records of the Assembly,* Special Supplement No. 151 (June 1936):25. Also see Archives de la S.D.N., Political, 1/15246/15227. For the best discussion about the League of Nations itself, see George Baer, *Test Case: Italy, Ethiopia, and the League of Nations* (Stanford: Hoover Institution Press, 1976).

93. James Dugan and Laurence Lafore, *Days of Emperor and Clown: The Italo-Ethiopian War, 1935–1936* (Garden City: Doubleday, 1973), p. 126.

94. W.D. Hubbard, *Fiasco in Ethiopia* (New York: Harper, 1936), p. 215.

95. Tinker, *Race, Conflict, and the International Order*, p. 41.

96. Vittorio Lanternari, *Movimenti religiosi di liberta e di salvezza dei popoli oppressi* (Milan: Fettrinelli, 1960), pp. 160–67.

97. See Angelo Del Boca, *The Ethiopian War*, translated by P.D. Cummins (Chicago: University of Chicago Press, 1969), p. 38; and Geiss, *Panafrikanismus*, chapter 17.

98. Marcus Garvey, in *Black Man* 1 (October 1935):1.

99. *Gazzetta del Popolo*, as cited in Del Boca, *The Ethiopian War*, pp. 230–31.

100. Angelo Piccioli, *Gli Annali dell'Africa Italiana*, August 1938, as cited in ibid., p. 231.

101. As cited in Antonio Banzi, *Razzismo fascista* (Palermo: Agate, 1939), pp. 226–31. Also see Renzo De Felice, *Mussolini il duce: Lo Stato totalitario, 1936–1940* (Rome: Einaudi, 1981), pp. 102ff.

102. See Pietro de Francisci et al., *Politica fascists della razza* (Rome: Istituo Nazionale di Cultura, 1940); the excellent study by Meir Michaelis, *Mussolini and the Jews* (Oxford: Clarendon, 1978); Andrew Canepa, "Half-Hearted Cynicism," *Patterns of Prejudice* 13 (1979):18–27; and A. James Gregor, *The Ideology of Fascism* (New York: Free Press, 1969), especially pp. 241–82.

103. Galeazzo Ciano, as cited in Gene Bernardini, "The Origins and Development of Racial Anti-Semitism in Fascist Italy," *Journal of Modern History* 49 (September 1977):448.

104. The words are those of Ronald Sanders, *Lost Tribes and Promised Lands* (Boston: Little, Brown, 1978), p. 378.

105. See Chapters 1 and 2; E.J. Young, *Gobineau und der Rassismus: Eine Kritik der anthropologischen Geschichtstheorie* (Meisenheim am Glan: Hain, 1968); and Nolte, *Three Faces of Fascism*, pp. 277–86.

106. Adolf Hitler, *Mein Kampf*, translated by Ralph Manheim (Boston: Houghton Mifflin, 1962 ed.), p. 339.

107. Ibid., pp. 624, 383, 57, 403, and 338.

108. Alfred Rosenberg, *Der Zukunftsweg einer deutschen Aussenpolitik* (Munich: Eher, 1927), pp. 19, 85, and 142.

109. Alfred Rosenberg, *Der Mythus des 20. Jahrhunderts* (Munich: Hoheneichen, 1930), passim. Also see Karl Saller, *Die Rassenlehre des Nationalsozialismus* (Darmstadt: Progress-Verlag, 1961).

110. Adolf Hitler to Otto Strasser, 21 May 1930, in Otto Strasser, *Ministersessel oder Revolution?* (Berlin: Verlag der Nationale Sozialist, 1933), pp. 12–14.

111. The details of these policies can be found in Lucy Dawidowicz, *The War Against the Jews* (New York: Holt, Rinehart, & Winston, 1975); and Joseph Tenenbaum, *Race and Reich* (New York: Twayne, 1956).

112. See, for example, "Die unerbittliche Sprache der Zahlen," *Neues Volk* 1 (November 1933):24–25; and various issues of *Der Stürmer* and *Rasse*.

113. Geiss, *Panafrikanismus*, pp. 235–36; and Ernst Presseisen, "Le Racisme et les japonais," *Revue d'histoire de la deuxième guerre mondiale* 13 (July 1963):1–14.

114. Wilhelm Frick, *Die Rassengesetzgebung des Dritten Reiches* (Munich: Eber, 1934), pp. 3–16, reprinting his speech of 15 February 1934. This rare publication is located at the Hoover Institution.

115. Germany, *Reichsgesetzblatt, 1935* (Berlin: Reichsdruckerei, 1935), 1:1142–47.

116. See Presseisen, "Le Racisme et les japonais," pp. 8–9.

117. *Neues Volk*, "Frankreich und die schwarze Gefahr" 2 (1934):7–14; "Wie Rassenfragen entstehen Weiss und Schwarz in Amerika" 4 (1936):9–15; "700 Jahre Rassenkampf" 5 (1937):16–21; "Rassenmischmasch" 5 (1937):22–23; and "Italiens Kolonialreich unter Rassenschuss" 6 (1938):26–31.

118. J.W. White, in Comité Intergouvernmental pour les réfugiés, *Actes du Comité* (Chambery: Imprimerie réunies, 1938), p. 13.

119. This discussion is based upon the very good study by Rita Thalmann and E. Feinermann, *La Nuit de Cristal* (Paris: Laffont, 1972), especially chapter 6.

120. The "Hossbach Memorandum" of 10 November 1937, in United States, Department of State, *Documents on German Foreign Policy, 1918-1945*, Series D (Washington, D.C.: Government Printing Office, 1949ff.), 1:29–39 [hereafter cited as *DGFP*].

121. Hitler, *Mein Kampf*, pp. 286, 651, 654, and 688. Also see Walter Gross, *Der deutsche Rassengedanke und die Welt* (Berlin: Junker & Dunnhaupt, 1939).

122. Adolf Hitler, as cited in Max Domarus (ed.), *Hitler, Reden und Proklamationen*, 2 vols. (Neustadt a.d. Aisch: Schmidt, 1962–63), 2:1058. On this point, also see the excellent discussion in Norman Rich, *Hitler's War Aims: Ideology, the Nazi State, and the Course of Expansion* (New York: Norton, 1973), especially 3–10 and 269n.; Klaus Hildebrand, *Deutsche Aussenpolitik, 1933-1945* (Stuttgart: Kohlhammer, 1971); and Gerhard Weinberg, *The Foreign Policy of Hitler's Germany, 1933-1936* (Chicago: University of Chicago Press, 1970) and *The Foreign Policy of Hitler's Germany, 1937-1939* (Chicago: University of Chicago Press, 1980). For a different point of view, see A.J.P. Taylor, *The Origins of the Second World War* (New York: Fawcett, 1965 ed.).

123. Adolf Hitler, 22 August 1939, in United States, *DGFP* 7:205.

124. Memorandum from Reinhard Heydrich, 21 September 1939, "Secret," Document 3363-PS from the International Military Tribunal at Nuremberg, as reproduced

in United States, War Department, *Nazi Conspiracy and Aggression*, 10 vols. (Washington, D.C.: Government Printing Office, 1946–48), 6:97–101.

125. Memorandum of Conference Between the Führer and Chief OKW on 17 October 1939, "Top Secret," Document 864-PS, in ibid., 3:619–21.

126. Decree of the Führer, 7 October 1939, Document 686-PS, in ibid., pp. 496–98.

127. For more detailed discussion, see Uwe Adam, *Judenpolitik im Dritten Reich* (Dusseldorf: Droste, 1972); Robert Koehl, *RKFDV* (Cambridge, Mass.: Harvard University Press, 1957); Rich, *Hitler's War Aims*, pp. 55–57; Dawidowicz, *The War Against the Jews*; Tenenbaum, *Race and Reich*; and Gerald Fleming, *Hitler and the Final Solution* (Berkeley: University of California Press, 1984).

128. See the stimulating discussion in Rich, *Hitler's War Aims*, pp. 150–51; and Max DuPrel and Willi Janke (eds.), *Die Niederlände im Umbruch der Zeiten* (Wurzburg: Triltsch, 1942).

129. As cited in Dawidowicz, *The War Against the Jews*, p. 361.

130. Arthur Seyss-Inquart, 22 May 1940, Document 2233-PS, International Military Tribunal, *Trial of the Major War Criminals*, 42 vols. (Nuremberg: International Military Tribunal, 1947–49), 29:402 [hereafter cited as *TMWC*].

131. Adolf Hitler, as cited in Gerald Reitlinger, *The House Built On Sand* (New York: Viking, 1960), p. 176.

132. Among many sources, see Hitler, *Mein Kampf*, pp. 654–67; Rosenberg, *Der Zukunftsweg einer deutschen Aussenpolitik*, p. 88; and Franz Halder, *Kriegstagebuch: Tägliche Aufzeichnungen des Chefs des Generalstabes des Heeres, 1939–1942*, Hans-Adolf Jacobsen (ed.), 3 vols. (Stuttgart: Kohlhammer, 1962–64), 2:336–37.

133. See Dawidowicz, *The War Against the Jews*, pp. 119ff.

134. Halder, *Kriegstagebuch* 2:336–37, entry for 30 March 1941; and the Geheime Kommandsache of 13 March 1941, Document 447-PS, International Military Tribunal, *TMWC* 26:53–58.

135. "The Einsatzgruppen Case," in International Military Tribunal, *Trials of War Criminals*, 15 vols. (Washington, D.C.: Government Printing Office, 1946–48), 4:412–13.

136. See *Das Schwarze Korps* 27 (July 1941); various issues of *Volkischer Beobachter* in the summer of 1941; Germany, Schutzstaffel, Rassenamt, *Volker, Volksgruppen und Volksstamme auf dem ehemaligen Gebiet der UdSSR* (Leipzig: Schwarzhaupter, 1942); and Alexander Dallin, *German Rule in Russia, 1941–1945* (London: Macmillan, 1957), pp. 67–70.

137. Germany, Reichsführer der SS, SS-Hauptamt, *Der Untermensch* (Berlin: Norland-Verlag, 1942). This remarkable publication as well as the private correspondence surrounding it is in the Heinrich Himmler Collection, File 286, Hoover Institution Archives.

138. Cited in R. Browne, *Race Relations in International Affairs* (Washington, D.C.: Public Affairs Press, 1961), p. 2.

139. Roy Preiswerk, "Race and Color in International Relations," *The Year Book of World Affairs, 1970* (New York: Praeger, 1970), p. 64n.

140. These are the words of Sir Frederick Maze, as cited in Christopher Thorne, "Racial Aspects of the Far Eastern War of 1941–1945," *Proceedings of the British Academy* 66 (1980):339, whose brilliantly written article provides the best treatment of this important subject.

141. See *Sydney Morning Herald*, 2 January 1942; "The Japanese," *Fortune* 25 (February 1942):53ff.; Christopher Thorne, *Allies of a Kind* (New York: Oxford

University Press, 1979), pp. 5–11 and 167–68; and L. Allen, *Singapore, 1941–1942* (London: Davis-Poynter, 1977), p. 54.

142. *Sydney Morning Herald,* 27 December 1941.

143. Letter from Walter White to Franklin Roosevelt, 4 May 1942, Eleanor Roosevelt Papers, Box 3855, Franklin D. Roosevelt Library, Hyde Park; Britain, PRO/FO, 371/ 27889; and A. Rhodes, *Propaganda: The Art of Persuasion: World War II* (New York: Chelsea House, 1976), pp. 248ff.

144. W.H. Elsbree, *Japan's Role in Southeast Asian Nationalist Movements, 1940–1945* (Cambridge, Mass.: Harvard University Press, 1953), p. 163.

145. The Goho Report, as cited in Thorne, "Racial Aspects of the Far Eastern War," p. 343.

146. As cited in ibid., p. 346.

147. See T.H. Haven, *Valley of Darkness* (New York: Norton, 1978); and S. Ienaga, *Japan's Last War* (Oxford: Oxford University Press, 1979).

148. D.R. Hughes and E. Kallen, *The Anatomy of Racism: The Canadian Dimension* (Montreal: Harvest House, 1974).

149. See United States, Commission on Wartime Relocation and Internment of Civilians, *Personal Justice Denied* (Washington, D.C.: Government Printing Office, 1982), pp. 1–27.

150. As cited in Jacobus tenBroek et al., *Prejudice, War and the Constitution* (Berkeley: University of California Press, 1975), p. 78.

151. Among many studies, see United States, Commission on Wartime Relocation and Internment of Civilians, *Personal Justice Denied*; Carey McWilliams, *Prejudice: Japanese Americans* (Boston: Little, Brown, 1944); Roger Daniels, *Concentration Camps USA* (New York: Holt, Rinehart, & Winston, 1971); Audrie Girdner and Anne Loftis, *The Great Betrayal* (New York: Macmillan, 1969); and Peter Irons, *Justice at War* (New York: Oxford University Press, 1983).

152. J.L. DeWitt, *Final Report: Japanese Evacuation* (Washington, D.C.: Government Printing Office, 1943), p. 34.

153. See Leon Poliakov, *The Aryan Myth: A History of Racist and Nationalist Ideas in Europe* (New York: New American Library, 1977), p. 1.

154. Minutes of the Wannsee Conference, 20 January 1942, "Top Secret," Document NG-2586, in International Military Tribunal, *Trials of War Criminals,* 13:210–17. The program of mass extermination actually began in practice during the summer of 1941.

155. Ibid.

156. Joseph Goebbels, entry of 27 March 1942, *Diaries, 1942–1943,* translated by Louis Lochner (New York: Doubleday, 1948), p. 147.

157. Mosse, *Toward the Final Solution,* p. 231.

158. See Rich, *Hitler's War Aims,* pp. 57 and 249–50.

159. See Germany, Politisches Archiv des Auswärtiges Amt, Abteilung Inland, Inland I Partei, Aktenzeichen 82-35, "Rassenfrage und Rassenfoerderung," Band 6; "Arbeitstagung der Judenreferenten der Deutschen Missionen in Europa," 3–4 April 1944, Document 3319-PS, in International Military Tribunal, *Trial of Major War Criminals,* 42 vols. (Nuremberg: International Military Tribunal, 1947–49), 32:164ff.; Rudolf Hoess, *Kommandant in Auschwitz. Autobiographische Aufzeichnungen* (Stuttgart: Deutsche Verlags, 1958); and Raul Hilberg (ed.), *Documents of Destruction* (Chicago: Quadrangle, 1971).

160. Adolf Hitler, "Mein politisches Testament," on display at the Imperial War Museum, London.

161. "Rede des Reichsführer SS," 4 October 1943, Document 1919-PS, International Military Tribunal, *TMWC* 29:110ff.

162. See Monty Penkower, *The Jews Were Expendable: Free World Diplomacy and the Holocaust* (Urbana: University of Illinois Press, 1983); and Martin Gilbert, *Auschwitz and the Allies* (New York: Holt, Rinehart, & Winston, 1981).

Chapter 5: The Turning Point

1. UNESCO, *Conference for the Establishment of the United Nations Educational, Scientific, and Cultural Organization,* ECO/CONF./29, 16 November 1945, p. 93.

2. Ruth Benedict, *Race and Racism* (London: Routledge, 1942), pp. viii and 141.

3. United States, National Archives and Record Service, Record Group 59, Alger Hiss Files, Box 2, "Official Statements of the United States Relating to the Promotion of the Observance of Basic Human Rights" [hereafter cited as U.S., National Archives].

4. Address of 6 January 1941, *The Public Papers and Addresses of Franklin D. Roosevelt,* 13 vols., Samuel Rosenman (ed.) (New York: Random House, 1938–50), 9:672.

5. See Britain, Public Record Office, Foreign Office [hereafter, PRO/FO], 371/67605, Minute from the Research Department, "Human Rights," 2 June 1947.

6. Britain, PRO/FO, 371/27889, "Advisability on a Statement on Relaxation of Racial Discrimination in Far East," 3–12 March 1941 [my emphasis].

7. Ministry of Information, as cited in Christopher Thorne, *Allies of a Kind* (Oxford: Oxford University Press, 1979), p. 162.

8. Britain, PRO/FO, 371/35917, Note by R. Wiseman, 16 June 1943, on the cover of the memorandum entitled "The 'White Australia' Policy."

9. As cited in Christopher Thorne, "Racial Aspects of the Far Eastern War of 1941–1945," *Proceedings of the British Academy* 66 (1980):357–58.

10. See the discussion in Chapter 4.

11. Joseph Stilwell Diaries, 18 February and 21 February 1942, Hoover Institution Archives.

12. Henry Stimson Diaries, as cited in Thorne, *Allies of a Kind,* p. 6.

13. George Padmore, *Pan-Africanism or Communism?* (New York: Roy, 1956), p. 290.

14. See John Hope Franklin, *From Slavery to Freedom* (New York: Knopf, 1984), pp. 434ff; Walter White, *A Rising Wind* (Garden City: Doubleday, 1945); N.A. Wynn, "The Impact of the Second World War on the American Negro," *Journal of Contemporary History* 6 (1971):42–53; and Richard Dalfiume, *Desegregation of the U.S. Armed Forces* (Columbia: University of Missouri Press, 1969).

15. United Nations Declaration on Jewish Massacres, 17 December 1942, in Great Britain, House of Commons, *Parliamentary Debates: Official Report* (London: His Majesty's Stationery Office, 1942), 385:2083.

16. See "Wartime Proposals for International Action," below.

17. Chaim Weizmann, as cited in Monty Penkower, *The Jews Were Expendable: Free World Diplomacy and the Holocaust* (Urbana: University of Illinois Press, 1983), p. 121.

18. See ibid., pp. 94–95 and 120; and Arthur Morse, *While Six Million Died* (New York: Random House, 1967).

19. "Churchill: 'Great Design in Africa,'" *Times* (London), 11 November 1942.

20. Winston Churchill, as cited in Thorne, *Allies of a Kind,* p. xxiii. Also see Lord Charles Moran, *Winston Churchill* (London: Constable, 1966), pp. 131 and 559.

21. Hugh Tinker, *Race, Conflict, and the International Order* (London: Macmillan, 1977), p. 47.

22. Mark Ethridge, as cited in Franklin, *From Slavery to Freedom*, p. 439.

23. Tinker, *Race, Conflict, and the International Order*, p. 46.

24. Britain, PRO/FO, 371/27889, file F/1899/17/23, "Statement on Relaxation of Racial Discrimination in Far East," and Thorne, *Allies of a Kind*, p. 202.

25. Jan Smuts to M.C. Gillett, 7 June 1942, in J. van der Poel (ed.), *Selections from the Smuts Papers*, 7 vols., (Cambridge: Cambridge University Press, 1973), 6:568.

26. See Thorne, "Racial Aspects of the Far Eastern War," p. 351, based upon Australian archival research.

27. "Dutch Diamonds," *Bombay Chronicle*, 14 February 1942, although his own comments seemed to make the matter worse.

28. Eleanor Roosevelt, as cited in Franklin, *From Slavery to Freedom*, p. 456.

29. As cited in Thorne, *Allies of a Kind*, p. 9.

30. A. Philip Randolph, as cited in Thorne, "Racial Aspects of the Far Eastern War," p. 355. Also see J. Anderson, *A. Philip Randolph* (New York: Harcourt, Brace, Jovanovich, 1973).

31. Walter White to Franklin Roosevelt, 4 May 1942, Eleanor Roosevelt Papers, Box 3855, Franklin D. Roosevelt Library, Hyde Park.

32. See Penkower, *The Jews Were Expendable;* and Morse, *While Six Million Died,* passim.

33. "Korematsu v. United States," *U.S. Supreme Court Reports* 323 (1944):233.

34. See various issues of *Neues Volk* and A. Rhodes, *Propaganda: The Art of Persuasion: World War II* (New York: Chelsea House, 1976), passim; and John Dower, *War Without Mercy: Race and Power in the Pacific* (New York: Pantheon, 1986).

35. Mohandas Gandhi to Franklin Roosevelt, 1 July 1942, in United States, Department of State, *Foreign Relations of the United States, 1942* (Washington, D.C.: Government Printing Office, 1960), 1:677–78 [hereafter cited as *FRUS*].

36. Penkower, *The Jews Were Expendable*, p. 97.

37. Franklin Roosevelt, as cited in Commission to Study the Organization of Peace, *International Safeguard of Human Rights* (New York: Commission to Study the Organization of Peace, 1944), p. 5.

38. Ibid., p. 8.

39. Ibid., p. 21.

40. Ibid., p. 11.

41. Britain, PRO/FO, 371/27889, file F1899/17/23, "Statement on Relaxation of Racial Discrimination in Far East."

42. Duff Cooper, as cited in Thorne, *Allies of a Kind*, p. 58.

43. H.J. van Mook, as cited in Thorne, "Racial Aspects of the Far Eastern War," p. 360.

44. William Phillips to Franklin Roosevelt, 19 April 1943, in United States, Department of State, *FRUS, 1943* 4:217–20.

45. Walter White, as cited in Thorne, "Racial Aspects of the Far Eastern War," pp. 355–56. Also see Walter White to Franklin Roosevelt, 4 May 1942, Eleanor Roosevelt Papers, Box 3855, Franklin D. Roosevelt Library, Hyde Park.

46. United Nations Declaration on Jewish Massacres, 17 December 1942, 385:2083. Also see Penkower, *The Jews Were Expendable*, pp. 87–92.

47. The best discussion can be found in Thorne, "Racial Aspects of the Far Eastern War," passim.

48. Geiss, *Panafrikanismus*, pp. 282–98.

49. Harold Moody, *News Letter* [of the League of Colored Peoples] 10 (June 1944):34–36.

50. See Immanuel Geiss, *Panafrikanismus: Zur Geschichte der Dekolonisation* (Frankfurt am Main: Europäische Verlagsanstalt, 1968), pp. 300–09.

51. Composed of G.H. Hackworth, Hamilton Fish Armstrong, Adolf Berle, Benjamin Cohen, Brooks Emery, James T. Shotwell (who became chairman of the Commission to Study the Organization of Peace). They were assisted by Durward Sandifer, John Halderman, Alice McDiarmid, and Lawrence Preuss.

52. U.S., National Archives, RG 59, Alger Hiss Files, Box 2, Alice McDiarmid, "The Legal Subcommittee," Secret, 22 September 1944.

53. U.S., National Archives, RG 59, Records of Harley A. Notter, Box 75, Advisory Commission on Post-War Foreign Policy, "Bill of Rights. Preliminary Draft," L. Document 2, Confidential, 31 July 1942.

54. Ibid., "Bill of Rights," L. Document 55, Secret, 3 December 1942.

55. Ibid., "Bill of Rights," L. Document 1, Secret, 31 July 1942.

56. Ibid., "Bill of Rights—International Implementation," L. Document 30, Secret, 4 November 1942.

57. Ibid.

58. Ibid.

59. U.S., National Archives, RG 59, Records of Harley A. Notter, Box 215, Advisory Commission on Post-War Foreign Policy, Alice McDiarmid, "Draft Commentary, First Revision" (discussing article 9, Human Rights).

60. See the report entitled "Japan and the Issue of Racial Equality at Paris," dated 3 February 1943 and sent to the Foreign Office by W.J. Gallman of the U.S. Embassy in London on 3 November 1943, in Britain, PRO/FO, 371/35949.

61. Wei Tao Ming to Cordell Hull, 3 June 1944 (transmitting text of the letter from Chiang K'ai-shek to Franklin Roosevelt), in United States, Department of State, *FRUS, 1944* 1:640.

62. "Tentative Chinese Proposals for a General International Organization," 23 August 1944, in ibid., 1:718.

63. "Race and Equality in the Peace," *Crisis* (October 1944).

64. Britain, PRO/FO, 371/40708, "Chinese Government's Memorandum on International Organization," Dr. Kung to Sir Alexander Cadogan at Dumbarton Oaks, Top Secret, 22 August 1944.

65. See extracts from the personal diary of Under Secretary of State Edward Stettinius, 29 August 1944, in United States, Department of State, *FRUS, 1944* 1:750.

66. Chinese representatives were not invited to this first phase due to the Soviets' desire not to jeopardize their position in the Far East with Japan but generally were kept informed of the meetings. See Joseph C. Grew Papers, MS Am 1687.3, Folders 118–20, Houghton Library, Harvard University.

67. On this unexplained shift, see Ruth Russell, *A History of the United Nations Charter* (Washington, D.C.: Brookings Institution, 1958), p. 329.

68. Memorandum from Edward Stettinius to Cordell Hull, "Progress Report on Dumbarton Oaks Conversations—Eighteenth Day," 9 September 1944, in U.S., Department of State, *FRUS, 1944* 1:789.

69. Ibid. Also see pp. 797 and 825.

70. Britain, PRO/FO, 371/40716, Telegram No. 5318 from Lord Halifax (Washington) to Foreign Office with addition from Alexander Cadogan, 29 September 1944. A letter, WR.208/126, "Secret and Immediate," from the Dominion Office on the following day warned the Foreign Office that this matter was obviously "of considerable importance" to the dominions.

71. As discussed above.

72. Plenary Record 3, Informal Record, Secret, 3 October 1944, File of Wellington Koo, "Washington, D.C. Conversations on International Organization" (on microfilm at Columbia University Law Library, New York).

73. Extract from the diary of Edward Stettinius, 27 September 1944, in U.S., Department of State, *FRUS, 1944* 1:890.

74. "Proposals for the Establishment of a General International Organization," in ibid.

75. Ibid., p. 998.

76. Joint Formulation Group, Record 3, Secret, 6 October 1944, File of Wellington Koo, "Washington, D.C. Conversations on International Organization" (on microfilm at Columbia University Law Library, New York).

77. Ernest Johnson, "A Voice at the Peace Table?" *Crisis* (November 1944):345.

78. Jan Smuts, Verbatim Minutes of the Sixth Plenary Session, 1 May 1945, in United Nations Information Organization, *Documents of the United Nations Conference on International Organization, San Francisco, 1945*, 22 vols. (London and New York: United Nations Conference on International Organization, 1946–55), 1:420–21 [hereafter cited as UNIO, *Documents*].

79. Harry Truman, Verbatim Minutes of the Opening Session, 25 April 1945, in ibid., pp. 113–15.

80. Jan Smuts, Verbatim Minutes of the Sixth Plenary Session, 1 May 1945, in ibid., p. 425.

81. Francis Forde, Verbatim Minutes of the Second Plenary Session, 27 April 1945, in ibid., p. 172.

82. Ramaswami Mudaliar, Verbatim Minutes of the Third Plenary Session, 28 April 1945, in ibid., p. 245.

83. See Britain, PRO/FO, 371/45016; and Russell, *History of the United Nations Charter*, pp. 568–69. This, in turn, had emerged from the Eighth International Conference of American States on 23 December 1938, as indicated by UN Document E/CN.4/Sub.2/3, "Constitutions, Declaration, and Other Instruments of International Organizations and Conferences Relating to the Prevention of Discrimination and Protection of Minorities," 8 October 1947.

84. Minutes of the Fifth Meeting of the U.S. Delegation, 9 April 1945, in U.S., Department of State, *FRUS, 1945* 1:223.

85. Minutes of the Sixth Meeting of the U.S. Delegation, 10 April 1945, in ibid., p. 228.

86. Britain, PRO/FO, 371/46324, Cecil Day (War Cabinet Office) to Sterndale Bennett (Foreign Office), Confidential, 17 February 1945, discussing a personal letter received from the permanent secretary of the New Zealand Department of External Affairs.

87. Comments of G.F. Hudson, 19 March 1945 in ibid.

88. Ibid.

89. W.E.B. Du Bois, *Color and Democracy* (New York: Harcourt, Brace, 1945), pp. 103 and 143.

90. Edward Stettinius, Verbatim Minutes of the First Plenary Session, 26 April 1945, in UNIO, *Documents* 1:126.

91. José Serrato, Verbatim Minutes of the Fourth Plenary Session, 28 April 1945, in ibid., p. 299.

92. See UNIO, *Documents* 3:34, 175, 269, 448, 453, 500, 527.

93. Britain, PRO/FO, 371/50703, handwritten comment in "Memorandum for Submission to His Majesty's Government for Their Consideration in View of the

San Francisco Conference," 12 April 1945. The backers included the Archbishop of Canterbury, the Archbishop of Westminster, the Chief Rabbi, and the Moderator of the Church of Scotland, among others.

94. Ibid.

95. Minutes of the Twenty-Sixth Meeting of the U.S. Delegation, 2 May 1945, in U.S., Department of State, *FRUS, 1945* 1:532. Among the consultants were Frederick Nolde of the Federal Council of Churches and Joseph Proskauer of the American Jewish Committee.

96. Edgar Brown, as cited in "Prominent Negroes to Speak," *San Francisco Chronicle*, 4 May 1945.

97. Mary McLeod Bethune, as cited in "Two Noted Negroes Here Seek a World Without Bias," ibid., 1 May 1945.

98. Franklin, *From Slavery to Freedom*, p. 458.

99. "A Declaration to the Nations of the World," issued by the Non-European United Committee, Cape Town, South Africa, 1945, as cited in W.E.B. Du Bois, *The World and Africa* (New York: International Publishers, 1965 ed.), pp. 39–41.

100. "Suggestions Presented by the Government of India for the Amendment of the Dumbarton Oaks Proposals," Document 2, G/14(h), 4 May 1945, in UNIO, *Documents* 3:527.

101. "Proposed Amendments . . . by the Philippine Delegation," Document 2, G/14(k), 5 May 1945, in ibid., p. 535.

102. Ibid., pp. 93–99.

103. See U.S., National Archives, RG 59, Box 2259, 501.BD Human Rights/11-1349, UNCIO CONS, Secret, Meeting 1, 2 May 1945.

104. "Review of Amendments to Dumbarton Oaks Proposals as Suggested by the Soviet Delegation," in U.S., Department of State, *FRUS, 1945*, 1:546, statement by Leo Pasvolsky. The formal amendment by the United States, China, Britain, and the Soviet Union supporting these principles came after these other proposed amendments and not before.

105. "Summary Report of the Sixth Meeting of Committee II/4," Document 404, II/4/17, 18 May 1945, in UNIO, *Documents* 10:453.

106. "Summary Report of the Eleventh Meeting of Committee II/4," Document 712, II/4/30, 31 May 1945, in ibid., p. 497.

107. "Verbatim Minutes of the Third Meeting of Commission II," Document 1144, II/16, 21 June 1945, in ibid., 8:134.

108. Ibid., pp. 138–39.

109. Russell, *History of the United Nations Charter*, p. 6.

110. See Commission to Study the Organization of Peace, *The United Nations and Human Rights* (Dobbs Ferry, N.Y.: Oceana Publications, 1968), pp. 2–3 and 43–44.

111. UNIO, *Documents* 5:311 and 17:230–31; and Russell, *History of the United Nations Charter*, pp. 806–07.

112. United Nations Charter, Preamble.

113. See U.S., Department of State, *The United Nations Conference on International Organization* (Washington, D.C.: Government Printing Office, 1946), pp. 93 and 202; and Russell, *History of the United Nations Charter*, p. 780.

114. United Nations Charter, Articles 55 and 56.

115. Document 2 6/7(h)(1), 4 May 1945, in UNIO, *Documents* 3:280.

116. Philip Jessup, as cited in Commission to Study the Organization of Peace, *International Safeguard of Human Rights*, p. 16.

117. Ibid., pp. 23–24.

118. "Statement of the Uruguayan Delegation," Document 995, I/1/41, 15 June 1945, in UNIO, *Documents* 6:627.

119. Minutes of the Fifty-First Meeting of the U.S. Delegation, 23 May 1945, in U.S., Department of State, *FRUS, 1945* 1:853–54.

120. Britain, PRO/FO, 371/46324, "World Organization: Racial Equality and Domestic Jurisdiction," 8 June 1945.

121. Ibid.

122. United Nations Charter, Article 2, paragraph 7. For a discussion of this clause in its wider context, see Russell, *History of the United Nations Charter,* pp. 900–10.

123. Minutes of the Fifty-First Meeting of the U.S. Delegation, 23 May 1945, in U.S., Department of State, *FRUS, 1945* 1:854.

124. See Verbatim Minutes of the Closing Plenary Session, 26 June 1945, in UNIO, *Documents* 1:688ff.

125. See Britain, PRO/FO, 371/40843.

126. United States, Congress, Senate, Committee on Foreign Relations, Discussion of 10 July 1945, in *The Charter of the United Nations: Hearings Before the Committee on Foreign Relations,* 79th Congress, 1st Session (Washington, D.C.: Government Printing Office, 1945), p. 311. This also should be seen in the context of the racial discussion in Congress relating to the Fair Employment Practices Commission, as evidenced in United States, Congress, *Congressional Record,* 79th Congress, 1st Session (Washington, D.C.: Government Printing Office, 1945), 91, pt. 5:6803–23, 6886–906, and 6991–7005.

127. Statement of W.E.B. Du Bois, 11 July 1945, Senate Committee on Foreign Relations, *The Charter of the United Nations: Hearings,* p. 392.

128. Lord Halifax, Verbatim Minutes of the Closing Plenary Session, 26 June 1945, in UNIO, *Documents* 1:698.

129. Jan Smuts, in ibid., p. 710.

130. Harry S. Truman, in ibid., pp. 715–16.

131. Lord Halifax, in ibid., p. 698.

132. See Hersch Lauterpacht, *International Law and Human Rights* (New York: Garland, 1973), passim.

133. "Draft Report of the Rapporteur of Committee II/4," Document 1091, II/4/44, Annex B, 19 June 1945, in UNIO, *Documents* 10:586.

134. Lauterpacht, *International Law and Human Rights,* pp. 3–47 and 145–65.

135. Mr. Alfaro, in United Nations, *Journal of the United Nations,* no. 54, Supplement A-A/P.V./50, 9 December 1946, p. 368.

136. See "Re Drummond Wren," *Ontario Reports* 4 (1945):778.

137. See Bert Lockwood, Jr., "The United Nations Charter and United States Civil Rights Litigation, 1946–1955," *Iowa Law Review* 69 (May 1984):901–56; and "The Impact of the Cold War," in Chapter 6.

138. Pertinax, "France Joining Big Four Envisaged," *New York Times,* 21 March 1945.

139. See Russell, *History of the United Nations Charter,* pp. 84–91 and 808–42.

140. United Nations Charter, Articles 73 through 91; Norman Bentwich and Andrew Martin, *A Commentary on the Charter of the United Nations* (London: Routledge & Kegan, 1950), pp. 141–62; and Russell, *A History of the United Nations Charter,* pp. 808ff.

141. See Chapter 7.

142. Ndabaningi Sithole, *African Nationalism* (London: Oxford University Press, 1959), p. 23.

143. See James Hooker, *Black Revolutionary: George Padmore's Path from Communism to Pan-Africanism* (London: Pall Mall, 1967), pp. 89ff.

144. George Padmore to W.E.B. Du Bois, 17 August 1945, as cited in Geiss, *Panafrikanismus*, p. 448.

145. The best discussions can be found in George Padmore, *Pan-Africanism or Communism? The Coming Struggle for Africa* (New York: Roy, 1956); Hooker, *Black Revolutionary*; and Geiss, *Panafrikanismus*, chapter 19.

146. Gershon Ashie-Nikoi, as cited in Du Bois, *The World and Africa*, p. 245.

147. Padmore, *Pan-Africanism or Communism?* p. 144.

148. See Kwane Nkrumah, *Towards Colonial Freedom* (London: Panaf, 1973 ed.), pp. 44–45; and Geiss, *Panafrikanismus*, pp. 450ff.

149. Theodore Bilbo, as cited in Ronald Segal, *The Race War* (New York: Bantam: 1967), p. 229.

150. See the discussion above in "The War as a Mirror."

151. "Treatment of Negroes a Blot on U.S.," *Sunday Standard* (Bombay), 8 July 1945; and "Shameful Act," *Morning Standard* (Bombay), 16 October 1945.

152. U.S., National Archives, RG 59, Box 4650, 811.4016/7-1145, Despatch No. 2169 from Howard Donovan (Bombay) to Secretary of State, Confidential, 11 July 1945.

153. This issue is discussed in more detail in Chapter 6.

154. I can find no concrete evidence that racial prejudice played any role in this military decision. Until such evidence is found, the subject will remain one of speculation. See the discussion in Thorne, *Allies of a Kind*, pp. 533–34; and Tinker, *Race, Conflict, and the International Order*, p. 51.

155. Mackenzie King, as cited in "Candid Diaries of Mackenzie King," *Times* (London), 3 January 1976.

156. See Penkower, *The Jews Were Expendable*, pp. 289–302; International Military Tribunal, *Trial of Major War Criminals*, 42 vols. (Nuremberg: International Military Tribunal, 1947–49); and United States, War Department, *Nazi Conspiracy and Aggression*, 10 vols. (Washington, D.C.: Government Printing Office, 1946–48).

157. The words are those of United States, Congress, House, Subcommittee on International Organizations, *Human Rights in the International Community and U.S. Foreign Policy, 1945–76* (Washington, D.C.: Government Printing Office, 1977), p. 1.

Chapter 6: Making a New Beginning

1. United Nations, General Assembly, *Official Records, Plenary Meetings of the General Assembly, Verbatim Record, 23 October–16 December 1946* (Flushing Meadow: United Nations, 1947), pp. 953ff. [hereafter cited as UN/GA].

2. Emile Saint-Lot, 9 November 1946, in ibid., pp. 958–59.

3. M.C. Chagla, 19 November 1946, in ibid., p. 973.

4. See Document A/149, "Treatment of Indians in the Union of South Africa: Text of Letter from Indian Delegation Requesting the Inclusion of an Item on the Agenda," 22 June 1946, in UN/GA, *Official Records, Joint Committee of the First and Sixth Committees, Summary Record of Meetings, 21–30 November 1946* (Lake Success: United Nations, 1946), pp. 52ff.

5. Vijaya Lakshmi Pandit, 25 October 1946, in UN/GA, *Official Records, Plenary Meetings, 1946*, pp. 731–33.

6. Vijaya Lakshmi Pandit, 21 November 1946, in UN/GA, *Official Records, Joint Committee of the First and Sixth Committees, Summary Record*, pp. 1–3.

7. Jan Smuts, 21 November 1946, in ibid., pp. 3–4.

8. Wellington Koo, 21 November 1946, in ibid., p. 7.

9. See the entire debate in ibid.

10. Vijaya Lakshmi Pandit, 7 December 1946, in UN/GA, *Official Records, Plenary Meetings, 1946*, pp. 1016–19.

11. Don Rafael de la Colina and Carlos Romulo, 8 December 1946, in ibid., pp. 1025 and 1028–29.

12. Jozef Winiewicz, 8 December 1946, in ibid., pp. 1039–40.

13. Ricardo Alfaro, 8 December 1946, in ibid., pp. 1026–27.

14. Jan Smuts, 7 December 1946, in ibid., p. 1009.

15. Hartley Shawcross, 8 December 1946, in ibid., pp. 1033–58.

16. Paul-Henri Spaak, 8 December 1946, in ibid., pp. 1051 and 1058.

17. Resolution 44 (I), "Treatment of Indians in the Union of South Africa," 8 December 1946, in UN/GA, *Official Records, Resolutions, 1946* (Lake Success: United Nations, 1947), p. 69.

18. See Hugh Tinker, *Race, Conflict, and the International Order* (London: Macmillan, 1977), p. 111.

19. *Crisis*, as cited in John Hope Franklin, *From Freedom to Slavery* (New York: Knopf, 1974 ed.), p. 460.

20. Walter White to Eleanor Roosevelt, 20 October 1947, in Eleanor Roosevelt Papers, Box 3766, Franklin D. Roosevelt Library, Hyde Park.

21. Copies of this lengthy petition can be found in the W.E.B. Du Bois Papers, Reel 86, Petitions, frames 1490–1545, Manuscript Division, Library of Congress; or in the Eleanor Roosevelt Papers, Box 3766, Franklin D. Roosevelt Library, Hyde Park.

22. "Statement of Dr. W.E.B. Du Bois to the Representatives of the Human Rights Commission and Its Parent Bodies, the Economic and Social Council and General Assembly," 23 October 1947, in the Du Bois Papers, Reel 60, Correspondence, frame 1079, Library of Congress.

23. See the report entitled "Press Reaction to the N.A.A.C.P. United Nations Petition," in the Du Bois Papers, Reel 60, Correspondence, frames 788ff., Library of Congress; U.S., National Archives, Record Group 59, Box 4651; and "Discrimination Against Negroes," *Free Press Journal* (Bombay), 28 October 1947; among many other examples.

24. H.H. Smythe to Cedric Dover, 3 November 1947, in the Du Bois Papers, Reel 60, Correspondence, frame 787, Library of Congress.

25. See "Preventing and Punishing Genocide," below.

26. Report by H.H. Smythe of the N.A.A.C.P. entitled "Afro-Americans Petitioning the United Nations for Equal Rights," in the Du Bois Papers, Reel 60, Correspondence, frames 708–09, Library of Congress.

27. Walter White to Eleanor Roosevelt, 25 October 1947, in Eleanor Roosevelt Papers, Box 3766, Franklin D. Roosevelt Library, Hyde Park.

28. See "Final Draft of a Commentary," in the Ernst Hamburger Papers, Box 6, Leo Baeck Institute, for a background discussion. Article 68 of the Charter empowered ECOSOC to create such a commission.

29. The words are those of the first director of the Division of Human Rights, John P. Humphrey, in his book entitled *Human Rights and the United Nations: A Great Adventure* (Dobbs Ferry: Transnational, 1983), p. 4.

30. See U.S., National Archives, RG 59, Boxes 2257 and 2258.

31. See Philip C. Jessup, "A Good Start," and Nathaniel Peffer, "A Too Remote Goal," both in *Commentary* (January 1946):56–59; and O. Frederick Nolde, "Possible Functions of the Commission on Human Rights," *Annals of the American Academy*

of Political and Social Science 243 (January 1946):144–49, among others in the same issue.

32. States represented were Norway, France, Belgium, Peru, India, China, the Soviet Union, Yugoslavia, and the United States.

33. Britain, Public Record Office, Foreign Office [hereafter, PRO/FO], 371/57317, "Commission on Human Rights," A.C.U. (46) 98, 25 March 1946.

34. Britain, PRO/FO, 371/57317, "Record of Meeting," A.C.U. (46) 125, 17 April 1946.

35. Henri Laugier, 29 April 1946, in his first speech to the nuclear commission, as cited in Britain, PRO/FO, 371/57318.

36. Eleanor Roosevelt, 2 May 1946, in UN Document E/HR/10, 6 May 1946.

37. See UN Document E/38, "Report of the Commission on Human Rights."

38. Britain, PRO/FO, 371/59739, memorandum from Berkeley, 15 June 1946.

39. Britain, PRO/FO, 371/57318, Telegram No. 599 from Ward to Cadogan, 14 June 1946, and Telegram No. 616 from Foreign Office to UN Delegation, 16 June 1946.

40. See Nikolai Feonov, in UN/ECOSOC, *Official Records, 1946* (New York: United Nations, 1946), pp. 35ff.

41. Resolution 2/9, "Commission on Human Rights," adopted 21 June 1946, in ibid., pp. 400–02.

42. UN Document E/259, "Report to the Economic and Social Council on the First Session of the Commission."

43. See the discussion in "Wartime Proposals for International Action," in Chapter 5.

44. Harry Truman, 26 June 1945, Verbatim Minutes of the Closing Plenary Session, in United Nations Information Organization, *Documents of the United Nations Conference on International Organization, San Francisco, 1945*, 22 vols. (London and New York: United Nations Conference on International Organization, 1946–55), 1:715–16.

45. See René Cassin, *La Pensée et l'action* (Paris: Lalou, 1972), pp. 103ff.; Britain, PRO/FO, 371/50716, Calder to Law, 16 May 1945; Ernst Hamburger Papers, Box 6, "Final Draft of a Commentary to the Universal Declaration of Human Rights," Leo Baeck Institute, New York; and Ministers of Foreign Affairs of the American Republics, Emergency Advisory Committee for Political Defense, "A Study of Conditions Necessary to Assure Political Defense," Third Annual Report, 2 January 1947.

46. Humphrey, *Human Rights and the United Nations*, p. 36. Also see Cassin, *La Pensée et l'action*, pp. 108–12.

47. On this point, see the excellent book by Howard Tolley, Jr., *The UN Commission on Human Rights* (Boulder, Colo.: Westview Press, 1987), p. 21.

48. Eleanor Roosevelt, "Statement Regarding Order of Work," a copy of which is enclosed in Britain, PRO/FO, 371/67606.

49. Britain, PRO/FO, 371/67606, letter from Geoffrey Wilson to Paul Gore-Booth, 19 June 1947.

50. V. Koretsky, as cited in Humphrey, *Human Rights and the United Nations*, p. 40. Also see U.S., National Archives, RG 59, Box 2256, 501.BD Human Rights/6-2147, Telegram 7594 from W. Austin to Department of State, Restricted, 21 June 1947.

51. Humphrey, *Human Rights and the United Nations*, p. 46. Also see Britain, PRO/FO, 371/67606, G. Wilson to W. Beckett, 21 July 1947, "Draft Written Statement."

52. See the discussion above in "The United Nations as the Forum and Focal Point."

53. See, among many others, France, Assemblée nationale, Chambre, *Rapport fait au nom de la commission des affaires étrangères, 26 February 1948* (Paris: Imprimerie nationale, 1948) at the Ministère des Affaires étrangères; Britain, PRO/FO, 371/72800, Telegram No. 514 from A. Cadogan to Foreign Office, 14 February 1948, and 371/72803, Letter No. U.2410/62, "The International Political Situation," from R.E. Ormerod to E.B. Boothby, 7 April 1948; U.S., National Archives, RG 59, Box 2256, 501.BD Human Rights/7-147, Memorandum of 1 July 1947 from Fahy and Rusk to Lovett; UN Document E/CN.4/Sub.2/7, "Draft Articles," 29 October 1947; and UN Document E/600, "Report of the Commission on Human Rights," 17 December 1947.

54. These words are from U.S., National Archives, RG 59, Box 2257, 501.BD Human Rights/3-348, letter from John Lockwood to James Hendrick, 3 March 1948; and Britain, PRO/FO, 371/67610, minute from W.E. Beckett to P.H. Gore-Booth, 9 December 1947.

55. The extensive work of the Working Party on Human Rights in London can be found in Britain, PRO/FO, 371/72800–07; and that of the Interdepartmental Committee on International Social Policy (ISP) and its Subcommittee on Human Rights in Washington within the files of U.S., National Archives, RG 59, 501.BD Human Rights, especially 4-347.

56. Humphrey, *Human Rights and the United Nations,* p. 63; and Cassin, *La Pensée et l'action,* pp. 112ff.

57. Britain, PRO/FO, 371/72806, Telegram No. 1523, from G. Wilson to Foreign Office, 18 May 1948.

58. For a detailed discussion of the relationship between nazism and particular articles in the Declaration, see United Nations, Sub-Commission on Prevention of Discrimination, Hernan Santa Cruz (rapporteur), UN Document E/CN.4/Sub.2/307/Rev.1, *Racial Discrimination,* pp. 252–66.

59. See "Preventing and Punishing Genocide," below.

60. Resolution 217 A (III), "Universal Declaration of Human Rights," 10 December 1948, in UN/GA, *Official Records, Resolutions, 1948,* pp. 171–77.

61. Cassin, *La Pensée et l'action,* p. 118.

62. Hernan Santa Cruz and Charles Malik, 9 December 1948, in UN/GA, *Official Records, Plenary Meetings, 1948* (Paris: United Nations, 1949), pp. 857 and 863.

63. Belarmino de Athayde and Mohammed Kahn, 10 December 1948, in ibid., pp. 878 and 890.

64. Eleanor Roosevelt, text of speech, in U.S., National Archives, RG 59, Box 2258, 501.BD Human Rights/12-848, in Telegram 1115 from J.F. Dulles to Department of State, 8 December 1948.

65. Zdenek Augenthaler and L.I. Kaminsky, 10 December 1948, in UN/GA, *Official Records, Plenary Meetings, 1948,* pp. 882 and 896–97.

66. Juliusz Katz-Suchy, 10 December 1948, in ibid., p. 904.

67. Andrei Vyshinsky, 9–10 December 1948, in ibid., pp. 854 and 924–27.

68. *Izvestiia,* 2 July 1949, as enclosed in both Britain, PRO/FO, 371/78949, letter from the British embassy in Moscow to Foreign Office, 5 July 1949; and U.S., National Archives, RG 59, Box 2259, 501.BD Human Rights/7-1249, despatch from U.S. embassy in Moscow to Department of State, 12 July 1949.

69. H.T. Andrews, 10 December 1948, in UN/GA, *Official Records, Plenary Meetings, 1948,* pp. 910–11.

70. See U.S., National Archives, RG 59, Box 2258, 501.BD Human Rights/1-2449 and /9-1448.

71. Britain, PRO/FO, 371/78936, note by W.E. Beckett, 23 July 1949.

72. U.S., National Archives, RG 59, Box 2258, 501.BD Human Rights/3-949; Britain, PRO/FO, 371/67606; Humphrey, *Human Rights and the United Nations*, pp. 46ff; and Walter Laqueur and Barry Rubin (ed.), *The Human Rights Reader* (New York: New American Library, 1979).

73. Frank Holman of the American Bar Association, as cited in "U.S. Delay Urged on U.N. Rights Plan," *New York Times*, 1 February 1949.

74. See Marc Bossuyt, *L'Interdiction de la discrimination dans le droit international des droit de l'homme* (Brussels: Bruylant, 1976), pp. 44–50; Raghubir Chakravarti, *Human Rights and the United Nations* (Calcutta: Progressive Publishers, 1958), pp. 75–78; and Warwick McKean, *Equality and Discrimination Under International Law* (Oxford: Clarendon Press, 1983), pp. 62–71.

75. Humphrey, *Human Rights and the United Nations*, p. 76. Also see the discussion in Albert Verdoodt, *La Naissance et signification de la Déclaration universelle des droits de l'homme* (Louvain: Naumelaerts, 1964); and United Nations, *United Nations Actions in the Field of Human Rights* (New York: United Nations, 1974); and Laqueur and Rubin (eds.), *The Human Rights Reader*, pp. 45–46; Egon Schwelb, *Human Rights and the International Community* (Chicago: Quadrangle Books, 1964), B.G. Ramcharan (ed.), *Human Rights: Thirty Years After the Declaration* (The Hague: Nijhoff, 1979).

76. Humphrey, *Human Rights and the United Nations*, pp. 48–49.

77. UN Document A/BUR/50, "Projet de résolution relatif au crime de genocide." The expression "race murder" is found in Britain, PRO/FO, 371/59795, Telegram No. 1920 from McKinnon Wood to W.E. Beckett, 23 November 1946.

78. Jaromir Spacek, 29 November 1946, in UN/GA, *Official Records, Sixth Committee, Summary Record of Meetings, 1946* (Lake Success: United Nations, 1947), p. 114.

79. Resolution 96 (I), "The Crime of Genocide," 11 December 1946, in UN/GA, *Official Records, Resolutions, 1946*, pp. 188–89.

80. See UN Document E/447, Draft Convention on the Prevention and Punishment of the Crime of Genocide; UN Document E/794, Report of the Ad Hoc Committee on Genocide, 26 May 1948; and UN/GA, *Official Records, Sixth Committee, 1948*, passim.

81. Britain, PRO/FO, 371/67517, Telegram No. 92 from Foreign Office to UK Delegation, "Secret," 18 April 1947.

82. Britain, PRO/FO, 371/67517, note by C.D.W. O'Neill, 29 July 1947. For archival material on the U.S. position, see U.S., National Archives, RG 59, Box 2255.

83. UN/GA, *Official Records, Plenary Meetings, 1948*, pp. 811, 822–23; and Pieter N. Drost, *The Crime of State: Genocide* (Leyden: Sythoff, 1959), p. ii.

84. See Britain, PRO/FO, 371/72693, Telegram No. 675, "Secret," from UK Delegation to Foreign Office, and Letter No. 25102/26/49, "Restricted," from Creech-Jones.

85. Resolution 260 (III), "Prevention and Punishment of the Crime of Genocide," 9 December 1948, in UN/GA, *Official Records, Resolutions, 1948*, pp. 174–78.

86. UN/GA, *Official Records, Plenary Meetings, 1948*, pp. 821, 834, and 844.

87. E.V. Evatt, 9 December 1948, in ibid., pp. 851–52.

88. Drost, *The Crime of State: Genocide*, pp. 119ff.; and Britain, PRO/FO, 371/78848, "The Genocide Convention," 2 March 1949, by J.L. Brierly.

89. See the debates in UN/GA, *Official Records, Plenary Meetings, 1948*, pp. 829ff.

90. The treaty entered into force in January 1951 without United States ratification. See "Convention pour la Prévention et la répression du crime de genocide," in UN, *Treaty Series* 78 (1951): 279ff.; Nehemiah Robinson, *The Genocide Covention: A*

Commentary (New York: Institute of Jewish Affairs, 1960); and UN Document E/ CN.4/Sub.2/80, "Contribution of the Convention," 7 December 1949.

91. See "Speeches and Majority Votes"—or "Iron and Blood"? in Chapter 9.

92. Winston Churchill, as cited in Herbert Feis, *From Trust to Terror* (New York: Norton, 1970), pp. 77–78. For the best discussion of the larger diplomatic context, see John Lewis Gaddis, *The United States and the Origins of the Cold War* (New York: Columbia University Press, 1972).

93. Joseph Stalin, as cited in ibid., p. 79.

94. Harry Truman, as cited in the *New York Times*, 13 March 1947.

95. See B. Ponomaryov, A. Gromyko, and V. Khvostov, *History of Soviet Foreign Policy, 1945–1970* (Moscow: Progress Publishers, 1974), pp. 158–59.

96. "Byrnes and the Balkans," *Crisis* (December 1945): 345.

97. *Unita*, 15 March 1946, enclosed in U.S., National Archives, RG 59, Box 4650, 811.4016/3-1846.

98. See *La Prensa*, 27 July 1946; *Epoca*, 14 March 1946; *Al Yaqdha*, 5 June 1946; and *Manchester Guardian*, 21 June 1946; among others, all assembled at the time by the Department of State in ibid., Box 4650.

99. "Off My Chest," *Bombay Chronicle*, 18 June 1946; and "American Race Prejudice," *Bombay Sentinel*, 18 June 1946.

100. *Trud*, 23 August 1946, as enclosed in U.S., National Archives, RG 59, Box 4650, 811.4016/8-2646, Despatch No. 355, Restricted, from Crawford to Secretary of State, 26 August 1946.

101. *Pravda*, 17 November 1946. Also see *Izvestiia*, 11 October 1946.

102. U.S., National Archives, RG 59, Box 4650, 811.4016/11-2046, Telegram No. 4180, Restricted, from W.B. Smith to Secretary of State, 20 November 1946.

103. Unfortunately, the impact of this external pressure has often been completely ignored in the study of the history of the U.S. civil rights movement.

104. U.S., National Archives, RG 59, Box 2256, 501.BD Human Rights/4-447, Memorandum from H. Notter to D. Rusk, 1 May 1947.

105. U.S., National Archives, RG 59, Box 2256, 501.BD Human Rights/4-2447, Letter from C. Fahy to Robert Carr, Restricted, 17 June 1947 [my emphasis].

106. U.S., National Archives, RG 59, Box 2256, 501.BD Human Rights/6-547, Memorandum from D. Rusk, 15 July 1947.

107. Letter from G. Marshall to R. Carr, 28 July 1947, in ibid.

108. Hersch Lauterpacht, *International Law and Human Rights* (New York: Garland, 1973), pp. 157–58.

109. United States, President's Committee on Civil Rights, *To Secure These Rights* (Washington, D.C.: Government Printing Office, 1947), pp. 111, 147–48, and 166.

110. See George Padmore, *How Russia Transformed Her Colonial Empire: A Challenge to the Imperialistic Powers* (London: Dobson, 1946); and Chapter 7 below.

111. Jervis Anderson, *A. Philip Randolph* (New York: Harcourt, Brace, Jovanovich, 1973), pp. 274ff.

112. See "The United Nations as the Forum and Focal Point," above, and UN Document E/CN.4/Sub.2/24.

113. "An Appeal to the World: A Statement on the Denial of Human Rights to Minorities in the Case of Citizens of Negro Descent in the United States of America and An Appeal to the United Nations for Redress," p. 20 (referring to Senator Theodore Bilbo and Representative John Rankin from Mississippi), in Eleanor Roosevelt Papers, Box 3766, Franklin D. Roosevelt Library, Hyde Park.

114. *Chicago Defender*, 1 November 1947; *New York World Telegram*, 20 October 1947; *New York Post*, 29 October 1947; among others, all in the Du Bois Papers, Reel 60, Correspondence, frames 787–89, in the Library of Congress.

115. *Morgantown Post*, 15 October 1947, in ibid. Also see U.S., Congress, *Congressional Record*, 80th Congress, 2nd Session (Washington: Government Printing Office, 1948), pp. 4270–71; U.S., National Archives, RG 59, 501.BD Human Rights, Box 2257; and "Second Class Citizens," *New Statesman and Nation* (3 April 1948).

116. See U.S., National Archives, RG 59, Box 2256, Memorandum from H. Notter to D. Rusk, "The Handling of Human Rights," 14 November 1947.

117. U.S., National Archives, RG 59, Box 2256, 501.BD Human Rights/8-1947, Circular Telegram of 19 August 1947, Confidential. Interestingly enough, the British Foreign Office sent out a similar letter, as evident in Britain, PRO/FO, 371/67600 and 67601.

118. U.S., National Archives, RG 59, Box 2256, 501.BD Human Rights/8-2647, Despatch No. 1575, Confidential, from D. Henry to Secretary of State, 26 August 1947.

119. See U.S., National Archives, RG 59, Boxes 2256 and 2257, 501.BD Human Rights, files 8/1947 through 10/2247.

120. U.S., National Archives, RG 59, Box 4651, especially file 811.4016/5-847. Also see the Indian newspapers, "U.N. Secretariat Staff Fear Racial Discrimination," *Morning Standard*, 26 July 1947; and "No Hope," *Free Press Journal*, 26 July 1947.

121. U.S., National Archives, RG 59, Box 4651, 811.4016/1-2248, Despatch No. 24 from P. Jester to Secretary of State, 22 January 1948.

122. See Box 4651 in ibid.

123. Despatch No. 77 from E.T. Smith to Secretary of State, 14 May 1948, in ibid.

124. "Washington's Color Bar," *Ceylon Observer*, 21 May 1949.

125. U.S., Congress, *Congressional Record*, 80th Congress, 2nd Session, pp. 4270–71; and Padmore, *How Russia Transformed Her Colonial Empire*.

126. See Eleanor Roosevelt Papers, Box 3766, in the Franklin D. Roosevelt Library, Hyde Park; and W.E.B. Du Bois Papers, Reel 60, Correspondence, letter from Du Bois to Eleanor Roosevelt, 14 October 1947, frame 809, in the Library of Congress.

127. See U.S., National Archives, RG 59, Box 2257, 501.BD Human Rights, various items; and her own comments as described in a memorandum from Du Bois to Walter White entitled "Meeting with Mrs. Eleanor Roosevelt," 1 July 1948, in Eleanor Roosevelt Papers, Box 3766, in the Franklin D. Roosevelt Library, Hyde Park.

128. Memorandum from Du Bois to Walter White, "Meeting with Mrs. Eleanor Roosevelt," 1 July 1948, in ibid.

129. Eleanor Roosevelt, "My Day," 9 February 1948.

130. See letter from Eleanor Roosevelt to Robert Lovett, 16 January 1948, in Eleanor Roosevelt Papers, Box 3762, in the Franklin D. Roosevelt Library, Hyde Park.

131. Humphrey, *Human Rights and the United Nations*, p. 5.

132. See Joseph Lash, *Eleanor: The Years Alone* (New York: New American Library, 1973), p. 99; and G. Petrov, "The Unbecoming Role of Eleanor Roosevelt," *Literary Gazette* 85 (23 October 1948), as enclosed in U.S., National Archives, RG 59, Box 2258, 501.BD Human Rights/11-548.

133. This is most evident in her famous "Struggle for Human Rights" speech delivered in Paris during September 1948, the text of which is in U.S., National Archives, RG 59, Box 2258, 501.BD Human Rights/9-2748.

134. "Oyama v. California," *U.S. Supreme Court Reports* 332 (1948):649–50, 662, and 674; "Shelley v. Kraemer," *U.S. Supreme Court Reports* 334 (1948); Bert Lockwood, Jr., "The United Nations Charter and United States Civil Rights Litigation, 1946–1955," *Iowa Law Review* 69 (May 1984):901–56; and McKean, *Equality and Discrimination Under International Law*, pp. 236–37.

135. U.S., National Archives, RG 59, Box 6, Project No. 121, "Laws and Regulations on Human Rights in the U.S."; and Franklin, *From Slavery to Freedom*, pp. 463–65.

136. Harry Truman, as cited in Barton Bernstein and Allen Matusow (eds.), *The Truman Administration: A Documentary History* (New York: Harper & Row, 1968), p. 114.

137. This is clearly evident when one compares the various draft proposals of resolutions, declarations, and conventions with those eventually adopted in the end. See U.S., National Archives, RG 59, Boxes 2257 and 2258; and Britain, PRO/FO, 371/72800–812.

Chapter 7: The End of Empire

1. On this point, see the excellent study by Hugh Tinker, *Race, Conflict, and the International Order* (London: Macmillan, 1977), p. 61.

2. C.T. Thorne, "External Political Pressures," in Vernon McKay (ed.), *African Diplomacy* (New York: Praeger, 1966), p. 145.

3. United Nations, Office of Public Information, *Yearbook of the United Nations, 1965* (New York: United Nations, 1967), pp. 801–03.

4. "Joint Statement by President Roosevelt and Prime Minister Churchill," 14 August 1941, in U.S., Department of State, *Foreign Relations of the United States* [hereafter, *FRUS*], *1941* 1: 367–68.

5. "Declaration by United Nations," 1 January 1942, in U.S., Department of State, *FRUS, 1942* 1:25–26.

6. See the discussion in "The War as a Mirror" and "The Beginnings with New Questions," in Chapter 5.

7. United Nations Charter, Article 1.

8. Ibid., Article 73. Also see Letter of 28 December 1945 from Walter White to Eleanor Roosevelt in Eleanor Roosevelt Papers, Box 4561, Franklin D. Roosevelt Library, Hyde Park.

9. Francis M. Forde, 21 June 1945, in Document 1144, 11/16, United Nations Information Office [hereafter, UNIO], *Documents* 8:135.

10. See Christopher Thorne, "Racial Aspects of the Far Eastern War of 1942–1945," *Proceedings of the British Academy* 66 (1980), pp. 365–67; France, Ministère des Colonies, *Conférence africaine de Brazzaville, 36 janvier–8 février 1944* (Paris: Imprimerie nationale, 1945); and George Padmore, "Anglo-American Plan for Control of Colonies," *Crisis* (November 1945): 355–57.

11. This developed throughout the war, as has been demonstrated so well by Wm. Roger Louis, *Imperialism at Bay: The United States and the Decolonization of the British Empire, 1941–1945* (New York: Oxford University Press, 1978).

12. Raymond Kennedy, "The Colonial Crisis and the Future," in Ralph Linton (ed.), *The Science of Man in the World Crisis* (New York: Columbia University Press, 1945), p. 308.

13. Raghubir Chakravarti, *Human Rights and the United Nations* (Calcutta: Progressive Publishers, 1958), p. 84.

14. Britain, Public Record Office, Foreign Office [hereafter, PRO/FO], 371/78945, Circular Despatch No. 25102/2/49, "Secret," from A. Creech Jones (Colonial Office) to Governors of the Colonies, 28 March 1949.

15. Britain, PRO/FO, 371/78945, letter from Lord Listowel (Colonial Office) to C.P. Mayhew, 8 April 1949.

16. This is evident in file UNE 1837/17314/96, in ibid.

17. Edmund Soper, *Racism: A World Issue* (New York: Negro Universities Press, 1947, 1969 reprint), p. 272.

18. Louis Snyder, *The Idea of Racialism* (Princeton: Van Nostrand, 1962), pp. 300–01.

19. See "The War as a Mirror" and "Wartime Proposals for International Action," in Chapter 5; and John Dower, *War Without Mercy: Race and Power in the Pacific* (New York: Pantheon, 1986).

20. Thorne, "Racial Aspects of the Far Eastern War," pp. 370–71; D.J. Steinberg, *Philippine Collaboration in World War II* (Ann Arbor: University of Michigan Press, 1967); and S.C. Bose, *Testament* (New Delhi: Rajkamal, 1946).

21. S. Sjahrir, *Out of Exile* (New York: Greenwood Press, 1969 reprint), pp. 248–49.

22. Tinker, *Race, Conflict, and the International Order*, pp. 49–50.

23. *Times* (London), "The Need for Stocktaking and Review," 13 March 1942; and "Capital, Labour, and the Colour Bar," 14 March 1942.

24. See Louis, *Imperialism at Bay*, p. 29; and Thorne, "Racial Aspects of the Far Eastern War," p. 373.

25. "The Post-Singapore War in the East," *Washington Post*, 21 February 1942.

26. The process was initially started by the Tydings-McDuffie Act of 1934. For more on this case, see Robert Smith, *Philippine Freedom, 1946–1958* (New York: Columbia University Press, 1958); and G. Grunder and W. Livezey, *The Philippines and the United States* (Norman: University of Oklahoma Press, 1951).

27. The words are those of Wm. Roger Louis, in his excellent book, *The British Empire in the Middle East, 1945–1951* (New York: Clarendon Press of Oxford University Press, 1984), p. 8. For a discussion of Churchill's attitudes, see Louis's *Imperialism at Bay*.

28. Ibid., p. 477. Also see R.J. Moore, *Escape from Empire: The Atlee Government and the Indian Problem* (New York: Clarendon Press of Oxford University Press, 1983); and Hugh Tinker, *Separate and Unequal* (Vancouver: University of British Columbia, 1976).

29. Working Committee Resolution, 7 August 1942, as cited in Thorne, "Racial Aspects of the Far Eastern War," p. 374.

30. See Josef Silverstein, *Burmese Politics: The Dilemma of National Unity* (New Brunswick: Rutgers University Press, 1980).

31. UN Document S/1417, "Commission des Nations Unies pour l'Indonésie: Rapport special au Conseil de sécurité sur la Conférence de la Table ronde," 10 November 1949; UN, Security Council, *Official Records, 1949* (Lake Success: United Nations, 1949), passim; George Kahin, *Nationalism and Revolution in Indonesia* (Ithaca: Cornell University Press, 1952); and Berhard Dahm, *Sukarnos Kampf um Indonesiens Unabhängigkeit* (Frankfurt am Main: Metzner, 1966).

32. Philippe Devillers, *Histoire du Viet-Nam de 1940 à 1952* (Paris: Seuil, 1952); France, Assemblée nationale, Chambre des Deputes, *Débats parlementaires, 1947–1954*, passim; Ho Chi Minh, *Selected Works*, 4 vols. (Hanoi: Foreign Languages Publishing House, 1961–62); and Britain, PRO/FO, 371/79165, Despatch No. 558, "Confidential," from Sir Harvey to C. Atlee, 13 September 1949.

33. Gen. Sir Gerard Templer, as cited in Richard L. Clutterbuck, *The Long, Long War* (New York: Praeger, 1966), p. 3. Also see Edgar O'Ballane, *Malaya: The Communist Insurgent War, 1948–1960* (Camden: Archon, 1966).

34. Bernard Porter, *The Lion's Share* (London: Longmans, 1975), p. 319.

35. Thomas G. Paterson et al., *American Foreign Policy: A History* (Lexington: D.C. Heath, 1977), pp. 525–27, citing the Department of State and Secretary Dean

Acheson. Also see New York Times, *The Pentagon Papers* (New York: Bantam, 1971), p. 14; and for a larger context, John Lewis Gaddis, *Strategies of Containment* (New York: Oxford University Press, 1982).

36. Communist Information Bureau, *For a Lasting Peace, For a People's Democracy,* no. 1 (10 November 1947), p. 2.

37. *Romania Libera,* 14 October 1949. Also see *Izvestiia,* 2 July 1949; U.S., National Archives, RG 59, Box 2259, 501.BD Human Rights/7-1249; Britain, PRO/FO, 371/ 78949; and "The Impact of the Cold War," in Chapter 6.

38. See the Soviet speeches in UN/GA, *Official Records, Plenary Meetings, 1948,* pp. 812–13, 838, 872, and 908–09; and *Official Records, Sixth Committee, Summary Record, 1948,* pp. 748–49, among many others; George Padmore, *Pan-Africanism or Communism?* (New York: Roy, 1956), pp. 268ff; and Fedor Leonidov, *Racism: An Ideological Weapon of Imperialism* (Moscow: Progress Publishers, 1965).

39. The quotation comes from Britain, PRO/FO, 371/78949, Letter 25102/2/49, Secret, from N. Huijsman (Colonial Office), to J.P. Duffy (Foreign Office), 12 October 1949.

40. U.S., National Archives, RG 59, Box 5, Research Project No. 108, "United States Attitude Toward Foreign Control Policies," dated 1949.

41. Memorandum from Walter White to Eleanor Roosevelt, 12 December 1950, in Eleanor Roosevelt Papers, Box 3855, Franklin D. Roosevelt Library, Hyde Park.

42. "Brown v. Board of Education," *U.S. Supreme Court Reports* 347 (1954): 483–96; and C. Vann Woodward, *The Strange Career of Jim Crow* (New York: University Press, 1957), p. 121.

43. John Foster Dulles, "International Unity," in U.S., Department of State, *Department of State Bulletin* 30 (21 June 1954):936.

44. U.S., Congress, Senate, Committee on Foreign Relations, *Nomination of John Foster Dulles, Secretary of State Designate,* 15 January 1953, 83rd Congress, 1st Session (Washington, D.C.: Government Printing Office, 1953), p. 10.

45. U.S., Department of State, *American Foreign Policy, 1950–1955: Basic Documents,* 2 vols. (Washington, D.C.: Government Printing Office, 1957), 2:2366–67, 2371–72, and 2373–80.

46. See "The Impact of the Cold War," in Chapter 6.

47. Paterson, *American Foreign Policy,* pp. 505–06.

48. Léo Hamon, "Non-engagement et neutralisme des nouveaux états," in J.B. Duroselle et J. Meyriat (eds.), *Les nouveaux Etats dans les relations internationales* (Paris: Colin, 1962), pp. 368 ff. Egypt, for example, was particularly inclined to take this point of view.

49. See "Racial Slavery and Separation," in Chapter 1.

50. Nkrumah, *Towards Colonial Freedom* (London: Panaf, 1973 3d.), p. 42.

51. Tinker, *Race, Conflict, and the International Order,* pp. 101–02; and the careful analysis in Louis, *The British Empire in the Middle East,* pp. 128–46.

52. Immanuel Geiss, *Panafrikanismus: Zur Geschichte der Dekolonisation* (Frankfurt am Main: Europäische Verlagsanstalt, 1968), pp. 318–21.

53. Tinker, *Race, Conflict, and the International Order,* pp. 102–03.

54. Jawaharlal Nehru, *India's Foreign Policy: Selected Speeches . . . 1946–1961* (New Delhi: Ministry of Information, 1961), pp. 242ff.

55. The signatories were the United States, Britain, France, Australia, New Zealand, the Philippines, Pakistan, and Thailand.

56. Donald Dozer, *Are We Good Neighbors?* (Gainesville: University of Florida Press, 1959), p. 353.

57. P. Queuille, *Histoire de l'afro-asiatisme jusqu'à Bandoung; la naissance du tiers-monde* (Paris: Payot, 1965).

58. Richard Wright, *The Color Curtain: A Report on the Bandung Conference* (New York: World Publishing, 1956), p. 83.

59. "Bangkok and Bandoeng," *Christian Science Monitor*, 23 January 1955. Also see A. Conte, *Bandoung, tournant de l'histoire* (Paris: Laffont, 1965); George Kahin, *The Asian-African Conference* (Port Washington: Kennikat Press, 1956); and *Times of India*, 19–25 April 1955.

60. Achmed Sukarno, in Republic of Indonesia, *The Asian-African Conference* (New Delhi: Information Service of Indonesia, 1955), pp. 13–18, which provides the official transcripts of the speeches.

61. Carlos Romulo, in ibid., p. 125.

62. Ibid., pp. 126–28.

63. See the fascinating discussion and insight on this point in Wright, *The Color Curtain*, pp. 113–16 and 175–96.

64. Final Communiqué of the Asian-African Conference, 24 April 1955, in Indonesia, *The Asian-African Conference*, pp. 208–15.

65. David Kimche, *The Afro-Asian Movement: Ideology and Foreign Policy of the Third World* (Jerusalem: Israel Universities Press, 1973), p. 80.

66. Léopold Senghor, as cited in Eugene Berg, *Non-alignment et nouvel ordre mondial* (Paris: Presses universitaires de France, 1980), p. 22.

67. Jawaharlal Nehru, as cited in *Times of India*, 25 April 1955. Also see his earlier speech about race, in "Racialism Poses Grave Threat," *Times of India*, 1 April 1955.

68. See W.A.C. Adie, "China, Russia, and the Third World," *China Quarterly* 11 (July–September 1962): 200–13; Bruce Larkin, *China and Africa* (Berkeley: University of California Press, 1971); and the official Soviet version in the chapter entitled "Soviet Assistance to the Independence Struggle of the Peoples of Asia and Africa," in B. Ponomaryov et al., *History of Soviet Foreign Policy* (Moscow: Progress Publishers, 1974), pp. 323–60.

69. "Through Indian Eyes," *Times of India*, 21 April 1955.

70. John Foster Dulles, "The Cost of Peace," U.S. Department of State, *Department of State Bulletin* 34 (18 June 1956): 999–1000.

71. See Kimche, *The Afro-Asian Movement*, pp. 126ff.

72. Oginga Odinga, *Not Yet Uhuru* (New York: Hill & Wang, 1967), p. 30.

73. See A. Césaire, *Cahier d'un retour au pays natal* (Paris: Bordas, 1947); Cheick Anta Diop, *Nations, nègres, et culture* (Paris: Editions africaines, 1955); and L.S. Senghor, *Les Fondements de l'africanité ou Négritude et arabité* (Paris: Présence africaine, 1967).

74. Pierre Boyer de Latour, *Vérités sur l'afrique du nord* (Paris: Plon, 1956); "Evolution de la question tunisienne," *Chronique de politique étrangère* 9 (July 1956): 506–28; and Stephane Bernard, *The Franco-Moroccan Conflict, 1943–1956* (New Haven: Yale University Press, 1968).

75. Kwane Nkrumah, as cited in Geiss, *Panafrikanismus*, pp. 327–28. Also see his own autobiography, Kwane Nkrumah, *Ghana* (New York: International Publishers, 1957); and D.E. Apter, *Ghana in Transition* (Princeton: Princeton University Press, 1963).

76. Cited in Kimche, *The Afro-Asian Movement*, p. 240.

77. W.E.B. DuBois, "Address to the All-African Peoples' Conference," in his book *The World and Africa* (New York: International Publishers, 1965 ed.), p. 310. At the

last moment, ill health prevented him from delivering his address in person, but it was presented by his wife.

78. Colin Legum, *Bandung, Cairo, and Accra* (London: African Bureau, 1958), passim; and Roland Oliver and A. Atmore, *Africa Since 1800* (Cambridge: Cambridge University Press, 1981), pp. 256–57.

79. Charles de Gaulle, as cited in W.W. Kulski, *De Gaulle and the World* (Syracuse: Syracuse University Press, 1966), p. 338.

80. Geiss, *Panafrikanismus*, pp. 328–30.

81. Robert Cornevin, *Histoire de l'afrique: colonisation, décolonisation, indépendance* (Paris: Payot, 1975), passim.

82. Harold Macmillan, 3 February 1960, Speech to Both Houses of Parliament at Cape Town, in Royal Institute of International Affairs, *Documents and Speeches on Commonwealth Affairs, 1952–1962* (London: Oxford University Press, 1963), p. 347.

83. Cornevin, *Histoire de l'afrique: colonisation, décolonisation, indépendance;* and René Viard, *La Fin de l'empire colonial français* (Paris: Maisonneuve et Larose, 1963).

84. See Odinga, *Not Yet Uhuru*, p. 245.

85. A.J. Luthuli, *Let My People Go!* (New York: McGraw-Hill, 1962). Also see A.J. Luthuli, *Luthuli Speaks* (Berlin: Solidarity Committee of the German Democratic Republic, 1982).

86. Organization of African Unity, *Charter of the Organization of African Unity* (Addis Ababa: Provisional Secretariat, 1963) [hereafter cited as OAU]. Also see "Die Gipfelkonferenz der unabhängigen Staaten Afrikas in Addis Abeba im Mai 1963," *Europa-Archiv* 18 (1963), 2:313–24.

87. OAU Document CIAS/Plen.2/Rev.2, 22–25 May 1963.

88. United Nations, *Everyman's United Nations*, pp. 6–7.

89. Cited in Amy Garvey, *Garvey and Garveyism* (New York: Collier, 1970), p. 310.

90. See Kimche, *The Afro-Asian Movement*, pp. 21–22 and 36–37; and McKay (ed.), *African Diplomacy*, passim.

91. Ibid., pp. 91–93; Thomas Hovet, *Bloc Politics in the United Nations* (Cambridge, Mass.: Harvard University Press, 1960); and Duroselle and Meyriat (eds.), *Les nouveaux Etats*.

92. See "The Beginnings with New Questions," in Chapter 5.

93. Letter 453-584, from Lyman C. White to Du Bois, 14 April 1947, in the Du Bois Papers, Reel 60, Correspondence, frame 922, Library of Congress.

94. This can be found in detail through the records of United Nations, Trusteeship Council, *Official Records, 1947–* (New York: United Nations, 1947–).

95. United Nations Charter, Article 73 (e).

96. Resolution 932 (X), "Progress Achieved by the Non-Self-Governing Territories in Pursuance of Chapter XI of the Charter," 8 November 1955, and Resolution 933 (X), "Renewal of the Committee on Information from Non-Self-Governing Territories," 8 November 1955, in UN/GA, *Resolutions, 1955*, p. 19.

97. F. van Langenhove, as cited in Crawford Young, "Decolonization in Africa," in L.H. Gann and Peter Duignan (eds.), *The History and Politics of Colonialism, 1914–1960* (Cambridge: Cambridge University Press, 1970), p. 462.

98. Mohieddine Fekini, 30 November 1960, in UN/GA, *Official Records, Plenary Meetings, 1960*, p. 1033.

99. Krishna Menon, 13 December 1960, in ibid., p. 1244.

100. Rafik Asha, 30 November 1960, in ibid., p. 1050.

101. Resolution 1514 (XV), "Declaration on the Granting of Independence to Colonial Countries and Peoples," 14 December 1960, in UN/GA, *Resolutions, 1960*, pp. 66–67.

102. The debates can be found in UN/GA, *Official Records, Plenary Meetings,* *1960,* pp. 981ff.

103. Ibid., p. 1274. The Dominican Republic also abstained.

104. Resolution 1654 (XVI), "The Situation with Regard to the Implementation of the Declaration on the Granting of Independence to Colonial Countries and Peoples," 27 November 1961, UN/GA, *Resolutions, 1961,* p. 65.

105. This was first known as the Special Committee of Seventeen but was expanded in 1962 and given much more authority as the Special Committee of Twenty-Four.

106. An excellent introduction can be found in UN Document A/5238, "Report of the Special Committee on the Situation with Regard to the Implementation of the Declaration Granting Independence to Colonial Countries and Peoples," 8 October 1962.

107. This expression "hard-core" is commonly used and can be found in print in United Nations, Office of Public Information, *Everyman's United Nations: A Summary of the Activities* (New York: United Nations, 1968 ed.), p. 165.

108. See Chapter 8.

109. See "Wartime Proposals for International Action" and "Human Rights, Racial Equality, and the Charter," in Chapter 5.

110. See "The United Nations as the Forum and Focal Point," "Setting Standards for Human Rights," and "Preventing and Punishing Genocide," in Chapter 6.

111. Britain, PRO/FO, 371/57317, Letter 25102/2/46, from A.H. Poynton to P.H. Gore-Booth, "Commission on Human Rights. Memorandum from the Colonial Office," 2 April 1946; and "Record of Meeting," A.C.U. (46) 125, 17 April 1946.

112. Among many examples, see Britain, PRO/FO, 371/67486, Telegram No. 206, Confidential, from Foreign Office to United Kingdom Representative on Human Rights Commission, 20 January 1947.

113. See "The United Nations as the Forum and Focal Point," Chapter 6. Also see Eleanor Roosevelt Papers, Boxes 3855, 4560, 4587, and 4588, in the Franklin D. Roosevelt Library, Hyde Park.

114. John P. Humphrey, *Human Rights and the United Nations,* (Dobbs Ferry: Transnational, 1983), p. 176.

115. Ibid., p. 28. Also see UN Document E/259. "Report to the Economic and Social Council on the First Session of the Commission," 1947, especially p. 6.

116. Howard Tolley, Jr., *The UN Commission on Human Rights* (Boulder, Colo.: Westview Press, 1987), Chapter 4.

117. Norman Bentwich, "Marking Time for Human Rights," *Contemporary Review* 192 (August 1957): 80–81. He placed much of the blame for this upon the colonial powers and the United States.

118. The best discussions can be found in Tolley, "The United Nations Commission on Human Rights"; and Jean-Bernard Marie, *La Commission des droits de l'homme de l'ONU* (Paris: Pedone, 1975).

119. Eleanor Roosevelt, *India and the Awakening East* (New York: Harper & Brothers, 1953), pp. xiii and 115.

120. Among many examples, see OAU, *Basic Documents and Resolutions* (Addis Ababa: Organization of African Unity, 1964).

121. Frantz Fanon, *Les damnés de la terre* (Paris: Masper, 1961). Translated by Constance Farrington as *The Wretched of the Earth* (New York: Grove Press, 1965). Also see Albert Memmi, *Portrait du colonisé* (Paris: Payot, 1973 ed.), first printed in 1965.

122. Mohammed Boucetta, 13 December 1960, in UN/GA, *Official Records, Plenary Meetings, 1960*, p. 1250.

123. United Nations, *Treaty Series*, no. 3822 in vol. 266 (1957): 3–87; no. 5181 in vol. 363 (1960): 31–41; and no. 6193 in vol. 429 (1962): 93–121.

124. This is discussed in more detail in Chapter 8.

125. See Resolution 1510 (XV), "Manifestations of Racial and National Hatred," 12 December 1960, in UN/GA, *Resolutions, 1960*, pp. 21–22; and UN Document E/CN.4/Sub.2/307/Rev.1, *Racial Discrimination*, especially chapter 12, "The Danger of the Revival of Nazism and Racial Intolerance," pp. 244ff.

126. See the discussions in Richard Jackson, *The Non-Aligned, the UN, and the Superpowers* (New York: Praeger, 1983); and Thomas M. Franck, *Nation Against Nation* (New York: Oxford University Press, 1985).

127. Dwight Eisenhower, as cited in Harold Isaacs, *The New World of Negro Americans* (New York: John Day, 1963), p. 13.

128. See Tinker, *Race, Conflict and the International Order*, p. 84.

129. Dean Rusk, as cited in Isaacs, *The New World of Negro Americans*, p. 19.

130. See Malcolm X, *The Autobiography of Malcolm X* (New York: Grove Press, 1965).

131. See Felix Ermacora, *Diskriminierungsschutz und Diskriminierungsverbot in der Arbeit der Vereinten Nationen* (Vienna: Braumuller, 1971), pp. 72ff.

132. Draft Declaration, in UN Document A/5603, "Report of the Third Committee," 12 November 1963.

133. See the debates in United Nations, Third Committee, *Official Records, Third Committee, Summary Records, 1963*.

134. Resolution 1904 (XVIII), "Declaration on the Elimination of All Forms of Racial Discrimination," 20 December 1963, in UN/GA, *Resolutions, 1963*, pp. 35ff. Also see "Rassendiskriminierung-Resolution," *Bulletin der Internationalen Juristen-Kommission* 19 (1964): 46–52; and Sir Rupert John, *Racism and Its Elimination* (New York: UNITAR, 1981), pp. 49–50.

135. Diallo Telli, 20 November 1963, in UN/GA, *Official Records, Plenary Meetings, 1963*, p. 4.

136. Moreno Salcedo, in ibid., p. 9.

137. Diallo Telli, in ibid., p. 13 [my emphasis].

138. Resolution 1906 (XVIII), "Preparation of a Draft International Convention on the Elimination of All Forms of Racial Discrimination," 20 November 1963; and Resolution 1960 (XVIII), "Draft International Covenants on Human Rights," 12 December 1963, in UN/GA, *Resolutions, 1963*, pp. 37–38 and 42–43.

139. See the lengthy discussion in Commission to Study the Organization of Peace, *The United Nations and Human Rights*, pp. 101ff; and Humphrey, *Human Rights and the United Nations*, passim.

140. Resolution 2106 A (XX), "International Convention on the Elimination of All Forms of Racial Discrimination," 21 December 1965, in UN/GA, *Resolutions, 1965*, pp. 47–51.

141. See N. Lerner, *The UN Convention on the Elimination of All Forms of Racial Discrimination* (Leiden: Sijthoff, 1970); Gerda Weinberger, *Gegen Rassismus und Rassendiskriminierung; Kampfdekade der UNO* (Berlin: Staatsverlag der DDR, 1976); Tolley, *The UN Commission on Human Rights*, chapter 5; and Marc Bossuyt, *L'Interdiction de la discrimination dans le droit international des droits de l'homme* (Brussels: Bruylant, 1976).

142. Egon Schwelb, "The International Convention on the Elimination of All Forms of Racial Discrimination," *International and Comparative Law Quarterly* 15

(1966): 1057. Also see Myres McDougal, Harold Lasswell, and Lung-chu Chen, *Human Rights and World Public Order* (New Haven: Yale University Press, 1980), pp. 587–88; and Warwick McKean, *Equality and Discrimination Under International Law* (Oxford: Clarendon Press, 1968), pp. 152–65.

143. See Thomas Buergenthal, "Implementing the UN Racial Convention," *Texas International Law Journal* 12 (Winter 1977): 187–221.

144. Resolution 2200 (XXI), "International Covenant on Economic, Social, and Cultural Rights," "International Covenant on Civil and Political Rights," and "Optional Protocol," 16 December 1966, in UN/GA, *Resolutions, 1966*, pp. 49–60.

145. Patricia Harris, 16 December 1966, in UN/GA, *Official Records, Plenary Meetings, 1966*, p. 12. Also see Dennis Driscoll, "The Development of Human Rights in International Law," in Walter Laqueur and Barry Rubin (eds.), *The Human Rights Reader* (New York: New American Library, 1979), pp. 45–50; and United Nations, *United Nations Actions in the Field of Human Rights* (New York: United Nations, 1974), pp. 20ff.

146. E.N. Nasinovsky, 16 December 1966, in UN/GA, *Official Records, Plenary Meetings, 1966.* p. 13.

147. The expression "Black Revolution," is used by Franklin, *From Slavery to Freedom,* pp. 476ff.

Chapter 8: A Decade for Action

1. See, for example, Wolf-Dieter Musch, *Das Rassendiskriminierungsverbot im englishen Recht und in der Europäischen Menschenrechtskonvention* (Heidelberg: Ruprecht-Karl-Universität, 1975).

2. These expressions, and many others like them, have been used in innumerable interviews with those involved in this process and those who observed it, including Jerome Shestack. Also see UN Document A/CONF.92/4, "General Introductory Paper Prepared by the Secretary General," 13 June 1978, p. 4; and Moshe Y. Sachs (ed.), *The United Nations: A Handbook* (New York: John Wiley & Sons, 1977), p. 103.

3. Resolution 2545 (XXIV), "Measures to Be Taken Against Nazism and Racial Intolerance," and Resolution 2544 (XXIV), "Program for the Observance in 1971 of the International Year for Action to Combat Racism and Racial Discrimination," 11 December 1969, in UN/GA, *Resolutions, 1969*, pp. 53–54.

4. Among many examples, see Resolution 2734 (XXV), "Declaration on the Strengthening of International Security," 16 December 1970, in UN/GA, *Resolutions, 1970*, pp. 22–24.

5. See Resolution 2646 (XXV), "Elimination of All Forms of Racial Discrimination," 30 November 1970, in ibid., pp. 71–72.

6. Resolution 2919 (XXVII), "Decade for Action to Combat Racism and Racial Discrimination," 15 November 1972, in UN/GA, *Resolutions, 1972*, p. 62.

7. Annex to Resolution 3057 (XXVIII), "Decade for Action to Combat Racism and Racial Discrimination," 2 November 1973, in UN/GA, *Resolutions, 1973*, p. 71.

8. "Program for the Decade for Action to Combat Racism and Racial Discrimination," in ibid., pp. 70–73.

9. See UN Document ST/HR/2, *United Nations Action in the Field of Human Rights,* pp. 41–44.

10. Resolution 3068 (XXVIII), "International Convention on the Suppression and Punishment of the Crime of *Apartheid,*" 30 November 1973, in UN/GA, *Resolutions, 1973*, pp. 75–77.

11. Verret of Haiti, 30 November 1973, in UN Document A/PV.2185.

12. Howard Tolley, Jr., *The UN Commission on Human Rights* (Boulder, Colo.: Westview Press, 1987), p. 87.

13. Resolution 1761 (XVII), "The Policies of *Apartheid* of the Government of the Republic of South Africa," 6 November 1962, in UN/GA, *Resolutions, 1962*, pp. 9–10; Resolution 2671 A (XXV), "The Policies of *Apartheid*," 8 December 1970, in UN/GA, *Resolutions, 1970*, pp. 31–32; and Resolution 2144 (XXI), "Question of the Violation of Human Rights," 26 October 1966, in UN/GA, *Resolutions, 1966*, pp. 46–48.

14. See United Nations, Centre Against Apartheid, *Publications of the Centre Against Apartheid (1967–1982)*, March 1983.

15. Resolution 31/6, J, "Program of Action Against *Apartheid*," 9 November 1976, in UN/GA, *Resolutions, 1976*, pp. 15–19; and UN Document A/CONF.92/4, "General Introductory Paper Prepared by the Secretary General," 13 June 1978, pp. 2ff. Also see "Combating South Africa over Namibia and Apartheid," below.

16. CERD publishes annual reports of its activities that are attached to the Supplements of the UN/GA, *Official Records*, each year. For the best summary, see UN Document A/CONF.92/8, reissued as CERD/1, "Committee on the Elimination of Racial Discrimination and the Progress Made Toward the Achievement of the Objectives of the International Convention . . . ," 1979.

17. Ibid., p. 22; and for an independent assessment, Thomas Buergenthal, "Implementing the UN Racial Convention," *Texas International Law Journal* 12 (Winter 1977): 187–221.

18. See Richard Wright, *The Color Curtain* (New York: World, 1956), passim.

19. See Chapters 4 and 5.

20. C.L. Sulzberger, "Strange Nonalliance," *New York Times*, 30 April 1971.

21. Resolution 3151 G (XXVIII), "Situation in South Africa Resulting from the Policies of *Apartheid*," 14 December 1973, in UN/GA, *Resolutions, 1973*, pp. 32–33.

22. Dowek, 22 November 1973, in UN Document A/PV.2176, pp. 90–91.

23. "Declaration of Mexico on the Equality of Women," July 1975, as cited in UN/GA, *Resolutions, 1975*, p. 84.

24. Resolution 77 (XII) of the Organization of African Unity, August 1975, as cited in ibid.

25. "Political Declaration and Strategy to Strengthen International Peace," August 1975, as cited in ibid.

26. Sharaf, 16 October 1975, in UN/GA, *Official Records, Third Committee, 1975*, p. 105.

27. Herzog, 17 October 1975, in ibid., p. 117.

28. Garment, 17 October 1975, in ibid., p. 113.

29. Resolution 3379 (XXX), "Elimination of All Forms of Racial Discrimination," 10 November 1975, in UN/GA, *Resolutions, 1975*, pp. 83–84.

30. Daniel Patrick Moynihan, as cited in Thomas M. Franck, *Nation Against Nation* (New York: Oxford University Press, 1985), pp. 206 and 209.

31. See Chapters 6 and 7 for discussions about the civil rights movement, and, for a treatment of Congress in the 1970s, American Association for the International Commission of Jurists, *Human Rights and U.S. Foreign Policy: The First Decade, 1973–1983* (New York: American Association for the International Commission of Jurists, 1984).

32. Richard Lillich, *International Human Rights Instruments: A Compilation of Treaties, Agreements, and Declarations of Especial Interest to the United States* (Buffalo: Hein, 1983), pp. 130ff.

33. See Chapters 5, 6, and 7.

34. Annex to Resolution 3057 (XXVIII), "Decade for Action to Combat Racism and Racial Discrimination," 2 November 1973, in UN/GA, *Resolutions, 1973,* pp. 70–71.

35. Resolution 3070 (XXVIII), "Importance of the Universal Realization of the Right of Peoples to Self-Determination," 30 November 1973, in ibid., p. 78. Also see the earlier Resolution 2784 (XXVI), "Elimination of All Forms of Racial Discrimination," 6 December 1971, in UN/GA, *Resolutions, 1971,* pp. 79–80.

36. United Nations, *Everyman's United Nations: A Summary* (New York: United Nations, 1968 ed.), p. 165.

37. Waldemar Nielsen, as cited in René Lemarchand (ed.), *American Policy in Southern Africa: The Stakes and the Stance* (Washington, D.C.: University Press of America, 1981 ed.), p. 13.

38. See William Minter, *Portuguese Africa and the West* (New York: Monthly Review Press, 1974); and S.J. Bosgra and Christian van Krimpen, *Portugal en de NATO* (Amsterdam: Angola Comite, 1971).

39. See "An Emerging 'Third World' and Independence in Africa," in Chapter 7.

40. Cited in Roland Oliver and A. Atmore, *Africa Since 1800* (Cambridge: Cambridge University Press, 1981), pp. 269–70.

41. Ibid., p. 276.

42. See UN/Security Council, Document S/4835, "Résolution adoptée par le Counseil de sécurité à la 956ème séance, le 9 juin 1961, concernant la situation en Angola"; Resolution 1807 (XVII), "Territories Under Portuguese Administration," 14 December 1962, and Resolution 1819 (XVII), "The Situation in Angola," 18 December 1962, in UN/GA, *Resolutions, 1962,* pp. 39–40 and 75; and Resolution 2107 (XX), "Question of Territories Under Portuguese Administration," 21 December 1965, in UN/GA, *Resolutions, 1965,* pp. 62–63.

43. Garin, 9 June 1961, in UN/Security Council, *Documents officiels,* 956ème séance, p. 7.

44. National Security Study Memorandum (NSSM) No. 39, written in 1969 and presented in 1970, as cited in Allen Isaacman and Jennifer Davis, "U.S. Policy Toward Mozambique, 1946–1976: 'The Defense of Colonialism and Regional Stability,'" and Gerald Bender, "Kissinger in Angola: Anatomy of Failure," in Lemarchand, *American Policy in Southern Africa,* pp. 35 and 68–69.

45. "Defending the 'Free World,'" *New York Times,* 9 December 1971.

46. Fourth Conference of Heads of State or Government of Non-Aligned Countries, "Resolution on Angola, Guinea-Bissau, the Cape Verde Islands, Mozambique, and Sao Tome e Principe," 9 September 1973, in UN Document NAC/ALG/CONF.4/Res.3.

47. See UN Document A/PV.2175, Plenary Meeting of 21 November 1973.

48. "A Whiff of Freedom for the Oldest Empire," *Time,* 6 May 1974.

49. "Portugal: Between Anarchy and Reaction," *Time,* 10 June 1974.

50. Antonio de Spinola, as cited in "End of the Last Empire," *Time,* 12 August 1974.

51. See Bender, "Kissinger in Angola," passim; and John A. Marcum, "Lessons of Angola," *Foreign Affairs* 54 (April 1976): 407–25.

52. Joaquim Peres, as cited in "End of the Last Empire," *Time,* 12 August 1974.

53. See Oliver and Atmore, *Africa Since 1800,* p. 285.

54. See "Dokumente zür Rhodesien-Krise," *Europa-Archiv* 21 (1966), 2:57–84 and 22 (1967), 2:55–69; Robert Cornevin, *Histoire de l'afrique* (Paris: Payot, 1976), 3:149ff.; and UN Document E/CN.4/Sub.2/370/Rev.1, *Racial Discrimination,* pp. 221–35.

55. U Thant, as cited in Gordon A. Craig, *Europe Since 1815* (New York: Holt, Rinehart, & Winston, 1971), p. 792.

56. Resolution 2138 (XXI) and Resolution 2151 (XXI), "Question of Southern Rhodesia," 22 October 1966, in UN/GA, *Resolutions, 1966*, pp. 68–69; and Resolution 253 (1968) and the discussion surrounding it in UN/Security Council, Document S/PV.1428, 29 May 1968.

57. "Rhodesia: Peace Between Black and White?" *Time*, 23 December 1974.

58. See "Is It a Breakthrough or a Breakdown in Rhodesia?" *Sunday Times* (London), 3 October 1976; and Oliver and Atmore, *Africa Since 1800*, pp. 282–86.

59. Jimmy Carter, *Keeping Faith* (New York: Bantam, 1982), p. 74, citing his speech as governor of Georgia.

60. "Inaugural Address," 24 January 1977, in Office of the Federal Register, National Archives and Records Service, *Weekly Compilation of Presidential Documents* 13 (January–June, 1977): 87–89.

61. Cyrus Vance, "Face the Nation," C.B.S. News, 27 February 1977.

62. Anthony Lake, "Pragmatism and Principle in U.S. Foreign Policy," Speech of 13 June 1977, as reproduced by the Bureau of Public Affairs, U.S. Department of State. Also see Lake's book, *The "Tar Baby" Option: American Policy Toward Southern Rhodesia* (New York: Columbia University Press, 1976).

63. "Ambassador to U.N.," *New York Times*, 17 December 1976.

64. "Young Says Africa Race War Would Start One in US," *New York Times*, 6 June 1977.

65. Andrew Young, "United States Reiterates Support for the Independence of Namibia and Zimbabwe at Maputo Conference," U.S. Department of State, *Department of State Bulletin* 77 (11 July 1977): 55. For an assessment of the Carter administration's policy toward Africa, see Winston Nagan, "The U.S. and South Africa: The Limits of 'Peaceful Change,'" in Lemarchand (ed.), *American Policy in Southern Africa*, pp. 225–77.

66. See "Text of the Maputo Declaration in Support of the Peoples of Zimbabwe and Namibia" and "Program of Action," 21 May 1977, in ibid., pp. 59–65.

67. Edgar Lockwood, "The Case of Zimbabwe," in Lemarchand (ed.), *American Policy in Southern Africa*, pp. 167–222, is excellent here, as are the daily reports in the *Times* (London) concerning the role of Lord Carrington and the Lancaster House negotiations of 1979.

68. The original text appeared in Annex to Resolution 3057 (XXVIII), "Decade for Action to Combat Racism and Racial Discrimination," 2 November 1973, in UN/GA, *Resolutions, 1973*, p. 72 [my emphasis].

69. UN Document A/CONF.92/4, "General Introductory Paper Prepared by the Secretary-General," 13 June 1978.

70. UN Document A/CONF.92/8, "A Study on the Work of the Committee on the Elimination of Racial Discrimination," 19 April 1978.

71. UN Document A/CONF.92/10, *Racial Discrimination*.

72. UN Documents A/CONF.92/11, "Adverse Consequences . . . "; A/CONF.92/14, "Report of the Ad Hoc Working Group . . . "; and A/CONF.92/21, "Report of the Special Committee . . . . "

73. See "Launching the Decade for Action to Combat Racism," above.

74. Jimmy Carter, "World Conference to Combat Racism," in U.S., Department of State, *Department of State Bulletin* 78 (November 1978): 48.

75. Examples can be seen clearly throughout the supporting materials submitted and speeches made during the conference itself, in UN Document series A/CONF.92.

76. Kurt Waldheim, in UN Document A/CONF.92/40, "Report of the World Conference to Combat Racism," pp. 29–32.

77. Ibid., pp. 6–7.

78. Ashour Gargoum, as cited in "Libyan Call for Armed Revolt Against Racism," *Times* (London), 22 August 1978. He offered to use the International Anti-Discrimination Organization with its headquarters in Tripoli for this purpose as well.

79. "Conference on Racism," *Times* (London), 21 August 1978.

80. UN Document A/CONF.92/40, "Report of the World Conference to Combat Racism," pp. 62–63.

81. Per Fischer, ambassador of the Federal Republic of Germany, as cited in New York Times News Service and Associated Press, 26 August 1978.

82. Interviews with J.M. Makatini, Jerome Shestack, Enayat Houshmand, Emmanuel Palmer, and Emmanuel Mompoint.

83. "Declaration," in UN Document A/CONF.92/4, "Report of the World Conference to Combat Racism," pp. 9–14.

84. "Program of Action," in ibid., pp. 15–26.

85. M.V. Molapo, in ibid., pp. 33–35. Also see Xinhua General Overseas News Service, "*Apartheid* Policy Condemned at Geneva Conference," 25 August 1978.

86. See "The United Nations as the Forum and Focal Point," in Chapter 6.

87. Humphrey, *Human Rights and the United Nations*, p. 14.

88. Johannes Strijdom, as cited in L.E. Neame, *The History of Apartheid: The Story of the Color War in South Africa* (New York: London House & Maxwell, 1963), pp. 131–32. Also see "Partnership with Blacks Rejected," *Times of India*, 22 April 1955.

89. See UN/GA, *Official Records*, Supplement No. 16, UN Documents A/2505 and A/2505/Add.1, "Report of the United Nations Commission on the Racial Situation in the Union of South Africa," 3 October 1953; Walter Limp, *Anatomie de l'apartheid* (Tournai: Casterman, 1972); Michael Banton, *Race Relations* (London: Tavistock, 1967), pp. 164ff.; Patrice de Comarmond and Claude Duchet (eds.), *Racisme et société* (Paris: Maspero, 1969), passim; and Leonard Thompson, *The Political Mythology of Apartheid* (New Haven: Yale University Press, 1985).

90. Colin Legum, "Color and Power in the South African Situation," in John Hope Franklin (ed.), *Color and Race* (Boston: Houghton Mifflin, 1968), p. 205. Also see Pierre van den Berghe, *Race and Racism: A Comparative Perspective* (New York: Wiley, 1967), pp. 96–111; George Fredrickson, *White Supremacy: A Comparative Study in American and South African History* (New York: Oxford University Press, 1981), pp. 240ff.; and John Laurence, *The Seeds of Disaster* (London: Gollancz, 1968).

91. Cornevin, *Histoire de l'afrique* 3:49.

92. Oliver and Atmore, *Africa Since 1800*, pp. 297–98. Also see "Violentes émeutes en Afrique du Sud," *Le Monde*, 22 March 1960.

93. See "The United Nations as the Forum and Focal Point," in Chapter 6; Resolution 616A (VII), "The Question of Race Conflict in South Africa Resulting from Policies of *Apartheid*," 5 December 1952, in UN/GA, *Resolutions, 1952*, p. 8; and UN Document E/CN.4/Sub.2/370/Rev.1, "Racial Discrimination," p. 205.

94. See Resolution 1598 (XV), "Question of Race Conflict in South Africa Resulting from the Policies of *Apartheid*," 13 April 1961, and Resolution 1663 (XVI), "Question of Race Conflict . . . ," 28 November 1961, in UN/GA, *Resolutions, 1961*, pp. 5–6 and 10–11; and Resolution 1568 (XV), "Question of South West Africa," 18 December 1960, in UN/GA, *Resolutions, 1960*, p. 33.

95. Resolution 134 (1960), "Question Relating to the Situation in the Union of South Africa," 1 April 1960, in UN/Security Council, *Resolutions, 1960*, pp. 1–2.

96. Kwame Nkrumah, as cited in "The Commonwealth: The Lengthening Shadow," *Time* (16 May 1960): 24.

97. *Daily Herald,* as cited in ibid., p. 25.

98. Nelson Mandela, 22 October 1962, as cited in Thomas Karis and Gwendolen Carter (eds.), *From Protest to Challenge: A Documentary History of African Politics in South Africa,* 4 vols. (Stanford: Hoover Institution Press, 1977), 3:725–31. Also see Nelson Mandela, *No Easy Walk to Freedom* (New York: Basic Books, 1965).

99. These included India, Ghana, Ethiopia, the Sudan, and Malaya, among others.

100. Resolution 1761 (XVII), "The Politics of *Apartheid* of the Government of the Republic of South Africa," 6 November 1962, in UN/GA, *Resolutions, 1962,* pp. 9–10.

101. Resolution 1881 (XVIII), "The Politics of *Apartheid* . . . ," 11 October 1963, in UN/GA, *Resolutions, 1963,* p. 19; and Resolution 190 (1964), "Question Relating to the Policies of *Apartheid,*" 9 June 1964, in UN/Security Council, *Resolutions, 1964,* pp. 12–13.

102. See the discussion in UN Document E/CN.4/Sub.2/370/Rev.1, "Racial Discrimination," pp. 206–07.

103. Ibid., p. 236.

104. Resolution 3111 (XXVIII), "Question of Namibia," 12 December 1973, in UN/GA, *Resolutions, 1973,* pp. 93–95.

105. General Assembly resolution, as cited in "3 Veto U.N. Ouster of South Africans," *New York Times,* 31 October 1974.

106. "South Africa Suspended by U.N. Assembly," *New York Times,* 13 November 1974.

107. See "Attacking the 'Hard Core' in Southern Africa," above.

108. Oliver and Atmore, *Africa Since 1800,* p. 305.

109. Steven Biko, as cited by Andrew Young, in U.S., Department of State, *Department of State Bulletin* 77 (12 December 1977): 861.

110. See "A Tragic Turn to Terrorism," *Newsweek,* 10 October 1977; "The Big Crackdown," *Newsweek,* 31 October 1977; and "Biko's Last Days," *Newsweek,* 28 November 1977.

111. R.L. Botha, as cited in Nagan, "The U.S. and South Africa," in Lemarchand (ed.), *American Policy in Southern Africa,* p. 237.

112. Resolution 31/6, "Policies of *Apartheid* of the Government of South Africa," J, "Program of Action Against *Apartheid,*" 9 November 1976, in UN/GA, *Resolutions, 1976,* pp. 15–19.

113. Andrew Young, 31 October 1977, in U.S., Department of State, *Department of State Bulletin.*

114. Resolution 417 (1977) of 31 October 1977, in UN Document S/RES/417 (1977); and Resolution 418 (1977) of 4 November 1977, in UN Document S/RES/418 (1977). It should be noted, however, that the United States, Britain, and France vetoed a proposal for more sweeping economic sanctions against South Africa.

115. Kurt Waldheim, 4 November 1977, in UN Document S/PV.2046, "Provisional Verbatim Record," p. 4.

116. The Gleneagles Agreement of June 1977, as reproduced in UN Document A/CONF.92/33, "Report Submitted to the Conference by the Commonwealth Secretariat," 19 July 1978.

117. See "Declaration on the Liberation of Namibia," in U.S., Department of State, *Department of State Bulletin* 77 (11 July 1977): 61–65.

118. "Text of Declaration," 26 August 1977, in ibid. (3 October 1977): 448–51.

119. See "Convening the World Conference to Combat Racism," above, and Resolution 435 (1978), "Question of Namibia," 29 September 1978, in UN/Security Council, *Resolutions, 1978,* p. 13.

120. See Resolution 34/24, "Implementation of the Program for the Decade for Action to Combat Racism and Racial Discrimination," 15 November 1979, in UN/ GA, *Resolutions, 1979,* pp. 162–64; Resolution 35/33, "Decade for Action to Combat Racism," 14 November 1980, in UN/GA, *Resolutions, 1980,* pp. 174–75; and William Johnston, "Namibia," and Winston Nagan, "The U.S. and South Africa," in Lemarchand (ed.), *American Policy in Southern Africa,* pp. 195–277.

121. R.L. Botha, as cited in Alfred Moleah, *Namibia: The Struggle for Liberation* (Wilmington: Disa Press, 1983), p. 208.

122. "South Africa Tells Its Terms," *New York Times,* 15 May 1979.

123. Moleah, *Namibia,* p. 223.

124. "Reagan and Southern Africa," *New York Times,* 16 February 1981.

125. See Moleah, *Namibia,* pp. 223–24; and George W. Shepherd, Jr., "Clues to Reagan's Africa Policy," *Africa Today* (4th Quarter 1980): 37–41.

126. "Reagan and Southern Africa," *New York Times,* 16 February 1981.

127. Ronald Reagan, as cited in Richard Deutsch, "Reagan's Unruly Review," *Africa Report* (May–June 1981): 23.

128. *Die Vaterland,* as cited in "Reagan's Views on South Africa Praised by Botha," *New York Times,* 5 March 1981.

129. Willie Breytenbach, as cited in "South Africa Sees a Friend in Reagan," *Wall Street Journal,* 27 March 1981.

130. See "U.S. Plans a Mission to Southern Africa," *New York Times,* 29 March 1981.

131. Communiqué from the Luanda Conference, 16 April 1981, as cited in Moleah, *Namibia,* p. 233.

132. "Non-Aligned Demand Oil Ban on Pretoria," *Times* (London), 20 April 1981. Also see Conférence internationale sur des sanctions contre l'Afrique du Sud, *Principaux documents* (New York: Centre des Nations Unies contre l'apartheid, 1981).

133. Chester Crocker, as cited in "U.S. Won't Take Sides in South Africa," *Washington Post,* 31 August 1981.

134. Olara Otunnu, as cited in Moleah, *Namibia,* p. 243.

135. George Bush, as cited in "Bush Remains Firm," *New York Times,* 22 November 1982. Also see "Bush Sees Angola Deal," *Times* (London), 20 November 1982.

136. Resolution 35/33, "Decade for Action to Combat Racism," 14 November 1980, in UN/GA, *Resolutions, 1980,* pp. 174–75.

137. See especially the working papers of the Sous-Comité sur le racisme, la discrimination raciale, l'apartheid et la décolonisation du Comité spécial des ONG pour les Droits de l'homme for its conference in Geneva, 5–8 July 1983; the background papers in UN Document series A/CONF.119; World Council of Churches, *Churches Responding to Racism in the 1980s* (Geneva: World Council of Churches, 1983); and Sir Rupert John, *Racism and Its Elimination* (New York: UNITAR, 1981), p. 28, on UNESCO's most recent Declaration on Race and Racial Prejudice.

138. Javier Perez de Cuellar, "Address by the Secretary-General," 1 August 1983, in UN Document A/CONF.119/26, "Report of the Second World Conference to Combat Racism and Racial Discrimination," pp. 33–34.

139. "Declaration of the Second World Conference to Combat Racism and Racial Discrimination," 12 August 1983, in ibid., pp. 11–17.

140. "Struggle Against Racism," Xinhua News Agency, 14 August 1983.

141. "Program of Action," in UN Document A/CONF.119/26, "Report of the Second World Conference to Combat Racism and Racial Discrimination," pp. 17–30.

142. Javier Perez de Cuellar, "Address by the Secretary-General," in ibid., pp. 33–35.

Epilogue: Toward the Future

1. "Declaration and Program of Action," 12 August 1983, in UN Document A/CONF.119/26, "Report of the Second World Conference to Combat Racism and Racial Discrimination," p. 13. Also see "Declaration of the International NGO Conference of Action Against Apartheid and Racism," Geneva, 5–8 July 1983, available from the Sous-Comité sur le racisme, la discrimination raciale, l'apartheid et la décolonisation du Comite special des ONG pour les Droits de l'homme.

2. Hector Charry-Samper, 1 August 1983, in UN Document A/CONF.119/26, "Report of the Second World Conference to Combat Racism and Racial Discrimination," p. 38.

3. See Sir Rupert John, *Racism and Its Elimination* (New York: UNITAR, 1981), pp. 79ff.; "Poor vs. Rich: A New Global Conflict," *Time*, 22 December 1975; and Ronald Segal, *The Race War* (New York: Bantam, 1967), p. 427.

4. For several specific examples see "Standards—and Double Standards," below. Also see the working papers of the Sous-Comité sur le racisme, la discrimination raciale, l'apartheid et la décolonisation du Comité spécial des ONG pour les Droits de l'homme for its conference in Geneva, 5–8 July 1983; the background papers in the UN Document A/CONF.119 series; World Council of Churches, *Churches Responding to Racism in the 1980s* (Geneva: World Council of Churches, 1983); Tilman Zulch (ed.), *In Auschwitz vergast, bis heute verfolgt* (Hamburg: Rowohlt, 1979); and, most recently, "A Chilling Wave of Racism," *Time*, 25 January 1988.

5. See Julius Lewin, *The Struggle for Racial Equality* (London: Longmans, 1967), p. 23.

6. David Lamb, *The Africans* (New York: Random House, 1982), p. 314.

7. See Moses Moscowitz, *The Politics and Dynamics of Human Rights* (Dobbs Ferry: Oceana, 1968), pp. 185–90.

8. The Manifesto on South Africa of 1969, known as the Lusaka Declaration, as cited in Moses Moscowitz, *International Concern with Human Rights* (Dobbs Ferry: Oceana, 1974), p. 66.

9. Ronald Reagan, as cited in "Railing Against Racism," *Time*, 24 December 1984.

10. See UN Document A/CONF.119/26, "Report of the Second World Conference to Combat Racism and Racial Discrimination," pp. 37–40.

11. Roy Preiswerk, "Race and Color in International Relations," *The Year Book of World Affairs, 1970* (New York: Praeger, 1970), p. 71.

12. Desmond Tutu, as cited in "Searching for New Worlds," *Time*, 29 October 1984.

13. Desmond Tutu, as cited in "Railing Against Racism," *Time*, 24 December 1984.

14. See "Ouverture et répression en Afrique du Sud," *Le Monde*, 23 February 1985.

15. See "Combating South Africa over Namibia and Apartheid," in Chapter 8.

16. Alan Boesak, as cited in "South Africa: The Fires of Anger," *Time*, 8 April 1985. Also see "Police Admit Minister's Version of South Africa Shooting Untrue," *Times* (London), 30 March 1985.

17. "Time to Cry Halt," *Rand Daily Mail,* 23 March 1985. Also see "Südafrika: Die Last der Gewalt," *Die Zeit,* 4 April 1985; and "South Africa: Is History Being Written in Blood?" *Manchester Guardian,* 11 May 1985.

18. P.W. Botha, as cited in "P.W. Criticised," *Rand Daily Mail,* 25 March 1985. Also see "Botha Refuses," *Times* (London), 26 March 1985.

19. "South Africa: The Fires of Anger," *Time,* 8 April 1985.

20. George Shultz, as cited in "System Evil, Shultz Says," *New York Times,* 22 March 1985.

21. "A Ritual Washing of Hands," *Washington Post,* as reproduced in the *Manchester Guardian Weekly,* 5 May 1985.

22. See "Declaration and Program of Action," 12 August 1983, in UN Document A/CONF.119/26, "Report of the Second World Conference to Combat Racism and Racial Discrimination," p. 14 [my emphasis].

23. "Report of the First Committee," in ibid., p. 63.

24. This expression is used frequently within the halls of the United Nations, as confirmed by numerous interviews.

25. Xinhua General Overseas News Service, "Chinese Delegation Leader Condemns South African Racism," 5 August 1983.

26. "Declaration of the International NGO Conference of Action Against Apartheid and Racism," 5–8 July 1983.

27. Desmond Tutu, as cited in "Railing Against Racism," *Time,* 24 December 1984.

28. "Declaration and Program of Action," 12 August 1983, in UN Document A/CONF.119/26, "Report of the Second World Conference to Combat Racism and Racial Discrimination," p. 15.

29. I am grateful to J.M. Makatini, chief representative of the African National Congress to the United Nations for a candid and helpful interview on this subject. Discussions with Leonard Jefferies and Lucy Webster also have been most helpful.

30. Interview with V. Tonchi.

31. I am indebted to Howard Tolley, Jr., for these expressions.

32. Warren Hewitt, director of the Bureau of International Organization Affairs in the U.S. Department of State provided an insightful discussion on this matter. Also see William Shawcross, Anthony Terry, and Peter Pringle, "The Barbarism the World Ignores," *Times* (London), reprinted in *Atlas* (June 1976): 20–22; Adda Bozeman, "How to Think About Human Rights," *Proceedings of the National Security Affairs Conference* (Washington, D.C.: National Defense University, 1977), pp. 1–16; and Daniel P. Moynihan, "The Politics of Human Rights," *Commentary* 64 (1977): 19–26.

33. Jeane Kirkpatrick, "Double Standards in Human Rights," 24 November 1981, in U.S. Department of State, Current Policy No. 353.

34. Statement by the British Council of Churches, in "Unease on Human Rights Issue," *Times* (London), 25 March 1985.

35. L. Irvine-Brown, in "Letters to the Editor," *Times* (London), 30 March 1985. It must also be said that the *Times,* among other Western papers, is usually accused by countries in the Third World of being biased in exactly the opposite direction.

36. Roelof Botha, as cited in "Deadly Rite of the Rainy Season," *Time,* 23 January 1984.

37. *Sunday Tribune,* as cited in ibid.

38. For a concise survey, see World Council of Churches, *Churches Responding to Racism in the 1980s,* especially p. 94. Also see Amnesty International, *Torture in the Eighties* (London: Amnesty International, 1985); and for an interesting discussion of

comparisons, Rhoda Howard, "Evaluating Human Rights in Africa: Some Problems of Implicit Comparisons," *Human Rights Quarterly* 6 (May 1984): 160–79.

39. Otto von Bismarck, 30 September 1862, in Gustav Rein et al., (eds.), *Bismarck: Werke in Auswahl*, 8 vols. (Stuttgart: Kohlhammer, 1965), 3:3.

40. Moscowitz, *International Concern for Human Rights*, p. v. Also see the discussion in David Forsythe, *Human Rights and World Politics* (Lincoln: University of Nebraska Press, 1983).

41. Colin Legum, "Color and Power in the South African Situation," in John Hope Franklin (ed.), *Color and Race* (Boston: Houghton Mifflin, 1968), p. 215.

42. Thomas M. Franck, *Nation Against Nation* (New York: Oxford University Press, 1985), p. 209.

43. This expression is frequently heard in both New York and Geneva, particularly among representatives of NGOs, who can often afford to be more blunt than official representatives of governments.

44. Javier Perez de Cuellar, 1 August 1983, in "Address by the Secretary-General," UN Document A/CONF.119/26, "Report of the Second World Conference to Combat Racism and Racial Discrimination," p. 35.

45. Hector Charry-Samper, in ibid., p. 36.

46. For daily accounts, see *Rand Daily Mail, Times* (London), *Le Monde, Die Zeit,* and *New York Times.*

47. Nelson Mandela, *No Easy Walk to Freedom* (New York: Basic Books, 1965), p. 31.

48. See "Combating South Africa over Namibia and Apartheid," in Chapter 8.

49. P.W. Botha, as cited in "New Security Clamp by Defiant Botha," *Times* (London), 13 June 1986.

50. *Mission to South Africa: The Commonwealth Report*, as cited in "An Awesome Tragedy Ahead," ibid.

51. David Owen, as cited in "Conference to Review British Stance on South Africa," *Rand Daily Mail*, 26 March 1985.

52. "Walking Toward Civil War," *Times* (London), 14 June 1986.

53. Edward Kennedy, as cited in "Eyeball to Eyeball: Reagan, Congress, and a Sanctions Veto," *Time*, 6 October 1986.

54. United States, Department of State, Secretary of State's Advisory Committee on South Africa, *A U.S. Policy Toward South Africa* (Washington, D.C.: Government Printing Office, 1987), p. vi.

55. See "Racial Dilemma of Disinvestment," *Rand Daily Mail*, 22 March 1985; and "Zulu Opposes Halt to Investment" and "Issues and Debate: Should U.S. Punish South Africa for Apartheid?" *New York Times*, 17 February 1985; and World Council of Churches, *Time to Withdraw* (Geneva: World Council of Churches, 1973), pp. 41–42.

56. Roelof Botha, as cited in "US Anti-SA Move Can Hurt," *Rand Daily Mail*, 13 March 1985.

57. Desmond Tutu, as cited in "South Africa Bans Most Antiapartheid Activities," *New York Times*, 25 February 1988.

58. World Council of Churches, *Churches Responding to Racism in the 1980s*, p. 106.

59. Romesh Chandra, "Address Before the International NGO Conference of Action Against Racism and Racial Discrimination," 5 July 1983, available from the Sous-Comité sur le racisme, la discrimination raciale, l'apartheid et la décolonisation du Comité spécial des ONG pour les Droits de l'homme.

60. Alhaji Maitama-Sule, "Africa, the United States, and South Africa," *Africa Report* (September–October, 1982), pp. 12–13.

61. Moleah, *Namibia*, pp. i and 315.

62. Desmond Tutu, as cited in "To Avert the Bloodbath," *Time*, 14 January 1985.

63. Segal, *The Race War*; and John, *Racism and Its Elimination*, p. 67.

64. Text of a display on apartheid, located at United Nations Headquarters. Also see Legum, "Color and Power in the South African Situation," p. 216.

65. Jerome M. Segal, "Violence Inevitable in South Africa," *Los Angeles Times*, 21 April 1987.

66. John Humphrey, *Human Rights and the United Nations* (Dobbs Ferry: Transnational, 1983), p. 13.

67. George Shultz, as cited in "South Africa: A Partial Victory for Romance," *Time*, 29 April 1985; and "Black Rage, White Fist," *Time*, 5 August 1985.

68. United States, Department of State, *A U.S. Policy Toward South Africa*, p. vi. Also see Chester Crocker, "A Democratic Future," 1 October 1987, United States, Department of State, Bureau of Public Affairs.

69. William Gray, as cited in "House Approves Sanctions Against Pretoria," *New York Times*, 6 June 1985.

70. Nederduitse Gereformeerde Kerk, as cited in "United No More," *Time*, 4 May 1987.

71. Johan Heyns, as cited in ibid.

72. "Declaration of Conscience," as reproduced in Julius Lewin, *The Struggle for Racial Equality* (London: Longmans, 1967), pp. 83–86.

73. Jan Hofmeyr, as cited in ibid., p. 48.

74. John F. Kennedy, as cited in Richard Kluger, *Simple Justice* (New York: Knopf, 1976), p. 756.

75. Kurt Waldheim, in UN Document A/CONF.92/40, "Report of the World Conference to Combat Racism," p. 33. Also see George Mosse, *Toward the Final Solution: A History of European Racism* (New York: Harper & Row, 1978), pp. 236–37.

76. Eleanor Roosevelt, as cited in Joseph P. Lash, *Eleanor: The Years Alone* (New York: New American Library, 1972), p. 72.

77. Maitama-Sule, "Africa, the United States, and South Africa," p. 13.

78. See Stanley Hoffmann, *Duties Beyond Borders* (Syracuse: Syracuse University Press, 1981), especially pp. 1–43 and 95–140; Thucydides, *The Peloponnesian War* (New York: Penguin Books, 1972 ed.), especially "The Melian Dialogue," pp. 400–408; Ernest W. Lefever (ed.), *Ethics and World Politics* (Baltimore: Johns Hopkins University Press, 1972); Paul Gordon Lauren, "Ethics and Intelligence," in James Maurer et al. (eds.), *Intelligence and Politics* (Boulder, Colo.: Westview Press, 1985); and Paul Gordon Lauren (ed.), *The China Hands' Legacy: Ethics and Diplomacy* (Boulder, Colo.: Westview Press, 1986); Kenneth Thompson (ed.), *Moral Dimensions of American Foreign Policy* (New Brunswick, N.J.: Transaction, 1984); and *Ethics and International Affairs*, vol. I (1987), passim.

79. See UN Document E/CN.4/Sub.2/288, "Special Study of Racial Discrimination," 25 July 1968, p. 20.

80. Hoffmann, *Duties Beyond Borders*, p. xii. Also see p. 95.

81. David Owen, 9 March 1977, as cited in U.S., Congress, *Congressional Record*, 95th Congress, 1st Session, p. 6851; and in Walter Laqueur and Barry Rubin (eds.), *The Human Rights Reader* (New York: New American Library, 1979), pp. 310–11.

82. Hector Charry-Samper, 1 August 1983, in UN Document A/CONF.119/26, "Report of the Second World Conference to Combat Racism," p. 37.

83. On this point see Sandra Vogelgesang, *American Dream, Global Nightmare* (New York: Norton, 1980), pp. 28 and 88.

84. See the Introduction; and U.S., Congress, House of Representatives, Committee on International Relations, *Human Rights in the International Community and in U.S. Foreign Policy* (Washington, D.C.: Government Printing Office, 1977).

85. Interviews with Jerome Shestack, Enayat Houshmand, Emmanuel Palmer, Emmanuel Mompoint, Joseph Stephandies, J.M. Makatini, T.C. Ragachari, and Sandra Vogelgesang.

86. Myres McDougal, Harold Lasswell, and Lung-chu Chen, *Human Rights and World Public Order* (New Haven: Yale University Press, 1980), p. 223.

87. Interview with Hania Semichi.

Selected Bibliography

Archival Sources

France. Archives diplomatiques du Ministère des Affaires étrangères, Paris.
Germany. Politisches Archiv des Auswärtiges Amt, Bonn.
Great Britain. Foreign Office Correspondence, Public Record Office, London.
Japan. Delegation to the Paris Peace Conference, Hoover Institution, Stanford.
League of Nations. Archives de la Société des nations, Geneva.
United States. American Mission to Negotiate Peace, Supreme Headquarters Records, Hoover Institution, Stanford.
United States. Department of State. National Archives, Washington, D.C.

Private Papers and Collections

Comité special des ONG pour les Droits de l'homme, Sous-Comité sur le racisme, la discrimination raciale, l'apartheid et la décolonisation. Geneva.
Du Bois, W.E.B. Library of Congress, Washington, D.C.
Grew, Joseph. Harvard University, Cambridge.
Hamburger, Ernst. Leo Baeck Institute, New York.
Himmler, Heinrich. Hoover Institution, Stanford.
Hiss, Alger. U.S. National Archives, Washington, D.C.
Institut für Zeitgeschichte, Munich.
Koo, Wellington. Columbia University, New York.
Lansing, Robert. Library of Congress, Manuscript Division, Washington, D.C.
Miller, David. Hoover Institution, Stanford.
Notter, Harley A. U.S. National Archives, Washington, D.C.
Roosevelt, Eleanor. Franklin D. Roosevelt Library, Hyde Park.
Stilwell, Joseph. Hoover Institution, Stanford.
Wilson, Woodrow. Library of Congress, Manuscript Division, Washington, D.C.

Published Documents

Canada. Parliament. House of Commons. *Official Debates.*
Commonwealth. Commonwealth Secretariat. Group of Eminent Persons. *Mission to South Africa.* Harmondsworth: Penguin, 1986.
Council of Europe. Commission européenne des Droits de l'Homme. *Compte rendu annuel.*
France. Assemblée nationale, Chambre des Députés. *Annales de la Chambre des Députés, Débats parlementaires.*
_____. *Rapports fait au nom de la commission des affaires étrangères.*
_____. Commissariat Général des Troupes Noires. *La Campagne allemande contre les troupes noires.* Paris: Gauthier-Villars, 1922.

————. Conférence de la Paix, 1919–1920. *Recueil des actes de la Conférence.* Paris: Imprimerie nationale, 1922.

————. Ministère des Affaires étrangères. "Les Troupes de Couleur dans l'armée française," *Recueil de documents étrangères.* Paris: Ministère des Affaires étrangères, 1922.

————. Ministère des Colonies. *Conférence africaine de Brazzaville.* Paris: Imprimerie nationale, 1945.

Germany. Austwärtiges Amt. *Die Grosse Politik der Europäischen Kabinette, 1871–1914.* 40 vols. Berlin: Deutsche Verlagsgesellschaft für Politik, 1922–27.

————. Reichsführer der SS, SS-Hauptamt. *Der Untermensch.* Berlin: Norland-Verlag, 1942.

————. Schutzstaffel, Rassenamt. *Völker, Volksgruppen und Volksstamme auf dem ehemaligen Gebiet der UdSSR.* Leipzig: Schwarzhaupter, 1942.

Great Britain. Foreign Office. *British and Foreign State Papers.*

————. Parliament. House of Commons. *The Parliamentary Debates.*

————. *Sessional Papers.*

————. Royal Institute of International Affairs. *Documents and Speeches on Commonwealth Affairs.* Oxford: Oxford University Press, 1963.

India. Ministry of Information. Jawaharlal Nehru, *India's Foreign Policy: Selected Speeches.* New Delhi: Ministry of Information, 1961.

Indonesia. *The Asian-African Conference.* New Delhi: Information Service of Indonesia, 1955.

International Labour Organisation. *Official Bulletin.*

International Military Tribunal. *Trial of the Major War Criminals.* 42 vols. Nuremberg: International Military Tribunal, 1947–49.

League of Nations. *Journal officiel.*

Ministers of Foreign Affairs of the American Republics. Emergency Advisory Committee for Political Defense. "A Study of Conditions Necessary to Assure Political Defense," Third Annual Report, 2 January 1947.

Organization of African Unity. *Basic Documents and Resolutions.*

————. *Charter of the Organization of African Unity.* Addis Ababa: Provisional Secretariat, 1963.

Organization of American States. La Comisión Interamericana de Derechos Humanos. *Actividades de la Comisión Interamericana de Derechos Humanos.* Washington, D.C.: Comisión Interamericana de Derechos Humanos, 1976.

————. *La Comisión Interamericana de Derechos Humanos.* Washington, D.C.: Comisión Interamericana de Derechos Humanos, 1970.

Soviet Union. Communist Information Bureau. *For a Lasting Peace, For a People's Democracy.* 1947.

————. Ministry of Foreign Affairs. *History of Soviet Foreign Policy,* edited by B. Ponomaryov. Moscow: Progress Publishers, 1974.

United Nations. Conférence internationale sur des sanctions contre l'Afrique du Sud, 1981. *Principaux documents.*

————. Economic and Social Council. Commission on Human Rights. *Official Records.*

————. Commission on Human Rights. Sub-Commission on the Prevention of Discrimination. *Official Records.*

————. Educational, Scientific, and Cultural Organization (UNESCO). *Records of the General Conference* and *Statements on Race.*

————. General Assembly. *Official Records, Verbatim Records,* and *Resolutions.*

————. Committee on the Elimination of Racial Discrimination (CERD). *Official Records.*

———. Decade for Action to Combat Racism and Racial Discrimination. *World Conference to Combat Racism and Racial Discrimination.* 1978 and 1983.

———. Special Committee Against *Apartheid. Official Records.*

———. Special Committee on the Situation with Regard to the Implementation of the Declaration on the Granting of Independence to Colonial Countries and Peoples. *Official Records.*

———. Third Committee. *Official Records.*

———. Security Council. *Official Records, Verbatim Records,* and *Resolutions.*

———. Trusteeship Council. *Official Records.*

United Nations Information Organization. *Documents of the United Nations Conference on International Organization, San Francisco, 1945.* 22 vols. London and New York: United Nations Information Organization, 1946–55.

United States. Commission on Wartime Relocation and Internment of Civilians. *Personal Justice Denied.* Washington, D.C.: Government Printing Office, 1982.

———. Congress. *Congressional Record.*

———. House. Subcommittee on International Organizations. *Human Rights in the International Community and U.S. Foreign Policy, 1945–1976.* Washington, D.C.: Government Printing Office, 1977.

———. Senate. Immigration Commission. *Reports of the Immigration Commission.*

———. Department of State. *Department of State Bulletin.*

———. *Documents on German Foreign Policy, 1918–1945.* Series D. Washington, D.C.: Government Printing Office, 1949–.

———. *Foreign Relations of the United States.*

———. *Treaties and Other International Agreements.*

———. *A U.S. Policy Toward South Africa.* Washington, D.C.: Government Printing Office, 1987.

———. President's Committee on Civil Rights. *To Secure These Rights.* Washington, D.C.: Government Printing Office, 1947.

———. Supreme Court. *U.S. Supreme Court Reports.*

———. War Department. *Nazi Conspiracy and Aggression.* 10 vols. Washington, D.C.: Government Printing Office, 1946–48.

Monographs

Adam, Uwe. *Judenpolitik im Dritten Reich.* Dusseldorf: Droste, 1972.

Asahi Shimbun. *The Pacific Rivals.* New York: Weatherhill/Asahi, 1972.

Baker, John R. *Race.* New York: Oxford University Press, 1974.

Banton, Michael. *Race Relations.* London: Tavistock, 1967.

Banzi, Antonio. *Razzismo fascista.* Palermo: Agate, 1939.

Barzun, Jacques. *Race: A Study in Superstition.* New York: Harper & Row, 1965.

Benedict, Ruth. *Race and Racism.* London: Routledge, 1942.

Bossuyt, Marc. *L'Interdiction de la discrimination dans le droit international des droits de l'homme.* Brussels: Bruylant, 1976.

Browne, R. *Race Relations in International Affairs.* Washington, D.C.: Public Affairs Press, 1961.

Bunch, Ralph. *A World View of Race.* Port Washington: Kennikat Press, 1968 ed.

Cassin, René. *La Pensée et l'action.* Paris: Lalou, 1972.

Césaire, A. *Cahier d'un retour au pays natal.* Paris: Bordas, 1947.

Chamberlain, Houston Stewart. *Die Grundlagen des neunzehnten Jahrhunderts.* Munchen: Bruckmann, 1907 ed.

Cohen, William. *The French Encounter with Africans: White Responses to Blacks.* Bloomington: University of Indiana Press, 1980.

Comarmond, Patrice de, and Duchet, Claude (eds.). *Racisme et société.* Paris: Maspero, 1969.

Commission to Study the Organization of Peace. *International Safeguard of Human Rights.* New York: Commission to Study the Organization of Peace, 1944.

————. *The United Nations and Human Rights.* Dobbs Ferry: Oceana, 1968.

Cornevin, Robert. *Histoire de l'afrique.* Paris: Payot, 1976.

Craig, Gordon A. *Europe Since 1815.* New York: Holt, Rinehart, & Winston, 1971.

Cronon, Edmund. *Black Moses: The Story of Marcus Garvey.* Madison: University of Wisconsin Press, 1969.

Curtin, Philip. *The Atlantic Slave Trade.* Madison: University of Wisconsin Press, 1969.

————. *The Image of Africa.* Madison: University of Wisconsin Press, 1964.

———— (ed.). *Imperialism.* New York: Walker, 1971.

Daniels, Roger. *The Politics of Prejudice: The Anti-Japanese Movement.* Berkeley: University of California Press, 1977.

Davidson, Basil. *The African Slave Trade.* Boston: Little, Brown, 1980.

Davis, David Brion. *The Problem of Slavery in the Age of Revolution.* Ithaca: Cornell University Press, 1975.

————. *The Problem of Slavery in Western Culture.* Ithaca: Cornell University Press, 1966.

————. *Slavery and Human Progress.* New York: Oxford University Press, 1984.

Dawidowicz, Lucy. *The War Against the Jews.* New York: Holt, Rinehart, & Winston, 1975.

Debien, Gabriel. *Les Esclaves aux antilles française.* Basse-Terre: Société d'histoire de la Guadeloupe, 1974.

Degler, Carl. *Neither Black Nor White.* New York: Macmillan, 1971.

Diop, C.A. *Nations, nègres, et culture.* Paris: Editions africaines, 1955.

Dower, John. *War Without Mercy: Race and Power in the Pacific.* New York: Pantheon, 1986.

Drost, Pieter. *The Crime of State: Genocide.* Leyden: Sythoff, 1959.

Du Bois, W.E.B. *Color and Democracy.* New York: Harcourt, Brace, 1945.

————. *Dusk of Dawn.* New York: Harcourt, Brace, 1940.

————. *The Suppression of the African Slave Trade.* Baton Rouge: Louisiana State University Press, 1969.

————. *The World and Africa.* New York: International Publishers, 1965 ed.

Duroselle, J.B., and Meyriat, J. (eds.). *Les nouveaux Etats dans les relations internationales.* Paris: Colin, 1962.

Elkins, Stanley. *Slavery.* Chicago: University of Chicago Press, 1968.

Elsbree, W.H. *Japan's Role in Southeast Asian Nationalist Movements.* Cambridge: Harvard University Press, 1953.

Ermacora, Felix. *Diskriminierungsschutz und Diskriminierungsverbot in der Arbeit der Vereinten Nationen.* Vienna: Braumuller, 1971.

Fanon, Frantz. *Les damnés de la terre.* Paris: Masper, 1961.

Felice, Renzo de. *Mussolini il duce: Lo Stato totalitario, 1936–1940.* Rome: Einaudi, 1981.

Fishel, Leslie Jr., and Quarles, Benjamin (eds.). *The Negro American.* Glenview: Scott, Foresman, and Co., 1967.

Fournier-Fabre. *Le Choc suprême ou la melée des races.* Paris: Ficker, 1921.

Francisci, Pietro de, et al. *Politica fascists della razza.* Rome: Istituo Nationale di Cultura, 1940.

Franck, Thomas M. *Nation Against Nation.* New York: Oxford University Press, 1985.

Franklin, John Hope. *From Slavery to Freedom.* New York: Knopf, 1974.

———— (ed.). *Color and Race.* Boston: Houghton Mifflin, 1968.

Fredrickson, George. *The Black Image in the White Mind.* New York: Harper & Row, 1971.

————. *White Supremacy: A Comparative Study in American and South African History.* New York: Oxford University Press, 1981.

Frick, Wilhelm. *Die Rassengesetzgebung des Dritten Reiches.* Munich: Eber, 1934.

Gann, L., and Duignan, Peter (eds.). *Colonialism in Africa.* Cambridge: Cambridge University Press, 1969.

Garvey, Amy. *Garvey and Garveyism.* New York: Collier, 1970.

Geiss, Immanuel. *Panafrikanismus: Zür Geschichte der Dekolonisation.* Frankfurt am Main: Europäische Verlagsanstalt, 1968.

Genovese, Eugene. *In Red and Black.* New York: Vintage, 1972.

Gobineau, Arthur de. *Essai sur l'inégalité des races humaines.* 2 vols. Paris: Firmin-Didot, 1938 ed.

Gossett, Thomas. *Race: The History of an Idea in America.* Dallas: Southern Methodist University Press, 1963.

Grant, Madison. *The Passing of the Great Race.* New York: Scribners, 1916.

Gumplowicz, Ludwig. *Der Rassenkampf.* Innsbruck: Wagner'sche univ.-buchhandlung, 1883.

Hanke, Louis. *Aristotle and the American Indians: A Study of Race Prejudice in the Modern World.* Bloomington: Indiana University Press, 1970.

Higham, John. *Strangers in the Land.* New Brunswick: Rutgers University Press, 1955.

Hitler, Adolf. *Mein Kampf.* Translated by Ralph Manheim. Boston: Houghton Mifflin, 1962 ed.

Hoffmann, Stanley. *Duties Beyond Borders.* Syracuse: Syracuse University Press, 1981.

Hovet, Thomas. *Bloc Politics in the United Nations.* Cambridge: Harvard University Press, 1960.

Hsiung, James (ed.). *Human Rights in East Asia.* New York: Paragon, 1985.

Hughes, D.R., and Kallen, E. *The Anatomy of Racism: The Canadian Dimension.* Montreal: Harvest House, 1974.

Humphrey, John P. *Human Rights and the United Nations: A Great Adventure.* Dobbs Ferry: Transnational, 1983.

Huttenback, Robert. *Gandhi in South Africa.* Ithaca: Cornell University Press, 1971.

————. *Racism and Empire.* Ithaca: Cornell University Press, 1976.

Iriye, Akira. *Pacific Estrangement.* Cambridge: Harvard University Press, 1972.

Irons, Peter. *Justice at War.* New York: Oxford University Press, 1983.

Ishii, Kikujiro. *Diplomatic Commentaries.* Baltimore: Johns Hopkins University Press, 1936.

Ito, Kazuo. *Issei.* Seattle: Japan Publications, 1973.

John, Sir Rupert. *Racism and Its Elimination.* New York: UNITAR, 1981.

Jordon, Winthrop. *White Over Black.* Chapel Hill: University of North Carolina Press, 1968.

Kahin, George. *The Asian-African Conference.* Port Washington: Kennikat Press, 1956.

Kajima, Morinosuke. *The Diplomacy of Japan.* Tokyo: Kajima Institute of International Peace, 1980.

Karis, Thomas, and Carter, G. (eds.). *From Protest to Challenge: A Documentary History of African Politics in South Africa.* 4 vols. Stanford: Hoover Institution Press, 1977.

Kiernam, V.G. *The Lords of Human Kind: Black Man, Yellow Man, and White Man in an Age of Empire.* Boston: Little, Brown, 1969.

Kimche, David. *The Afro-Asian Movement: Ideology and Foreign Policy of the Third World.* Jerusalem: Israel Universities Press, 1973.

Lake, Anthony. *The "Tar Baby" Option: American Policy Toward Southern Rhodesia.* New York: Columbia University Press, 1976.

Lamb, David. *The Africans.* New York: Random House, 1982.

Laqueur, Walter, and Rubin, Barry (eds.). *The Human Rights Reader.* New York: New American Library, 1979.

Larkin, Bruce. *China and Africa.* Berkeley: University of California Press, 1971.

Las Casas, Bartholomé de. *In Defense of the Indians.* Translated and edited by S. Poole. DeKalb: Northern Illinois University Press, 1974.

Lash, Donald. *Asia in the Making of Europe.* Chicago: University of Chicago Press, 1965.

Lauren, Paul Gordon (ed.). *The China Hand's Legacy: Ethics and Diplomacy.* Boulder, Colo.: Westview Press, 1986.

_____. *Diplomats and Bureaucrats.* Stanford: Hoover Institution Press, 1974.

Lauterpacht, Hersh. *International Law and Human Rights.* New York: Garland, 1973.

Lee, Changso, and DeVos, George. *Koreans in Japan: Ethnic Conflict and Accommodation.* Berkeley: University of California Press, 1981.

Lefever, Ernest (ed.). *Ethics and World Politics.* Baltimore: Johns Hopkins University Press, 1972.

Legum, Colin. *Bandung, Cairo, and Accra.* London: African Bureau, 1958.

Lemarchand, René (ed.). *American Policy in Southern Africa: The Stakes and the Stance.* Washington, D.C.: University Press of America, 1981 ed.

Lerner, Nathan. *The UN Convention on the Elimination of All Forms of Racial Discrimination.* Leiden: Sijthoff, 1970.

Leroy-Beaulieu, Paul. *De la colonisation chez les peuples modernes.* Paris: Guillaumin, 1874.

Lewin, Julius. *The Struggle for Racial Equality.* London: Longmans, 1967.

Lillich, Richard. *International Human Rights Instruments: A Compilation of Treaties, Agreements, and Declarations.* Buffalo: Hein, 1983.

Louis, Wm. Roger. *The British Empire in the Middle East.* New York: Clarendon Press, 1984.

_____. *Imperialism at Bay.* New York: Oxford University Press, 1978.

Luthuli, A.J. *Let My People Go!* New York: McGraw-Hill, 1962.

Mandela, Nelson. *No Easy Walk to Freedom.* New York: Basic Books, 1965.

McDougal, Myres; Lasswell, Harold; and Chen, Lung-chu. *Human Rights and World Public Order.* New Haven: Yale University Press, 1980.

McKay, Vernon (ed.). *African Diplomacy.* New York: Praeger, 1966.

McKean, Warwick. *Equality and Discrimination Under International Law.* Oxford: Clarendon Press, 1983.

Madariaga, Salvador de. *The Fall of the Spanish American Empire.* New York: Collier, 1963.

Malcolm X. *The Autobiography of Malcolm X.* New York: Grove, 1965.

Mannix, Daniel, and Cowley, M. *Black Cargoes.* New York: Viking, 1962.

Marie, Jean-Bernard. *La Commission des droits de l'homme de l'ONU.* Paris: Pedone, 1975.

Martin, Gaston. *Histoire de l'esclavage dans les colonies françaises.* Paris: Presses universitaires de France, 1948.

Martinkus-Zemp, Ada. *Le Blanc et le noir.* Paris: Nizet, 1975.

Mason, Philip. *Patterns of Dominance.* New York: Oxford University Press, 1970.
Mee, Charles. *The End of Order: Versailles, 1919.* New York: Dutton, 1980.
Memmi, Albert. *Portrait du colonisé.* Paris: Payot, 1973 ed.
_____. *Le Racisme.* Paris: Gallimard, 1982.
Meyerson, Ignace (ed.). *Problèmes de couleur.* Paris: S.E.V.P.E.N., 1957.
Miller, David Hunter. *The Drafting of the Covenant.* New York: Putnam, 1928.
Miller, Kelly. *The World War for Human Rights.* New York: Negro Universities Press, 1969 reprint.
Miller, Stuart. *The Unwelcomed Immigrant.* Berkeley: University of California Press, 1974.
Moleah, Alfred. *Namibia: The Struggle for Liberation.* Wilmington: Disa Press, 1983.
Montagu, Ashley. *Man's Most Dangerous Myth.* New York: Harper Brothers, 1952.
_____. *Statement on Race.* New York: Oxford University Press, 1972.
Morgan, Edmund S. *American Slavery, American Freedom.* New York: Norton, 1975.
Morner, Magnus. *Race Mixture in the History of Latin America.* Boston: Little, Brown, 1967.
Moscowitz, Moses. *International Concern with Human Rights.* Dobbs Ferry: Oceana, 1974.
_____. *The Politics and Dynamics of Human Rights.* Dobbs Ferry: Oceana, 1968.
Mosse, George. *Toward the Final Solution: A History of European Racism.* New York: Harper & Row, 1978.
Mower, A. Glenn, Jr. *Human Rights and American Foreign Policy: The Carter and Reagan Experiences.* Westport, Conn.: Greenwood, 1985.
_____. *The United States, the United Nations, and Human Rights.* Westport, Conn.: Greenwood, 1979.
Musch, Wolf-Dieter. *Das Rassendiskriminierungsverbot im englishen Recht und in der Europäischen Menschenrechtskonvention.* Heidelberg: Ruprecht-Karl-Universität, 1975.
Myrdal, Gunnar. *An American Dilemma: The Negro Problem and Modern Democracy.* New York: Harper, 1944.
Neame, L.F. *The History of Apartheid: The Story of the Color War in South Africa.* New York: London House & Maxwell, 1963.
Newby, I.A. (ed.). *The Development of Segregationist Thought.* Homeward, Ill.: Dorsey, 1968.
Nkrumah, Kwane. *Ghana.* New York: International Publishers, 1957.
_____. *Towards Colonial Freedom.* London: Panaf, 1973 ed.
Noer, Thomas. *Cold War and Black Liberation: The United States and White Rule in Africa, 1948–1968.* Columbia: University of Missouri Press, 1985.
Odinga, Oginga. *Not Yet Uhuru.* New York: Hill & Wang, 1967.
Oliver, Roland, and Atmore, A. *Africa Since 1800.* Cambridge: Cambridge University Press, 1981.
Oliver, Sydney. *White Capital and Colored Labor.* London: Hogarth Press, 1929 ed.
Padmore, George. *Pan-Africanism or Communism?* New York: Roy, 1971.
Pagliaro, Harold (ed.). *Racism in the Eighteenth Century.* Cleveland: Case Western Reserve University Press, 1973.
Palley, C. *The Constitutional History and Law of Southern Rhodesia.* New York: Oxford University Press, 1966.
Penkower, Monty. *The Jews Were Expendable: Free World Diplomacy and the Holocaust.* Urbana: University of Illinois Press, 1983.
Poliakov, Leon. *The Aryan Myth: A History of Racist and Nationalist Ideas in Europe.* New York: New American Library, 1977.
Porter, Bernard. *The Lion's Share.* London: Longmans, 1975.

Powell, Philip. *Tree of Hate.* New York: Basic Books, 1971.

Queuille, P. *Histoire de l'afro-asiatisme jusqu'à Bandoung: la naissance du tiers-monde.* Paris: Payot, 1965.

Redkey, Edwin. *Black Exodus.* New Haven: Yale University Press, 1969.

Rich, Norman. *Hitler's War Aims.* New York: Norton, 1973.

Roberts, J.M. *History of the World.* New York: Knopf, 1976.

Roosevelt, Eleanor. *India and the Awakening East.* New York: Harper & Brothers, 1953.

Rosenberg, Alfred. *Der Mythus des 20. Jahrhunderts.* Munich: Hoheneichen, 1930.

———. *Der Zukunftsweg einer deutschen Aussenpolitik.* Munich: Eher, 1927.

Rotberg, Robert, and Mazrui, Ali (eds.). *Protest and Power in Black Africa.* New York: Oxford University Press, 1970.

Saller, Karl. *Die Rassenlehre des Nationalsozialismus.* Darmstadt: Progress-Verlag, 1961.

Sanders, Ronald. *Lost Tribes and Promised Lands.* Boston: Little, Brown, 1978.

Segal, Ronald. *The Race War.* New York: Bantam, 1967.

Senghor, Léopold. *Négritude et civilization de l'universel.* Paris: Seuil, 1977.

Shepherd, George. *The Study of Race in American Foreign Policy and International Relations.* Denver: University of Denver Press, 1969.

Shepherd, George, and Lemelle, Tilden (eds). *Race Among Nations: A Conceptual Approach.* Lexington: Heath, 1970.

Simpson, G.E., and Yinger, J.M. *Racial and Cultural Minorities.* New York: Harper & Row, 1965.

Snyder, Louis. *The Idea of Racialism.* Princeton: Van Nostrand, 1962.

Soper, Edmund. *Racism: A World Issue.* New York: Negro Universities Press, 1947, 1969 reprint.

Sowell, Thomas. *The Economics and Politics of Race: An International Perspective.* New York: Morrow, 1985.

Stanton, William. *The Leopard's Spots.* Chicago: University of Chicago Press, 1960.

Stoddard, T. Lothrop. *The Revolt Against Civilization: The Menace of the Under Man.* New York: Scribner's, 1922.

———. *The Rising Tide of Color Against White World Supremacy.* New York: Scribner's, 1921.

Tannenbaum, Frank. *Slave and Citizen: The Negro in the Americas.* New York: Vintage, 1963.

tenBroek, Jacobus, et al. *Prejudice, War, and the Constitution.* Berkeley: University of California Press, 1975.

Tenenbaum, Joseph. *Race and Reich.* New York: Twayne, 1956.

Thorne, Christopher. *Allies of a Kind.* New York: Oxford University Press, 1979.

Tinker, Hugh. *Race, Conflict, and the International Order.* London: Macmillan, 1977.

———. *Separate and Unequal.* Vancouver: University of British Columbia, 1976.

Tobias, Phil. *The Meaning of Race.* Johannesburg: South African Institute of Race Relations, 1961.

Tocqueville, Alexis de. *Democracy in America.* Edited by Phillips Bradley. New York: Vintage, 1945.

Tolley, Howard, Jr. *The UN Commission on Human Rights.* Boulder, Colo.: Westview Press, 1987.

Uhlig, Mark (ed.). *Apartheid in Crisis.* New York: Vintage, 1986.

Vacher de Lapouge, Georges. *L'Aryen.* Paris: Fontemoing, 1899.

van den Berghe, Pierre. *Race and Racism: A Comparative Perspective.* New York: Wiley, 1967.

Van Dyke, Vernon. *Human Rights, Ethnicity, and Discrimination.* Westport: Greenwood Press, 1985.

———. *Human Rights, the United States, and World Community.* New York: Oxford University Press, 1970.

Vierdag, E.W. *The Concept of Discrimination in International Law.* The Hague: Nijhoff, 1973.

Vogelgesang, Sandra. *American Dream, Global Nightmare.* New York: Norton, 1980.

Walters, F.P. *A History of the League of Nations.* 2 vols. London: Oxford University Press, 1952.

Weale, B.B. Putnam. *The Conflict of Color: The Threatened Upheaval Throughout the World.* New York: Macmillan, 1910.

Weinberger, Gerda. *Gegen Rassismus und Rassendiskriminierung: Kampfdekade der UNO.* Berlin: Staatsverlag der DDR, 1976.

Weston, Rubin. *Racism in U.S. Imperialism.* Columbia: University of South Carolina Press, 1972.

Williams, Eric. *Capitalism and Slavery.* New York: Capricorn Books, 1966.

Williamson, Joel. *The Crucible of Race.* New York: Oxford University Press, 1984.

Wilson, William J. *Power, Racism, and Privilege: Race Relations in Theoretical and Sociohistorical Perspectives.* New York: The Free Press, 1976.

Woodward, C. Vann. *The Strange Career of Jim Crow.* New York: Oxford University Press, 1957.

World Council of Churches. *Churches Responding to Racism in the 1980s.* Geneva: World Council of Churches, 1983.

Wright, Richard. *The Color Curtain.* New York: World, 1956.

Young, E.J. *Gobineau und der Rassismus: Eine Kritik der anthropologischen Geschichtstheorie.* Meisenheim am Glan: Hain, 1968.

Articles

Adie, W.A.C. "China, Russia, and the Third World." *China Quarterly* 11 (July–September 1962): 200–13.

Arendt, Hannah. "Race Thinking Before Racism." *Review of Politics* 6 (January 1944): 36–73.

Bentwich, Norman. "Marking Time for Human Rights." *Contemporary Review* 192 (August 1957): 80–83.

Bernardini, Gene. "The Origins and Development of Racial Anti-Semitism in Fascist Italy." *Journal of Modern History* 49 (1977): 431–53.

"Biko's Last Days." *Newsweek*, 28 November 1977.

"Black Rage, White Fist." *Time*, 5 August 1985.

Buergenthal, Thomas. "Implementing the UN Racial Convention," *Texas International Law Journal* 12 (Winter 1977): 187–221.

Canepa, Andrew. "Half-Hearted Cynicism." *Patterns of Prejudice* 13 (1979): 18–27.

Carlyle, Thomas. "Occasional Discourse on the Nigger Question." *Frazer's Magazine* 40 (1849): 670–79.

Contee, Clarence. "Du Bois, the NAACP, and the Pan-African Congress of 1919." *Journal of Negro History* 57 (January 1972): 13–28.

Deutsch, Richard. "Reagan's Unruly Review." *Africa Report* (May–June 1981): 23–26.

"Dokumente zür Rhodesien-Krise." *Europa-Archiv* 21 (1966), 2: 57–84 and 22 (1967), 2: 55–69.

Du Bois, W.E.B. "Opinion." *Crisis* 18 (May 1919): 7.

"End of the Last Empire." *Time*, 12 August 1974.

"Frankreich und die schwarze Gefahr." *Neues Volk* 2 (1934): 7–14.

Fritz, Harry. "Racism and Democracy in Tocqueville's America." *Social Science Journal* 13 (October 1976): 65–75.

Graham, Richard. "Causes for the Abolition of Negro Slavery in Brazil." *Hispanic American Historical Review* 46 (May 1966): 123–37.

Hellwig, David. "Black Leaders and U.S. Immigration Policy, 1917–1929." *Journal of Negro History* 66 (Summer 1981): 110–27.

Humphrey, John. "The Memoirs of John P. Humphrey, The First Director of the United Nations Division of Human Rights." *Human Rights Quarterly* 5 (November 1983): 387–439.

Isaacs, Harold. "Color in World Affairs." *Foreign Affairs* 47 (January 1969): 235–50.

Johnson, Ernest. "A Voice at the Peace Table?" *Crisis* (November 1944).

Kennedy, Philip. "Race and American Expansion in Cuba and Puerto Rico." *Journal of Black Studies* 1 (March 1971): 306–16.

Lasch, Christopher. "The Anti-Imperialists, the Philippines, and the Inequality of Man." *Journal of Southern History* 24 (August 1958): 319–31.

Lauren, Paul Gordon. "First Principles of Racial Equality: History and the Politics and Diplomacy of Human Rights Provisions in the United Nations Charter." *Human Rights Quarterly* 5 (Winter 1983): 1–26.

————. "Human Rights in History: Diplomacy and Racial Equality at the Paris Peace Conference." *Diplomatic History* 2 (Summer 1978): 257–78.

Lerch, Eugene. "Der Rassenwahn von Gobineau zur UNESCO Erklärung." *Der Monat* (1950).

Lincoln, C. Eric. "The Race Problem and International Relations." *New South* 21 (Fall 1966): 2–14.

Lockwood, Bert, Jr. "The United Nations Charter and United States Civil Rights Litigation, 1946–1955." *Iowa Law Review* 69 (May 1984): 901–56.

Maitama-Sule, Alhaji. "Africa, the United States, and South Africa." *Africa Report* (September–October 1982): 12–13.

Marcum, John. "Lessons of Angola." *Foreign Affairs* 54 (April 1976): 407–25.

Preiswerk, Roy. "Race and Color in International Relations." *The Year Book of World Affairs, 1970.* New York: Praeger, 1970.

Presseisen, Ernst. "Le Racisme et les japonais." *Revue d'histoire de la deuxième guerre mondiale* 13 (July 1963): 1–14.

Putney, Martha. "The Slave Trade in French Diplomacy." *Journal of Negro History* 60 (July 1975): 411–27.

"Race and Equality in the Peace." *Crisis* (October 1944).

"Railing Against Racism." *Time*, 24 December 1984.

"Rassenmischmasch." *Neues Volk* 5 (1937): 22–23.

Schreiber, Marc. "L'Année internationale de la lutte contre le racisme et la discrimination raciale." *Revue des Droits de l'Homme* 4 (1971): 311–40.

Schwelb, Egon. "The International Convention." *International and Comparative Law Quarterly* 15 (1966): 996–1059.

Shepherd, George W. "Clues to Reagan's African Policy." *Africa Today* (4th Quarter 1980): 37–41.

"700 Jahre Rassenkampf." *Neues Volk* 5 (1937): 16–21.

Sio, Arnold. "Interpretations of Slavery." *Comparative Studies in Society and History* 7 (April 1965): 289–308.

"South Africa: The Fires of Anger." *Time*, 8 April 1985.

Thorne, Christopher. "Racial Aspects of the Far Eastern War of 1941–1945." *Proceedings of the British Academy* 66 (1980).

Tolley, Howard, Jr. "Decision Making at the United Nations Commission on Human Rights, 1979–82." *Human Rights Quarterly* 5 (Winter 1983): 27–57.

Wynn, N.A. "The Impact of the Second World War on the American Negro." *Journal of Contemporary History* 6 (1971): 42–53.

Newspapers

L'Action française
The Age (Melbourne)
African Times and Orient Review
Asahi
Bombay Chronicle
Bombay Sentinel
Ceylon Observer
Chicago Defender
Chicago Tribune
Christian Science Monitor
Courrier d'Haiphong
Courrier Saigonnais
Epoca
Frankischer Kurier
Free Press Journal (Bombay)
Hochi
Indépendance Belge
Izvestiia
Japan Times
Kokumin
Lagos Observer
Los Angeles Times
Manchester Guardian
Le Monde
Morning Standard (Bombay)
News Letter [of the League of Colored Peoples]
New York Herald
New York Times
New York World Telegram
Nichinichi
Il Popolo d'Italia
Pravda
La Prensa
Rand Daily Mail
Rasse
Romania Libera
San Francisco Chronicle
Der Stürmer
Sun (New York)
Sunday Standard (Bombay)
Sydney Morning Herald
Times (London)
Times of India
Trud

Unita
Victoria Daily Colonist
Volkischer Beobachter
Wall Street Journal
Washington Post
Xinhua General Overseas News Service
Yorozu
Die Zeit

Index